CORRESPONDENCE

THE COLLECTED WORKS OF JOSEPH CAMPBELL

Thou Art That: Transforming Religious Metaphor

The Inner Reaches of Outer Space: Metaphor as Myth and as Religion

The Flight of the Wild Gander: Selected Essays 1944–1968

The Hero's Journey: Joseph Campbell on His Life and Work

Myths of Light: Eastern Metaphors of the Eternal

Mythic Worlds, Modern Words: Joseph Campbell on the Art of James Joyce

Pathways to Bliss: Mythology and Personal Transformation

A Skeleton Key to Finnegans Wake: Unlocking James Joyce's Masterwork

The Mythic Dimension: Selected Essays 1959–1987

The Hero with a Thousand Faces

Mythic Imagination: Collected Short Fiction

Goddesses: Mysteries of the Feminine Divine

Romance of the Grail: The Magic and Mystery of Arthurian Myth

Asian Journals: India and Japan

The Ecstasy of Being: Mythology and Dance

Correspondence: 1927–1987

More titles forthcoming

CORRESPONDENCE

1927–1987

Joseph Campbell

EDITED BY EVANS LANSING SMITH, PhD,
AND DENNIS PATRICK SLATTERY, PhD

New World Library
Novato, California

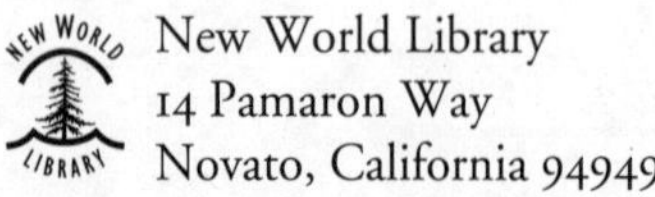
New World Library
14 Pamaron Way
Novato, California 94949

Text design by Tona Pearce Myers

Library of Congress Cataloging-in-Publication Data
Names: Campbell, Joseph, 1904-1987, author. | Smith, Evans Lansing, date, editor. | Slattery, Dennis Patrick, date, editor. | Joseph Campbell Foundation.
Title: Correspondence : 1927-1987 / Joseph Campbell ; edited by Evans Lansing Smith, PhD, and Dennis Patrick Slattery, PhD ; Joseph Campbell Foundation.
Description: Novato, California : New World Library, [2018] | Includes bibliographical references and index.
Identifiers: LCCN 2018028676 | ISBN 9781608683253 (alk. paper)
Subjects: LCSH: Campbell, Joseph, 1904-1987--Correspondence. | Mythologists--United States--Correspondence. | Religion historians--United States--Correspondence. | Authors, American--20th century--Correspondence. | College teachers--United States--Correspondence. | Intellectuals--Correspondence.
Classification: LCC BL303.6.C35 A4 2018 | DDC 200.92--dc23
LC record available at https://lccn.loc.gov/2018028676

First printing, January 2019
ISBN 978-1-60868-325-3
Printed in Canada on 100% postconsumer-waste recycled paper

New World Library is proud to be a Gold Certified Environmentally Responsible Publisher. Publisher certification awarded by Green Press Initiative. www.greenpressinitiative.org

10 9 8 7 6 5 4 3 2 1

*With gratitude to the McTaggart Foundation,
whose generous support made this volume possible*

The pillars of Nature's temple are alive
and sometimes yield perplexing messages;
forests of symbols between us and the shrine
remark our passage with accustomed eyes.

Like long-held echoes, blending somewhere else
into one deep and shadowy unison
as limitless as darkness and as day,
the sounds, the scents, the colors correspond.

There are odors succulent as young flesh,
sweet as flutes, and green as any grass,
while others—rich, corrupt and masterful—

possess the power of such infinite things
as incense, amber, benjamin and musk,
to praise the senses' raptures and the mind's.

Charles Baudelaire, "Correspondences,"
translated by Richard Howard

CONTENTS

ABOUT THE COLLECTED WORKS OF JOSEPH CAMPBELL

AT HIS DEATH in 1987, Joseph Campbell left a significant body of published work that explored his lifelong passion, the complex of universal myths and symbols that he called humankind's "one great story." He also left, however, a large volume of unreleased work: uncollected articles, notes, letters, and diaries, as well as audio- and videotape-recorded lectures.

The Joseph Campbell Foundation—founded in 1990 to preserve, protect, and perpetuate Campbell's work—has undertaken to create a digital archive of his papers and recordings and to publish The Collected Works of Joseph Campbell.

THE COLLECTED WORKS OF JOSEPH CAMPBELL
Robert Walter, Executive Editor
David Kudler, Managing Editor

FOREWORD

Letter Writing

The Imagination's Personal Genre

Working with Evans Lansing Smith on this edited volume of mythologist Joseph Campbell's correspondence—including letters sent to him as well as letters about him—has made me reconsider this form of communication, which today has found its often diminished structure in emails, tweets, and Facebook posts (the venues continue to grow). For many of us, these new iterations have enhanced the thrill of receiving a handwritten letter or card, which carries a charge the other vehicles lack.

In my study at home I have stored in a closet a half dozen shoeboxes containing letters and cards—some typed, most handwritten, from friends, professional connections, former students, and colleagues, as well as from individuals who have read one of my books and wanted to share a thought, an insight, a feeling, or simple gratitude for my writing it. Other cards or notes contain a congregation of signatures from a class of students, each with some written note of encouragement for my health at a time of illness. Each note is signed. These moments of deep connection make any endeavors of teaching or writing worth all the effort. Their personal communication carries what C.G. Jung and others before him called a *mana* energy:[1] something numinous is present in the cursive, even in the typed letters with handwritten signatures, that technology has largely canceled out. In those shoeboxes a host of souls rest; as individuals, they continue to live in my study and in my memory.

Historically, of course, letter writing was the most commonly practiced form of communicating with others. It carried *affect*—feeling and emotion on a different register. Letters have their own vocabulary, their own at times sentimental rhetoric. Today a handwritten letter by a prominent figure in history, passed or still alive, will sell for an enormous monetary figure—surely a testimony to the personal nature of the correspondence and to the individual's embodied presence in a letter written, as we say, "in their own hand."

Letter writing shares many features with journal writing. The letters in this volume, whether from Campbell himself or to him or to someone about him, reveal qualities of a person. Letters allow and even promote such affect, usually in the form of affection; in others, by posing challenges or questions about Campbell's ideas. Something was stirred in the writers, and they wished to share it with him and/or others.

The audience for the letter is very specific and direct: it is crafted for a designated individual. This "transport vehicle" (a term Campbell used to describe the power of a good metaphor) conveys the writer's original character in an intimate and direct way through cursive writing. Of course, a handwritten letter will take days to arrive by mail, but even so, its hands-on quality makes it memorable. A postcard is a letter in a more public venue: anyone can read it, yet its words are often no less intimate for being widely accessible.

I think that the letter's bodily presence in handwritten format and its witness to temporality, conveyed in its date, create in the recipient's imagination something of the writer's spirit, energy, and even Beingness. The unique appearance of handwriting, perhaps with words crossed out or corrected, or punctuation changed during a proofreading, attests to the writer's embodied engagement.

Handwritten letters conjure up ontological presences, unlike emails, which are psychological or simply informational presences.

Real letters communicate something specific to another person: a plan, a deep reflection, a musing that does not have to be proved or researched and that may appear nowhere else. A letter is transported as a vehicle of emotion to another specific person, often with affection and respect. One handles these forms of communication, which create a communion between writer and receiver. They often present a shared memory, which I think is the greatest gift. History enters the personal communiqué.

Specificity is the golden link in this chain. I think of one letter in this collection, from February 29, 1940, which the novelist Thomas Mann wrote to Campbell thanking him for his kind words about Mann's book *Lotte in Weimar* (see page 232 below). He says that his pleasure was heightened in learning that Campbell read the publication in the original German. He goes on to tell Campbell what a delight it was to meet him and his wife, Jean Erdman. The letter is typed, with a handwritten signature. As I read the original document, I felt connected to Mann and Campbell in a new way, knowing I was touching the letter that Mann had signed and that Campbell had held when reading it. My own history entered at this moment, because Mann's fictional works were formidable influences in my undergraduate and graduate work in comparative literature: my master's thesis was in part dedicated to two short stories by this German artist.

In his short missive, I learned something of Mann's own temperament, his warmth and generosity, affectionately shown to the mythologist and extended to include his wife. The letter is memorable as a historical document, but it is more—it shows the living presence of Mann and Campbell on one page. It also captures and expresses an important moment in each of their lives. Both men and their spouses are present in a fully human way on the page, as Mann speaks from the heart as well as the intellect in conveying his deep respect and admiration for Campbell. I realize that I am not reading something that happened in the past, but am instead part of a living history. History lives in the original document, which was handled by both men and now by me, the reader of years later. It gave me chills.

Mann's signature, with a line running beneath it and with a period at the end, reveals his personality; perhaps it was a regular habit to sign his name that way. Typed letters like this one and others that are corrected, perhaps with an arrow running under some words to show where others would better appear in another arrangement—these split the difference between machine-made words and exclusively handwritten ones. Marked after being typed, they show a level of care, of proofreading. Fortunately, their writers did not retype them to erase these human tracings, which remain to give the missives a level of historical presence, even evidence of rethinking, to fashion history's moment, not to eviscerate it.

The embodied trace in these letters is palpable and may conjure in the reader, as it has in me, a feeling of shared intimacy. Yes, some individual characters and words may be beyond deciphering; such is part of the trade-off for enjoying a handwritten letter or even signature! Cursive writing becomes a rhetorical puzzle: "What did he or she mean right here? I cannot read it! What am I missing?" So the letter has gaps, holes, even pockets of ambiguity. I make my best guess; I rejoice in my own frustration when this happens to me. It is so like life, ever beckoning us to interpret or revise a previous reading, or to reread and puzzle anew over the blurs into some version of clarity, perhaps of our own invention. We can rejoice in the ambiguity of the correspondence this way: *This is a letter for me alone to decipher. What an honor! I will have another go at it tomorrow. It will be worth the wait and the additional effort.*

Dennis Patrick Slattery, PhD
New Braunfels, Texas
June 14, 2017

INTRODUCTION

Joseph Campbell's Correspondence

A Portrait of an Epoch

Camille Paglia, in her essay "Erich Neumann: Theorist of the Great Mother," argued:

> Post-structuralism did manifest damage to two generations of students who deserved a generous and expansive introduction to the richness of the humanities and who were instead force-fed with cynicism and cant. I fail to see that American students are emerging today even from elite universities with a broad or discerning knowledge of arts and letters. Nor has post-structuralism produced any major new critics—certainly none of the towering scholarly stature once typical of prominent professors who had been educated in the first half of the twentieth century.[1]

What can be the remedy for the dire straits that the humanities find themselves in as a result of such poststructural demagoguery? To move toward an answer, and to apply it to the work of Joseph Campbell, let me offer another quotation, from Andrea Wulf's recent book about Alexander von Humboldt:

> Alexander von Humboldt has been largely forgotten in the English-speaking world. He was one of the last polymaths, and died at a time when scientific disciplines were hardening

> into tightly fenced and more specialized fields. Consequently his more holistic approach—a scientific method that included art, history, poetry and politics alongside hard data—has fallen out of favour. By the beginning of the twentieth century, there was little room for a man whose knowledge had bridged a vast range of subjects. As scientists crawled into their narrow areas of expertise, dividing and further subdividing, they lost Humboldt's interdisciplinary methods and his concept of nature as a global force.[2]

If we substitute the names of any one of the many scholars of towering stature who flourished before the French Invasion of the seventies and eighties—Erich Neumann, Carl Jung, Marija Gimbutas, Northrop Frye, Joseph Campbell—I think we can find our way toward a flickering light in the darkness. We need the kind of holistic vision and mastery of interdisciplinary studies, bridging the vast range of knowledge that Andrea Wulf celebrates in Humboldt, if we are to find our way forward to forging new paradigms and worldviews that can embrace the complexities of our current crisis, which is so painfully manifest in our education, our divisive politics (both national and global), and our ecosystems.

After Campbell died, he was viciously maligned by a small coterie of academics who were apparently incapable of assessing his contribution to American life, culture, and education. From what they wrote, it seems that many of these critics had not actually read those remarkable books or experienced his remarkable lectures in person, but were just rehashing received opinions. Something similar happened to Marija Gimbutas, who was discredited by people whose knowledge of her work was completely secondhand—a sad indication of how rigidly dogmatic academic intellectuals can become under the pressures of publication, tenure, and promotion, all dictated by party lines.[3] One result of such an approach is that in *Sacred Narrative*, an otherwise fine anthology of essays about myth edited by Alan Dundes, Campbell is the only one not allowed to speak for himself with an excerpt from his work.[4] Instead we get Robert Segal's synopsis and attack—a very poor substitute indeed.[5]

One posthumous attack on Campbell came from Brendan Gill, who wrote in the *New York Review of Books* that Campbell hated Freud.[6] This didn't sound correct to me, so I went back to *Creative Mythology*, which at many points celebrates Freud's works, referring to *The Interpretation of Dreams* as "epochal" and acknowledging Freud as one of the great creative spirits of our age.[7] Indeed the very first sentence of Campbell's famous *Hero with a Thousand Faces*, in the preface, is a quotation from Freud, and there are no fewer than fifteen other references to Freud scattered throughout the book—all of them favorable, without any trace of the hatred Gill erroneously attributed to Campbell.[8] Key references to Freud—at least forty-two of them—permeate the entire tetralogy of *The Masks of God*. Furthermore, in an odd transitional sentence, Gill referred to "another example of his bigotry," where the word *bigotry* refers to Campbell's belief in the sanctity of marriage![9] How that kind of commitment could be seen as bigotry eluded me then, and still does.

Among the other critical voices from this time—which should have been devoted to celebrating what the *Chronicle of Higher Education* called Campbell's unique contribution to deep learning in America—was that of Indologist Wendy Doniger, who wrote that Campbell was the "bane of her existence," in apparent disregard for his extensive contributions to Sanskrit studies, both in editing the posthumous works of Heinrich Zimmer and in his extraordinary ability to communicate many of the essential doctrines of Hinduism and Buddhism to lay audiences, many of whom left his lectures with a direct experience of the mysteries of those teachings that no amount of scholarly commentary could provide.[10] The same critic also wrote that for Campbell *The Tibetan Book of the Dead* and Dante's *Divine Comedy* were "the same" thing—another grossly inaccurate statement.[11] I heard Campbell speak about both works many times, and he never said anything of the sort. In fact, he paid scrupulous attention to the unique details of each of the texts, fully acknowledging their cultural differences.

The letters that were written to and about Joseph Campbell

while he was alive, and to his wife, Jean Erdman, after he died, tell a very different story. They come from an astonishing diversity of individuals who were touched and inspired by his books and lectures. This remarkable web of correspondents extends well beyond the halls of academia. It shows how widely influential Campbell's work was, inspiring creative endeavors and subtle shifts in many people's lives. His work emerged at a time when it was still possible in higher education to embrace the notion of a Renaissance man, by which I mean one whose scholarship embraces the many disciplines of which Campbell showed a mastery: anthropology, literature, depth psychology, religious studies, art history, and of course comparative mythology. That he could assimilate these materials and transmit the inner wisdom of so many of the world's spiritual and cultural traditions was the essence of his genius as a writer and educator. During magical moments in his lectures, one didn't simply get information about such subjects as kundalini yoga and Buddhism; one experienced them directly, in flashes of inspired transmission.

When we began work on this project, the notion was that it would be devoted entirely to letters written by Campbell. But as I undertook the laborious process of transcribing JPEG images of the letters from the archives into editable documents in Microsoft Word, it became clear to me that much of the excitement and energy of the materials lies in the dynamic exchanges between Campbell and a wide range of correspondents: academics (Mircea Eliade, Henry Corbin), anthropologists (Margaret Mead), journalists (Bill Moyers), poets and novelists (Thomas Mann, Gary Snyder, Carolyn Kizer), literary critics (Stanley Edgar Hyman, Edmund Wilson, Ted Spivey), Orientalists (Ananda K. Coomaraswamy, Hermann Goetz), and many others—including Campbell's dearest friends (Angela Gregory, Ed Ricketts), whose letters are among the most precious in the selection that follows.

What unfolded then was a kind of epistolary narrative, with multiple voices and points of view, dramatic conflict and resolution, character development, and even mystery. It became a portrait not just of Campbell but of a remarkable generation of artists, dancers, filmmakers, musicians, spiritual seekers, poets, and novelists, all engaged in the creative powers unleashed by mythology. Hence emerged my plan to structure this volume with a focus on correspondence associated with the critical decades of Campbell's extraordinary career of publication and on many of his remarkable books. This narrative also includes the stories of how the books were born and the collaborative labor that made possible such publications as *The Mythic Image.*

In order to provide a framework for the scope of Campbell's lifetime achievement, we begin this volume with an "overture" in the form of an overview of his life and work written by Robert Walter, Joseph Campbell's literary executor and executive editor of his Collected Works, on the occasion of the centennial of Campbell's birth. The overture provides those not familiar with his work with a summary of the opera that unfolds in the subsequent chapters of this volume—a biography, primarily in Campbell's own words, that covers many of the major works and episodes in his lifelong engagement with myth. These chapters are organized by decades and the work that Campbell produced in them. While the overall framework for the book is chronological, I decided to gather all letters by the same correspondent together in the chapter in which the correspondence began, even if later letters spanned later decades. The purpose of the selection is to provide an epistolary narrative of his remarkable career, even if that will occasionally involve letters from Campbell's correspondents in the absence of his direct replies.

The first chapter covers the decade from the late 1920s up through the 1930s, before the rather miraculous decade of the 1940s, when his first publications emerged like a volcanic eruption of creativity. The subject of the former I call "Wanderings—Paris to Pacific Grove" in chapter 1; the subject of the latter I call "a decade *mirabilis*" in chapter 2. Chapter 3 is devoted to the 1950s, a remarkable period of production centered on the publication of papers from the Eranos Yearbooks. One of the most important correspondents during this period was the literary critic Stanley Edgar Hyman, husband of author Shirley Jackson. Chapter 4 focuses on the 1960s, when the extraordinary sequence of four books, *The Masks of God*, was written. Written during this decade are illuminating letters by such figures as Alan Watts, Henry Murray, Hermann Goetz, and Mircea Eliade. Chapter 5 takes up the problem of Campbell's political views and includes the correspondence with Thomas Mann—who rightly took Campbell to task for his lack of understanding of the situation in Nazi Germany. Two extraordinary landmarks in the history of American book publishing are at the center of the final chapters. Chapter 6, devoted to the 1970s and *The Mythic Image*, provides a unique glimpse into the complex negotiations with Princeton University Press. Chapter 7 focuses on Campbell's last decade, when he produced his magnificent masterpiece the *Historical Atlas of World Mythology*. Finally, as a coda, we include testimonials and letters of condolence written to Jean Erdman after Campbell's death.

Evans Lansing Smith, PhD
Pacifica Graduate Institute
Carpinteria, California
August 1, 2017

NOTES ON THE TEXT

We have attempted to present the letters collected here as closely as we could to the way they were written: we have attempted to retain the writers' spelling, diacritical marks, and, where possible, formatting, occasionally adding [*sic*] to indicate a typo or other error in the original. Where the vicissitudes of penmanship and time have made a passage more opaque, we have interpreted words and names to the best of our abilities. Informational and editorial comments are set between letters in italics. Where it was important to elucidate a reference, we have added endnotes or, in certain cases, bracketed additions.

One thing we made the very conscious decision to change were street addresses. To protect the privacy of current residents of these buildings, we have redacted street numbers throughout the text.

OVERTURE

About Joseph Campbell

On the Occasion of His Centennial

Over one hundred years ago, on March 26th, 1904, Joseph John Campbell was born in White Plains, New York. Joe, as he came to be known, was the first child of a middle-class Roman Catholic couple, Charles and Josephine Campbell.

Joe's earliest years were largely unremarkable; but then, when he was seven years old, his father took him and his younger brother, Charlie, to see *Buffalo Bill's Wild West* show. The evening was a high point in Joe's life; for, although the cowboys were clearly the show's stars, as Joe would later write, he "became fascinated, seized, obsessed, by the figure of a naked American Indian with his ear to the ground, a bow and arrow in his hand, and a look of special knowledge in his eyes."[1]

It was Arthur Schopenhauer, the philosopher whose writings would later greatly influence Campbell, who observed that

> ...the experiences and illuminations of childhood and early youth become in later life the types, standards and patterns of all subsequent knowledge and experience, or as it were, the categories according to which all later things are classified—not always consciously, however. And so it is that in our childhood years the foundation is laid of our later view of

Joseph Campbell, 1984

> the world, and therewith as well of its superficiality or depth: it will be in later years unfolded and fulfilled, not essentially changed.[2]

And so it was with young Joseph Campbell. Even as he actively practiced (until well into his twenties) the faith of his forebears, he became consumed with Native American culture; his worldview was arguably shaped by the dynamic tension between these two mythological perspectives. On the one hand, he was immersed in the rituals, symbols, and rich traditions of his Irish Catholic heritage; on the other, he was obsessed with primitive (or, as he later preferred, "primal") people's direct experience of what he came to describe as "the continuously created dynamic display of an absolutely transcendent, yet universally immanent, *mysterium tremendum et fascinans*, which is the ground at once of the whole spectacle and of oneself."[3]

By the age of ten, Joe had read every book on American Indians in the children's section of his local library and was admitted to the adult stacks, where he eventually read the entire multivolume *Reports of the Bureau of American Ethnology.* He worked on wampum belts, started his own "tribe" (named the "Lenni-Lenape" after the Delaware tribe that had originally inhabited the New York metropolitan area), and frequented the American Museum of Natural History, where he became fascinated with totem poles and masks, thus beginning a lifelong exploration of that museum's vast collection.

After spending much of his thirteenth year recuperating from a respiratory illness, Joe briefly attended Iona, a private school in Westchester, New York, before his mother enrolled him at Canterbury, a Catholic residential school in New Milford, Connecticut. His high school years were rich and rewarding, though marked by a major tragedy: in 1919, the Campbell home was consumed by a fire that killed his grandmother and destroyed all the family's possessions.

Joe graduated from Canterbury in 1921, and the following September, entered Dartmouth College; but he was soon disillusioned with the social scene and disappointed by a lack of academic rigor, so he transferred to Columbia University, where he excelled: while specializing in medieval literature, he played in a jazz band, and became a star runner. In 1924, while on a steamship journey to Europe with his family, Joe met and befriended Jiddu Krishnamurti, the young messiah-elect of the Theosophical Society, thus beginning a friendship that would be renewed intermittently over the next five years.

After earning a BA from Columbia (1925) and receiving an MA (1927) for his work in Arthurian Studies, Joe was awarded a Proudfit Traveling Fellowship to continue his studies at the University of Paris (1927–28). Then, after he had received and rejected an offer to teach at his high school alma mater, his fellowship was renewed and he traveled to Germany to resume his studies at the University of Munich (1928–29).

It was during this period in Europe that Joe was first exposed to those modernist masters—notably, the sculptor Antoine Bourdelle, Pablo Picasso and Paul Klee, James Joyce and Thomas Mann, Sigmund Freud and Carl Jung—whose art and insights would greatly influence his own work. These encounters would eventually lead him to theorize that all myths are the creative products of the human psyche, that artists are a culture's mythmakers, and that mythologies are creative manifestations of humankind's universal need to explain psychological, social, cosmological, and spiritual realities.

When Joe returned from Europe late in August of 1929, he was at a crossroad, unable to decide what to do with his life. With the onset of the Great Depression, he found himself with no hope of obtaining a teaching job; and so he spent most of the next two years reconnecting with his family, reading, renewing old acquaintances, and writing copious entries in his journal. Then, late in 1931, after exploring and rejecting the possibility of a doctoral program or teaching job at Columbia, he decided, like countless young men before and since, to "hit the road," to undertake a cross-country journey in which he hoped to experience "the soul of America" and, in the process, perhaps discover the purpose of his life. In January of 1932, when he was leaving Los Angeles, where he had been studying Russian in order to read *War and Peace* in the vernacular, he pondered his future in this journal entry:

> I begin to think that I have a genius for working like an ox over totally irrelevant subjects.... I am filled with an excruciating sense of never having gotten anywhere—but when I sit down and try to discover where it is I want to get, I'm at a loss.... The thought of growing into a professor gives me the creeps. A lifetime to be spent trying to kid myself and my pupils into believing that the thing that we are looking for is in books! I don't know where it is—but I feel just now pretty sure that it isn't in books.—It isn't in travel.—It isn't in California.—It isn't in New York.... Where is it? And what is it, after all?
>
> Thus one real result of my Los Angeles stay was the elimination of Anthropology from the running. I suddenly realized that all of my primitive and American Indian excitement might easily be incorporated in a literary career.—I am convinced now that no field but that of English literature would have permitted me the almost unlimited roaming about from this to that which I have been enjoying. A science would buckle me down—and would probably yield no more important fruit than literature may yield me!—If I want to justify my existence, and continue to be obsessed with the notion that I've got to do something for humanity—well, teaching ought to quell that obsession—and if I can ever get around to an intelligent view of matters, intelligent criticism of contemporary values ought to be useful to the world. This gets back again to Krishna's dictum: "The best way to help mankind is through the perfection of yourself."[4]

His travels next carried him north to San Francisco, then back south to Pacific Grove, where he spent the better part of a year in the company of Carol and John Steinbeck and marine biologist Ed Ricketts. During this time, he wrestled with his writing, discovered the poems of Robinson Jeffers, first read Oswald Spengler's *Decline of the West*, and wrote to some seventy colleges and universities in an unsuccessful attempt to secure employment. Finally, he was offered a teaching position at the Canterbury School. He returned to the East Coast, where he endured an unhappy year as a Canterbury housemaster, the one bright moment being when he sold his first short story ("Strictly Platonic") to *Liberty* magazine. Then, in 1933, he moved to a cottage without running water on Maverick Road in Woodstock, New York, where he spent a year reading and writing. In 1934, he was offered and accepted a position in the literature department at Sarah Lawrence College, a post he would retain for thirty-eight years.

In 1938 he married one of his students, Jean Erdman, who would become a major presence in the emerging field of modern dance, first as a star dancer in Martha Graham's fledgling troupe and later as dancer/choreographer of her own company.

Even as he continued his teaching career, Joe's life continued to unfold serendipitously. In 1940, he was introduced to Swami Nikhilananda, who enlisted his help in producing a new translation of *The Gospel of Sri Ramakrishna* (published 1942). Subsequently, Nikhilananda introduced Joe to the Indologist Heinrich Zimmer, who introduced him to a member of the editorial board at the Bollingen Foundation. Bollingen, which had been founded by Paul and Mary Mellon to "develop scholarship and research in the liberal arts and sciences and other fields of cultural endeavor generally," was embarking upon an ambitious publishing project, the Bollingen Series. Joe was invited to contribute an "Introduction and Commentary" to the first Bollingen publication, *Where the Two Came to Their Father: A Navaho War Ceremonial*, text and paintings recorded by Maud Oakes, given by Jeff King (Bollingen Series I: 1943).

When Zimmer died unexpectedly in 1943 at the age of fifty-two, his widow, Christiana, and Mary Mellon asked Joe to oversee the publication of his unfinished works. Joe would eventually edit and complete four volumes from Zimmer's posthumous papers: *Myths and Symbols in Indian Art and Civilization* (Bollingen Series

VI: 1946), *The King and the Corpse* (Bollingen Series XI: 1948), *Philosophies of India* (Bollingen Series XXVI: 1951), and a two-volume opus, *The Art of Indian Asia* (Bollingen Series XXXIX: 1955).

Joe, meanwhile, followed his initial Bollingen contribution with a "Folkloristic Commentary" to *Grimm's Fairy Tales* (1944); he also coauthored (with Henry Morton Robinson) *A Skeleton Key to Finnegans Wake* (1944), the first major study of James Joyce's notoriously complex novel.

His first, full-length, solo authorial endeavor, *The Hero with a Thousand Faces* (Bollingen Series XVII: 1949), was published to acclaim and brought him the first of numerous awards and honors: the National Institute of Arts and Letters Award for Contributions to Creative Literature. In this study of the myth of the hero, Campbell posits the existence of a Monomyth (a word he borrowed from James Joyce), a universal pattern that is the essence of, and common to, heroic tales in every culture. While outlining the basic stages of this mythic cycle, he also explores common variations in the hero's journey, which, he argues, is an operative metaphor, not only for an individual, but for a culture as well. *The Hero* would prove to have a major influence on generations of creative artists—from the Abstract Expressionists in the 1950s to contemporary filmmakers today—and would, in time, come to be acclaimed as a classic.

Joe would eventually author dozens of articles and numerous other books, including *The Masks of God: Primitive Mythology* (Volume 1, 1959), *Oriental Mythology* (Volume 2, 1962), *Occidental Mythology* (Volume 3, 1964), and *Creative Mythology* (Volume 4, 1968); *The Flight of the Wild Gander: Explorations in the Mythological Dimension* (1969); *Myths to Live By* (1972); *The Mythic Image* (1974); *The Inner Reaches of Outer Space: Metaphor as Myth and as Religion* (1986); and five books in his unfinished, four-volume, multipart *Historical Atlas of World Mythology* (1983–87).

He was also a prolific editor. Over the years, he edited *The Portable Arabian Nights* (1952) and was general editor of the series Man and Myth (1953–54), which included major works by Maya Deren

(*Divine Horsemen: The Living Gods of Haiti*, 1953), Carl Kerenyi (*The Gods of the Greeks*, 1954), and Alan Watts (*Myth and Ritual in Christianity*, 1954). He also edited *The Portable Jung* (1972), as well as six volumes of *Papers from the Eranos Yearbooks* (Bollingen Series XXX): *Spirit and Nature* (1954), *The Mysteries* (1955), *Man and Time* (1957), *Spiritual Disciplines* (1960), *Man and Transformation* (1964), and *The Mystic Vision* (1969).

But his many publications notwithstanding, it was arguably as a public speaker that Joe had his greatest popular impact. From the time of his first public lecture in 1940—a talk at the Ramakrishna-Vivekananda Center entitled "Sri Ramakrishna's Message to the West"—it was apparent that he was an erudite but accessible lecturer, a gifted storyteller, and a witty raconteur. In the ensuing years, he was asked more and more often to speak at different venues on various topics. In 1956, he was invited to speak at the State Department's Foreign Service Institute; working without notes, he delivered two straight days of lectures. His talks were so well received, he was invited back annually for the next seventeen years. In the mid-1950s, he also undertook a series of public lectures at the Cooper Union in New York City; these talks drew an ever-larger, increasingly diverse audience, and soon became a regular event.

Joe first lectured at Esalen Institute in Big Sur, California, in 1965. Each year thereafter, he returned to Big Sur to share his latest thoughts, insights, and stories. And as the years passed, he came to look forward more and more to his annual sojourns to the place he called "paradise on the Pacific Coast." Although he retired from teaching at Sarah Lawrence in 1972 to devote himself to his writing, he continued to undertake two month-long lecture tours each year.

In 1985, Joe was awarded the National Arts Club Gold Medal of Honor in Literature. At the award ceremony, James Hillman remarked, "No one in our century—not Freud, not Thomas Mann, not Lévi-Strauss—has so brought the mythical sense of the world and its eternal figures back into our everyday consciousness."

Joseph Campbell died unexpectedly in 1987 after a brief struggle with cancer. In 1988, millions were introduced to his ideas by the broadcast on PBS of *Joseph Campbell and the Power of Myth with Bill Moyers,* six hours of an electrifying conversation that the two men had videotaped over the course of several years. When he died, *Newsweek* magazine noted that "Campbell has become one of the rarest of intellectuals in American life: a serious thinker who has been embraced by the popular culture."

In his later years, Joe was fond of recalling how Schopenhauer, in his essay "On the Apparent Intention in the Fate of the Individual,"[5] wrote of the curious feeling one can have, of there being an author somewhere writing the novel of our lives, in such a way that through events that seem to us to be chance happenings there is actually a plot unfolding of which we have no knowledge.

Looking back over Joe's life, one cannot help but feel that it proves the truth of Schopenhauer's observation.

ROBERT WALTER
SAN ANSELMO, CALIFORNIA
MARCH 26, 2004

Joseph Campbell, circa 1927

CHAPTER 1

Wanderings—Paris to Pacific Grove

1927–1939

The wanderings I refer to here focus on a critical period in Campbell's life, starting with his meeting Angela Gregory in the studio of the sculptor Antoine Bourdelle in Paris. (Angela studied with Bourdelle in his studio—today the Musée Bourdelle, on Rue Antoine Bourdelle—from 1926 to 1928.)

The purpose of Campbell's trip was to pursue his studies in the Arthurian romances of the Middle Ages, beginning with a year of lessons in Old French in Paris, followed by a critical year in Munich, when his view of the romances dramatically expanded to include influences coming into Europe from the Middle East and the Orient.[1]

It was in Paris in 1927 that Angela Gregory sculpted her portrait bust of Campbell—and helped him to understand Brancusi's Bird in Space *and the abstract paintings of Mondrian. While Campbell sat for the portrait, Bourdelle would engage the young couple in philosophical discourse on the nature of art that would have a lasting impact on Campbell's thought. And it was here that Campbell reconnected with Jiddu Krishnamurti, whom he had first met during a transatlantic crossing in 1924, and this reconnection would prove a dramatic turning point in Campbell's life.*

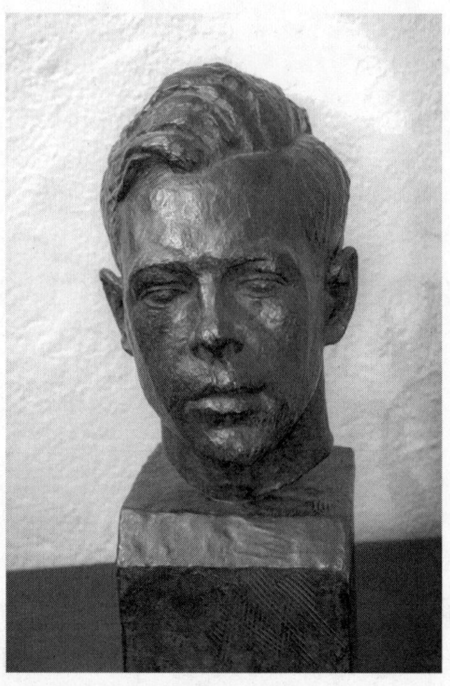

Bust of Joseph Campbell by Angela Gregory, 1927

Campbell continued his correspondence with Angela right up to the end of his life, after she had gone on to become a major figure in American sculpture, exhibiting her work at the Tuileries in Paris, the National Gallery in Washington, and the Metropolitan Museum in New York (where one may also find a cast of Bourdelle's Hercules the Archer*). In 1982 she was named Chevalier de l'Ordre des Arts et des Lettres by the French minister of culture. Several of her monumental sculptures adorn the city of New Orleans, and her studio there, on Pine Street, was a meeting place for musicians, French diplomats, and such luminaries as Thornton Wilder and Kirk Douglas. Perhaps most importantly for this volume, it was here that Jean Erdman visited Gregory after Campbell's death to pay tribute to her for the critical role she had played during the time in Paris.*

After Campbell returned from Paris, the stock market crashed,

Antoine Bourdelle, with his *Hercules*, 1909

and he used the money he had made playing saxophone to get into an old black Ford and drive it all the way to California. He stopped over briefly along the way to see Angela Gregory, crossed the state of Texas (which he noted had the worst roads in all the United States), and came to California, stopping over for a brief spell in Los Angeles, and Berkeley, where he reconnected briefly with his friend Adele Davis, with whom he had exchanged kisses on a cruise through the Caribbean in December 1929. From Berkeley, Campbell drove south to visit another friend, Idell Henning, whom he had met on ship returning from Honolulu in 1925—and whose sister Carol was married to John Steinbeck. So why not go down to Pacific Grove, where the Steinbecks lived, for a visit?

The following letter is from Angela Gregory to her father (excerpted in Stephen Larsen and Robin Larsen, A Fire in the Mind, *86–87).*

December 1927

Mr. Stone and his young friend Joseph Campbell—the Columbia boy—dashed up—and we danced all evening. He's a very nice boy—clean open face—and rather unusual in that he doesn't drink and doesn't smoke. He declines very graciously—each time. It was indeed amusing to dance with a 20th century youth who has enthusiasm and zest, and talks heatedly about religions and "what's beauty?"…

I was very interested when I found out that he knows Krishnamurti, the young Hindu Messiah—intimately. It is he who posed for Bourdelle last fall and swept him off his feet with his wonderful personality. Campbell was so thrilled to find that I was interested in Krishna—having been boosted by his book *The Kingdom of Happiness*, which Mrs. Miller gave me to read when I was "all in" at the hospital last summer. After the dance—which always ends at 11 o'clock—we adjourned to our studio bringing a Mr. Jones along also. We fed them on cheese and crackers and a little Chartreuse which I have had for over a year.

The following two letters are from Campbell to Angela Gregory.

Rue de Staël
Paris
Feb. 21[, 1928]

Dear Angela—
At last I've seen Chartres!—and I'll probably never get over it. The light was dim and the windows gleamed like unearthly things—and all about were the shadow curves of gothic vaulting. A nice old fellow

took me up to the towers and into the vaultings, and let me pat some of the less dangerous gargoyles. The whole visit was a dream.

You and your mother have seen Chartres, I suppose. If you haven't, though you really ought to before long. Walk down the nave and don't look back till you reach the croisée. You get a thrill to last you a lifetime.

I've also been to the Rodin Museum and the contrast with your little Bourdel's [*sic*] studio is quite interesting. The lack of variety and of repose I found surprising and I can't help thinking of all the wonderful variety "chez Bourdel." Everything Rodin ever did seems to be throbbing and uncomfortable.

In spite of all my recent "artistic sightseeing" my own efforts at creating a masterpiece have subsided. "Croquis"[2] has been getting along without me. It's a shame too, 'cause when you left I promised myself that by the time you came back I should be doing marvelous things.

Feb. 26

Your letter has been resting in a somewhat out of the way corner while I've been wrestling with a catch up on the correspondence campaign. It seems to me better not to scribble away like lightning on a letter to someone to whom I really wanted to write. I hope that you will excuse the delay which my strategy involved.

I'm glad that you got all excited about Avignon and all lackadaisical in the warm southern sunshine. It would have been rather a pity I think, had either reaction been at all otherwise. To be really happy in life one has to relax into a grand spell of utter laziness every so often—and this spell should be punctuated with not too violent spurts of enthusiasm. I was afraid that your holiday would be spoiled by too much excitement and too little languor—but your letter confesses that the sunshine did the trick—The only trouble with your letter was its note of penitence. Now, half the good which you might derive from a luxurious laziness will be scurried away by a feeling of penitence, and anyhow, penitential psalms were never meant to be sung by youth. Folks who spend their work times thinking about holidays—and their holiday times worrying about the work which isn't being done, should begin tuning up for a real good penitential psalm, it seems to me. Folks who do such marvelous things as you do, on the other hand, and who know how to relax away when the sunshine tingles through them—folks who come from New Orleans (let's say) should never be sad about things.—I'm delighted, therefore, when I think about the holiday which you and your mother are having, and it's lucky, for me what part of myself got shut up in your baggage.

Paris has begun to think about summertime and the wish has tempted a few picturesque souls into the folly of eating their meals on the sidewalks. Parisian sunshine has more to do with pleasantness than with temperature and consequently there are many ice cold potatoes poked into chattering mouths, every noontime.

[The final page is illegible.]

Rue de Staël
May 5, 1928

Dear Angela,
Thank you very much for the vernissage invitation and for the help which you gave me in figuring out the complicated plan of the palais. After my expedition into the fantastic regions at the far end of the long hall I hunted around for you and your mother though I had no luck.

When I see you again I shall ask about "Oiseau dans l'espace"[3] and the nice red and black quadrangles painted upon the white backgrounds.

Sincerely,
Joe

Hotel Metropole
London, W.C.2.
July 17, 1928 6.05 a.m.

Dear Angela:
Things have been whizzing. First it was the business of leaving Paris—books, books, books! Then it was an exciting stop in London—new clothes!! Then it was a dizzy trip through Ireland—And now it's back in London for a while. Getting away from Paris was a panic. Ireland was funny little dream. And London is the most wonderful city on earth. It makes Paris seem a wee bit like an overgrown summer camp.

My trip through Ireland was a riot. I started away on the night train third class; and the darned train was so well packed with people going to Dublin that I sat out in the corridor on one half of my suitcase. The other half of the suitcase was occupied by a little Irish girl who went to sleep on my shoulder before the night was out. When we landed in Ireland the little Irish girl woke up and promised to help me look at Dublin. She had four brothers, three sisters and two automobiles. The whole crowd got together and whirled me from one grand thing to another—I took a three day look at Cork and the lakes of Killarney, kissed the Blarney stone and fell in a bog.

Finally, I decided to come back to London. Now I have just landed after the sort of night that one can spend nowhere except in a third class compartment. London has not yet rolled out of bed, and Joe has not yet rolled into bed.—Ireland is O.K.

Just before leaving Paris I had a delightful talk with Krishnamurti. He filled my head with astonishment at his own magnificence.

Next day—3 p.m.

Oodles has happened. I've seen Mother and Alice [Campbell's sister] and received all in a bunch <u>three</u> letters from you. Three good, long, exciting letters they are. And there are some snaps of you at Canterbury.

You are having a really thrilling reaction to America, and I enjoy every word you have to say about the place.

And you are where palm trees grow!—You know—I think that palm trees are the loveliest things that God managed to design during those six hectic days when He was creating things.

I'm glad that the artistic career is coming nicely along. And won't it be great to see you some day, sculpting away, flourishing in your studio. I hope that the bronze of my head may be ready in time for the next visits. Monsieur Bourdelle thinks he'll not have it when I return to Paris next month—but the one never knows—does one! I'm a bit worried about the plaster moulds of Adelaide and myself simply because I don't know where they are. Monsieur Tailleur seemed completely in the dark when I was talking with him about them and I feel stupid not knowing where to go for them.

Now isn't it exciting to think that I was the one who snapped that cute picture of you with the four-leaf clover! Even to have clicked a camera shutter is to have lived, when the snap turns out like that.—As for the picture of myself: it hasn't appeared just yet.

I'm looking eagerly forward to the trip which I'm going to take this summer. I'm going with Mother and Alice to visit a few of the cathedral towns in France, and perhaps to visit Krishna in Holland. I'm thoroughly excited about the talk I had with Krishna. He has helped me to select a star worth aiming at. What the star is named I don't quite know—what it looks like I somehow feel. But Krishna is there—in the star—and he is beautiful. It is thrilling to think that my own searching helped me to select some time ago the constellation into which Krishna's star is set. I've gotten a fairly good start along the way which goes up to it.—And now, after my talk with Krishna, I'm quite sure that my dreams have not been mere illusions, and I know that the way which I have been seeking exists. Krishna more than anyone I know, is like the person I have wanted to be.

During the past few weeks my studies have taken an awful slump. Things have been in a constant whirl. But very soon I shall be at it again. With the new start that I've got on things it will be interesting to see what I think about!—and what I read about! Just now I'm not quite sure what my "new life" is going to be like.

I've been talking with Mother and Alice about you, and they are hoping almost as much as I am that you may be back again next year. They'll probably have a little apartment in Paris—on the left bank—in the midst of all those dear places and things that seem to me, now that I'm away from them, just about as delightful as can be.

Please don't be afraid to write me long letters when you want to. I love to hear from you—and to write to you. You always make me think about very lovely things—

My love to Mother dear

As always,

Joe

Campbell with his sister, Alice, at Chartres Cathedral

Aux coins d'A. Savoy & Cie
rue de Faubourg Poissonière
August 21, 1928—at Deauville

Dear Angela—
After a delightful visit to Krishnamurti's castle in Holland, I can scarcely think of anything but the wisdom and beauty of my friend. I walked with him in the woodlands which are all about his home. He answered me my questions and thrilled to the beauty of the trees. He gave me a great deal to think about, and set me off on a quest for something which I scarcely understand.

Every time I talk with Krishna something new amazes me.

Krishna's place in Holland is called Eerde—and it was given to him by the baron who owned it. There are five thousand acres of lovely woodlands, with a fine old castle set in the midst of everything. A moat is around the castle, and in it are goldfish as big as carp, water-lillies, and white swans. Gardens are there with an old wall around them, and outside the wall are the trees. The place is peaceful and very beautiful.

When I arrived, there was a Hindu lady sitting in the sunshine on the bridge which crosses the moat. Her husband was standing beside her, and neither was saying a word.

Almost two miles from the castle there is a huge camp. During the first week in August three thousand people were there to hear Krishna. They came from fifty-odd countries—Iceland, Java, Brasil...

Krishna is going to sit for Bourdelle during the last two weeks of September.

I'm glad that chez-vous things are beginning to settle down a bit—for when there is lots of work to be done, and lots of rushing about, it's hard for a person to think, or even to wonder. I'm very proud of the first bit of work done in this studio—Things must be lovely there—with you amongst them all.

Word has just come from the foundry to say that our head has been cast. Soon Mother, Alice, and I shall be in Paris, and then I'll see about sending the head along to your exhibit. October 27 to November 5, n'est-ce pas? We'll get it there in time, I'm quite sure.

Paris was beautiful as I came into it Saturday evening. I was all excited—but before I'd been two hours in the place I found some long-lost friends, and the beauty of the city became of secondary importance. One of the friends was my track coach, and the other was Jackson Sholz, the fellow with whom I spent my first month in Paris.[4] Sunday we found two of the Olympic gym team, and while my friends were testing French champagne I was practicing handstands—to everyone's amazement. The champagne, I guess, was lots better than the handstands were.

Mr. Stone was away on a trip through Normandy, so that I didn't discover how the summertime has been treating him. But I guess he must be in pretty good trim, or he'd not attempt to travel.

Thanks, Angel, for the nice things you said in your August first letter—I'm hoping for the best, so far as my star is concerned, and I'm beginning to discover the way that leads to it. You know, I hope, that you've had a lot to do with this business...things started to happen while you were turning my head into something artistic.

I've never been able to tell you much about things which you've made me feel. That is because you've made me feel so much. And I'll not start now to say things,—for I think that you understand.

Affectionately,

Joe

Please excuse all the inkinesses—my pen dropped into the sand, and messed things up a bit—

Jiddu Krishnamurti

Le Royal
Blvd. Raspail—
August 27–31, 1928

(From now till October my address is # rue Schoelcher, XIVe)

Dear Angela—
At last our bronze has arrived. Mother loves it and if it were not very fine I should certainly feel jealous. But I too love our chef-d'oeuvre. So much gleams through the rich bronze of the beauty which human lives express when they are noble—so much is there of the vision toward which I was turning while you were at work—that it's difficult to think of our head simply as something rescued from the past. I think that your art has expressed whatever there may be of noble beauty in the future, and it seems to me much more than a glowing spark snatched from a beautiful moment.

Thank you for the news about Chartres. Of course I shall be eager to claim my prize; but it makes me unhappy to think of your unhappy reason for letting your paintings go.—"It's going to take more than magic to get me back to Paris next year!"—That sounds as though your spirits were sinking a little. "It takes a lot to make me feel inspired…and a certain blankness seems to surround me now."—I know that the constant drumming of things around one can upset the pulse of one's heart. Environment can engulf us in pleasures and pains. But after all it's inside our own hearts that beauty reposes. Pleasures and pains affect the body; and if our dreamings have never released our souls, then pleasures and pains will upset our mental and emotional tranquility. Aggravations and disappointments—and even a certain blankness can help the soul to grow in understanding, once the soul has learned to feed upon whatever comes its way.

Marcus Aurelius was a very wise man, and if you'll pardon me a moment I should misquote something which he wrote once.—When a flame is young it must be carefully guarded, and fed with things which will help it to grow. But when the flame has reached a certain height, and attained a certain vigor, then everything which comes its way is its food—everything helps it to grow. The soul is like that.

Angel, I think that chez-vous and chez-moi there are souls which have attained a certain vigor. Our mental attitude—our wisdom should help these souls to grow—to mount with every experience. When we shall have lived this intensely we should have truth in our hearts and beauty—then our work will be great because we shall be great ourselves.

And now that I've gotten all that off my chest:—

Mother wants another bronze—so that she'll not be lonesome while this little fellow—who already is the family pet—is in America. I'd like to know what you would have me do about this.

The bronze who sits before me will be off to you this week I expect—you may keep him if you want as long as he makes himself useful and agreeable, for if Mother has a bronze number 2 to keep her company in Paris, bronze number 1 will stay in America—and there will be no one in New York for a while to appreciate our masterpiece. It would be nice, I think, if he could live with you while we're bumping around the world.

Of course I shall sincerely appreciate your kindness if you will tenderly watch over the Chartres picture for me, until your departure for Paris—or else until my own return home. I should be afraid either to carry it about Europe and Asia, or to pack it away in some storage place. I want now simply to buy it so that I may think of it as mine.—But if you come to Paris next winter, and can't think of anything to do with Chartres and me—simply send both of us to Krueger—Tobin Co., # Park Ave, New York City—you can address me and Mother and Chartres to me—!

The letter which you received from Bourdelle must have been delightful—the little quotations sound exactly like le maître: "Le seul succès véritable vient de la bonne qualité de l'esprit, c'est à dire des réalités de l'âme."[5] That's good enough for a motto!—It says a very great deal—and the more one thinks about it the more it says. Bourdelle is a wise little man—and even to think of him is inspiration.

I've bought Alice the collection of his sketches and sculptings which you have, and I'm quite surprised and delighted to find how much I feel now when I look at something of Bourdelle's. Last year, when I looked at your pictures, Bourdelle's work seemed simply strange to me, and it told me little—but now I can feel the strength and beauty of it, and it seems to me strange that not very long ago I was blind to this beauty. Of course I know whom to thank for my sight…

I hope that you've recovered now from the upset you had when the heat wave came along—that must have been an awful jolt to your enthusiasms.—But the trip, let's hope, made up for things a little—I can't imagine why anyone should go to the Gulf of Mexico for coolness!!—But then, of course, I've never been to the Gulf, so I shouldn't be talking.

Monday the Campbells move to # rue Schoelcher, XIVe,

where I shall stay till the first of October. Krishnamurti is my reason for spending another month in Paris. He's coming back here about the middle of September, and in October I'm going back to Holland with him. After a week or so up there I'll finally get started to Munich.

Paris is being pleasant enough—but frankly I'm tired of the place.

Good bye for a while, Angela—and please don't work too hard—

As always,
Joe

Thank you muchly for the money order—Please excuse the lecture on page 2.

---

rue Schoelcher—Paris XIVe
Sept 9, 1928

Dear Angela—
Now I envy thee with deep green envy—many gleaming nuggets of gold would I give (had I such strange things about me) to see that Maya collection which you went to see with the dashing young hero of the expedition. But there is consolation for me in many of my own excitements. These I shall recount to thee without much more ado.

First off—here we are safe at last in our own studio. It's very grand—up near the lion who sits with his back to Montparnasse. The business of getting settled was a bit more than the business of getting settled usually is! A great many things fell apart when we touched them and had to be fixed!!

We overlook the Montparnasse cemetery; and when we were coming home last Friday, we thought it would be good to return by way of the grave yard. Under my arm was a "dry point" we had bought, of a silly-looking little girl about to pick an apple. When we turned to leave the cemetery a policeman told me that it was his duty to arrest us, and when I politely asked why, he said that people are not allowed to leave French cemeteries with bundles under their arms. "How do I know that you didn't take that thing from a tomb?"—said he—"By looking at it" said I—"Yes," he said, "but people could take things from tombs, and therefore I have to arrest you." I was trying not to laugh, and my appreciation of the policeman's mental anguish was what saved me. There he stood, having dedicated his life to the business of keeping people from leaving Montparnasse cemetery with bundles. There I stood, attempting to leave Montparnasse cemetery with a bundle. His common sense told him that the picture never came from any tomb—but his duty told him to arrest people leaving Montparnasse cemetery with bundles—two francs dissolved the dilemma, but left the bewildered gentleman wagging his head.

Mother had not been in France long enough to understand why it took two francs to explain an obvious fact to a policeman.

Next—I'm studying German and feeling all thrilled about it. Until I get away from Paris, I shall of course feel somewhat wicked for liking the language—but in spite of the guilt I'm going at it with a wallop. The big thrill came when I found that it was possible to plow through a history of India, written in schönes Deutsch. Mr. Stone has been warning me that the Germans do not write the language they speak—and he has been telling me that if I learn to struggle through a German text I shall accomplish a tough year's work. But I find now—not exactly to my amazement—that German texts are being very pleasant and exciting things indeed.

And now—thank you very very much for the advice to Alice which you sent along with your last letter. Alice sends many thank yous—and Mother says the greatest hope she has just now is that you may be the little teacher we're looking for. I have that hope too, for many reasons.

Yes—in Beauvais we all went to see le tête de Christ. The museum was closed, but the concierge let us in just the same, and told us about la petite Américaine qui l'avait croquée.[6] Now what do you think of that?

Whether I shall go to la Touraine and la Provence before leaving la belle France I'm not at all sure. Krishnamurti and Deutschland are very much on my mind just now, and for the moment I've lost all interest in the beautiful places. I'd like to feel myself making some headway along the path that's before me—You see, in just about a year I leave Europe for the east,[7] and I'd like to have everything—including myself—well in hand by that time.

Listen:

"We are not mere mirrors of what is happening outside us, we are rather transformers of the energies of the universe. The artist, therefore, must train himself to know 'things-as-they-are.' The outer universe must pour through his senses in a larger measure than with ordinary men. But then his mind has to come into play, for he must transform, he must not merely reproduce.

"Each artist must profess all the faiths and philosophies in the world, and yet none. He must be a rounded being in his inner nature. Yet, because he is going to discover for himself something which was never discovered before, he cannot be identified as the believer exclusively in any one religion or cult. He must be certain of what he is himself and what is the purpose of the world, so that his transformation of the universe may have more than a temporary merit. To create something for eternity he must find serenity among his ideas. Everything that the artist is as an individual is reflected in everything which he creates.

"Art does not tell us of any one individual's passion, love, or regret, in this or that particular situation, but it tells us of Passion, and Love, and Regret themselves. We go behind then, in art, from the particular-in-time to the general-in-eternity. However small be the size of the thing the true artist creates, there is in that thing something of the totality of the universe."

Now what do you think of all that? It rings [an] echo in my mind of things which Bourdelle used to say. That's a bit of wisdom which a Hindu gentleman named Jinarajadasa had to give me.[8] He seems a very wise little man.

Enclosed is an invoice for the bronze head which ought to be on its way to you by this time. The Tailleur people had a sad story to tell me about some things which you say they lost. The story is that the things must be somewhere in the excelsior—that they couldn't be anywhere in Tailleur's place because everything was packed up chez-vous. He asked me to tell you to look carefully about—I said that I would, and now I've done it...

Now it's late and I must go beddy-bye—

Good night, Angel—

As always

Joe

No, I don't seem to remember the Collins person who wrote "The Rome Express"

Are you kidding me when you say: "your generous remarks apropos long letters"?—Really, I meant to sound enthusiastic not merely generous about your letters, and I'm afraid now that my expression of my emotion must have been something of a flop. The enthusiasm persists, nevertheless—and with each letter it considerably augments in quality and quantity.—So there...

This letter from Campbell to Angela Gregory is excerpted from Larsen and Larsen, A Fire in the Mind, *157–58).*

December, 1931

I arrived in Baton Rouge shortly before sundown, went immediately to the courthouse... which I circumambulated and explored... Those on the Eastward wing I couldn't get to see very well because of the diminishing light, but those on the Westward looked mighty fine.[9]

When I came away from the courthouse, it was pretty near dark.

I drove down to the river and—behold—a blast of red behind the black silhouette of a levee and in the clear blue above the red, a brilliant evening star! The Mississippi was a hot, molten reflection of the red and the blue. It broke the colors into blocks and tossed them around. I never had seen such a thing for simple sensuous beauty in all my life. The boats on the river were black hulks and their lights glided along slowly. It was enough to tighten something in your throat—but the woolly state of Texas I conjure out of mind into the realms of eternal night. Any state that can be so enormous ought to be drawn and quartered and cut into bits unless it can also build itself a set of respectable roads! To be prodigious and mountainous may perhaps not be any crime, but to furnish the weary traveler with the punkest roads in the Republic so that his passage through the monotony becomes in every conceivable manner delayed, held up and hindered, *that* I declare, well *that is* abominable, *abominable.* I was denied the pleasure of meeting your brother by just these roads. I went into mud up to my hubs and floundered for an hour getting out, burned all the tread from my two back tires and ran a delightful nail into my front left—result, sweat and delay. Sunday I drove to Van Horn, 535 miles, ran into snow and another bum mess of road and denounced Texas to the night…

Arizona was marvelous, sublime if there ever was a sublime. I drove through it with my heart in my throat and my eyes everywhere but on the road. First a desert of sage and cactus, then a building up of lumpy hills and a growing into larger hills. A beautiful road wound in and around and then bursts into a canyon! Sheer, runny, buff, tawny, drawn straight painted walls, striped, mottled, naked, tremendous, piled one on top of another, overwhelming. For two hours I went driving through the canyons between Globe and the city of Phoenix, winding in and out, up and down, like a mouse in a city of walls. After that, I thought there was nothing but I came then to the desert and the beauty of the drifted dunes, gentle, undulating, warm and rich with the ruddy sands, I passed from the grip of the sublime to that of the beautiful. The desert was a good deal more voluptuous, I think, than any girl I've ever seen.

After the desert came a parody of mountains made out of boulders, billions of great boulders stacked into heaps as big as the Catskills and after that again came the green of the coast and the blue of the sea.

This letter from Campbell to Angela Gregory is excerpted from Larsen and Larsen, A Fire in the Mind, *177–78.*

March 3, 1932

I discovered a lot of old friends there, titles and authors I hadn't thought about in more than a dozen years.[10] Amongst the newer books I found one by Robert Gessner about the Indian situation today in this glorious republic. *Massacre* was the name of it.[11] I read the book last night and it made me more than a little sick. It made me positively ashamed of myself for ever having been proud of anything that this glorious republic has ever achieved! I shall recommend the book to everyone I know. I shall particularly recommend the book to people who hunt for scandals in India and in Russia and to people who get very lofty and noble when they think about America's conspicuous assistance to the starving Armenians and to the Japanese.

Campbell to Angela Gregory:

March 11, 1932

Within the past week I have managed to put anthropology into the subservient position which I feel sure it ought to occupy in my plans and I have conclusively decided that my major emphasis should be on literature and history rather than on science. It is quite possible (and in fact I believe *desirable*) to consider primitive [cultures as being comparable to our own].

I seem to be getting deeper into myself in this place than gotten in a long while and I'm a bit afraid to pull up stakes un[illegible] I know exactly how everything stands with me. I think you will understand how that might be and I think you will understand too why I should postpone my hop to New Orleans until I have caught this bug which seems to be just ahead of me now! I sincerely appreciate Franz Blom's enthusiasm and general invitation.[12] I hope that my hesitancy about taking advantage of them is not offensive. But what I feel is contagious foreign enthusiasm might cloud my whole raw self over again and send me whirling off again in another wild direction. I'm sick of whirling off in wild directions, and this time, by jiggers, I'm going to hop after something that I'll be glad to catch if I catch it. Two years plunging after the magazine short story and then the sickening realization that I'd rather be digging ditches. Two years plunging after Krishna's Absolute and then the sudden realization that there wasn't any such thing! Two years plunging after the objective facts of scholarship and the realization that these twinkling objective facts hadn't the least bearing on the conduct of my own life! And now? Two years of what? *And then,* what? I wonder if you can blame me, Angela dear, if I hesitate a moment! I wish I could lose myself sometimes in this clear blue sky or in this blue sea or in these green hills so that everything might be gone except whatever intoxications there may be in the present moment.

The following letter to Angela Gregory from 1932 is taken from Larsen and Larsen, A Fire in the Mind, *198–99.*

I have lately had such a thrill in me that it has positively been all I can do to keep my heart from thumping out of me. With the Canterbury job ahead and $150 left to last me till September, I have relaxed into a perfectly glorious loaf. All I do is go around feeling how fine things are, how happy I am to be living, how amazingly sweet the world is! It is glorious. And the strange thing is that I seem to be learning more about myself, about life and art, than I learned in the years of reading and fretting that have just passed. Here I sit in my funny little shanty looking out over housetops to the Bay of Monterey and all inside me is the tingling of my joy!! It is a most amazing thing.

The other night a crowd of us climbed one of the mountains in the neighborhood. On top of it we sat to gaze at the moon and the spangle of stars. There was a warm gentle breeze. There was the yowling of a distant dog that echoed in the night, and the whole world was so fine and so magical that for a long while the four of us sat there simply feeling it all.

"There's something unreal about it," [Tal] said. I had felt that too. "There's something unreal about this whole thing," I said, "the past two months have been unreal, like a piece cut out of a dream." One of the fellows was a biologist with a short beard and a scientific coolness.[13] "Isn't that true," he marveled, "and the funny part of it is we're all so conscious of the fact that we're so happy." Another while we sat there drinking in the wonder and then a young artist named Rich said the thing that really told the story. He was standing like a sentinel behind us, plucking his stubby moustache and looking out over the hills. "We're dead," he said, "we all died at once and now this is heaven."

When Rich said that it was almost as though I knew he was right. There are six of us here, two married couples, and two bachelors, and we've clicked into this inseparable gang![14] And there swims around us such a luminous cloud of delightedness that we don't know quite how real it is. And this cloud is teaching me more somehow than I thought there was to learn!

Campbell to Angela Gregory, spring 1933:

By the way about a month ago Alice and I made a swell discovery about Picasso, Archipenko, abstraction, etc.[15] Archie had been up to dinner at Alice's and we had been talking about abstraction. Archie had been trying to explain the thing, but neither of us got it. When he went home, I felt uncomfortable and bewildered so that Alice and I continued to talk. Finally Alice said, "They seem to mean something about geometry. There's something geometric about it." And then the whole thing clicked. Spengler!! I suddenly realized that Western geometry was Analytic and not Euclidean. I made a dive for chapter one, "The Meaning of Numbers." I knew exactly the page I wanted and with elaborate explanations I read it to Alice. Function instead of proportion, operation instead of construction, dynamics instead of statics, infinite space instead of limited body. I gave her a one-hour lecture on the principles of Analytic Geometry and the Calculus and suggested that next morning she try to sculpt with an eye to the operation of functions in infinite space instead of the construction and proportion of limited bodies.

It was all very tenuous, but next morning Archipenko looked at her work and smiled and said, "You've got it." And that same day I went to look at a collection of Picasso's and for the first time I really caught on to them. They seem to me now about the finest pictures I've ever seen!!! And so I've been having a top notch thrill as you can perhaps imagine.

The following two letters from Campbell to Angela Gregory are excerpted from Larsen and Larsen, A Fire in the Mind, *217–18.*

May 11, 1933

If two qualities are such that the first is given, the value of the second is thereby determined, the second quality is said to define the first or to be a function of the first. For instance, a girl lifts up her right arm. Her right breast lifts and "smallens." The higher the arm, the higher and smaller the breast. The position and size of the breast is a function of the position of the arm.

Now your good Greek in considering this delightful fact limits his attention to the actual young girl. So how can she lift her arm just so high and only so high... [how far] will your good Greek go? Our Westerner however, might ask himself, "Why limit my attention?" If the girl could lift her arm higher, higher, higher toward infinity, the breast would rise always relative to the lift of the arm, become smaller, always relative to the lift of the arm—approaching infinity in his height and zero in smallness... Why limit ourselves to the actual? Why not follow out implications towards infinity, why not?

(Of course there is a great deal more to the whole business, but that, it seems to me, is a fair introduction.)

April 12, 1933

I feel extremely good about things, because I've determined definitely to go back to my writing for keeps—or until I shatter completely. I shall have saved the enormous sum of $300 and I hope to make it last about ten months. If I don't sell a story by then (next March) I don't know what will become of me, but at any rate I'm excited about the impending adventure.

This letter from Campbell to Angela is excerpted from Larsen and Larsen, A Fire in the Mind, *223.*

July, 1933

This all has to do, it seems to me, with a feeling for the mystery behind phenomena.... There is furthermore, I begin to believe, a difference between feminine and masculine world-feelings which would tend to express itself in the work of woman and man artists. The whole subject touches intimately the final questions of being—and it is nothing to be sneezed at!...

Thus art need not be either propagandistic for contemporary politics or indifferent to them. It is essentially another expression field for something more fundamental and deep-running than either art or politics, economics, science, society or religion. It is a self-subsisting discipline, that mysterious soul-relationship to the contemporary and corresponding politics.

Campbell to Angela Gregory:

August, 1933

His work [Archipenko's] is barren as pure abstraction is barren. Bourdelle and Epstein seem to me now the prime representatives of soul perception. (I can't think of a really good name for it!) Abstraction seeks to impose form, the other seeks to discover personality.

Pine Street
New Orleans
October 13
—1978—

Joe—
How truly dear it was of you to write me as you have. Your letter carried my thoughts rushing back to those wonderful, exciting years when we were exchanging new found inspiration—in Bourdelle's studio—in Chartres and at every turn—or so it seemed.

It is with deep felt, poignant appreciation that I now learn from you that our friendship has meant as much to you all these years as it always has to me.

All the wonder and excitement of life is still always with me. I think the magic qualities of living for so many busy, happy years is achieving the very quality of Truth which you have so beautifully conveyed.

Thank you Joe and may you go on to even greater achievements in your work (in which I have felt great pride)—and in your own dear self discovery.

I'll be thinking of you on the 21st—remembering—and remembering.

Perhaps someday our paths will cross again—

Until then—a thousand thanks for the Joe of my youth and the Joe of now.

Devotedly—

Angela

Joseph Campbell
Kalakaua Avenue
Honolulu, Hawaii 96815
June 25, 1982

My Darling—

I have to tell you how very deeply I appreciate the beautiful letter that arrived today: the first letter to appear in my new mailbox. That my words have contributed so much to the restoration and shaping of your lovable life means more to me than anything I have heard from the world in response to my writing and teaching. It is as though you had become, in truth, my child, the golden daughter of my whole life's quest; and at this stage and period of that life (looking back on what was accomplished) I can tell you that the knowledge that you are out there, in health, so beautiful, gives me joy as well, and a sense—for which I can now thank you—of fulfillment.

You were dear to let me know all this. My thanks and my love

Ever

Joe

Angela Gregory, Studio
Pine
New Orleans, Louisiana
March 19, 1984

Dear Joe—
Your delightful & heart warming message at Christmas was deeply appreciated.

For years I've wanted to "pull together" my memories of the days in Bourdelle's studio—and now in the twilight of my career I am doing just that. I find I have vast material—diaries & letters written home during those inspiring and thrilling years—

Having been <u>stunned</u> last October to find myself celebrating my 80th Birthday & realizing that you too will be doing the same on March 26—I thought you'd enjoy the following—written home from Paris in 1928.

"Last week we were kept busy celebrating 'les fêtes de Joseph.' He was 24 last Monday the 26th & much excitement was caused by his mother sending him a wonderful bunch of roses—via the Manager of the hotel where his father usually stays in Paris. The Manager added a lovely Birthday cake and a bottle of Champagne—so Joe burst in to ask if he couldn't have a party in our studio Tuesday afternoon.

"The party was composed of [undecipherable] Mr. Stone, Joe & me—& one of the girls lent me her Victrola & we had much 'cheer,' Mr. Stone drank most of the champagne—he loves it so!"

I recall that the cork popped onto the tin roof of Dr. Wadleigh's little chapel!

Dear Joe—may your 80th Birthday be as happy—
With affectionate memories—
As ever,
Angela

Angela Gregory, Studio
Pine
New Orleans, Louisiana
October 6, 1985

Dear Joe:
Your very beautiful letter of February 21, 1985 has remained unacknowledged for many reasons.

First, I must confess I delayed because I was hoping to receive "The Way of Art" you said you would send me in the spring.[16] I am keenly anxious to read it, and particularly as you quote Bourdelle.

The second reason for my silence was because in searching through your letters for Bourdelle quotes, I was overwhelmed with the quantity and quality of all you have written me, not only about Bourdelle, but about Krishnamurti and his influence on your life.

The night we met at 4, Rue de Cheuvreuse, you said to me, "So, you are studying sculpture. I don't know a thing about art." (Yes! You did!). When I caught my breath, by way of conversation I mentioned that many interesting people visited Bourdelle's studio, and I added "Yesterday, I opened the door for Krishnamurti." That remark was quite important as it turned out.

In a letter home dated March 25, 1928, I wrote "about 8:30 this morning!, Zezette phoned to tell me that Mme. Bourdelle asked her to let me know that Krishnamurti had lunch with them the day before and they had spoken to him of Joe C. and he had begged them to tell Joe to speak to him after his conference which was to be Tuesday night at the Theosophical Society Hall—I sent Joe a pneumatique which he found when he went to his room at 7:00—he turned up at the conference an hour later. (I recall that the only seat left was a strapotin [*sic*].) He (Krishnamurti) grasped Joe's hand as he went down the aisle and they had a chat with one another afterwards."

And, as you wrote me in July of 1928, from London—"just before leaving Paris, I had a delightful talk with Krishna. He filled my head with astonishment at his own magnificence. Krishna, more than anyone I know, is like the person I have wanted to be"[17] ...I find that I have so many exciting things that you wrote me about Krishnamurti and Bourdelle and it is fascinating to me that you found "that he and Bourdelle have so much in common."

Bourdelle changed my life and Krishna, yours—and the strange or destined crossing of our lives is interesting to think about all these years later. Lest you think I am spending my "golden years" reliving the past, I hasten to explain that several years ago, the Director of the Southeastern Architectural Archive of Tulane University became interested in preserving my professional papers and drawings, etc., pertaining to my career.[18]

These unearthed long forgotten letters and documents, among them many of your letters to me over the years, I find now are in large part the story of those formative years of your life.

My Bourdelle book is progressing thanks to these letters and records that have been preserved of a twenty-year-old American in Paris in the twenties! At this point I should not only thank you for your interest and enthusiasm about my Bourdelle memoirs, but it is high time after all these years that I thank you for the part that you have played in the shaping of my career and life, both of which have turned out to be very wonderful.

As ever,
Angela

P.S. Pardon me for sending you a typed letter.

Angela Gregory, Studio
Pine
New Orleans, Louisiana
October 8, 1986

Dear, dear Joe—

Your book is very beautiful—and I am deeply touched by the words you have inscribed to me.

I am very proud & extremely happy to learn that "a lifetime

ago"—that the sparks of inspiration (that changed my life) emanating from that darling bien cher Maitre—Bourdelle—also had such a deep and lasting influence upon your life and work.

Merci mille fois—

My gratitude and my love—

Angela

Following is a postcard from Angela Gregory.

New Orleans—
Mardi Gras 1987

Dear Joe—

Your exuberant Christmas card was appreciated—my greetings never saw the light—because I delayed hoping to be able to send you a copy of the sermon of the Rev. Dr. Marsden.

I found it most intriguing that the publication of the Unitarian Church in N.O. should be the one to give you such a truth.

"The Book"—is finally finished—I fear you will groan when I say that both Nancy Penrose and I want you to see what I quoted and said about you.[19] I know how awful it will be for you to be burdened with another ms—but we'd mark the pertinent areas—for you to cast your eyes upon—& feel grateful for your having seen it—Best wishes to continued success—& affectionate good wishes

Angela

Angela Gregory, Studio
Pine
New Orleans, Louisiana
Saturday, August 5, 1989

Dear Jean

I tried in vain to phone you last night—hence this note. Southern hospitality triumphs and so my cousins Lawrence Brès Eustis and his wife Tae will meet you next Sunday the 13th when you arrive in New Orleans. They will be at the exit of the plane—and Lawrence is thin with greying hair—(a retired geologist) and will take you safely to the Ramada Inn! My nephew who lives in N.O. will unfortunately be out of town and was upset over the Taxi idea—Lawrence & Tae are thoughtful & I do feel better about your safety—

With much anticipation—Angela

This letter from Jean Erdman to Angela Gregory is undated, although Gregory's reply, which follows it, suggests that it was written on September 7, 1989.

Dearest Angela

Each day I awake with thoughts of you and your kindness & generosity in sharing your memories of Joe + Paris in 1927, 28, 29 etc. (the late Twenties)—bringing to life so vividly all the people important to him there—the most treasured of all, of course, being you—yourself.

And it is wonderful, now, for me to know the artist who created the portrait of him that has drawn expressions of praise from all who have seen it in our N.Y. apartment.

I want very much to share something with you—a part of the worldly rewards that have come to me because of the success of his ideas, teachings, and writings.[20] I know that Joe would be delighted to have found himself, finally, in such a bountiful State.

So, enclosed in this note is a check which brings much love and gratitude to you for what you have done for me and, also, for what you have meant to Joe.

Affectionately, your friend—

Jean

Angela Gregory, Studio
Pine
New Orleans, Louisiana
September 17, 1989

Very dear Jean:
I have been trying to find adequate words to tell you how deeply touched I have been by your letter of September 7th.

Actually, I too have thought of you each day since we met and realized what an utterly wonderful and extraordinary event it was to meet you and hear you read in my studio Joe's letters to me of a lifetime. And in so doing have a unique and lasting picture of the growth of his brilliant mind and delightful personality.

You are extraordinarily generous to share with me some of the "worldly rewards" that are the result of Joe's ideas, teaching and writings. I really cannot find words to express what your friendship means to me. After considerable hesitation I accept it with sincere appreciation in memory of my friendship with Joe and now my friendship with you.

(At this point the phone rang and it was your dear voice calling me from half around the world…yes the same wave length!!)

Meeting you dear Jean has been a wonderful climax to my beautiful friendship with Joe.

Devotedly,
Angela

Ed Ricketts

The 1932 trip to Pacific Grove would lead to critical encounters in Campbell's early life—both intellectual and erotic. Campbell became fast friends with novelist John Steinbeck and marine biologist Ed Ricketts.

Ricketts is best known for Between Pacific Tides *(1939), a pioneering study of intertidal ecology, and for his influence on Steinbeck, which resulted in their collaboration on* The Sea of Cortez, *later republished as* The Log from the Sea of Cortez *(1951). Ricketts was fictionalized as "Doc" in Steinbeck's 1945 novel* Cannery Row. *The letters exchanged with Ed Ricketts show the lasting impact of the natural sciences on Campbell's work, and particularly on what Ricketts precociously called emergence and "non-teleological teleology," a notion derived from his extensive studies of the marine animals of the Pacific Coast and from his work in the laboratories of the canneries on Monterey Bay.*

In the background of these letters is the dramatic story of the night in 1932 when everyone drank too much grain alcohol, which Ricketts cut with fruit juice, and Campbell fell in love with Carol Steinbeck, who was sitting in the branches of the tree opposite his own perch. Although their relations seemed to have gone no further than lying together and kissing, Campbell's feelings put a strain on his relationship with Steinbeck (Larsen and Larsen, A Fire in the Mind, *173–200).*

The two settled their differences more or less amicably. Campbell took the opportunity later that year to accompany Ed Ricketts on an expedition to Alaska, but the friendship between Steinbeck and Campbell cooled. Steinbeck and Carol were later divorced (Larsen and Larsen, A Fire in the Mind, *210–11).*

This incident was almost certainly the foundation of Campbell's lifelong fascination with the myth of Tristan and Isolde, with its love potions, its adulterous passion, and the union of love and death. Stephen and Robin Larsen tell this story in their biography of Campbell, A Fire in the Mind. *It can also be found in Campbell's journals from this period, which are excerpted in* A Fire in the Mind.

Beretania Street
Honolulu, Hawaii
August 22, 1939

Dear Ed—
Greetings!
I expect to land in San Francisco August 30, and should like to drop in on you before starting across the continent. As soon as I can get my car out of storage I shall start from Pacific Grove—Carmel—Monterey to hunt you out. The trip for New York must be started the following day; and so, only an afternoon and evening—after seven years!—will be available for review of Weltanschauungen. I hope you will have an hour or two to share.

That something has happened to me since our last word will be evident to you, when you see a wife beside me, in the front seat of the car. The marriage is already fifteen months old, and shows good prospects for the months to come. My presence in Honolulu is the consequence—or rather a consequence of the wedding: Jean's home was Honolulu, and we are visiting her family.

As for the project I had in hand when you last saw me—namely the quest for a synthesis of Spengler and Jung: I have been diligently at work on the project these seven silent years. Joyce's new work, "Finnegans Wake," is the closest thing I have found to a complete resolution of the problem. I have spent most of my summer trying to digest the book. It may take me another seven years to exhaust its implications: more probably, it will take me a lifetime!—but I can say that my little Spengler-Jung brain wave was indeed something!

John [Steinbeck] has rung the bell, I see. Of course, I am not surprised. Give him my regards, congratulations, and best wishes for a big career, if you see him. And I hope Carol is still around, to enjoy the spoils of conquest!

I am looking forward eagerly to the visit, old man. Every time I see a rocky coast I think of you in your boots. Jean has heard more about you than about any single experience of my wander-years. It will be a great disappointment to both of us if we fail to find you in Pacific Grove.

Regards to your little family.

Faithfully—Joe

The following letter is from Ed Ricketts.

August 25, 1939

Dear Joe:

I shall be perfectly delighted to see you.

A good many things have happened to me also in those seven years. Externally most important: little less than three years ago the lab burnt down—result of electrical fire in cannery next door which swept this part of the waterfront. Everything I had destroyed, library especially. Just before that Father died, whom you will remember as my right hand man. And a little before that Nan and I had a permanent split-up. Ed Jr. is with me, getting along fine; the girls are with Nan in Washington. My book finally came out, as you no doubt will have seen. When my files burnt up in this holocaust, I lost your address and so lost possibility of touch with you. Ed Jr. only was here when your friend called up and I never did get even his name.

In continuation of the things we discussed I have worked up three essays that pretty well sum up the world outlook, or rather the inlook, that I have found developing in myself more and more during the years. Unfortunately for the progress of things of that sort, however, I have had such an adjustment problem to finances and personal difficulties that much of the time I havn't [*sic*] either energy or morale for acuteness of this type. I have another zoological book projected; big job, mostly hack work, don't know if I'll do it or not. Loss of my library was a blow. I got another Spengler, several Jung things, some medieval philosophy, but mostly poetry. I got my morale up to the point of working on new scientific library only recently.

Xenia and John Cage, whom she married—modern composer, are in town.[21] Ritch and Tal back here to stay from Alaska. He is becoming consequential pot. John and Crl [*sic*] just left; will be back for week end. Most of the news. I'll be so glad to see you. And I have a sense of welcome towards your wife.

If you don't mind sleeping uncomfortably there is a room for both of you here.

\# Waverly Place
New York, N.Y.
September 14, 1939

Dear Ed: I am going to let your three papers serve as excuse for three more letters. With college-opening at hand, I have had time to read the work only once through, and swiftly. The present letter is simply an exclamation of pleased surprise.—I am even a little glad, now, that seven years went by with hardly an exchange of words between us; for, if we had been discussing our problems as we encountered them, nothing quite as pretty as this could have taken place! You begin with Jeffers quotations that I tried to memorize while driving across the continent, after our year of crazy beginnings. Then you present a series of ideas that corresponds essentially with the series that I too encountered in following the Jeffers lead. You cannot imagine what a profoundly gratifying experience it has been to discover that we have been walking parallel ways. I am only sorry that I have written no statement of my own, so that you might have an experience similar to the one I have just enjoyed!—I shall have time, later, to consider the papers more carefully and to discuss them a bit.

It was fine seeing you, if only for an evening, after all this time. Jean was smart enough to perceive that you and your life-way stand close to the source of her husband's enlightenment. She and I are looking forward to a longer stay on the peninsula. (—When?—Don't know.—) Meanwhile, I shall do something to bring my ideas into cogent order. I always feel that I am on the brink of something like a unified field theory, and keep my pen waiting for the one root word but now I shall try to put things down: perhaps the effort of exposition will do the trick.—Joyce has penned a root word, and so, I am going to begin with an analysis of "Finnegans Wake." (Half seriously I wonder whether anything else remains for the modern literati to do!)

Jung's "Secret of the Golden Flower" will arrive in a week or two, from Jean and me, in recognition of a superior evening, night, and morning, and in anticipation of renewed fellowship.

Sincerely,

Joe

From Ed Ricketts (1939):

Dear Joe:

Your most welcome letter came some time back, and the book arrived this morning. Many, many thanks to you. I had been dallying with the idea of getting the Secret of the Golden Flower for a couple of years; it's hard to pick up such out-of-the-way things locally.

I have started attempts toward publishing those three essays. Sent them first to Harpers and they came back just a couple of days ago, and only a few days after John who was with de Kruif in Michigan, had wired me for dope on the one on non-teleology and had then, with de Kruif, unbeknownst to me, wired to Harpers asking them to make a typed transcription of the essay charged and sent to Hon. He apparently tho[ught] that that influence would call the things to their attention, in addition to his wanting a copy of the revised essay.

Now I try Atlantic Monthly, then Yale Review, then Southern Review, then Partisan Review, but I think none will take them. So there I'll be. Guess I'll have to be well known before I can publish the darn things and that may never be.

I am to do another job for Stanford—a manual of the invertebrates of the SF Bay area. Won't take long, a year or so if I can get to it. And there are a lot of ideas coming up based on those indicated in the essays, but that's slow and spotty. Tal is having more fun even than before with Finnigan's [*sic*] Wake; I have been reading the new Wickes "Inner World of Man." Bureau of Fisheries assistant from Manila has just been here, leaving me more than half tempted to go over there for a couple of months collecting etc. when I can raise the steamship fare. I had planned to spend next summer up north, but now I think I may stay here after all. So come along and spend the vacation in P[acific] G[rove]'s good dripping fog. I liked your Jean very much as you both no doubt realized. We'll take lots of pleasant trips; I know the mountains hereabouts now fairly well.

\# Waverly Place
New York City
December 10, 1939

Dear Ed—
I knew that if I waited long enough, time would clear the obstructions from my room and it would become possible for me to get to my pen, to this sheet of paper, to the three essays buried under the debris of college duties, to the sense of calm and the mood for reflection: the congenial circumstance has now presented itself; a quiet Sunday stands before me; I take my vorpal pen in hand and confront my pleasure.

First let me thank you for the letter of two months ago, whereby I learned of your attempts to publish these three essays, of your new project for a manual of the invertebrates of the SF Bay area, of Tal's fun with Finnegans Wake, of your possible seduction to Manila, and of your kind hope that Jean and I may return to Pacific Grove for next summer. Note that I am writing with considerable attention to a mildly amorphous, yet stilted decorum! Explanation:—the past two months have been devoted to the composition of a chapter on James Joyce;[22] and since I am not a writer, by any means, the effort to come up to my subject has sprained my good right hand: it now moves the pen with the most elaborate show of semicolons, adjectives, complex constructions—over compensations of every possible kind for the fundamental lack of craft. I thought that a letter to Pacific Grove would not betray me!—I perceive that I am betrayed at every point. It is far too early for me to say anything about next summer, but I think that Jean will probably be dancing at Bennington, Vt., and that I shall be up to my nostrils in this book that I'm trying to write. It's a fierce job. My collaborator is an old hand at hack writing, and without his optimistic back-slapping I should have let the damn thing go, long before this. But I read my stuff to him about once a month, and give him material for a sort of introductory chapter which he is trying to compose; the conflabs buck me up for another spell, and I return to the heartbreaking task. The worst of it is, that with my college work and with my determination to continue my private studies, very little time is left me for writing: and, since I have to learn to write—literally have to learn to write—the situation looks very bad. We tell ourselves and our possible publisher that our book will be ready next fall—but I doubt whether it will ever be ready.

A moment ago I mentioned, with a high-toned flourish, "my private studies." They have recently taken an abrupt swerve to the east. I have begun, in fact, what I hope may be an extended study of Hindu philosophy. I am trying to rehabilitate my Sanskrit, and have reached the fourth verse of the Mandukya Upanishad, in which one is introduced to the wonders of the exalted syllable, Aum. I find secreted in this syllable, not only the key to Finnegan, but even the long required synthesis of Dante, Goethe, Schopenhauer, Nietzsche, Spengler, Frobenius, Freud, Jung and Thomas Mann!! I find, also, a basis for correlation between the studies of folklore, metaphysics, and aesthetics, which have been contending, the past few years, for my attention.—All sounds very very hysterical, I know; but I am really quite sober, and shall have, next time I see you, enough to fill even more than a breakfast hour.

That was a swell breakfast, Ed. Jean and I liked it better than anything that happened to us during our handsome summer.

Now I can turn to the first of your three essays—saving the latter two as excuses for letters in the future—and can begin by declaring that it is, precisely as you told me it would be,—a proof that our thoughts have been following parallel ways since our discoveries of old time.

I think, in the first place, that the introductory Jeffers quotations, as they stand, are a bit too diffuse. Perhaps if the Whitman and Biblical texts were used as introductory mottoes the purpose would be served. I note that you quote Jeffers in the body of the essay. It might be well to save Jeffers for that point, when his somewhat difficult statements will be less confusing to the timid reader. The Whitman and Biblical quotations are simply swell: set beside each other they invite the mind to take its own leap. Their power seems to me to be obscured a little by the Jeffers dynamite as close to hand.

Page 4— I should name, if I were you, the Hemingway novel referred to.—I should refer "the mind knows, grown adult" to Jeffers.

Page 7— here, I admit, where you quote "tragedy that breaks man's face and white fire flies out of it" the entire passage might be inserted. This is an important point in your essay, and it could bear the pause and cogitation which the Jeffers passage would touch off. You might then, with an introductory sentence or two, present the quotation from "The Women at Point Sur," which is to serve you in the paragraph following.

I should give my authority for the quotation at the bottom of the page.

Page 9— an "r" is omitted from p<u>r</u>erequisite.

Page 11— the polarities and solutions indicated remain a bit obscure, I think: though a bit of looking certainly clarifies them, I do not know whether an uninitiate would know what to do about the words "hyperthyroidism," "the Roan Stallion," "the Fitzgerald contraction." Perhaps an example or two more, from common life!

Page 13— do I recognize myself in the very intellectual youth who had led a cloistered life and determined that what he needed was to suffer?—(Bull's eye!) the phrase "decimated by one third or more" is self-contradictory. "Decimated" means, reduced by one tenth.

Page 15— up <u>to</u> the sentence "In the inward growth of an individual..." this paragraph is obscure. From the word "In..." to the end, it is splendid. I think that the first nine lines might be pinned to the end of the paragraph, where their point would be more apparent than it is at present. This would not destroy the power of the paragraph on totalitarian forms.

This is the third time I have read the essay, and I hope that I may hold it, to read again. It is really a beauty. I am not surprised that the journals have failed to take it: it is a bit (not to say an enormous bit!) off the God damned beaten-track. But if you hang on to this thing a few years, and continue to develop your point, I should not be surprised to see a handsome little volume. The small magazines, read only by the cultists, are already susceptible to work of this temper, and that is a kind of prelude to things ahead. I think, for instance, of "The Phoenix," published in Woodstock, N.Y. by a few Lawrence enthusiasts. "Transition" might be interested. I do not know whether it is worth the bother to publish in such papers, but I note, in the "Transitions" of ten years ago, many of the names that are pronounced with respect today. Meanwhile, I shall keep my eyes open for someone who might know. I have lost touch with the magazine world, the past few years.

My quiet Sunday has nearly spent itself. I must turn to my Upanishad. I have enjoyed myself, these couple of hours, refreshing my contact with Protean Ed, the man of the sea. With symptoms of obeisance I dispatch my few impertinent suggestions—and hope to write soon again.

Kindest regards to the peninsulites: affectionate regards, in fact.

Joe

Waverly Place
New York, N.Y.
May 19, 1940

Dear Ed—

I have finally got around to my second reading of your second essay,—too late, perhaps, to be of any use to you, but not too late to furnish myself with a welcome breath of Monterey Peninsula's good ozone. My studies have progressed, but very slowly; and although I have worked hard, every week-end, trying to pen my explication of Finnegans Wake, I have only some seventy thousand unsatisfactory words to show for myself. I have not managed, yet, to discover even a starting point from which to introduce the innocent reader to that grandiose image which my own eye now perceives, through the perplexing work murk of the very difficult text.—Meanwhile, I have been trying to familiarize myself with Irish folklore, history, and geography, while studying to discover every possible clue to Joyce's interpretation of these local materials.

And I have taken a slight but very stimulating dip into the ocean of Sanskrit philosophy (if one may use such a term!). India has probably formulated all the answers to all the questions, and the cool, rational, matter-of-fact slokas are a great delight to read. Joyce has leaned heavily on the Hindus. Their systematic reference of all folklore forms to philosophical foundations, their presentation of "truth," as well through images as through words; their recognition of Brahmanism in everything, and their dedication of art to the celebrations of this recognition; their entirely non-sentimental emphasis upon the "collective" rather than the "personal" unconscious; their strict attention to the fine nuances of craftsmanship; their sublime irony; etc. etc. etc.—are traits not dissimilar from the characteristic traits of Joyce. Furthermore, it is certain that before the English destroyed Ireland, there flourished a Gaelic poetry and philosophy of profoundly oriental cast. Joyce is something of a primordial Irishman, and, consequently, something of an oriental. So that Finnegans Wake, Irish folklore, and Sanskrit philosophy are three aspects of a single problem: it is the problem to which we turned our attention that unforgettable season: the problem which you are confronting in your essays.

Before discussing your second essay in general, let me note a few items, page by page:

p. 1.— The word "spirit" does not mean literally "a wind."

It is related to the Latin spirare which means to breathe,

and spiritus, which means a breathing, breath. This is close to wind, but not quite the same thing.—If you look again at page 135 of Jung's Two Essays (your reference) you will perceive that the word which he gives for "wind" is the Greek pneuma (πνεῦμα), which means both "spirit" and "wind," and is related to the Latin spiritus not etymologically but only semantically.—You may say: "A related picture is suggested by the Latin origins of the word "spirit," literally "a breath"; as a form receives or is acted upon by a breath of life, the spirit."—Breath, of course, is wind; and so, even in English, the word spirit may be used to mean "wind," but the archaic meaning of the word cannot be said to be "wind." It is unnecessary to refer to any authority for the statement spirit = breath; the etymology may be found in any good dictionary.

p. 4.— What is the meaning of "holistic tenderness"? Holism is a philosophy which declares that the determining factors in evolution are entire organisms and not the constituent parts of organisms. You may have a big idea here, but the statement requires clarification.

p. 6. anlage should be capitalized: Anlage (noun!)

p. 9.— Discuss "emergent." This is an important element in your thesis, and the reader should not be left to work the meaning out for himself.

p. 12. "over-balancedly" is awkward enough to stop the reader, a moment, in his tracks.

In general, I think that you have, perhaps, two essays here instead of one. At any rate, the relationship of part II to part III is not made clear. Part III is very very good. It should be introduced by a somewhat modified Part I.—In Part I you should state very clearly what you mean by "a spiritual morphology of poetry," and you should lead, then, directly into Part III.—The paragraph beginning

"Although *how* is commonly considered at the expense of *what*, poetic content as the expression of a metaphysic" should either be linked more closely to the discussion of "spirit," by explanations of some kind, or be transferred to your concluding paragraphs in Part IV, where it would be immediately comprehensible.—The paragraph beginning "The citations of such poems as appear..." etc. should either be omitted or confided to a footnote.

Part II should follow, rather than precede Part III. It might be turned into an amplification of the problem. Part III is really very clear and convincing, whereas Part II is obscure. I believe that the obscurities would vanish if we could digest, first, the thesis of Part III.—I think that Laotze's sonnets and the poetry of the Upanishads fit into your D classification. I should expect Avesta to furnish examples of Class D poetry; and I wonder whether something may not exist in the biblical Psalms.

But there remains to be considered the relation of content to form. This is really (I think) the problem of Part II. Perhaps you could discuss a "Class E" in which the class D content is perfectly rendered. (For the artist, as you no doubt know, *form is content*. In heaven, form and meaning are identical. It is only the dross of earthly "matter" which obscures from the eye the soul which is embodied. Ideally the word is to be made flesh.) This would involve such a discussion as you outline on page 3, and it would bring to culmination, rather than introduce, your argument.

I am going to save Essay III for my holiday, which begins next month.—Let me, meanwhile, thank you for your letter of December 16.—I should like to be going to Pacific Grove this summer, but my attempt to write down what I can about Finnegans Wake is going to hold me close to my library. Jean, furthermore, will be in Bennington,—dancing. Her trip west, this winter, was lovely. She wanted to stop off and pay you a visit, but she was whisked so rapidly up the coast, that she had no time. In Seattle, she met Xenia, and heard that you and John were collaborating on a work of some kind. That sounded to me very exciting. I look forward to greeting the result.

Some say I shall know enough to talk with you again about art and metaphysics. I am on the brink of a great new synthesis (new for me, that is to say: it appears to be well known to the entire world east of Suez!). Next winter I shall be giving a course on "James Joyce" and another on "Folklore and Myth": I expect to work out my great concoction during the nights of preparation for my classes.—I'm convinced that there are in this country very few who have even begun to get behind the most obvious "ideals" of "practical materialism": we are living in a kind of desert, where occasional hermits are to be discovered. So I halloo to you across the entire continent.

Yours
Joe

Mexico City
July 5, 1940

Dear Joe:
Your letter arrived just as I was preparing to come here, so I brought it along and have just got to it.

I have just revised—I hope for the last time—"The Philosophy of Breaking Through," and have incorporated your suggestions throughout. I found them all apropos, significant and practical.[23]

Have also been working on the two forthcoming books, especially on the bibliography of the Gulf of Calif section which may develop into sort of a handbook and also of the Panamic province animals. I found a fine biological library here, or rather two of them. At the institute of biology—a fine outfit affliliated to the not-so-good national university—they grin delightedly and hand me practically any book I ask for. Things I shouldn't expect to find anywhere on the Pacific coast of US unless possibly at Univ of Calif Life Science Library.

I may get a chance to work on the poetry essay but I doubt it. You weren't a bit too late with your pertinent suggestions. I am most grateful, for the help even more than for the attention and consideration which are most welcome. I shall look forward to your comments on the non-teleological item.

Now I think that these three essays, together with one or two more in the offing, may not be publishable until—if ever—I get well known. If Jon and I do these two things which we plan and which are well commenced, I may after that have sufficient position in order to get out a volume of essays. May be difficult tho even at that. And with a world at war, and with a US war probably coming on, may be impracticable. But anyway...

I think your synthesis promises better and more than anything I've heard of for many a day. I suppose it will reach only a highly restricted audience, but it seems awfully important to me. It ought to be done. Must be awfully thankless work, considering prerequisites, difficulties and limited audience, but I hope that something will stimulate you so as to keep you at it. All art is in one sense dedicated to the recognition of the all in everything altho it's not generally recognized. The diamond is universally sought in all fields as the symbol of the most persistent and permanent thing in the world. It has no other value except in the crafts. Oh by the way I use the term holistic in the sense that Jan Smuts considers it in his essay "Holism" in XIV Encycl Brit; may stand a definition; tho: a light: the integration of the parts being other (and more, than) the sum of the parts, an emergent.

Lots to do; home next week, and much work before that. Good luck in your work, and best regards to both of you.

[The following was a handwritten, somewhat illegible addition from Ricketts at the end of the letter.]

For indicating of validity of "light" of "enlightenment" pun in line with emergent "Phil of Breaking Thru" or in poetry essay "there is not enough darkness in all the world to put out the light of one small candle"

Inscription of dog's tombstone read some where in the Alps

1941

Waverly Place
New York City
December 26, 1941

Dear Ed:

I simply have to tell you how much I enjoyed reading *Sea of Cortez.*[24] In the first place, of course, there were my own grand recollections of our epochal voyage of a decade ago: so many of the moments I recognize again; and so many of the charming little intertidal personalities returned with their timeless physiognomies!! On the level of personal reminiscence, the book was enormously enjoyed.—And I was glad to see that that marvelous form of living which we met during those weeks on deck, namely, a form directly in touch with the mother zone between the tides, and with the innumerable little children of the teeming shallows; and a form at the same time moving along the shore-line of contemporary society and contemporary thought, languid and lazy from the standpoint of megalopolitan busyness, deep and terrifically impelling nevertheless:—I was glad that this form had at last received its book-form; for I am still the man who hardly believes in a thing until it has gotten itself between covers. And I think that the book form discovered by you and John is perhaps as close to the life form itself as a book could possibly be to life. The on-and-on carelessness of the first two hundred pages, with the cans of beer and the vague chewing of the fat; and then, emerging out of all this, the great solid realization of the "non-teleological thinking"; and then again, that moment just before the entering of Guaymas, when a realization of two realistic worlds, in the most moving way presents itself; gradually, meanwhile, the dominant theme of the work is emerging and from this remark and from that, we understand that society itself is an organism, that these little intertidal societies and the great human societies and manifestations of common principles; more than that: we understand that the little and the great societies are themselves units in a sublime, all inclusive organism, which breathes and goes on, in dreamlike half-consciousness of its own life processes, oxidizing its own substance yet sustaining its wonderful form. Suddenly, then, the life goes out of the trip and we are on our way back to the laboratory to follow this great thing through in a more exact set of terms, linking it into the fantastic thought-net of the modern scientific workers, whose thoughts somehow (as mysteriously as possible) duplicated the marvels of the fact worlds, and several in their own way the prodigious yet profoundly intimate mysteries of that which simply is because it simply is. Ed, it's a great great book—dreamlike and with no end of implications—sound implications—all-sustaining implications: everything from the beer cans to the phyletic catalogue is singing with the music of the spheres.

That is to say, I enjoyed the book very much.—And it should do something to help the critics discover the standpoint from which John has been writing his novels.

Since my last letter, I have been pushing slowly forward, as through a swamp, toward that great synthesizing middle-point which we all glimpsed those days of the great intuitions. My work on Finnegans Wake has continued, and my work on Mythology has completely matched it.[25] During the past six months the world of the myths has been revealing to me those simple, wonderful forms that underlie and sustain the bewildering pell-mell: I hope, within the next few years, to be able to send you a few papers, written in the jargon of another science, to supplement the discoveries of your lab!

I am hoping that we may see you before long. As soon as the way to Hawaii is open we shall go west again. Meanwhile, good luck, enthusiastic congratulations, and from both Jean and myself warmest greetings,

Yours

Joe

Dec. 31, 1941

Dear Joe:
Glad to hear from you. Even tho, to get such a response, I had to write a book!

You got the jist of what was intended, not only better than anyone else, but as no one else. Not one of the critics to date knew, or at least stated their knowledge, of what it was all about. All of them however liked it (except old sour puss Joe Jacobson, whose man Friday regards philosophical speculation as confusing!), and several quoted very significant parts, still without getting a sense of the whole.

I was very charmed with the book. Jn certainly built it carefully. The increasing hints towards purity of thinking, then building up toward the center of the book, on Easter Sunday, with the non-tel essay. The little waves at the start and the little waves at the finish, and the working out of the microcosm-macrocosm thing towards the end. I read it over more than I do lots of other things still. Well, it's nice to like something you have a hand in. I figured you'd like it too. Right down your alley. And doubly so because you had a hand in some of the ideas and collecting details both.

Incidentally, Henry Miller was here for a while. I think he's on that same track, more fiercely than clearly, but not unclearly. Some of it comes out pretty plainly in the most recent thing "The Colossus of Mauroussi." I think he's a good guy. He also read, apparently liked very much, and praised very highly those three essays of mine. You may have run into him; last I heard he was headed for the east.

I'll look forward to seeing your work on Finnegan's Wake and on mythology. It really ought to be done. Only trouble, there again, is the matter of erudition. Both on the part of the writer and reader. I have barely glanced at the book, and know Ulysses not much better. Altho I have the latter in the Mod. Libr. Edition. In order to see the whole picture, a person has to put so darn much time into it! And human energy so limited. This is the way I seem always to end a letter. End of the page.

Ed

Until Aug 15th, 1942
Hoodsport, Wash.

Dear Joe:

Odd summers I'm likely to be anywhere but PG. Spending this month and part of August in the Puget Sound country. Forgot entirely about your possible plans for coming thru California, but if I had recalled, I should have realized in any case that Pearl Harbor changed all that.

We have some mighty pretty collecting up here. Gonionemus chiefly. You recall: the little pulsating jellyfish that we took in the eel grass of Jamestown Bay, near where the Grampus was anchored.[26]

And some unpretty weather. Pretty if you like rain. And a little exploring around, despite the gas shortage which isn't very serious here. I had five or six projects in mind. A couple of scientific papers to work on—the last echoes of the Sea of Cortes work. And some ideas on internationalism to work on. Maybe a little war work. But not many of them seem to be getting done. University of Washington is working up to a fine school. The library is v.g. Next best to U Calif which is better than anything west of the Miss and good in any terms. At that tho, in the west we must depend on libraries that you people back there would find pretty inadequate.

Yes, I'm afraid this winter may be very destructive. Collectivism is upon us, and better that it should come from within, even tho forced as a response to a world that will fight us that way, than that we should have it crammed down our throats by an outside enemy. The eternal verities will be with us still but they may take a form so new that those accustomed to the old lights may not recognize them. Altho I must say that, comparing the present with the witch hunting I remember from World War I, this country has been doing pretty well in the matter of sanities and kindnesses. That last sentence deserves a paragraph mark; it really has no previous connection.

Nevertheless I'd think it would be good if you got your ideas out, and if possible published. All the objectiveness and depth that can be made available ought to be. At best, and this is nearly best for a war, all belligerencies drag along a lot of biases. Tend to declare things as black and white that otherwise would be worked out as special cases.

Reading Koestler, Hitler carefully. Probably a little of Dan Gibb's "Search for Sanity," Farrar Reinhart and pretty fair but I fear terribly verbose. Toni (girl friend, on the scene since you were here)[27] getting into Boodin, and I fear will read Spengler completely thru carefully, which is more than I've ever done. The copy you sent me burned up when the lab burnt, but I got the one volume edition since, and peck at it now and then. I'd say that it's surely the depth behind the Hitler dialectic.

I wish I could sit in on your two courses next year. Some one ought to abstract the whole thing, get the feeling of it so it can be perpetuated other than esoterically in the minds of the pupils. Oh incidentally, the McIntire (New Directions) Faust seems to me to be a fine job. Only good translation I've found. I hope he goes ahead with the 2nd part.

Say hello to Jean. Come on out when you can. Winter holidays maybe, if still there is any travel left for non-essentials in the war effort. Us. Altho merely as a balance wheel, such as we may be making a real contribution.

Ed

Sept. 23, 1944

Dear Joe:
The time of Xen's[28] visit here was very full and very pleasant. Left not much leisure for letters. Now she's en route back there I'll put in some office time.

Very grateful to you for sending on the new book. I have dipped into it only the least bit, but already from that little I am confirmed in what I would have assumed sight unseen. Certainly a front line, firing line of a most important issue, more so because not well known popularly. The one that underlies all others. However did you manage to get so much lively interest in what I would have expected to be a rather dry guide!

We got your Navajo portfolio.[29] Wonderful reproductions! Xenia said you were disappointed in them. Have to see the originals to understand that. I was badly disappointed in the Sea of Cortes color illustrations. In the black and white too, for that matter.

Cannery Row about the same. Busier than ever. The lovely nice sporting house, Flora Woods, was a war casualty. Too much gold star mothers,[30] and slightly unreal attitude of Army Me Corps (which I was in for about a year as Xen no doubt mentioned; 2nd time in the army for me, 1st world war too). Toni has been working on local paper, but recently quit. Doesn't want full time work. In any case we keep too busy. But still a little beer gets drunk, so I suppose everything is alright.

I have been working on my little animals, on and off. An ultimate manual on the Pacific Coast marine invertebrates. Which has to be preceded by more exploration. Chiefly a trip to Bering Sea, Aleutians, Gulf of Alaska over to Kamchatka. And lord only knows when I can get up there. But I can work on the prerequisites. Also lots of dope on a projected popular book on the Japanese Mandated islands,[31] on which, by devious ways I got to be something of an expert. But that's probably out now, with military turn of events. And I would have finished it in any case only if I got publisher's contract, which seems not to be forthcoming.

John is publishing book on Cannery Row which should retire me, in self defense, from the public eye for a few weeks after publication.[32] Aside from that phase, and excluding few sentimentalities, it could be a good book. Tortilla-flatish.

In the meantime I have been chemisting for a past year. Into that directly from the army where I was doing clinical laboratory work. All of which made hash of my own programme but the threads are still there and maybe I can pick things up again.

My best to Jean.

I'm assuming that you know we'd like very well to see you people again.

The following letter to Ricketts is excerpted in Larsen and Larsen, A Fire in the Mind, *162.*

Oct. 1, 1944

Monterey Peninsula is the Earthly Paradise.... I have still a deep nostalgia for those wonderful days, when everything that has happened since was taking shape. That was, for me at least, the moment of the great death-and-rebirth that Jung is always talking about; and all of you who were involved in the "agony" are symbolic dominants in what is left to me of my psyche.

Waverly Place
New York 14, N.Y.
April 21, 1946

Dear Ed—
The wheels of destiny are going to be rolling us westward again this summer, and we are wondering whether you are to be in Pacific Grove. We expect to leave S.F. for Honolulu, June 20 and

to return Sept. 11. Shall you be at home, in the neighborhood of either of those dates?

There should be a lot for us to talk about. Xenia has been keeping us more or less in touch with your movements; and I should say you had been exposed to a few major experiences. My own major experiences have been very much on the bookish side, but illuminating in their own way. All my time has been devoted to the mythological, and I am beginning to feel somewhat at home with the gods. The ramifications of this mythological matter into all departments of life and art now seem to me the great world-redeeming marvel to be brooded. I am sure that the laws of mythology are the laws of "spiritual biology," and that a good confab with yourself will make this quite clear to me.

I hope we shall be able to see you.

Yours,

Joe

Ap 29—1946

Dear Joe:

Very good news. I'll certainly be glad to see you.

We'll probably be away when you come through June 30th. But back long before Sept. 11th.

Expect to leave here about May 22nd for a long collecting trip—something like we took that good year but not so elaborate. West coast of Vanc Id (where we spent last summer also). Queen Charlotte Ids, Prince Rupert, perhaps on up to Stewart-BC-Hyder Alaska. Then I think I'll be finished with the Canadian outer coast line. Gulf of Alaska next. Then when, if ever, I get out to the Aleutians, Bering Sea, maybe Kamchatka, I'll have covered the entire area from Panama to Asia well enough at least to start on the manual. Almost 50 now; give me anyway twenty more years of good health, not too much restriction financially and I think I can do it. Or lay a good foundation for the next guy.

Yes, I've been in the army, working since at a regular bread and butter job. More or less. At regular hours. Biochemist. Which should amuse anyone who knows how I hate math, and how little chem I know. Now on part time, and building up PBL again as a commercial supply house.[33] I have used it for 5 years chiefly as a research headquarters. But back again for a season after my summer leave of absence, and when the canneries open up full blast. I have been on biol-fisheries research also, mostly for myself, partly for Cal Pack (cannery) and I've certainly dug up some amusing things about the plankton. By what magic the annual peak of a 7 year mean curve for SCalif comes at precisely the same week as that of a 6 year curve of different years in the Aleutians is more than I can figure. If we had long period data on this, all sorts of ideas might be justified. Just now it all seems pretty close to the primitive jumping off place biologically; anything could happen. A marvelous calendar for the little bugs to coordinate into! Trouble so far in understanding it has been that the single year and single locality variations have been so immense, no one bothered to construct a mean curve.

Ed [Ricketts's son] is back from three years in the army, most of it overseas. He's fine. Wonderful photographer, wonderful musician, wonderful mathematician. Going up with us too, and then into Cal Tech on the GI bill of rights if his qualifications fit. Did the most interesting army work I've almost ever heard about: one of 5 EM [enlisted men] and 4 officers who had charge of the signal corps annex of the SWPI [Southwest Pacific Islands] invasion plans. Got a T/S [technical sergeant], working his own hours, lived mostly in hotel, worked sometimes very hard but of course with the greatest sense of significance and drank apparently plenty of beer. Toni has come here with me since you went thru last. As Xen no doubt will have told you. A pretty cerebrate gal; I imagine you two will get on fine, but those things are beyond prediction. Anyway, come on, we'll be so glad to see you and Jean. Happy Days, Ed.

Oct. 25, 1946

Dear Joe:
Many thanks to you for all the fine things. The pretty things. That legend of the Jew and the soldier at the bridge is certainly something. Seems like you're blossoming out as a writer at a great rate. I have to readjust my mind to think of you that way. As a thinker and a teacher, but not until now as a writer.

I have been looking thru the Key again in connection with picking up the Wake from time to time. I certainly agree with you that those last few pages are among the best, quite <u>the</u> best, in modern literature. Perhaps in any western literature. How such depths can be evoked thru the printed word is more than I can see.

Things happened since you were here. Xenia of course came on. We havn't seen as much of her as we hoped, but she's kept busy looking after the kids, and we may see, oh of course we will, more of her before she goes on. Changed. More level. Still thank heavens you can't even prevent a screwball from being at least a little screwballish. And Toni came back with Kay from the hospital.[34] Who is doing fine; seems to be suffering from some anxiety and insecurity, but usually handles it well. Of course she's really been through a lot.

And my work on the little animals goes on. I applied for a Guggenheim. Think I have a good chance for it. The Foundation people themselves finally suggested I apply after Schmidt of the Field Museum had apparently written them about me. So I may have another good trip next summer despite hospital bills.

Very little CalPack work here this fall. And of course I put in the added time to good advantage otherwise. Everyone very downcast about the sardine situation. And well they should be! Just another instance of greed, lack of foresight, lack of seeing beyond a narrow individual segment of a large picture. For years the canners and reduction plant operators and fishermen have been warned they were taking too many fish. They refused to listen, selected their evidence, petitioned for more and more permits, put pressure on the Fish and Game Comm., lobbied the legislators, always got their way. And now so sad. No fish. Of course they'll come back, the situation will straighten itself out after a bad time. But it's all so unnecessary. Need for the fish has increased many fold during the past ten years. But the fish themselves havn't increased in any such fashion. Like the auto traffic in NY, per Fortune's recent survey, it's all tied up with the refusal of the average person to see any picture larger than his own. Then when the social pressure hits him, he wants to put the blame outside, never take his share. I think of that very often in driving. I come into an intersection, look in the rear view mirror—unless I'm terribly in a hurry—and consider how many cars on the other street can go by unstopped if I pause a second longer. In other words, just what the corssing [*sic*] cop has to do. If everyone would do that just the least bit, a greater good would be served for a greater number, including the guy himself on some other occasions if not then. But damn few people ever consider that. And if they won't do it in a thing like that, how much less so in larger and more important items. So the lumberman takes all the timber and beats his children out of an equal share in forest products of the region. And all the while the Swedes, thru conservation, get now each year more out of their forests than they got 110 years ago when the present program was instituted. Now the same thing happens to the fish. And it makes it so much harder to explain, when you know that there are peaks and troughs anyway, and that even if they didn't take too many there'd be some bad years. But not so bad, of course. And not so disastrously long. Here this year, many fishermen will suffer, their fine boats will be foreclosed, some of the new reduction plants will go broke. A pity they were allowed ever to be built, especially at this time with difficult materials priorities. And people go without homes of their own while the unused reduction plants promise to stay idle. Now I see one of the social values of organized religion. I've thought so little of them I never realized that before. If people won't of their own accord achieve a sense of balance with something suprapersonal, you beat it into them. Well, I'd rather be an ecologist and have for stock in trade that sense of integration with a whole picture without which any field zoologist must be lost. Or, I suppose, an integrator of myths and literature.

I think Jean is fine. If she wants a vacation from concert dancing and from New York, bring her here for awhile. She will go well with this bunch, like and be liked. If you people would spend a summer here, I think there would be many good times, and you'd get some work done. That fine Wings Over Jordan negro choir comes here tonight; if they still have the wicked soprano it'll be good. Well, why don't I get to work. Read a vitamin or two. Assay a protein for my living.

Ed

Waverly Place
New York 14, N.Y.
April 3, 1947

Dear Ed—and Toni—
Thank you for sending me the two handsome articles. In the first place, anything from Ed's lab has fetish-value in my life; I thank you first therefore (on religious grounds) for the mere sending of these priceless objects. I perform meditations before, around, and over them, three times a day, between meals. In the second place, they are good, and have yielded both delight and information to your devotee. I thank you, second, therefore (on literary and scientific grounds) for the prose. On this point I pause, a moment, to dilate. Toni on Steinbeck is the only word on Steinbeck worth two cents—so far as I know; and she, I would say, is worth her ink's weight in gold. Toni my dear (excuse me, Ed) you are bright, and you write with competence, and I feel I know and like you better and much more than one evening's public companionship would seem to explain. The answer is probably (alright Ed, you can come back now) that Ed is simply infallible. Which brings me to the

critical problem of the sardine (excuse me, Toni): the enemy, it seems to me, is Dr. Miller. "Until we know more about the relation in the movements and spawning of sardines and survival of young fish to ocean temperatures, ocean currents and other hydrographic conditions," Dr. Miller said, "it is impossible to anticipate such fluctuations in the catch or to account for them after they have occurred."

Dear Ed,

Doesn't it seem a disgrace that such men, everywhere, in every department of learning, sit in the chairs, while you and I, with our dear Toni and Jean, are trying to make ends meet? Like the farmer-in-the-Dell? In the familiar pattern of dust to dust and ashes to ashes, their bodies disintegrate, but their souls go marching on. The released elements, in the form of a rain of particles, constantly enrich the dark deeper layers (that's us), but then, when, by the process called "upwelling," fertilizer is brought to the surface, these here now denizens of the upper layers, receiving all the light to permit developments, simply grow so rapidly that they deplete the fertilizer and are as badly in need of diatoms as ever. There's a Curve to elucidate that one, I'm sure.

Good luck, old boy, on the Guggenheim. The news of the second edition is great news. Let me know when it appears.

Yours,

Joe

P.S. Faber and Faber, London, are publishing an edition of The Skeleton Key. The page proofs were here a couple of months ago. Also, the first printing of the Zimmer book has already sold out.[35] My second Zimmer volume is in the press, and I am about to commence work on the third. The whole winter has gone into my revision of the MS of my own myth book, on which I have been working, it now seems, since the fall of Man.

Dear Toni,
Your essay on John's wayward cosmos is a beautiful summary of a lot of things that Ed used to be talking about back there in Those Were The Days and He Was Their Hero. Returning to me now, with your (dear) touch to them, and at this time when I have been far from the incense of formaldehyde [spelling accident] for so long that I have faintly lost the nose for it, the impact on my thought is considerable. I sense the possibility of a non-teleological teleology, if you know what I mean [seriously!]. Well perhaps that's something we're going to have to talk about some day. Anyhow, it fits in some way with myth and the idea of Involuntary Bliss.

Bliss to thee, Toni, and joy to Ed.

Yours also,

Joe

P.S. Jean joins in greetings.

April 11, 1947

Dear Joe:
Your letter lifted Toni more perhaps even than it did me. She was a very tickled gal. "To be included, so nice," was her note.

Sign on P[acific] G[rove] church announcing sermon. "After Easter, what." Did you like the article in recent Life on Medieval Europe. I was surprised how clearly they got over what I think is the substance of those times. Very significant that we, who among nations move most swiftly to the break-up, should have ourselves destroyed Mt. Cassino monastery, Thomas Aquinas nurturing place. We destroyed our grandfather's house. I fear there'll be many a bad time before our children build its equivalent.

A thing you'll like in the new Ed BPT. The plankton essay. Or did I tell you. If not, you'll be interested. If so, only a little bored.

The man who for thirty years has been laboriously counting the organisms per typical liter of sea water daily, then composited weekly, finally retired discouraged. The fluctuations (he himself calls them pulses) vary from a few hundred to hundreds of thousands within a few days or within a few miles. The university refused to publish any more of his figures after seven reports. But did publish some of the summaries—which lacked the details some of us would have liked for combinings. Anyway, after investigation the limitations of mean curves for this material, I constructed 3-station-composite means curve for the 7 year period in S Calif. Out of data from a single station in the Aleutians for 6 different years I also constructed a mean year's calendar based also on daily readings. These both came to peak in the <u>same week</u>. There was a huge secondary peak in the north (reflecting the usual northern autumnal re-growth which doesn't occur in the south) but there was a corresponding but smaller polygon peaking at the same week. The 5 or 6 smaller bumps all came to peak in or near the same weeks! Isn't that fabulous. If substantiated by the 25 year figures, which have been got and could be made available if a person had the money to get them tabulated and worked up, this would reflect a primitive biological rhythm operative over the whole of the north Pacific, the same presumably in any large group of years.

So we both strike fertile ground. For you're doing so certainly. And sounds as tho you're at it steadily. I did not get the Guggenheim. A pity. I was counting on it rather, since they suggested I apply. That'll make this summer different. I had figured on going again to the Queen Charlottes, then taking that three year's work as basis for a book "The Outer Shores." Now it'll have to be deferred a year, perhaps indefinitely. Kay's operations and a couple of other unexpected items see to that! Toni did a job on Jeffers, also another little thing called something about are we losing our minds. I'll send them on. Now she prances around here half clothed, well not even half, saying come on now get ready to go to Barbara and Ellwoods. I forget if you knew them. They do well. He traded paintings for a Packard Station wagon. And has now an entire block of wooded hill near his house and some added lots. I have just bought two of them and will hope eventually to put a lab up since I can't get waterfrontage for love or money. And this is too valuable and high taxed for me to hold onto indefinitely. oh that impatient gal. here we go. To jean and Joe from Toni and Ed.[36]

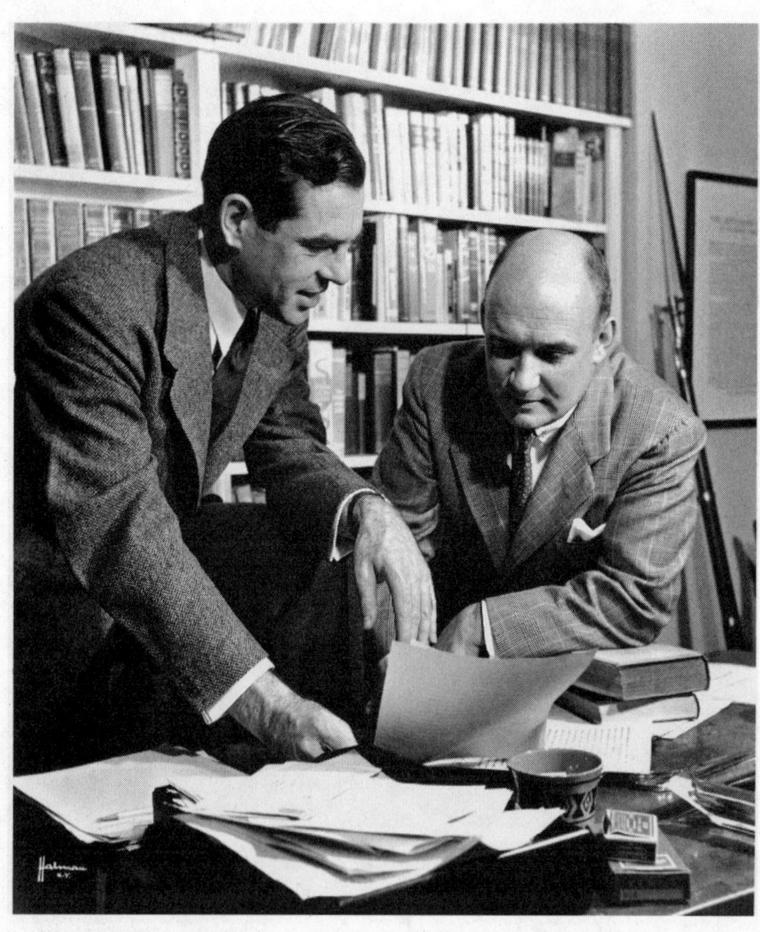

Joseph Campbell and Henry Morton Robinson, circa 1944

CHAPTER 2

Decade *Mirabilis*

The 1940s

Campbell found work at Sarah Lawrence College in Bronxville, New York, in March 1934. He would teach there for the next thirty-eight years, beginning one of the most extraordinary careers in American education. The position provided him with the secure employment that would enable him to begin his writing career, with a series of remarkable publications in the decade of the 1940s—the subject of this chapter. During this period, he produced his first books: commentary on Where the Two Came to Their Father, A Skeleton Key to Finnegans Wake, *and* The Hero with a Thousand Faces. *It boggles the mind to think how one could manage this while editing and publishing the voluminous posthumous papers left behind by Heinrich Zimmer (*The King and the Corpse, Myths and Symbols in Indian Art, Philosophies of India, *and, later,* The Art of Indian Asia*). To top all of this off, at the end of the decade Campbell read through all of the papers from the Eranos Yearbooks, in French, Italian, English, and German, to lay the foundations for his six-volume selection, produced during the 1950s (the period covered in chapter 3).*

Although there seem to be no letters directly between Campbell and Heinrich Zimmer during this decade mirabilis, *there are letters that give us glimpses into the stages of production associated with those remarkable books—and with crucial responses to them, like the one from Roger Sherman Loomis, Campbell's mentor at Columbia. Loomis was so completely committed to his view of the Celtic origins of the Arthurian romances that he responded with bewildered contempt to Zimmer's* The King and the Corpse. *This work espoused a broadly comparative approach to Celtic and Asian mythologies that would become the keystone of Campbell's work.*

Campbell's reply to Loomis is one of the most important letters in this volume. It is a manifesto of sorts, marking a crucial transition in Campbell's career, catalyzed by his studies in Paris and Munich in the twenties and by his pivotal meetings with Heinrich Zimmer, beginning in 1942, when Campbell attended a series of Zimmer's lectures at Columbia on Indian art and philosophy. The story of those encounters is told in Larsen and Larsen, A Fire in the Mind, *and in a 1980 interview Campbell did for* Parabola *magazine. After Zimmer died of pneumonia, suddenly and unexpectedly, in March 1943, Campbell spent nearly ten years editing the papers left behind.*

Among the correspondents from this period, the most important is surely Ananda K. Coomaraswamy, then the curator of the Oriental collection at the Boston Museum of Fine Arts. Coomaraswamy was himself not well during these years (1945–47), but his expertise in Sanskrit enabled him to offer critical notes, suggestions, and contributions to The King and the Corpse. *His footnotes in that beautiful book are acknowledged by his initials, and the letters written to Campbell during the final stages of its preparation demonstrate his commitment to the project—quite movingly, in the shadow of his death in 1947, a year before its publication.*

The other key correspondent of this period was the novelist Henry Morton Robinson (September 7, 1898–January 13, 1961). He is best known for A Skeleton Key to Finnegans Wake, *written with Campbell and published in 1944, and for his 1950 novel* The Cardinal.

Maud Oakes (1903–1990) was an artist, ethnologist, and writer who spent her life recording the indigenous cultures of Native American tribes, including the Navajo of the American Southwest and the Mam of Guatemala. She is best known for her books recording these tribes' ceremonies, art, and stories. These include Where the Two Came to Their Father: A Navaho War Ceremony *(with commentary by Campbell),* The Two Crosses of Todos Santos: Survivals of Mayan Religious Ritual*, and* Beyond the Windy Place.

Maud Oakes in Guatemala, 1948

Coolidge, New Mexico
[No date]

Dear Jo:
Just a line to say hello and send you a description of things that go on out here, and my first meeting with Jeff. Did Mima give you the letter that described the first meeting last year with Jeff?

Please keep the enclosed letter as I want it for my files and you can give it back when we meet in New York.

The skins that I am to paint on and that were promised in

March have not yet come, so I am returning to New York the middle of May. Wolff can not do the reproductions from the skins so I shall have to do another set on paper.

Best of luck to you, and will see you soon.

Sincerely,

Maud

Coolidge, New Mexico
March 23, 1943

Dear Jo
What sad news about Zimmer—I can't get it out of my mind—his poor wife and boys what will become of them?—I know what a great loss it must be to you his going—for I have known him such a short time and I feel it very much. Am awaiting the coming of Jeff King the medicine man and then you shall hear more from me. Have heard good news from the people I wrote on the Pueblo affair. Best of luck to you,

Maud

From Stanley Young, editor of Where the Two Came to Their Father.

Harcourt, Brace and Company, Inc.
Publishers
Madison Avenue, New York
June 25, 1943

Dear Joe:
I have now finished my second reading of your introductory and I think it is a most perceptive and stimulating signpost to lead us into the enchanted land of mythology. I was about to say that the writing was "beautiful, sweet, glorious, stunning, and delicious"

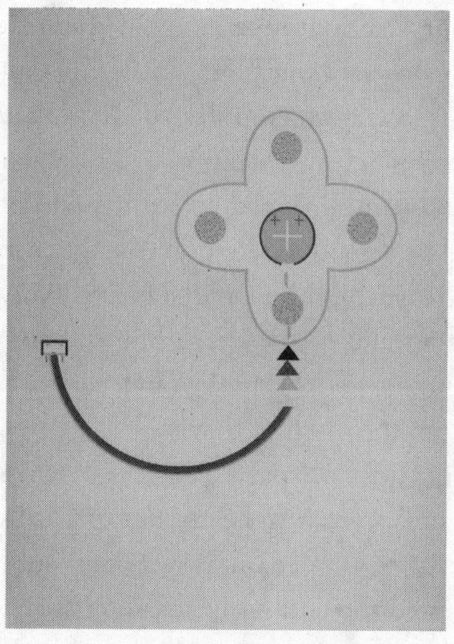

Sand painting by Jeff King of "The Mountain around Which Moving Was Done" from *Where the Two Came to Their Father*

but then I realized I would be hoisting you on your own petard. (See cuts in ms.!)

I don't know if editors are born of careless women, hence monsters, but I do know they can think of monstrous things whenever they get near a manuscript. So I shall begin: the first impression of the script in its present form is that sections two to four, having to do with M. Oakes and her task in getting the myth, seem out of key with the solid body of the introduction. This I feel very strongly. In my opinion this part should be lifted entirely, and with some compression, be re-told by Maud Oakes herself, under a separate heading. As the bulk of these sections is taken from Maud Oakes' letters, it would be a simple matter to cast it all into the first person—that is, if Maud is agreeable. Both your work on interpreting the myth, and her part in gathering would, to my mind, be immeasurably strengthened by this division. There is an unspannable gap between the colloquial style of Maud Oake's [*sic*] story and your interpretation of the myth as the matter is now presented.

So far as your own writing is concerned independent of these two sections (2–4) I have very little to say, except of a technical nature. PP. 12–15 could be compressed. Part Four gets down to business and moves informatively to page 43 where, for me, it becomes long and somewhat tedious to the end of that section. I think this would be a good area to examine for cutting. Sometimes your vast knowledge of the whole subject of mythology comes between the reader and his desire to know about the myth he is waiting to hear in this book. I think you need constantly to keep in mind, and refer to, the myth of <u>this</u> book.

The Catholic stuff on page 46 I must say as a devout ex-protestant, yet still protesting heathen, can hardly please a publisher and is sure to be jumped on. Better cut it out or tone it down.

I have suggested the cutting of Jeff's anecdote on p. 30 which seems fairly irrelevant and not anything to make Jeff die of laughter. But maybe I should go to the nearest hogan.[1]

Now to little points: is it CHILD BORN OF THE WATER or CHILD BORN FOR THE WATER? The ms. is inconsistent about this. Put the fine yellow insertions into the ms. when it gets retyped. Use footnotes in your introductory where pages and publishers are mentioned, and check the "asides" in Jeff's telling of the myth. Where it is Jeff's aside, it should remain in parenthesis, but where it is Maud Oakes it should go into a footnote, in order not break the spell of the tale-telling.

Also, in the re-typing, ask your girl to use the symbol (--) for a dash, instead of three smacks. Printers put it down as it comes to them, you know. The dash, by the way, is used pretty liberally throughout, in many cases too often, I think.

You are going to stylize the ms. in every way possible so I need not mention the matter of keeping Beauty Way consistently in (or out) of quotes, keeping "hogan" lower case, etc.

You will find words ringed throughout the manuscript which either Mary Mellon or I have questioned for one reason or another.[2] Colloquial phrases have been questioned, too liberal a dose of adjectives has been questioned or cut, and occasionally a sentence or a phrase or a paragraph will show two vertical lines at the side which suggest revision.

I am unable to know how far you have gone in cutting the introduction or in making revisions of your own. I should judge that you yourself have probably caught, by now, many of the things I have indicated. You wrote this very quickly and naturally there were sure to be revisions. I hope you won't be defensive about these suggestions from a hardened professional and that some of them will make sense to you. When they don't, please tell me and let us discuss them.

After all these thrusts and demands, I repeat my personal pleasure over the grand job you did. Wolff needs the manuscript not later than July 15th, so persevere with the finished copy, complete with titles, tables of contents, etc. I think titles should be used at the opening of each section of the introductory.

If you have any questions, let me have them. Naturally, I know you and Maud Oakes will want to discuss with me the suggested organic change for sections 2–4. Cut your own part as you can without destroying the fine structure you have built up.

Yours,
Stanley Young

Waverly Place
New York City
June 27, 1943

Dear Stanley,
I have typed out sections 2 and 3 in the first person, with addition of the corrections suggested by Maud and yourself, and with some deletions. I am sending copies to both Maud and yourself. This is not my notion of what the final draft should be. Maud will have to season it to her own taste. The final draft should be made next week-end.

My feelings about the present offering are as follows:

1. This story told in the first person has to me a disagreeable flavor. Perhaps it could be put back into the third person and stand separate from my introduction.
2. This story, given as preface describing the collection of the present materials is much too long. It should be reduced to an account of the work with Jeff King. But such reduction would deprive the book of one of its most charming feathers, namely, the most vivid introduction to the contemporary Navaho world that has yet been written. This, it seems to me, would be a great loss indeed.
3. This story, given at full length in the third person, and separate from my introduction, chops the book into too many units. This entire story, together with Maud's description of the pictures, might stand as the introduction; my general discussion of the mythology should, in that case, be omitted. I should not like it to stand as a kind of appendix. I would return to you half of my fee, and I would keep my sections for use somewhere else.
4. If it is finally decided to give Maud's story in a separate preface, I think that section 2 of the present enclosure, where the rite of Jeff King is discussed, should be lifted back to my Introduction. It could be sparked up a bit, and made to serve as transition from my general discussion of Navaho lore to my specific discussion of the rite and legend of the present opus. Also, it would give to my dervish dance a bit of solid Navaho ground to stand on.

My positive suggestions, in the order of my preference, are as follows:

Plan 1. Leave the introduction intact. Let me tidy up the style of Maud's section. Let me sparkle up Jeff King's section to make the transition into my discussion less sudden.—I really feel that much more is to be lost by breaking this thing up than is to be gained (but I am not the guy to put up a fight for any of my ideas, particularly when it is somebody else who is paying for them). I have during the past twenty-four hours carefully questioned the worthies who read the second carbon copy of the paper, and all agree that, when read through in one sweep, the transitions are easily made, the development is orderly and exciting, the introduction to the subject matter is easy and agreeable to follow, the intensity of the experience mounts to a climax about midway through, and then gradually returns to the level from which an easy step can be made into the simple style of the myth. All this is what the author intended. After careful rereading, I feel that, though I slobbered over frequently in the gush of my florid celtic style, I made no mistakes in organization.

Plan 2. Put Maud's section in a separate Preface. Let it remain in the third person. (How it is to be justified in its length, I do not know.) Let Jeff's section remain in my Introduction, to be sparkled up with a couple of drops of my patented cosmic extract.

Plan 3. Let Maud's section, Jeff's section, and Maud's description of the pictures constitute the introduction. My comparative-mythological discussion should, in this case, be omitted entirely.

Plan 4. Let a brief statement in the first person, by Maud, describe the collection of this legend and picture-series. Let Jeff's section remain with my introduction, as in Plan 2.

You will understand, I am sure, that although my feelings, as author, are strong in this matter (and all for Plan 1), my feelings as a human being are not, and I shall present no obstacles to any decision you may finally make (unless it is to include my introduction as a kind of co-introduction, to follow or to precede a preface, or introduction, giving all the necessary facts for the simple reading of the story). I take my cue in matters of this kind from a wonderful little upholsterer, who does work for us, now and then: the patron or employer must be satisfied.

I have gone through your text corrections and find them excellent. I shall follow them to the letter. They give me a good feeling. I expect to be ready to hand my text over to a typist Wednesday or Thursday, so I shall be grateful for an early statement of what you think should be done about this awkward, nasty matter or arrangement.

Please note: the title of our piece, according to Father Berard's latest pronouncement, is Where the Two Came to Their Father.

My warmest thanks to you for your advice in the matter of the present text, and in the matter of my Myth book as well. I feel that you have already done much to let me know what the budding author must understand about the publisher.

Hope you had a wonderful swim: my best to Nancy,

Yours

The following is from Campbell to Kurt Wolff, founder and publisher of Pantheon Books, original publisher of the Bollingen Series.

Waverly Place
New York, 14, N.Y.
July 16, 1943

Dear Mr. Wolff:

Enclosed is the blurb for which you asked.

Last night and the morning I reread the legend of Jeff King with that pesky lady in Connecticut in mind. While I should not like to have her correct my introduction, I now think that it might not be a bad thing to have somebody go through the Legend and take out commas. I punctuated the piece very heavily, because it seems to me very compact. But a fresh eye might find that I had overladen the pages. This is the only doubt that I feel as I wake up this morning. It would be a four hour job for someone, and since the Jeff King sections do not begin until page 100, no printing time would be lost.

During the summer I shall work on the Zimmer manuscript, which I hope to have ready by Thanksgiving Day. Stanley asked me to compose a little statement for the advertising copy; I shall send him something this week-end.

Thank you very much for the advice and help that you are giving us. With kindest regards,

Yours very sincerely
[Joseph Campbell]

The following two letters from Oakes concern Princeton University Press's 1969 hardcover rerelease of Where the Two Came to Their Father.

c/o Jerome Hill
Sugar Bowl
Norden Calif 95724
August 27, 1967

Dear Jo:
Your letter was forwarded to me here where I came several days ago.

Sugar Bowl is a heavenly spot situated 7000 feet altitude. We work, walk, cook and drink wine with delicious food. We are the cooks and we help each other with our new projects.

I agree with all you say in your letter. After talking to you on the phone that day I sent off all that stuff without rereading the book. I agree that nothing should be changed except the switch around and the two lines you want cut out: I do think it is important to put that six months after the collecting of the myth I went out again to check with Jeff King about the myth. This was Paul Radin's suggestion.

Yes! I heard that Jeff King had received an award but never

heard the details. I wonder if the Navaho Bureau of Affairs, or what ever it is called would have the details? The address is Window Rock and whether it is in Arizona or New Mexico I don't know and can't find out up here.

As to the paragraph. I can't help out much out here. I remember one thing that is interesting. When Mima [Mary Mellon] and Stanley started the [Bollingen] Foundation and wondered what manuscript they should commence with Zimmer said something like this. "If we were in Germany we would commence any new venture in publishing with the Old Guard," so that is why they decided on Where the Two Came to Their Father. When I return to Big Sur in a week or so, probably the end of the month, I will try to get the data on the award if you want me to.

If I do not go to Europe I will certainly be at your Big Sur seminar and I hope you will look on "Little Star Way" as a place to rest and eat when you want it.

Love to you and Jean
Maud

P.S. you could put the note about the recheck of myth on p. 45 or 56 or bring it into the text.

Maud Oakes
Partington Ridge
Big Sur, Calif. 93920
Sept 21, 1967

Dear Jo:
Just a line to say hello! And to say I shall be out here for your seminar.

Have just returned from spending the night with Jo and Helena H[enderson].[3] We spoke of you and your time here.

First, you should know that there is a great deal of hepatitis (sp.?) on the Pacific Coast and especially Big Sur. It is really an epidemic, and many people at the Hot Springs, Esalen, have had shots against it. I have had them and many of my friends. If you are going to eat at the Hot Springs I would suggest your having them. The Hendersons are staying with me and sleeping in Henry Miller's house next door. If you don't mind sharing a bath with the Hendersons and sleeping in my studio, which is Henry Miller's, I could have a bed moved in there and you would be comfortable. This way you could have all your meals here at my house and not run the danger of dishes not properly washed. The Hot Springs have ordered elec dish washers, but they have not come. This is just a suggestion and may not fit in with your plans.

I shall attend your San F. lecture as well as here, so if you want a lift out here after your morning lecture I would be delighted to drive you out route 1 along the ocean. The Hendersons have offered to take you back to San F.

Have you heard about the Zen Mt. retreat? It is in the mountains back of Carmel. Situated in a valley between high Mts. and by natural Hot Springs. It is run by real Zen priests from Japan and with very dedicated followers. If you have time I could drive you over there. I remember how much you loved Japan.

How is the book coming on and who is checking on the color plates?

Love to you and Jean,
Maud

P.S. The hepatitis was carried by the Hippies using unclean needles.

The following correspondence has to do with A Skeleton Key to Finnegans Wake, *which Campbell wrote with Henry Morton Robinson, whom he calls "Rondo."*

Waverly Place
New York City
Dec. 31, 1940

Dear Rondo:
The handsomest little penknife arrived, and I thank you. I'm glad the pies are still welcomed by your household, and that you are all big and strong enough to eat them. I feel like a Dutch uncle, every year indulging himself to a little touch of domesticity.

As for the great work. It's still, but very slowly, progressing. This winter I am having to work very hard at my college work, and the time I have had on hand for Big Mister Finnegan has been very little. Nevertheless, I see myself with a few great strides of the end of this heartbreaking task of constructing a skeleton outline of the work. Furthermore, I have reviewed carefully <u>The Portrait of the Artist as a Young Man</u> and <u>Ulysses</u>, looking for clues, and I have assembled a promising lot of material which I have not yet had time to evaluate. My stack of notes is steadily increasing, and my plan of attack is clarifying itself.—That is all I have to report!

When I finish the present task, I am going to begin work on some of the major themes, comparing the passages in which they occur and attempting to settle my mind about them. It is then that I shall hope to cash in on your wit. For the present, I have only this dull grind to accomplish (and, believe me, it is dull), week by week putting pages behind me, trying to establish my "outline."

Many thanks again for the little knife. It sits now close at hand, contributing its share to the progress of our work.

Best wishes for the new year to your entire household from ourselves.

Sincerely,
Joe

P.S. the word "work" occurs six times in the above page and a half, and expresses the only thought on my mind!!

Waverly Place
N.Y. City
March 31, 1942

Dear Rondo:
When I read the enclosed article, immediately it came into my head that you might find, in this study, material for a stunning Readers Digest article. I wrote Zimmer to see whether he would let me send it to you, and he was delighted to think that "the subject of Hindu mythology" might win the eye of the American public. The point, as you will immediately see, is that the stories which he here presents are drawn from traditional Indian sources and illustrate the answer to that question which all newspaper writers love to ask these days: "How does mysterious India think? and specifically, how does India think about history and dictatorships and the overthrow of dictators?" It is an amusing coincidence that one of the dictators of the present collection, namely Mura, uses as his power-gesture precisely the Hitler greeting. And you will see that the Indian formula for victory, namely an unforeseen synthesis of the pairs of opposites, producing a new redeemer, can be illustrated as well with modern examples (Capitalistic England & America with Communistic Russia) as with ancient mythological (Shiva with Vishnu!).

The article as it stands, composed in very bad English for a scholarly audience, is of course not at all fit for the Readers Digest—but if you think this theme a good one, willing hands will toil to put India before the American eye!

Meanwhile you perhaps may wonder what can have become of the great enterprise of Finnegan. It has advanced another long and heavy step, but is far from ready for your valuable help. There is simply no end to this goddamn job. I am hoping to be able, late this spring, to begin working on the final stage of the problem—the stage of composing a text to be read. As soon as I complete the first pages I shall be at your feet for help.

And how are you, anyhow?

Jean joins me in sending kindest greetings to you and your tiny ones and their mother.

Sincerely

Joe

P.S. If you wish to communicate directly with the author of the enclosed article, his address is Dr. Henry Zimmer, # Woodland Avenue, New Rochelle, N.Y.

Waverly Place
New York City
May 30, 1943

Dear Rondo—
I am simply amazed at your job of compression. I find it difficult to think what you left out, and yet I know some six thousand words have disappeared. It is a fine little piece—and should come into the field of contemporary American criticism like a small visitor from another planet. I am not surprised it widened Cousins' eyes.[4]

The task, let me say the miracle, of deleting 500 words more without defacement to the manuscript was beyond my poor power—but I did get rid of the half-thousand words. I send you a pretty retyped edition to save you the apoplexy. Careful count will reveal that 520 words have been cut out. More careful collation with the original will show that 600 were cut out and eighty added—the additions to bridge the gaps and to touch up one or two little points. The addition of the three words "and Broadway hits" on page 10 does something quite magical to the discussion of Shaun and brings the entire paper into lively connection with our popular series!

Thank you for the appreciation of my rendition of Finnegans Wake, Part II. I am sure we have the only key that will ever be made to that seven-sealed cave of smoke. Part I, sections 2 and 3, are the densest chapters in the library of European fiction!

I hope the enclosed corrections please. If more cuts are required, I think they should come from the Shem and Shaun paragraphs—but I have not the heart to make them!

Yours,

Joe

Woodstock, N.Y.
Tuesday (No date)

Dear Rondo:

Yesterday I worked on the first chapter and found the Demonstration section excellent. The Synopsis is based on a very early version of our interpretation and requires some revising, which I am trying to supply. I am going to stress the lines that keep the work tied together, so that the reader, from the start, will be conscious of the unity of the composition. I worked yesterday on this task, and it started very encouragingly. You are entirely right about the need for a synthesis of this kind in this place. Perhaps this review of the Wake will make a good article for Cousins.

Jean and I enjoyed very much the party Sunday evening. Indeed, it has been an entirely wonderful summer—thanks primarily and almost totally to yourself and Gerty. We look forward to seeing you in New York, where, Deus volens, our Entitled Mamafesta Memorializing the Most Highest shall open its leaves to day.[5]

Yours,

Joe

The following letter refers to Robinson's novel The Perfect Round, *then recently published. The novel inspired David Carradine's 1983 film* Americana.

Waverly Place
New York 14, N.Y.
October 14, 1945

Dear Rondo:
<u>The Perfect Round</u> arrived yesterday, and I have just finished it. The book is full of very strange and moving images. I enjoyed the Dedalus-Earwicker undertones. The merry-go-round, the dog-fight, the incident in the pipe, the barge episodes, and the Ulster County background materials, add up to something pretty potent. And the development of the wild plot is strong and convincing. I must thank you for a fine experience, as well as a few fresh ideas about the linkage of symbolic images to the scrap-materials of life.

Jean and I have had (are having) an impossible Fall. First, our apartment wasn't yet painted when we returned, and two weeks down the drain while we waited around. Then my mother passed through with Alice's little Anne (3 yrs old) on the way to Hawaii, and we had a bit to do there. Next, Jean's mother writes that she is arriving from Hawaii—first visit since Pearl Harbor—and we have been going crazy trying to find a room (success came to us only yesterday!). Finally, concerts, dance-classes, galley proofs, odd jobs, my myth book ms., and a million other things, have had to be faced. The fine summer—hardly a month away—seems years away already.

Please give our love to Gertie; we are still searching for a casserole to match the one we broke!! Hope to see you soon.

Yours,
Joe

Waverly Place
New York 14, N.Y.
November 18, 1945

Dear Rondo:
Thank you for your very nice letter of last week. I am delighted to hear that your novel is finding its public, in spite of the New York

reviews. I read only two of the reviews (the one in the N.Y. Times and the one in the issue of the Saturday Review that happens to be carrying my own Roheim article) and found them very wishy-washy, as though the reviewers both suspected there might be more in the book than they had found, and yet were unwilling to say that it carried profundities. For myself, I thought that the fault in the book lay in what might be called the "intermittent character of its symbolic continuity": this, however, is a fault which it shares with Ulysses and Finnegans Wake, and perhaps this is of a piece with the character of modern life. What I mean is, that, though the basic symbolic image fills the entire work, the several phases of its life-reference (political, social, psychological, metaphysical) are not kept active simultaneously and throughout, but present themselves, one or two at a time, momentarily, and then disappear. In one section of the book (the quest for the leather belt) the literal, physical aspect of the adventure took over and the overtones fairly dwindled out. But against this quality of allegorical irregularity, the narrative itself had a firmness and inevitability that supplied a good stout string of continuity, and there was a quite charming lyrical quality that pervaded the whole. I think you found a rich and fruitful image, and developed it with great facility, furnishing not only a darn good story, but a number of indelible, almost "mythological" scenes.

The editing of the Joyce letters is a project that might yield some very interesting and important glimpses into the Ulysses–Finnegans Wake secrets. I have a feeling it is something we should try to keep in the family, so to speak; and yet, I am so deep under sea, with all my present tasks, that I do not know whether I am going to be able to be of much help this time. It is just possible that the collecting and deciphering might turn out to be a prodigious task, in which case the camels' backs might crack in the middle, right at the hump. Have you any idea of the probable dimensions of the project?

Good to hear about Tony Robinson, Quarterback. I am sure he must be having a marvelous time. We are hoping to see his proud parents one of these fine wintry days. Best wishes for a substantial turkey.

Yours,

Joe

The following two letters to Robinson were sent together.

Waverly Place
New York 14, N.Y.
March 13, 1946

What big ears you have, Grandpa, he said.

And by what miracle may the information have got from the quiet of my study to the hurly-burly of your hue and cry, within a week?

But I can explain myself; and it is non-actionable, though a goddam nuisance.

I thought it would be nice to refer my desirable reader to a single excellent series of reference books, as often as possible, instead of to every volume in the N.Y. library.[6] And so, wherever I could, I took my texts from The Mythology of All Races, XIII vols Marshall Jones & Co., Boston. Old Mr. Jones wrote me that he was delighted, etc., but that, unfortunately he had just sold the plates of the whole series to Macmillan. Macmillan deliberated the problem for 2 months, and then decided that since they had not yet brought out <u>their</u> edition of the volumes, they would prefer not to have the series quoted at this time. Result: a fine job for Joe, scouting out new sources in umpteen non-English dialects. The work is done. I have now only to revise my footnotes and change a few paragraphs of the text; and Macmillan can shove their thirteen volumes up their chimney (if they are so fortunate).

Brockway has been incubating my manuscript ever since I handed it to him, and so there are no copyright suits in the offing. All will have been repaired by this time next week.

Dear Rondo:
It was swell to hear from you, and to learn the news about the wonderful little family. Jean and I have been having an extraordinarily busy winter: coping with our several families-in-law while dancing and writing respectively. The Zimmer volume has gone through 4 sets of proofs; the agony of an index; and all the marvels of Greek, Sanskrit, German, French, Latin, and English typographies. It will appear two seconds before my death. My own myth book has been ready for some time now, but lying in Brockway's apartment. Zimmer volume #2 is almost ready for the publisher. And I have decided to take another year off from teaching.

Jean & I expect to go to Honolulu this summer, so there won't be any nice Mavericking with the Robinson's. But we hope to have a look at you before we depart—somehow. Meanwhile, love to you all—and thanks, Rondo, for your quick word in response to the rumor.—Yours Joe

---

Waverly Place
New York 14, N.Y.
October 2, 1946

Dear Rondo—
Back from Never-Never Land, fat, subdued in mental vigor, trying to pick up life where it left off, and thinking to spend our following summer among the mosquito-swamps of the Maverick (where there will be time for work), I recall, with pleasure and no little pride, a phone-call received from my great colleague of the filled fountain pen, somewhat to the tune of his kind willingness to cast a sympathetic eye upon the pages of my boomeranging myth book. Sensible of many earlier favors, days of our youth spent among the frangible Queen Anne's Lace of the manured fields, evenings by the fire, mornings by the dozen, nights with our wives (two sparkling daughters of), and no little desirous of your further regard, I

now (with your kind permission) write to know whether it would be convenient for you, within the next few days, to receive my burden by registered mail. With love to your sweet Gertrude, and to the father, son, and pretty twilling-bugs, hoping that their summer was greatly profitable both to purse and to the psychosomatic system, yearning to see you, one and all, in the earliest possible nick of time, I am (and Jean joins me in my cry of love),

Your most humble admirer,

Joseph

The following letter refers to Robinson's novel The Great Snow *(1947).*

Waverly Place
New York 14, N.Y.
March 30, 1947

Dear Rondo:

"The Great Snow" began yesterday morning and ended about ten minutes ago. I am really impressed. Of course, I am not able to read your novels with clean eyes: there are too many bifocal interferences from the Maverick; also, the echoes of Ulysses and Finnegans Wake ring for me in a special way. Nevertheless, I am sure that such accidental sights and sounds are not enough to obscure the book entirely. I am reasonably certain that the major portion of my pleasure and instruction was the fruit of your art and intention.

You are developing, it seems to me, a technique of symbolic composition that is primarily your own (even though utilizing, now and then, the devices and figures of the Master), and I think that you have gained greatly in control and compression since "The Perfect Round." There are more levels visible to the mind in the present book, and fewer interruptions of the symbolic treatment. Your theme is very strong and important, and its play many-faceted. I find only here and there, in some of the mechanical, surgical, and athletic details, elements that have not been digested and assimilated into the symbolic context (or perhaps I should say, which I was unable to experience as symbol, instead of as fact or evidence). For example, the rubber sheet was excellent, but the splinter remained, I think just a splinter, and the motorcycle engine only a machine. The business with the hawk was really grand; so too the development of the whole context of the snow. The book is full of vivid and very eloquent scenes. It is packed with feeling, thought, and sensation. I was reluctant to put it down and go to bed. And I felt when I was finished that I had learned something very valuable about the art of being human. For all of which I thank you sincerely, kind sir, and send to you my profound congratulations, expressions of respect, and confident best wishes for your Opus III.

Love to the household.

Yours,

Joe

Waverly Place
New York 14, N.Y.
December 9, 1947

Dear Rondo—

Last summer, in what may have been a weak moment, you declared that you would like to feast your soul again on my myth book. Wolff has read it and wishes to publish it; we are now in the process of building for backing from the Bollingen Foundation. Meanwhile, I intend to go over the whole thing once more, this winter, to decide on the pictures to be used and to make my last adjustments of the text. Wolff found the going hard after the first hundred pages or so, but his reader had no great difficulties and was enthusiastic. I want to make the thing as easy and pleasant as I can, and so am planning to make one more heroic effort. Wolff's complaints were essentially the same as yours; I thought I had smoothed all that out, but it seems I haven't. And so, with the hope that this is not an imposition on your time and friendship,

I am sending the manuscript, with the humble request that if you can bring yourself to look at it again, will you graciously please put a signal in the margins where to go off the rails? I think two things are necessary: 1. abridgment of many of the stories (but I don't know which!), and 2. summing ups and looking ahead (but I don't know where!). In other words: I am a willing hand but a numb brain, eager to work but afraid to ruin the whole damn thing.

On the other hand, if you are too busy or just too tired to bring yourself to this operation, do not think for a minute that I might not understand, that I might be the least bit offended, or that I might have even a subconscious reaction. Actually, I feel that it is an imposition on my part to send this on to you at all.—and if it were not for that weak moment of yours last summer, I should certainly not pressure to do so.

The work this fall has proceeded in good style. I hope to finish the first half of Zimmer #3 by January 1 (the first half will amount to 286 pages). Zimmer #2 is about to leave the press (publication date probably some time in January). And my own myth book has been brought to the state that you soon shall see. The return to College has been pleasant and interesting. New York has been lively and full of events. And I think that if it were not for my need for sleep now and then I could get everything done that I have to do.

I have been wondering about your successful clergyman and trying to guess where he might be now. Bishop yet? And are there going to be any women in his life? When I think of all the trouble I have had simply trying to write down stories already told a million times, I marvel more and more at the man who tells a story for the <u>first</u> time. My heart goes out to you and I wish you courage.

Love and kisses to all the pretty ones, and a mighty handshake for the young hero of the family.—And listen, Rondo, if this MS is just a pain in the neck, dump it into that ditch out where the squash plants bloom and I shall be the first to understand.

Yours,

Joe

Waverly Place
New York 14, N.Y.
May 24, 1949

Rondo, my pal,
You done good by the old pencil-chewer, believe me! It's as good as ambrosia to know that such things can be said about the new opus, even if the hermetic knower who writes them is the one who told me to write the book. You were generous to take time out from your Cardinal-Carnival[7] to do this pretty thing. And let me say—there's a ping in your writing that's as exhilarating as a brisk plunge. I would have enjoyed reading the review, even if it had been about the work of someone I didn't know.

Jean and I have been hoping to be able to accept your invitation, of some months ago, for a weekend on the Maverick; but Jean's work has been so demanding, this spring, that we have been pinned to New York. She is now in Pittsburgh, teaching, and will be back for only a couple of days in June; just before we set off for the University of Colorado, where she will again be teaching. After that we sail for Honolulu. And then we come back to New York just in time for her to put her company in shape for a concert in October. Which is pretty thick. She is so tired that I may soon be able to persuade her not to accept every invitation that comes in the mail. But meanwhile, I've been getting a lot of work done myself; so I don't have too good a stance from which to argue. Perhaps we're both just nuts.

I find myself thinking every so often about your Cardinal, and wondering how he is. You must be seeking like a vestry by now. Priests, priests everywhere, in and out of every cell in your brain, stepping across the synapses and paying visits to the inside of your closed eyes! It must be something. Good wishes to the one with the red hat.

And my love to the twinkling daughters of; as well as a firm handshake for the pole-vaulter. I do wish that I were going to be seeing you and Gerty this season.

Yours,

Joe

Waverly Place
New York 14, N.Y.
March 20, 1950

Rondo, my dear man—

You've written a wonderful book [*The Cardinal*]. The mail brought it Friday afternoon. I've been reading it every possible second since. Finished five minutes ago (4:20 p.m.) without skipping a syllable, having been fascinated from first to last. The work flows majestically, all the way, with a great rich diapason: a book of life moved by divine grace, with many really noble scenes and a remarkable multifaceted eloquence. It is a poem that fully justifies—and expresses—your faith in the popular tongue as a possible vehicle of the supreme message (Dante's faith). And finally, it is a novel that brings to handsome flowering the art that was budding in your two earlier works. In sum: I was delighted, impressed, and proud.

So that I thank you from the bottom of my heart, Rondo, for this beautiful book, with its inscription celebrating a friendship that is one of the warmest jewels in my treasury and Jean's. I thank you also for the prominence of my own name in the first page and the last of this volume, which, to date, is the finest trophy of our common adventure into the marvelous labyrinth. You have here given us a flower that matches in beauty, magnitude, and perfume, anything known to me in the modern American garden of letters; if the next continues the rate of the development from 1 to 2 and from 2 to 3, we shall have to look far to find its fellow. Bravo! Bravissimo! And a profound obeisance!

Jean and I were delighted by your visit of the other evening. It was lovely that we could all be around a table again—as it has been lovely in the past—and will be lovely in the future. So here's to that future, Rondo, with a great acclaim to its promise in your present.

Jean joins in love and pride and applause.

Yours ever

Joe

The first page of the following letter to Robinson is missing.

...how, having heard from you last year what you were doing and then seeing the partially finished opus, brought the whole thing out very vividly. My thoughts are now that before going on with my pedantic, semi-scholarly performances, I should try my hand at the paramount task of the writer, namely, a novel of some kind. In the past I have thought about such a project, but now I think I should really begin to plan to get around to it. My next book, therefore, may turn out to be an attempt of some kind—in which case I shall be following, at a disciplinary distance, in the footsteps of the Master,—three novels and a half behind.

Jean has returned to her studies greatly refreshed—and improved in technique her two hour course with Hannele. We seem to be heading full tilt for the winter season, in spite of the general weight, all around us, of this terrific heat. The proofs for my myth book should arrive any day now and I have a beautiful set of plates for it. Zimmer #3 is all but finished, and Zimmer #4 is going to be comparatively easy. On the whole, I feel that I have put a great mountain range behind me, and that the going, henceforward, should be a little less rugged. If it is, I shall owe a lot of the numerous lessons learned in the various rooms of the Maverick domicile where I last week had such a fine holiday. My thanks to you and Gerty for a delicious psychomatic renovation.

Affectionately,

Joe

Waverly Place
New York 14, N.Y.
Aug. 24, 1960

Dear Rondo—
It was good of you to call Sunday and a great pleasure to hear your voice; also, to receive your letter the next day. I am greatly relieved to know that the idea of letting our little opus stand as it is appealed to you, and I know that it will do as well in its present form as it would with a few dickerings here and there. The book is still the only way to get in to Finnegans Wake. The next thing necessary is a ten volume work on the subject, and I am willing to leave the fashioning of that to somebody else.

Somehow your remarks about the writer's task gave me new heart for the pages ahead. I do not forget that it was you who turned my nose from reading to the writing desk, and I guess the voice of the old guru will always have magic for his school.

The volume on Oriental Mythology that I am writing is giving me a great tussle, largely because of the cross-currents of my own emotional relationship to the materials; but the worst part of the job is now behind me and I foresee clear sailing from here to the finish—which ought to be, though it may not be quite, Oct. 1.[8]

When you are free and feel like it, give me a ring, and meanwhile best wishes and affectionate greetings from us both

Yours ever,

Joe

P.S. If you phone, please dial, let the phone ring twice, hang up, dial again, and I'll be there. That's what's know as "the signal." It has absolute priority.

The following letter is apparently from a man attempting to translate Finnegans Wake*, or parts of it, into Hungarian.*

Dr. Endre Biró
Budapest, VIII
Baross—u 3.
May 29, 1963

Dear Mr Robinson or Mr Campbell or both / sorry for the curious beginning / but what follows will be stil more strange. Pardon me to address you with this extravagant letter. The oddities begin with the poorness of my knowledge of English, being swift to mate errthors stern to check myself, my incapacity reaching the depth of evry conceivable grammatical and orthographical mistakes. Next item of the curasity is my being an admirer of the work of James Joyce, jusque à Finnegans Wake. The next oddity is that I make, it is some sort of surprise even for me, translations of little selected parts in hun-gulash in my dusk mother tunga. Perhaps it is not so odd, that I have no other aim with my efforts as making amusement to myself and to some friends. The extravagancy No N. is that I am not some sort of a young enthusiastic philologist, but a sciencist, professor of biochemistry etc. / and the only connection of my fields of interest is to read finnegannian echoes in the oceans of dry scientific English I am force to read—which doing gives some refreshment /

Now to do all the diddies in one dedal, I want to ask from you some help with my translations. In spite of all difficulties I could make some round passages / as: the Mookse and the Gripes, Shem the Penman, The museyroom, a bit of the Gracehoper and the Andt etc. / but in all of them, besides the necessary blanks, which do not distrurbe the movement, there are some little and very important passages which I could not master. They are mostly only debris of sentences where I have no guess of the "litteral" meaning / although I have only of what it would mean and of the "musical" function of it too, but I don't know in what direction to commence the curious wheedling with which I arrive at the thing I call "translātion." / By the way it is not further apart from the original as the French ones published by André Bouchet—May I take some time from you, by asking you for some explanations?

To begin with: / the numbers are pages of the 1939 Faber and Faber ed. /

p. 155 "Tugurios-in-Newrobe or Tukurios-in-Ashies"—Europe and Asia I do hear in it, but what the "Tug..." and "Tuk..."?

p. 156 I don't undertsan stillabel of "...for par the unicum of..." and of "that brokenarked traveller...and what is what the Gripes added: "Mee are...etc.

p. 157 what is with "that Skand"...what is "sokaparlour"?

p. 159 "The romescot nattleshaker..." what is it for the snakes of snaking rattle? Is it somebody who collects pieces, as in the churches, instead of the applaus? Or am I wholly wrong? This rounding up of the lecture scene would be very important to get the whole of my rendering.

p. 170 "when he yeat ye abblokooken...etc." I hear in the excellent record, read by Cyril Cusack that it must be some classic poetry distorted, as the next item, the Yeats poem "when you are old etc." but I have no idea what it is?

p. 194 From: "bride leaves her"...to did ye hear...etc." I have only Very cloudy ideas about the "sense" of this passage would be very necessary from the rithmical point of I can't do it with only two "old the news of the great big world"; it sounds poor.

Still two other questions not referring to the text: You make somewhere a quotation in your "Key" like this: "Let stand his deed though clearly it is a mitake" / something like that, momentarily I do not find if. / Is it from Finnegans wake?

Mr. Ellman mentions a quotation from Edgar Quinet, which is the only true one made by Joyce in Finnegan. Where is it quoted? Ellman states only the place where it is transcribed in finneganolese. / p. 14–15/

I feel I must apologuise again for my fantastic letter and as a modest recompense for the truble I am asking you to take, I give here a few hungarian words I have picked up in Finnegan. It may have some interest for you. / Some were quoted by Moholy-Nagy, but I cant quote his study exactly now. /

p. 171 "feherbour" / talkind on the drinking habits of Shem / fehérbor = white wine

p. 176 "ahone ahaza" = a hon, a hasa, two patriotically coloured expressions for "patrie," with article

p. 184 in the "aria" on eggs: "somekat on toyast" = sonka és tojá = han and eggs.

p. 184 "ochiuri" means in rumanian eggs-on-the-plate / the word means "eyes"

p. 177 "kavehazs" = "kávéház = koffeehous / pronounced with the most open wovels you can imagine.

Excuse me again for beseting you in this way, and hoping for an answer if you would have some time for it

Sincerely yours,

Dr. Endre BIRÓ

Heinrich Zimmer (December 6, 1890–March 20, 1943) was the son of Heinrich Friedrich Zimmer, the great scholar of Celtic philology. A professor of Indology at Heidelberg University, he was dismissed in 1938 because of his anti-Nazi views. From 1941 to 1943, he lectured at Columbia University. Zimmer influenced the work of C. G. Jung as well as that of Thomas Mann, who dedicated his novel The Transposed Heads *to him. The first volume of the Bollingen Series (1943) was dedicated to his memory. The series published four of Zimmer's posthumous works, completed and edited by Campbell:* Myths and Symbols in Indian Art and Civilization *(1946),* The King and the

Corpse *(1948),* Philosophies of India *(1951), and* The Art of Indian Asia *(two volumes, 1955).*

Heinrich Zimmer (right) with Bollingen Foundation cofounder Paul Mellon, circa 1943

Elizabeth Shepley Sergeant was a journalist with an interest in Pueblo culture. She wrote a number of "literary portraits"—short biographies of authors and academics—for Harper's Magazine *from the 1920s through the 1940s. From the correspondence below, it is clear that she was preparing an introductory biography of Zimmer for* Myths and Symbols in Indian Art and Civilization. *Sergeant's portrait of Zimmer was not ultimately included in the published work, which includes only a short editor's foreword by Campbell.*

Waverly Place
New York 14, N.Y.
March 30, 1944

Dear Miss Sergeant,
I am glad the Zimmer lectures will help you. You are very kind to suggest sending me comments on the language of the chapters; I shall eagerly welcome every suggestion and hint. The first draft is only a half-way step between the lecture notes and the finished book. I expect to do a lot of revising, and a bit of help from someone who has not lost bearings in the sea of Germanisms will mean a great deal. It is queer the way the text seduces one; after an hour or so it becomes, for me at least, almost impossible to discover where English begins and ends. What I meant, finally, is a clean flow of English prose! Hence, you will be doing me a great favor if you will mark up and comment on the copy in your hands! And when you come again to New York, we must see each other again, for another talk. You have a standing invitation to have dinner with Jean and me, whenever you find yourself free to do so.

About Zimmer's special approach to Indian philosophy. He was particularly interested in the powerful influence of Dravidian, pre-Aryan forms on the development of Hindu, Buddhist, and Jain belief, cult, art, and yoga. The rich life-affirmation of the swelling hips and breasts of the Indian tree-goddesses, serpent queens, and land-demonesses, the wonderful mother-goddesses and their vigorous, full-bellied hero-consorts, represented a world of native life-power, "life-sap" as he always liked to say, with which he spontaneously identified himself. Indeed, when he would throw on the screen the picture of a Yaksha, and rhapsodize on the abundant life-sap of the sturdy form, it was impossible not to see that his own physique was a precise duplicate to that of the figure in the picture, and not to realize that he knew very well that he was talking as much about himself as about the ageless fertility demon of the most ancient Indian worship. Classical Vedānta, with its strong hankering for "release," he declared was all right for rarified

Brahmins, but not at all the thing for us cruder folk of the West. The popular myths spoke to us more directly; karma-yoga and bhakti-yoga (action-yoga and devotion-yoga) were something from which we could greatly profit; and finally the sophisticated refinement of the affirmative way in the Tantric philosophy of modern Hinduism (see Woodroffe) and in the Māhayāna, the presented as the highest triumphs of Oriental thought. The Boddhisattva ideal was his highest inspiration: here the antithesis of Samsara (time world) and Nirvana (Eternity, freedom) is transcended, and, in the profoundest way, the passing moment and the changeless infinite are recognized as but two aspects of the Unspeakable. Thus Bhoya (the life of pleasure and pain) and Yoga (the discipline of the spirit) can be one and the same.

All of which is simply to say, that while Zimmer would give its due to the Classical Vedānta, his great delight was in the heterodox philosophies (at once simpler and more sophisticated), and in the great pictorial-philosophies of the myths. Vishnu, Shiva, the goddess, Māhayāna Buddhism, Tantra, Hindu Art, the Purānas, the vegetation demons,—these, it seems to me, were his great loves. These represented a vital principle, antedating and surviving the episode of the Aryan conquest.—And in the Classical Brahmanical teachings, he favored the life-wisdom of the house-priest over the world negation of a Shankaracharya.—Whereas we are used to thinking of Oriental thought as quietistic and negative, Zimmer revealed it to be a roaring Yea.

I hope this answers your question. If it is obscure or off the point I shall be glad to try again.—Meanwhile, best wishes—and you may keep the manuscript, by the way, as long as you like.

Yours sincerely,
Joseph Campbell

Waverly Place
New York 14, N.Y.
September 9, 1944

Dear Miss Sergeant,
Many thanks for your sweet letter of some weeks ago. Jean and I have just returned to the city, and I have collapsed into a fairly uninterrupted sleep. During the Nantucket holiday I typed and scribbled everyday from 8 a.m. to 10 p.m., and lay awake every night revolving the book in my mind. We dashed back to New York for the opening of college; and when I learned that my presence would not be required on the campus until Monday, sleep came over me, and has remained. The present letter is the great effort of today! The moment the signature goes onto the end of it, I shall return to the horizontal and remain till dinner time. I can remember nothing to match this in the whole course of my days.

The myth book is finished, anyhow, and is now being typed; and the Grimm commentary will be out in a few weeks. Meanwhile, the Finnegan book is selling very fast, and my thoughts are beginning to lean forward to the Zimmer manuscript. I hope to be able to resume work about the fifteenth of September.

It will be a couple of weeks, I am afraid, before my social life can be resumed. The opening weeks of college are full of oddments, and I know I shall be coming home with thoughts only of sleep. But as soon as the air clears again, we must have another visit. Perhaps the first week of October?

Best wishes to you from us both,
Yours,
Joseph Campbell

Waverly Place
New York 14, N.Y.
June 25, 1944

Dear Miss Sergeant,
I have waited to see Mrs. Zimmer before replying to your letter. I do not think you have to worry about your piece just going "into the archives"; the only question is whether it should go into the present volume or into the one for which I originally proposed it. Mrs. Zimmer liked the piece, and was not the least adverse to its appearance in the later volume, where (if I am not mistaken) it will be entirely at home. That volume will be a collection of the Celtic and Indian myth-interpretations on which he was working precisely the moment of his death. They represented a new phase in his work, and were addressed, as it were, rather to his friends than to the world. The intimacy of these papers would not only justify, but even invite such a thing as a biography.

When I received your letter telling me that Stanley Young had thought it should go in the first volume, I saw the point of an introduction at the start of the series; but I think that Mrs. Zimmer's point is the sounder in the long run, namely, that the biography will be much more fitting in the more intimate, warmer volume. I can promise you, the book will be a charmer and you will be delighted to find yourself amidst it.

Mr. Young has not seen the Zimmer manuscripts and so has no idea what is coming. His judgment, on the basis of what he can know of the matter, is quite sound, I am sure; but I think that he too will heartily agree to Mrs. Zimmer's point when he receives the later manuscript. I expect to work on the Zimmer materials without interruption, until they are all out of my hands—work beginning next September 15. How long it will take, I cannot say; the wait, however, will not be unbearable! I think that within two years everything will be in order.

Your paper, as you say, is an introduction to Zimmer. Therefore it should go in the volume that is really "Zimmer." The present work is, rather, "India" via Zimmer; and I think it will hold its own in those terms. On the other hand, the "Zimmer" book, without your study, would be missing something.

I am very sorry that this complication has presented itself, to upset your work. But I know that it is only a momentary flare—originating largely from an unpredicted suggestion which suddenly frightened Mrs. Zimmer. We have both been a little afraid that the Bollingen office would begin slicing around the Zimmer volumes, and this seemed a preliminary portent. Hence the slightly hysterical vibrations! The whole relationship of Mrs. Zimmer to the Bollingen Series is a very delicate one, and I should not like to see it complicated by quarrels around the very first of the volumes. Mr. Young has a way of belittling creative, as opposed to executive, thought, which made her see black—that is why she spoke to you as she did about Heinz, the Bollingen, and Stanley Young.

I expected to see you Wednesday; but I am still available, even though in Nantucket. Our address will be Siasconset, Mass, and I shall be delighted to see your paper.

—Best wishes,
sincerely,
Joseph Campbell

Siasconset, Mass
July 16, 1944

Dear Miss Sergeant,
I like the piece. Zimmer comes very much alive in it. The analysis of his development is illuminating and convincing. There is nothing that I can say by way of finding fault, nor can I suggest any improvement.

I have suggested "von" Hoffmansthal instead of "Von," and on page 12 have suggested the deletion of the word Prussian. Zimmer himself didn't employ it at that point; his remark suggested rather that military men were pretty much what they are, whether Prussian, American, or French; and I do not think he was the one to support the American legend of something particularly unpleasant about the Prussian. Those are my only offerings.—I hope that everybody else concerned in this complicated affair likes the sketch as well as I do. It seems to me, it would require hardly a touch to fit into the volume I have in mind.

Personally, I don't see why this sketch could not be used both for the Bollingen book and for your own volume of sketches. What Young would think of such a thing, I don't know; but the books would have quite different publics.—I have no idea, either, how quickly Young will publish the books as I finish them. The first book will certainly appear this winter. I expect to complete the second and third by spring and to work on the fourth (the one in which I should like to see your sketch) next summer. The work may go either faster or slower than I expect, but I hope it will go fast! Two more volumes remain (I think) to be done after the fourth; and I want to be through with this editing work by 1946.

I am at present working to get my little myth book in shape for the Sept. 1 date-line. Reading it over, I found it had to be entirely rewritten, from page one to page last! Writing an entire book in 6 weeks is a bit of an assignment. If my second version is half as bad as my first, I shall blow up the island and go down with the ship!

Do not worry about returning the Zimmer manuscript this holiday. I shan't begin work on it until the fifteenth of September. College opens the seventh, and the first week is always a jam.

Jean and I are beginning to acquire tans. The past five days have been poorish, and so we are afraid we may already be losing them, and if my book becomes too harsh a taskmaster, we may never see the sun again. But for the moment, we are looking forward to a beautiful summer.

I hope your back is better and that the work is in a good state. I shall be interested to hear what comes of the Atlantic Monthly.

Jean joins in good wishes,

Sincerely yours

Joseph Campbell

Waverly Place
New York 14, N.Y.
December 24, 1944

Dear Miss Sergeant:

Thank you for your kind letter of some two weeks ago. I have been on the point of replying to it, day by day. With Jean's dance problems piling up (she had an important audition last Sunday), college term closing (no end of reports to be written), Christmas shopping insisting on itself, and my work on the Zimmer manuscript proceeding through a very difficult area (the section on the dancing Shiva), I have had so much to do, that my whole system of social correspondence has simply run into a snarl. The present letter, therefore, is very late. I had hopes to be able to search some good book on American folklore that I might recommend to you, but that good work too has remained unaccomplished. Actually, that is a very difficult field—principally because the collecting and evaluating has been carried on by an extraordinarily crotchety, unimaginative crew. The materials lie scattered in a hundred local "Folklore Society" filing cabinets, and in the dreary pages of the American Folklore Journal. No decent compilation (to my knowledge at least) has ever been published. Botkin's book was particularly disappointing, because Botkin (president of the Am. Folklore Society) is precisely the one to have given us <u>the</u> authoritative job—and his book is a mess. My personal opinion <u>is</u> that there is no good—even moderately good—collection of American folklore; but I wanted to verify this opinion before handing it on to you. My personal suspicion, furthermore, is that there is no such thing as American folklore. The celebrated "tall tale" tradition and the sourdough anecdotes around such figures as Mike Fink, Buffalo Bill, and Paul Bunyon don't add up to much, and finally aren't very amusing. Botkin's collection reads like a string of Rotary Club after-dinner boredoms. I think, perhaps "progress" isn't quite the soil for folklore.

I am very sorry to hear that your sciatica has been so bad.[9] The recent damps cannot have helped it any.—And thank you for your sweet invitation to us to pay another little visit. These holidays are going to be frightfully busy, and I am sure we shall be unable even to think of leaving New York. Jean is having a concert February fourth, and I am hoping to have finished this Zimmer book by that time. I have still to hunt out a million petty references and straighten out the picture problem. The re-writing is going very slowly. Somehow, I can sink hours into a page.

I have not had time, yet, to consult Simon & Schuster on the revisions of my myth book. I do not know whether they want great or little changes. Nor have I consulted with Young–Mrs. Zimmer Dr. Block & Co. on the problem of the next Zimmer volume. Everything is just where it was when we talked together at the little French place, and I do not see how I can bring our affairs to their next pass until I conclude the present assignment. The task is a much heavier one than I thought it would be; on the other hand, the book is turning out much better than I expected. On the whole, I am greatly pleased—though my finances, meanwhile, are heading for collapse!!

Best wishes for the Christmas season and the New Year
—Yours, Joseph C.

Woodstock, N.Y.
June 22, 1945

Dear Miss Sergeant,
Jean and I are very sorry that our shift of plan deprived us of the visit to Palisades. The preparations for Jean's three concerts (Thursday evening, Saturday afternoon and evening) made such heavy

demands on our time, that it was impossible to begin our packing before Sunday. We had to put the apartment in shape for painters; and this turned out to be such a job, that we were not ready to start away until Monday, 4 p.m. It would have been impossible for us to have lunch with you that day. The whole operation—concerts plus departure—was simply tremendous.

You were very kind to ask us, and then to get in touch with us by phone; and we were looking forward to our visit. But, somehow, we always underestimate our packing problems. That is an annual shock to us. We shall never learn.

The Zimmer volume went to press the week before our departure, and I have just begun the conversations preliminary to Volume II.[10] This will be the collection of papers that I described to you last Fall, the book to which your paper on Zimmer might well serve as introduction. I shall not have the material ready for publication before May 1, 1946, and so do not think there should be any hurry about your negotiations with Mrs. Z and Mr. Young. In fact, I think it would probably be best to wait until November or so, when we shall have begun to have some idea of the size and character of the volume. This summer I shall be working on a book of my own. I shall not touch the Zimmer material until the Fall.

Many thanks again for your kind invitation and our regrets that we were unable to make connections. Jean joins me in best wishes.

—Yours sincerely,

Joseph C.

Waverly Place
New York 14, N.Y.
June 11, 1946

Dear Miss Sergeant,

I am sending you, today, a copy of the manuscript. This is not quite the final draft: I plan to go over the whole thing once more. But it is close enough to give you a good idea of what the book is to be.

Another friend of mine has been kind enough to agree to go over the manuscript during the summer, and make suggestions. I should be very grateful to you, therefore, if you would mail it to her when you have had time to read it:

Mrs. Peter Geiger
East 71 Street
New York, N.Y.

If you can get it to her by the middle of August, that will be time enough.

Yesterday I had a long talk about the book with Mr. Barrett,[11] at the Bollingen; and he now has your name, with all the details. Since the book is not to go to press until November or so, there will be plenty of time in the Fall for us to discuss the Introduction. It is just possible that Dr. Jung may write something for the present volume; but Mr. Barrett agrees with me that if your biography should be squeezed out by the Words of the Master, it might well be placed in one of the coming volumes. I now foresee at least four more! Two on philosophy, one on art, and one of miscellaneous papers (perhaps, however, two or three of miscellaneous papers). I shall start work on the first of the philosophy volumes, the end of September.

Jean and I are leaving tomorrow for Honolulu. We shall be back, about September 15. Best wishes to you for the summer. And I hope you enjoy the manuscript.

Yours
Joseph Campbell

Waverly Place
New York 14, N.Y.
November 3, 1946

Dear Miss Sergeant,

Thank you for your two letters, one of the summer, one of the fall. I am sorry that my quite quite wild summer interfered with the replies. Jean and I had so many family rites to attend to in Honolulu, that neither of us was able to get a stroke of work done: and the moment I returned to my desk in New York, I received notice that I was called to jury duty. You can perhaps imagine the lovely state of my affairs. To give you a notion: I have not yet <u>seen</u> Mr. Barrett, at Bollingen. He has my manuscript, which I gave him last June; but I do not know what (if anything) has been done about it. I am hoping to have a conference with him within the next week or ten days, and I shall discuss with him then the whole case to the Zimmer series. I have not heard what effect the death of Mrs. M. will have upon these publications; nor do I yet know whether Dr. Jung was asked to do a preface. As soon as I am back in the picture, I shall let you know how things are.

Best wishes to you.
Sincerely,
Joseph Campbell

Waverly Place
New York 14, N.Y.
November 17, 1946

Dear Miss Sergeant,
I had my first talk with Barrett the other day and found that Mary Mellon was the only person connected with the Bollingen Series who had read my MS. She had not communicated her ideas about it to Barrett, except to say that it was an exciting book. I now have to wait for him to read it. But he tells me that he hopes to publish the volume by next summer, and as I imagine I shall be hearing from him again pretty soon—within the next month. I wish to revise certain pages, but shall do nothing about this until I hear from him. And so we shall have a good two months, at least, before the MS goes to press.

Meanwhile, nothing was done (apparently) about the Jung introduction, and so the way is as clear as ever for something by your good self. I think you should now write to Mr. Barrett. I shall be seeing him again in a couple of weeks, to hear what he has to say about the MS, and if he has your letter in his hands by that time, it will be possible for me to talk with him about the project. You may say that you and I have frequently spoken about it, and that I have declared myself favorable to such an introduction, with the proviso, of course, that the biography should meet with no objections from Mrs. Zimmer.

Jean and I are very busy, these days: she, preparing her concert (Dec. 7 & 8), and I typing to recover some of the ground lost during the summer. She joins me in sending to you our kindest regards.

Yours sincerely
Joseph Campbell

Waverly Place
New York 14, N.Y.
April 20, 1947

Dear Miss Sergeant,
Thank you for returning the MS and for your note last week. I am sorry to hear the really bad news of your difficulties with your landlords. It is a rough deal you are receiving, and I am sure it is a wonder that your health has not failed you entirely under the strain.

As for the Bollingen business: the manuscript seems, at last, to have gone to the printers, and publication seems to be scheduled for the fall. I think it would be well for you to get in touch with Mr. Barrett. I do not know what decisions they are going to make about a possible introduction to this volume, but I have told Mr. Barrett all about you, and have suggested that whether this volume or for a later one, it would be well for Bollingen to be in possession of such a biography as you would write. I have already started work on Zimmer #3, and have contracted for 4 and 5. There will probably be a #6 and perhaps even a #7. When Mr. Barrett finally got around to reading the present MS he thought that it would be large and substantial enough to carry itself; but I have not seen him for several weeks and do not know what he thinks at present.—My supposition would be that you should do your portrait for the Harpers series, if Barrett doesn't want it right away; and then it should be sold to Bollingen for use in one or another of these Zimmer volumes. I do think that Barrett will wish to have it once he sees it.

My own myth book comes in for a revision every time I turn around. There are still a number of chapters that displease me, but which I cannot seem to solve to my own satisfaction. I spent the winter on it, but am still unwilling to let it go. My hope is that after the revision I am planning for next August, I shall be rid of it, for keeps.

The first Zimmer book is selling very well. It is already going to press for a second printing. And I think that the second will be even more popular. As for the third—we shall very soon see.

Jean joins me in sending our kindest regards. Let us see if you come to the city.

Yours cordially,
Joseph Campbell[12]

Waverly Place
New York 14, N.Y.
Wednesday—[No date]

Dear Miss Sergeant,
Enclosed are the first pages of the Zimmer book. I had started to revise, as you will see, and so the MS is in places a mess.

Jean and I had a delightful holiday with you, Sunday. In my hurry to make the bus I neglected to deliver the parting word; but it was a wonderful, refreshing excursion, and we thought every bit of the countryside simply marvelous. The trip home was brief and pleasant; exactly one hour from my sprint to our opening of this door. The strawberry shortcake is still a treasure of recollection!

Thank you for letting me read your biographical sketch of Zimmer. I shall be delighted to see it again—if you wish—when it is completed. Meanwhile, the enclosed morsel may supply a fresh phrase or two. You are about to read one of the most wonderful myth fragments I have ever seen!

Best wishes for the remainder of your task and for the summer. We expect to leave about the 28th for Nantucket, and if we don't see you earlier shall have our next good visit in the fall. Jean will have to try to beat that dessert!

Yours sincerely
Joseph Campbell

The following letter, from an unidentified employee of the Bollingen Foundation, concerns the 1960 publication of Papers from the Eranos Yearbooks, Volume 4: Spiritual Discipline.

Apr. 1, 1960

Dear Joe:
Thanks (also to Christiane) for the Zimmer notes. I happened to find your piece in Partisan Rev., which I had saved, and I added some details—justifiable, I would say, in view of Z.'s importance in and to the B S and just general importance. Is it true that he never traveled to the East? I seem to recall that from our days working on the A of I A. I'm a bit dissatisfied with my remark about his linguistic learning, which sounds naïve, and perhaps you'll think of another way of indicating the breadth of his scholarship. Could you just mark up one of these and send it back (to # E 62). Show to Christiane if you think best.

The volume is practically wound up now, though I still must receive biogr. Sketches of Rousselle and Bernoulli, which Rhein Vlg. Promised to send; v. Cammerlocher has persistently eluded all our efforts and I have had to sketch him in almost as a ghost, based on dim recollections of Mrs Jacobi. You'll see proofs of all these sketches and other end matter; front matter; and the plates, which turned out quite well.

Ever,

B

Jacqueline Kennedy Onassis (1929–1994) was the First Lady of the United States from 1961 to 1963. She served as an editor, at Viking and then Doubleday, from 1975 until her death.

Gotham Book Mart & Gallery Inc.
West 47th St.
New York, N.Y. 10036

January 10, 1986

Mr. Joseph Campbell
Waverly Place Apt. 14
New York, New York 10014

Dear Mr. Campbell,
Mrs. Jacqueline Onassis is a very good customer and we try to select something special to send each Christmas. This year we selected your two-volume ART OF INDIA, published in 1955.

Her letter of appreciation was so enthusiastic, we thought you might enjoy seeing a copy.

Frances and I enjoyed your recent lecture very much and she appreciated your warm acknowledgement when she said good-night. On January 1, 1986 she began her ninety-ninth year. We are looking forward to celebrating her one-hundredth birthday. At the moment, she is in Florida recovering from a minor hip operation. She still speaks with great enthusiasm about your Frances Steloff lecture at Skidmore College.

Best wishes for the New Year.

Sincerely,

Andreas Brown

June 6 1986

Dear Andreas
I am overwhelmed by the treasure you gave me for Christmas—the Bollingen 1955 Arts of Southern Asia by my hero Joseph Campbell.

There is no book I would treasure or appreciate more. Your thoughtfulness and sensitivity in sending it to me is deeply appreciated—Your two books, on Christmas day, just boosted my India Library into World Class status! Thank you dear Andreas and all my happiest wishes for the New Year—

Gratefully,
Jackie

The following letter is from Heinrich Zimmer's daughter, Maya Rauch.

Maya Rauch
Jorstensteig 14
CH 8044 Zürich

New York, 13.XII.90

Dear Jean Erdman:
When I crossed Waverly Place yesterday, I felt again, what it meant for me, to have seen the working-room of your husband, as there are but few people I am so grateful to for what he has done, as for him saving the work of Heinrich Zimmer, which he had started during his last years. All would have been lost—if there would not have been Joseph Campbell—and I am well aware, that he was perhaps the only one capable to do the work. I hope we meet again—I wish you all the best for the Holidays and the New Year.

Your
Maya

Ananda K. Coomaraswamy with his wife, Stella Bloch, 1922

Ananda K. Coomaraswamy (August 22, 1877–September 9, 1947) was a Sri Lankan Tamil philosopher and metaphysician, as well as a pioneering historian and philosopher of Indian art, and an early interpreter of Indian culture to the West. In particular, he has been described as "the groundbreaking theorist who was largely responsible for introducing ancient Indian art to the West." In 1933 Coomaraswamy's title at Boston's Museum of Fine Arts (MFA) changed from curator to fellow for research in Indian, Persian, and Mohammedan art. He served at the MFA until his death in Needham, Massachusetts, in 1947. During his long career, he was instrumental in bringing Eastern art to the West. In fact, while at the MFA, he built the first substantial collection of Indian art in the United States. He also helped establish the collections of Persian art at the MFA and at the Freer Gallery of Art in Washington, D.C.

Museum of Fine Arts
Boston, Massachusetts
May 25, 1945

Dear Mr. Campbell,
I am very glad to hear Dr. Zimmer's material is taking shape. I enclose a print of the subject you need. It should be acknowledged as 'Photo of the Archeological Survey of India': and returned to me after use. Many thanks for your kind words of appreciation I look forward to the publication eagerly.

Very sincerely,
Ananda K Coomaraswamy

Museum of Fine Arts
Boston 15, Mass.
June 12, 1945

Dear Mr. Campbell,
I am not acquainted with your own studies. It is just possible you would like me to look over the spellings of Skr. Words in the galley proofs. If so, I would be happy to do this. It is equally possible you need no help in that direction. If so don't bother to reply.

AK Coomaraswamy

Museum of Fine Arts
Boston 15, Mass.
Oct 10 1945

Dear Mr. Campbell,
I don't know what you will think of my suggestions. A few are, of coursc, indispensable; but you are the Editor and it is for you to decide about the others. I presume you will write a short Introduction, in which, if you want to use my notes (to which I feel sure Z. would have

agreed) you could say that a few explanatory notes in square brackets and initialize AKC have been added by Dr. Ananda Coomaraswamy.[13] That is what I would wish, but as I say, it is for you to decide.

A few of the spelling corrections are not separately noted in the typescript.

If you should not like my suggestions, please return the typescript to me, as I might find it useful in writing a review later.

Very sincerely,
Ananda K Coomaraswamy

Museum of Fine Arts
Boston 15, Mass.
October 11, 1945

Yours of 10th received. Let me have you comment on what I have done so far before I do more. (By the way I think you might ask the publishers to give me 3 copies in consideration of my work on the proofs)

AKC

Museum of Fine Arts
Boston 15, Mass.
October 15, 1945

Thanks. I will [undecipherable] the remainder in the same way. Please send me a copy of my pieces on <u>tapas</u> and the <u>lotus</u> as I want to add a line to each, and have no copy. I think you did a really wonderful job.

AK Coomaraswamy

P.S. You might like to read my article in the current issue of <u>Psychiatry</u>.[14]

Museum of Fine Arts
Boston 15, Mass.
October 20, 1945

Dear Mr. Campbell,
Herewith an installment. Balance will follow this week. A few minor points are noted in the galleys. I have aimed to say nothing that Z. would not himself have approved, as that seemed to me necessary to orient the reader. The only note that really involves a correction is that in the Trimūrti, but I have worded that judiciously. Galleys 44-48 and 71-end herewith.

Very sincerely,
AK Coomaraswamy

Museum of Fine Arts
Boston, Massachusetts
October 23, 1945

Dear Mr. Campbell,
Enclosed is all I'm able to do. As aforesaid, decisions are for you. Obviously the text could be annotated ad lib, but that I have not tried to do.

In general criticism I will only say that while Z's adherence to and exposition of exclusively medieval sources—too much neglected and looked down upon by 'scholars'—this does occasionally result in a perhaps inevitable neglect of the intrinsic primordial senses of some formulae. Some of the later chapters are rather long drawn out. Anyway I'm very glad you have rescued all this material and hope it will be read.

Very sincerely,
AK Coomaraswamy

Museum of Fine Arts
Boston 15, Mass.
October 25, 1945

I omitted Galley 59, last note, continue

[But Māhavīra, 'great Hero,' is already Indra's epithet in the Rig Veda, just as by implication (-- jit) he is a 'Conqueror' (jina), and these epithets are inherited alike in Jainism and Buddhism.—AKC.]

Museum of Fine Arts
Boston 15, Mass.
December 3, 1945

I return the proof. I have not read it thoroughly but chiefly for my part. Not in Galley p. 142 docta is correct (not "doctrina"). I am referring to Cusa's and others doctrine of "learned ignorance"

AKC

Museum of Fine Arts
Boston 15, Massachusetts
June 5, 1947

Dear Professor Campbell,

I should have answered yours of May 25 before now, but have been rather unwell during the last 2 months, and this has slowed up both my work and correspondence. I do not know of any ancient or modern representation of Satī herself, and I think you will have to use one of Pārvatī.

I'm glad to hear the Myths and Symbols is doing so well. I have been reading with very great interest Zimmers Der Weg zum Selbst [The way to the Self] (Zürich, 1944), and I think it would be a very good thing if the Pantheon Press would publish a translation. It seems to me very nearly equal in importance to the Memories of Sri Ramakrishna.

By the way I enjoyed your Chimera article on Finnegan's Wake [*sic*], tho' I have not read the latter. When is your 'comparative mythology' to be ready?[15]

You probably have seen my Brother's Keeper.

With very kind wishes,

Ananda K Coomaraswamy

Museum of Fine Arts
Boston 15, Mass.
July 5, 1947

In your review of Der Weg zum Selbst you effectively criticise Jung's usual position. But in Two Essays in Analytical Psychology, 1928, p. 268 he really does contrast the empirical ego with the unknowable self

AKC

Museum of Fine Arts
Boston, Massachusetts
August 1, 1947

Dear Campbell

Many thanks for your kind note. I think by far the best translator for Der Weg zum Selbst would be Dr. Murray Fowler (# Brattle St. Cambridge Mass). I can't say whether I can write a short introduction—I would like to—but am not as strong as I was and have orders not to undertake any new work—I needn't say this leaves me with plenty of unfinished work in hand. Incidentally I mentioned Der Weg zum Selbst also to Harpers so perhaps Bollingen Pr. had better hasten their arrangements. I will try to write for it, anyway. Of course, I shall be happy to run through proofs of any of Zimmer's books.

I am sending you "Symplegades" shortly. It may be useful for your general mythology!

I hope "Woodstock" will be sufficient address.

Very [undecipherable]

Ananda K Coomaraswamy

Museum of Fine Arts
Boston, Massachusetts

August 15, 1947

Dear Professor Campbell,
Proofs received. So far I note

Galley 29: ? add note referring to my "The Loathly Bride" in Speculum XX

Galley 44: Gawain is the real hero of early English chivalry (as often emphasized by J. L. Weston)

Galley 55: "portcullis," add note: Cf. AKC "Symplegades" in Studies and Essays in the History of Science and Learning offered in Homage to George Sarton on the Occasion of his Sixtieth Birthday, ed. M.F. Ashley Montagu, New York, 1947, pp. 463–488.

Galley 57: "bridge": ? add note referring to D.L. Coomaraswamy, "The Perilous Bridge of Welfare" in HJAS 8

Galley 62, note 1, add: H.B. Wheatley, ed., Merlin (2 vols., EETS, 1899).

Galley 25, note 1, add: See also Coomaraswamy, A.K., "Sir Gawain and the Green Knight" in Speculum XIX,—a study of the decapitation motive, with Oriental parallels

Galley 79 line 13 from bottom, mind-born sons, add note: Kāma, the God of Love, being the "first born" of these seeds of mind, Rigveda 10.129.4.

Galley 55 "horse for cart," a great degradation; metaphysically = exchange of solar vehicle for human body, the latter being a "cart" in the sense of the Platonic, and Indian "chariot symbolism." This is the point at which Gawain, as every solar hero does once, "hesitates" ("May this cup be taken from me"; the Buddha's hesitation to preach; etc.).[16] Hence the importance of what to a casual reader seems a minor point.

Very sincerely,
AK Coomaraswamy

I do not very much relish the "dilettante" business of the beginning!

Museum of Fine Arts
Boston, Massachusetts
August 17, 1947

Dear Campbell,

Galley 12 note 1: ? add: Cf. René Guénon, Aperçus sur l'initiation, Paris, 1946.

The following remarks are more for you than intended for use in the book

Galley 89 A more literal translation of Satī would be "She who Is" (cf. "He who Is" as the truest name of God, Katha Up., Damascene, etc.)

Galley 7 l.44: the voice of tradition would say, not "to resign oneself" but, "to rely upon the Self"

Galley 8 lines 10–11 again, the voice of tradition would say exactly the opposite,—"Can the ego, whose demons… clutches, put itself to death? Can if become what it is?" Cf. Philo LA 3.41—and the whole tradition of "self-naughting," dragon slaying.

below, I would say Nemo contra diabolum nisi Deus ipse!

below, "Heaven and Earth,"—the macrocosmic archetype of all weddings

Galley 10, flaying motive, cf. my "Sir Gawain…" p. 6, note

3. Also Euthydemus 285; and as cited in The Legacy of Islam p. 216 "I came forth from Bayazid-ness like a snake from its skin"; Radin, Road to Life and Death, p. 112; Goodenough, By Light, Light, 300, 305

Galley 11 "chess" in its original aspect of a conflict in which the players stake themselves, cf. O. Rank, Art and Artist, ch. 10 "Game destiny (? insert ref. to this).

"day and night... Chinese formulation,"—and as for Heracleitus, frs. 36, 43, 46 (and many other sources for the "contraries (Symplegades)!

Galley 12 note 1 add: Cf. René Guénon, Aperçus sur l'initiation, Paris, 1946.

1.5 from bottom: cf SB 13.2.8.1 "now the Gods, ascending, knew not the way to the heavenly world, but the horse knew it"

Galley 13 the rolling ball reminds one of the wheel and rolling apple that Cuchullain follows on his way to Scathach's realm beyond the "bridge"

As for the Bird, one must remember that the "speech of birds" is the language of angelic communication

Galley 15 last line "the mortal and the divine",—cf. AA 2.3.7 as quoted in my "Hares and Dreams" p. 2[17]

Galley 25 note 2, on Curoi cf pp. 71, 357, 378 in Brown, Origin of the Grail Legend, and in Iwain, 1903, 53f., and 80, 81. I don't need to say that "Life and "Death" are both equally nomina Dei. "Green" stands for either or both! In fact all this is probably quite superfluous for you; you probably are familiar with all the Arthurian bibliography (Loomis, Brown, Krappe, Scott, et al)! On the conflict with Māra—see my discussion of the Māra Dharsana in the B.C. Law Volume I "Some Sources of Buddhist Iconography" (the archetype being Indra's conflict with Vritra)

Galley 26 top: Mathnawī 2.2525 "What is 'beheading'?

Slaying the carnal soul (nafs = Heb. Nefesh) in the Holy War".

Galley 27 and of No return; = Brahmaloka, Upanisads, passim; nothing "hopeless" about that! for cf. JUB 3.28.5 "Who having cast off this world would desire to return again? He would be only there!" As Dante says, however, we must die to live up there. The Hero's return to the cave (as in the Republic) is a deliberate descent, a voluntary sacrifice, not that he would prefer "to be only there." I think Z. misses a little of this.[18]

Museum of Fine Arts
Boston, Massachusetts
Aug. 23, 1947

Dear Campbell,
I leave it to you just how and how much of my notes to insert. One way would be to use initials and brackets (as before) only where a new idea is added, not where additional ref. (esp. to my own work) is added; but do what you think best.

Many thanks for your kind birthday wishes,—which were read with others at a dinner at the Harvard Club yesterday.

Henceforth I have to conserve my energies to try and finish the most important of the unfinished tasks in hand; as much as possible, anyhow, before we retire to the Himalayas for good next year!

Very sincerely,
Ananda K Coomaraswamy[19]

Campbell sent the following letter to the director of Princeton University Press concerning the manuscript that would become Coomaraswamy: Selected Papers, Volume 1: Traditional Art and Symbolism *(1977); Selected Papers, Volume 2: Metaphysics (1978); and* Volume 3: Life and Work *(1978). Edited by Roger Lipsey, they constitute Bollingen Series 89, published by Princeton University Press.*

Waverly Place
New York, New York 10014

December 20, 1971

Mr. Herbert S. Bailey, Jr.
The Princeton University Press
Princeton, N.J. 08540

Dear Herb:

This letter is about [Roger] Lipsey's work.

First let me say that I am delighted to know that he is the person to whom the editing of Coomaraswamy's Nachlass [Unpublished works] has been assigned. He knows the matter thoroughly—probably more thoroughly than anybody alive. He has skill in organization, literary grace, and a certain gently critical attitude toward his author. Further, he is well acquainted not only with the life and works of Coomaraswamy, but also with the lives and works of those by whom Coomaraswamy was variously influenced, the literary and other movements with which he was from time to time associated, and, in general, the orders of scholarship and philosophy from which he drew ideas.

The great problem, however, to which you have already called my attention is the great length of Mr. Lipsey's offering, and it is to this that I wish to address myself. I do not feel that I can recommend publication of the work as it stands.

In the first place, it seems to me we have actually two works here, a biography (Part I), and a critical analysis and exposition of the author's works (Part II). I can understand why Mr. Lipsey wished to link them. They do indeed supplement and support each other. But they can be appreciated separately, and, in fact, have not the same ranges or qualities of appeal. Furthermore, there are certain stylistic features, which, while appropriate for Part II, are not so, as they appear in Part I.

I felt distinctly in Part I that I was reading an excellent Ph.D. thesis, and it was not until I got well into Part II that I felt myself out of the schoolroom. The lavish use of quotations, which in the second part serves generally (though even here not always) to carry the reading forward, in Part I interrupts the flow. Already in Sections I–III these interruptions are annoying. One feels (and knows) that with a little harder work the author could have extracted their essential thoughts and rerendered these in his own prose. By about the middle of Section IV the undigested quoted passages, continually recurring, become intolerable. We are now encountering long quotes, furthermore, not from Coomaraswamy only, but from other authors as well. Sections IV–V I found particularly tedious. The pattern is of too much quoting, and then, thinly spun out discussions of whatever themes emerge. Besides, Coomaraswamy's thinking at this early stage of his career was in itself not particularly interesting. We certainly do not need all these pages to make the point that he found the influence of the West deleterious to the arts and crafts of the Orient. Section VI, on the Appreciation of Indian Art in Britain, 1843–1911, is in its matter a bit more interesting; but again, too full of quotes and too long.—And so on!—The best Section, I felt, the most alive, was number XI: AKC in America: First Ten Years. Then again, the old pattern returned of too many quotes and too long interspersed among thin, meandering discussions of ideas. The bibliographie raisonnée of Section XIII gives the sense of an overload, without due selection, and in Section XIV, The World of a Scholar, we are overloaded again, this time with quotes from the letters of every scholar who ever wrote a word either to or about Coomaraswamy.

In short, while we certainly have an excellent Ph.D. thesis in these pages, I do not believe that we have yet a publishable book. What is most wanted is concision. The quotes should be digested and their sense conveyed in the author's prose; the somewhat too relaxed, prolix discussions and elucidations of ideas and books, tightened up and sharpened; some of the personalities characterized (if possible) more vividly; and, in general, more attention given to the elicitation of a reader's interest in the story of a colorful life during a richly interesting period, than to proving to Professor X that a great amount of meticulous and fruitful research was accomplished.

In Part II, the story is different. The lavish use of quotation is more appropriate to a work of criticism than to a biography; yet even here, I feel, there is a bit too much. Something would have to be done about a first chapter, of course, if Part II were published separately. Section XVII, "Tradition," with which this part of the work begins, has more to do with René Guénon than with AKC, and again, it rambles too leisurely a pace. For me, things begin to get going in Section XVIII, "Traditional Art"; Section XIX, "Traditional Aesthetics," brought us to the meat of Coomaraswamy; and with Section XX, "Symbolism," I felt that something valuable was being given us that we could perhaps not ourselves have better derived from a reading of Coomaraswamy's own works.

And this brings me to another aspect of our problem.

Princeton University Press is about to bring out in the Bollingen Series a volume or two of the selected papers of A.K. Coomaraswamy. It is not clear to me that a well chosen arrangement of these would not give, in as many pages, a richer and better idea of Coomaraswamy's contribution than Part II of Dr. Lipsey's work. I do not know what the plans are for these volumes; but it might just be possible to ask Dr. Lipsey to prepare two introductions for two separate collections: one, of the earlier writings, introduced by the matter of Part I of Lipsey's thesis (greatly abridged, with the quotes left out, and the master's life more sharply sketched); and another, of his important later papers of the period, post 1932, introduced by the matter of Lipsey's work Part II (again left out, or rather reduced to references to the matter of the text).

In any case, this manuscript (I am sure) should not be published in its present state. The revision of Part I would have to be total (as above suggested), and of Part II, considerable, and the two, if then brought out, should be separate works, published rather as handbooks to the Bollingen volumes than as independent sources. Or better (again as above suggested) their material, excellently organized and researched as it is, might best be turned into introductions to Volumes One and Two (perhaps) of the master's own works.

Amen!—and I hope that one or another of these suggestions may be of use.

Sincerely,
Joseph Campbell

P.S. I shall be mailing the manuscript next week, when the Christmas rush in the post office will have ended.

Géza Róheim (September 12, 1891–June 7, 1953) was a Hungarian psychoanalyst and anthropologist. He was the first psychoanalytically trained anthropologist to do field research, and later developed a general cultural theory. Róheim is best known for his (with his wife, Ilonka) nine-month stay at or near Hermannsburg Lutheran Mission in central Australia in 1929—a trip that generated great interest in psychoanalytic circles—and for his subsequent writings about Arrernte and Pitjantjatjara people. His research was used to support Freud's disciple Ernest Jones in his debate with Bronislaw Malinowski over the existence of the Oedipus complex in matrilineal societies. Róheim also did fieldwork in Melanesia, North America, and the Horn of Africa. His theory of culture stressed its rootedness in the long period of juvenile dependence in humans, allowing for exploration and play.

Dr. Geza Roheim
West 85th Street
New York City
2 May 1945

Dear Mr. Campbell:
I have to thank you for the excellent review of my book.[20] The spirit of the whole is contained in your rendering.

I remain very sincerely yours.
Geza Roheim

Dr. Geza Roheim
West 85th Street
New York City
Dec 30, 1949

Dear Dr. Campbell!
I read your paper in Samiksā on the cult of the Siva Linga (Vol III. No 1). What interests me especially is this: has Shiva anything to do with dreaming?

I would be much obliged for any information you could give me. With thanks and Seasons Greetings.

Sincerely yours,
Geza Roheim

Dr. Geza Roheim
West 85th Street
New York City
Jan 9, 1950

Dear Dr. Campbell!
Thank you for your letter and for the references. But I don't think I expressed myself quite clearly. What I meant was: is Siva regarded as the god who gives dreams or sleep like for instance Hermes?

The doctrine you mention about the three states is interesting. I would like to read the proofs when they come out. It may have something to do with a dream theory I am working on. I am sending you some reprints with very best wishes, cordially yours,

Geza Roheim

Dr. Geza Roheim
West 85th Street
New York City
September 15, 1951

Dear Dr. Campbell!
Thank you for sending me this very interesting book. It will take me some time till I grasp the meaning of the whole thing but I have some hunches already. Also, thank you for your excellent paper in the "Festschrift."

Cordially yours,
Geza Roheim

Roger Sherman Loomis (October 31, 1887–October 11, 1966) was an American scholar and an authority on medieval and Arthurian literature. He is perhaps best known for showing that the roots of Arthurian legend, in particular the Holy Grail, lie in native Celtic mythology. He was the director for Campbell's master's thesis at Columbia University. (The thesis, called "The Dolorous Stroke," can be found in Campbell's posthumous collection Romance of the Grail: The Magic and Mystery of Arthurian Myth.*)*

April 1, 1948

Dear Campbell,
I have received your book—or rather Zimmer's[21]—and thank you for thinking of me. I think the stories are told with a great deal of perspicacity and feeling. I like the re-telling of Gawain and the Green Knight.

But frankly, I think the Zimmer-Coomaraswamy approach to Arthurian romances is simply mad. And I mean it. And Zimmer's plea to abandon the standards of rationality and trust to the emotional response to symbolism and cryptic meanings seems to me to make of comparative mythology a Mad Hatter's tea-party, where every learned lunatic is as good as any other. It is an invitation to irresponsible day-dreaming.

Take the interpretation of GGK. The Green Knight is Death and his wife is Life—on the analogy of a Hindu story! The analogy is extremely vague and there can have been no historical contact between India and England in the 14th century. To ignore the origins of GGK, through perfectly demonstrable channels in Irish and Welsh myth is a flagrant violation of the first principles of honest scholarship and common sense—which are after all the same.

As you know, I am a firm believer in the existence of meanings in the stories which lie behind Arthurian romance, and in Celtic Myth I made some guesses, some of which I still hold and others which I have long since rejected, as to what those meanings were. Since the sources were predominantly Celtic, it is in Celtic texts that the earlier meanings must be sought and not in the mythologies of the Sioux, the Patagonians, the Babylonians, or the Parsees. I hope you agree with me.

If you think there is anything to be said for Zimmer's fantasies, I should be glad to discuss the matter with you, but at present am inclined to think him one more victim of the view that the one mythology one knows well is a key to unlock all other mythologies—no matter how remote in space and time.

Yours sincerely,
Roger Loomis

April 7, 1948

Dear Loomis—
Thank you for your letter about the book. I found it on my desk when I returned this morning after our Easter Holiday. I see your point, that the proper way to study the Arthurian romances is by looking back to Celtic rather than afield to Indian and Patagonian mythology. In fact I felt the force of just that point when I started working on these papers, and so tried to cushion it by placing that

piece about dilettantism out in front, as well as by stressing, wherever possible, Zimmer's statement that this was not a scholarly book with philological-historical pretensions, but a playful exercise—an attempt to see what the old stories could suggest and say to the modern imagination. However, you are right: the book is not as innocent as it would like to be; it does have scholarly pretensions, as well as implications, and these leave it open to scholarly criticism and attack.

My own feeling about Zimmer's comparative approach (and Coomaraswamy's too, which is somewhat different, yet open to many of the same objections) is not as clear and strong as yours (obviously since [if] it were I could not have produced the present opus); for the thing that puzzles me and impresses me most about the mythologies with which I am acquainted is that they continually treat of identical themes in much the same way. I should say that the old boys of the [eighteen] eighties and nineties had made that point pretty clear: Bastian, Lang, Frazer, Wundt, and the rest. I know that in each region special applications are given the themes, so that a reading made in Timbuctoo will not quite apply (and perhaps not apply at all) to the special problems of Lhasa and Tenochtitlan; nevertheless, it is also very clear that such readings often <u>do</u> apply. And this is the reason why I do not feel that the dangerous approach of Zimmer is altogether mad.

Furthermore, there is this odd and uncomfortable business about psychoanalysis and the recurrence of archaic mythological figures and situations in contemporary dreams. I do not think that it is possible to dismiss the material that has accumulated and been published during the past forty years; nor should I think it would be quite in keeping with the first principles of honest scholarship to disregard the problems that the evidence poses. I know that Zimmer was very much interested in these problems, and that his theory about letting the myths operate on the imagination was based on an idea that fantasies are never really free but follow laws which remain constant in the human psyche, whether in 14th century England, 2nd century India, 20th century Germany, or on the plains of the Sioux. From this standpoint a historical connection between two regions would not have to be demonstrated to permit of a legitimate scholarly comparison.

For example, take the case that you cite of Gawain and Green Knight. I should not think that a historical connection between England and India in the 14th century would have to be demonstrated before sound scholarship could acquiesce to the suggestion that a man with an axe meant death to the hero and a beautiful woman in bed, life. Common sense would here seem to be on the side of Zimmer, and would suggest also that if those figures did not mean something pretty close to that for the Celts, then there must have been something really peculiar about the Celts. In your Celtic Myth you run these heroes back to Cuchulinn and Curoi, whom you identify as the young and old sun-god, and you associate the beheading game with the theme of year-renewal. But this is precisely the symbol, in many mythologies, for the death-and-resurrection, or "regeneration," theme. Zimmer, in fact, agrees with all of these identifications. You admit yourself, however (p. 61), that the formula as it appears in GGK does not fit with the solar formula, as one would have expected it to appear. "The Irish fili[22] who concocted the story," you write, "doubtless cared more about pleasing his patrons than about the hopeless task of making myths logical. So he merely remarked: 'So much the worse for the myth!' and gave us this charming story." In other words, the peculiar formative factor at work, in this case at least, was not mythological exclusively; and your guess as to what the non-mythological factor was seems to me to represent a flight of scholarly fantasy no less questionable than (and finally not very different from) Zimmer's—but with the disadvantage of not interpreting the story as it stands or telling us why old sun myths were being used for entertainment purposes. Also, there remains the psychological question as to why a story of this kind entertains. What is it saying to us, and what did it say to the fili's patron?—These are the questions with which Zimmer was entertaining himself, and, frankly, I cannot see how his answers conflict in any way with your identification of GGK with the sun formula and pluck-buffet game. Curoi

(Terror, son of Great Fear) and Blathnat (the Persephone of his yonder world) seem to me not misnamed under Zimmer's titles, Death and Life;—or am I crazy? Also in point:—the sun in the underworld is not infrequently the lord of the dead (viz. Osiris, Minos).

As for the historical connections between the British Isles and the Orient: 1. Is it not true that the Neolithic diffusion of the basic arts of civilization (which took place following the development of agriculture, cattle-culture, etc., in the Near East, about 6000 B.C.) carried westward all the way to Ireland, as well as eastward into India and China? Do not most of the basic themes and symbols of all our high-culture mythologies go back at least to that period? 2. Is it not true that during the third and second millenniums B.C. the little boats of the Aegean-mariners were poking out beyond the Gates of Hercules, up the coast to Cornwall, north to Scotland, and even across, then, to Sweden and Denmark? This was the great period of the Babylonian myths, and there was actually a connection between Mesopotamia and India at this time. The Buddhist and Puranic myths of India point back to this period. Is it then too wild to suggest that between these and the myths at the other end of the line there might be some connection? 3. Is it not true that there were also overland connections between the Mediterranean and the north throughout these centuries (amber trade and bronze diffusion)? 4. Did not the Celts enter Ireland with iron; and was not the knowledge of iron derived from the Near Eastern area? 5. Do not yourself point out the Celtic-Greek parallels? (the Greeks are linked in many ways to the Orient). 6. Is there no basis for Jess[i]e Weston's contention that the beliefs in certain Eastern mystery religions were carried with the Roman armies into Gaul and Britain?[23] 7. Was there not in Ireland a considerable neo-Platonic influence precisely during the centuries when the Christian poets were at work (cf. Scotus Ergina)?—Richard Garbe has demonstrated the influence of the Sankhya Philosophy (which lies behind Buddhism) on the neo-Platonic philosophers. 8. Did the crusades not bring the best men of Europe into touch with the Near Eastern civilization? And what about the court of Fredk II? Was not the entire Pancatantra translated from Sanskrit into Persian into Arabic into Hebrew into Latin—thus entering Europe c.1270 A.D.? Have not the Finnish folklorists demonstrated a continuous passage of folk-materials into Europe from the Southeast?—11. Is it permissible to say that there can have been no historical contact between India and England in the 14th century?

The story that Zimmer cites in connection with the testing of Sir Gawain is not just "a Hindu story," but the legend of the testing of the Buddha—which is simply the world's most celebrated instance of the testing theme.[24] Zimmer does not assert that the Buddha story influenced the Gawain, but that they are two instances of the same essential problem; and yet I think that if one put oneself to it, it might not be very hard, after all, to demonstrate the possibility of an actual influence. For example: Mani, the prophet of Manichaeism in the Roman empire was immense. St. Augustin was a Manichaean in his youth, and his influence on the thinking of 14th century England is not to be denied. Furthermore, there were Buddhists in Alexandria; Barlaam and Josephat were the Buddha; and who will say how much Buddhism there is in Gnosticism, how much Gnosticism in the Albigensian heresy, or how much of the Albigensians in the Grail romances?—I don't think that one need deny the Celtic origins of the beheading game and the heroes involved in order to believe that your Irish fili may well have had some Oriental thoughts in his mind when he reshaped his tale for the entertainment of his lordly patron (perhaps just back from a chat with Hafiz in the neighborhood of Bagdad).

Finally, as to whether myths in general are to be read in psychological terms (Zimmer), metaphysical (Coomaraswamy), or purely naturalistic (solar myths, vegetation myths, etc., without psychological or metaphysical content): that is a large, overall problem that concerns the entire subject of mythology and not just this province or that. If the psychological approach is valid in India, it is valid also in Ireland or Yucatan, and one does not have to be a Mad Hatter to make the transfer.

Now that, briefly, is my defense of the King and the Corpse. I started out to thank you for your kind letter, telling me (as I asked you to) exactly what you thought, and I find that I have composed what is practically an article. I was really delighted to hear that you liked the retelling of the stories. And I hope that my letter, if it does not demonstrate the science of my author, will at least make clear why it is that while I agree with you wholeheartedly in your requirement that the Irish origins of the Arthurian tales should not be ignored, I also followed with considerable enthusiasm Zimmer's psychological reading of the symbols. Apparently, I am one of those detestable middlemen who can joyfully bow, without the least sense of incongruity, to both sides.

Again, my thanks—and if you think you would like to go on discussing this fine business, I should be honored and delighted to try to handle my foil.

I very much enjoyed our luncheon the other day. Perhaps you would like to join me, one of these fine noon-or-dinner-times, at the New York A[thletic] C[lub].

With my kindest regards to Mrs. Loomis, and still again my thanks for your vigorous letter.

Sincerely yours
[Joseph Campbell]

Morningside Drive
New York City 27, N.Y.

Dear Campbell,
I appreciate your long and friendly letter. These are things we must discuss, and no luncheon will be sufficient to cover more than a fifth of the subject. So I accept your proposal for dinner at the A.C. and invite you to a continuation at some French or Italian restaurant another evening. My calendar seems free this week except for Wednesday.

Just one thing. "Celtic Myth and Arthurian Romance" was written twenty-seven years ago, and though I still think it was right in the main thesis, there is a lot I have outgrown—especially so far as the Grail chapters go. So I'm no longer responsible for all I said in that book; in fact, there has been inserted in copies during the last ten years or so a printed warning to the reader.

Yours cordially,
Roger Loomis

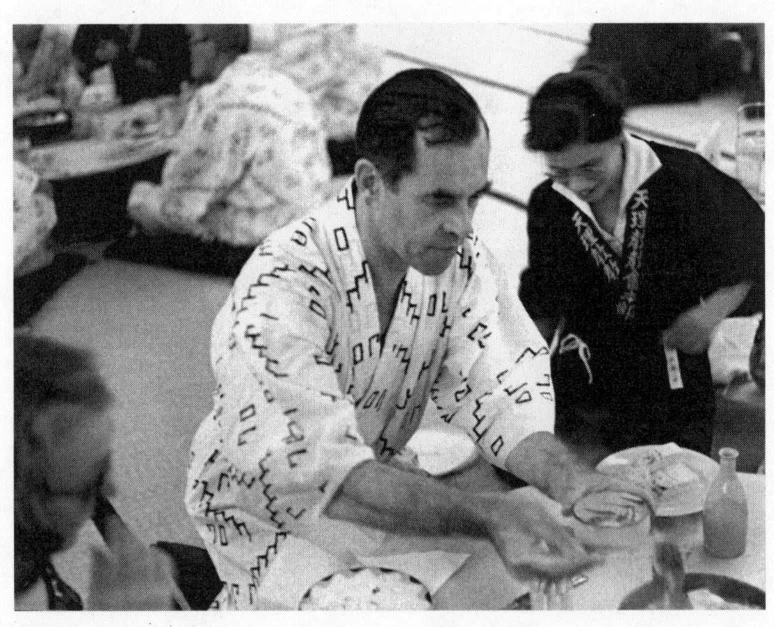

Joseph Campbell enjoying a meal in Japan, 1955

CHAPTER 3

The Banquet Years

The 1950s

In November 1949, after a year spent reading all the Eranos Jahrbücher *(Eranos Yearbooks), Campbell handed in a compendium report, abstracting each of the 140 lectures, analyzing them by geography, religion, length, and scientific discipline, choosing the seventy-eight lectures he considered the best, and arranging those as seven volumes. He argued eloquently for each volume of his scheme.*[1]

After the publication of The Hero with a Thousand Faces *in 1949, Campbell undertook to complete the Zimmer posthuma, took a series of epic voyages, and began to work on the monumental tetralogy* The Masks of God. *In the summer of 1953, Campbell and Erdman went to the Eranos Conference in Ascona. Afterward, they visited C. G. Jung at his tower in Bollingen, Switzerland, and then went on to France to see the Paleolithic caves of the Dordogne, including the grand sanctuary of Lascaux. The Campbells would return to Eranos in 1957 and 1959, when Campbell gave talks titled "Renewal Myths and Rites of the Primitive Hunters and Planters" and "The Symbol without Meaning." In 1954 to 1955 Campbell undertook his journeys to the East, to explore Hinduism in India and Buddhism from Sri Lanka to*

Japan,[2] *returning in 1958 to speak at the International Congress of the History of Religions Association in Tokyo.*

It was also during the 1950s that Campbell began work on several important presentations and publications. During the late fall and early winter of 1950, in a series of all-night sessions, he collaborated with Maya Deren, helping her put into shape the manuscripts that would become the book Divine Horsemen: The Living Gods of Haiti. *It was published the next year. Around the same time, he began work on the* Portable Arabian Nights *for the Viking Press series. It was published in 1952. He also began regular trips to Washington, D.C., from 1956–59, to give greatly appreciated lectures at the Foreign Service Institute.*

Henry Corbin (April 14, 1903–October 7, 1978) was a philosopher, theologian, Iranologist, and professor of Islamic Studies.

Campbell met Corbin at the Eranos meeting in the summer of 1953. Shortly thereafter he and Jean visited Jung at his retreat at Bollingen, Switzerland (Larsen and Larsen, A Fire in the Mind, *359–64).*

Following is a translation of Corbin's handwritten letter shown on the next page.

Rue de l'Odeon
Paris VI
September 12, 1953

My dear sir,
Perhaps you have not forgotten the little rendezvous that we had together at Ascona. Both my wife and I very much rejoice everyday at the prospect of seeing you. We have been told by your hotel that you will arrive today, Saturday. And so would you like to come have tea in our little home, in all cordial simplicity, tomorrow, Sunday, around 5:30 to 6 o'clock? We will await you with great

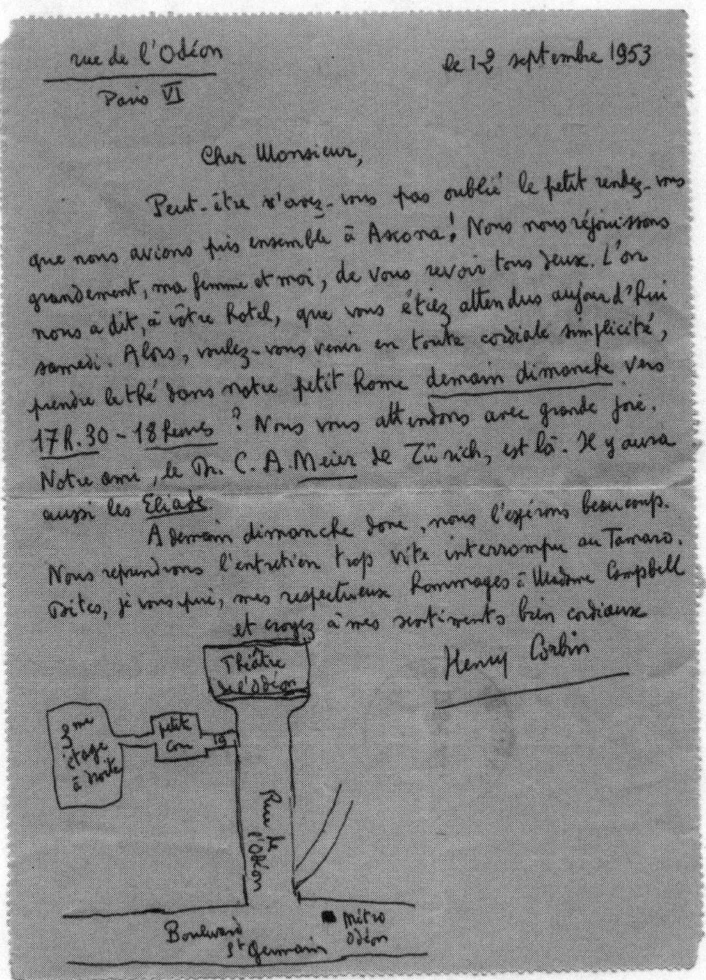

rue de l'Odéon
Paris VI

le 12 septembre 1953

Cher Monsieur,

Peut-être n'avez-vous pas oublié le petit rendez-vous que nous avions pris ensemble à Ascona! Nous nous réjouissons grandement, ma femme et moi, de vous revoir tous deux. L'on nous a dit, à votre hotel, que vous étiez attendus aujourd'hui samedi. Alors, voulez-vous venir en toute cordiale simplicité, prendre le thé dans notre petit home demain dimanche vers 17h.30 - 18 heures? Nous vous attendons avec grande joie. Notre ami, le Dr. C. A. Meier de Zürich, est là. Il y aura aussi les Eliade.

A demain dimanche donc, nous l'espérons beaucoup. Nous reprendrons l'entretien trop vite interrompu au Tamaro. Dites, je vous prie, mes respectueux hommages à Madame Campbell et croyez à mes sentiments bien cordiaux

Henry Corbin

A facsimile of Corbin's letter of September 12, 1953

joy. Our friend Dr. D.A. Meier from Zurich will be there, and also the Eliades.

Tomorrow Sunday, then, we hope. We can take up the conversation too quickly interrupted in Tamaro. Please give my respectful greetings to Mrs. Campbell and trust in my very cordial feelings.

Henry Corbin

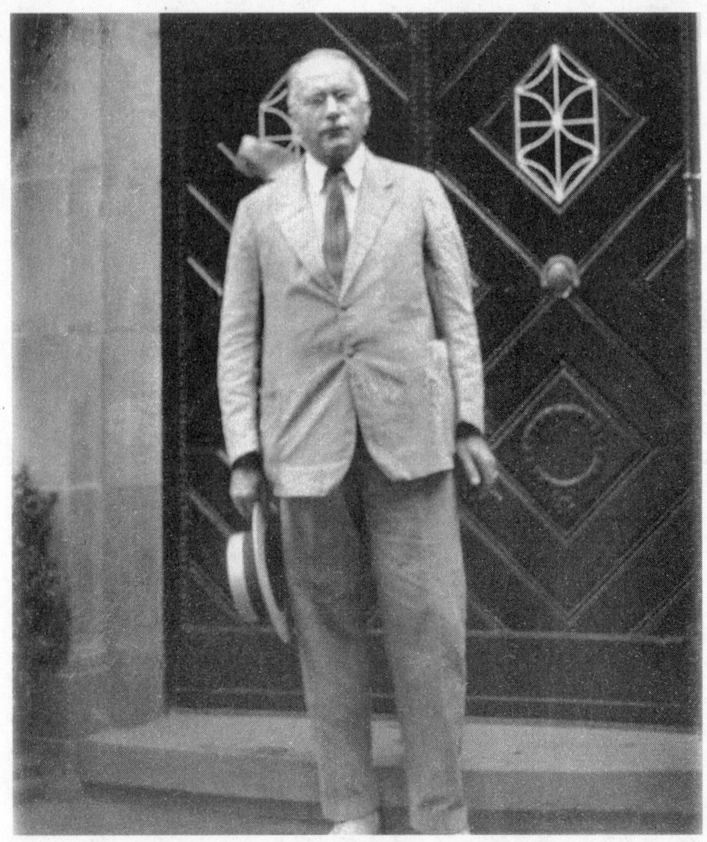

C. G. Jung

C. G. Jung was the founder of analytical psychology, a therapeutic practice based on the creative engagement of the energies of the deep psyche, through an exploration of the archetypal imagery of dreams and their relationship to the myths of the collective unconscious. His work had a profound impact on a diversity of disciplines, including anthropology, art, literature, mythology, philosophy, and theology.

Küsnacht-Zürich
Seestrasse 228

Nov. 4, 1953

Mr. Joseph Campbell
c/o Bollingen Foundation Inc.
New York 21, N.Y.

Dear Mr. Campbell,
Thank you ever so much for kindly sending me your very beautiful book. I had already seen it before and have duly admired it. You are certainly shaping after my late friend Heinrich Zimmer. It is the same style and outlook. I am glad to have made your personal acquaintance this summer.

With my compliments to Mrs. Campbell and my best wishes,
Sincerely yours,
C. G. Jung

Stanley Edgar Hyman (1919–70) was a literary critic who wrote primarily about critical methods: the distinct strategies critics use in approaching literary texts. Though most likely to be remembered today as the husband of writer Shirley Jackson, he was influential in developing literary theory in the 1940s and 1950s. Equally skeptical of every major critical methodology of his time, he worked out an early instance of a critical theory, exploring ways that critics can be foiled by their own methods. "Each critic," Hyman wrote in The Armed Vision, *"tends to have a master metaphor or series of metaphors in terms of which he sees the critical function. . . . This metaphor then shapes, informs, and sometimes limits his work." Hyman saw it as his task to point out these overriding themes by which other critics tacitly organized their work and their thinking.*

Waverly Place
New York 14, N.Y.
April 20, 1950

Dear Stanley,
Thank you for the copy of the twelve propositions. There is only one sentence, or rather phrase, on the page that catches me up, and that is the one about myth arising out of the ritual and <u>not vice versa</u>. I think that perhaps there are cases vice versa. However, even in these (if they exist) the correlation with the ritual is what is important. I liked very much your handling of the relationship of literature to myth: that is the point where the literary critic usually goes crazy (as Slochower did).[3] I'm adding One Warm Saturday, Castaway, and Captain Carpenter to my reading schedule, following your own magnum opus. I didn't realize that you were working directly on this problem of mythology—and it was a great delight to me to find that you were.

A delight also to find myself talking with you and Shirley, when I had expected to walk into a den of stuffed lions.

Best wishes to both—and again my thanks for this page (which will not be quoted without due credit: cross my heart,

Yours,

Joe

Waverly Place
New York 14, N.Y.
May 6, 1950

Dear Stanley,
Thank you for your kind letter. I haven't yet had a chance to read what you wrote about me, but I did catch a glimpse of the 1948 article in the S[arah] L[awrence] C[ollege] library (1949 volume at the binder's, or something) and in general agreed with your

sentiments. I thought the attack on Stith Thompson (no friend of mine, by the way) rather overdone, however.[4] The Finnish School, unless I am greatly mistaken, does not represent Nordic prejudice, but on the contrary, traces a great number of the tales of Europe back to non-European sources. Moreover, though this idea reconstructing archetypal tales may be something for Cloud-Cuckoo Land, they have brought a new precision into the art of collecting, as well as a new view of the oral migration of tales, and we are all, I think, now standing on their shoulders. They represent one of the few fairly solid spots in this tricky bog, and Thompson, as one their leading Trojans, deserves, I think, respectful handling. It seemed to me not quite cricket to give everybody in the lot a general kicking around and then hold up an unidentified group of promising young people as the true, though as yet invisible, benefactors of the science.

You are right, in the main, about the collectors; and Bodkin's book,[5] of course, was a calamity; but even here, I think it probable that we owe more to the collectors than you gave them. It is a curious job they've elected, and I doubt whether anyone with much wit would take it on; yet even the worst of their rubbish heaps yields bits of gold.—You see, I'm a softy! Give me a crumb, and I'll not quarrel much about the basket that it's in.

But, having got a load of your fighting vocabulary, I confess I'm a little bit scared. I should like very much to receive copies of the two pieces, so that I may study them properly, here, in the protection of my room; and I'll be glad, then, to give you my views. Jane Harrison[6] happens to be one of my pets, so it can't be that we're terribly far apart.

Looking forward to the shock,

Yours,

Joe

Waverly Place
New York 14, N.Y.
May 15, 1950

Dear Stanley.
Thank you for the copies of the Kenyon Review. I've now read the articles carefully, and find them excellent. This discussion in the middle of the 1948 piece, which I could only glimpse in the rush of the college day, gives good firm ground, I think, for your criticisms of Thompson; and I see that you have given him decent credit for what we owe him. My only serious criticism for your position is that you rest too complacently on the ritual theory, and even specifically on the fertility-ritual theory! Whether mankind's earliest rituals were fertility rituals remains a great question. Freud's Totem and Taboo, for example, suggests something very different, and the Doctor himself declares that he cannot comprise in his totem theory the rituals of the Goddess Mother of the agricultural societies.—What has always impressed me is the remarkable similarity in all the rituals, whether totemistic, shamanistic, agricultural, or rites of passage, and the question of the reason for their form, and for their constant character throughout the world, has teased my mind. I have been unable not to ask: Why is "the which the rite enacts or once enacted" always the same? Frazer has answered with an association theory that is no longer tenable—no longer, that is to say, since Freud opened the trap-door into the unconscious. How the question is to be answered in strictly Freudian terms, however, has not been settled, by any means.

I thought that as a result of your easy answer you stopped short of the problem that I—at least—was trying to face, and so missed all my wonderful discoveries. Also, your dogmatism carried you on a crusade against Euhemerism that went too far. Millions of legends are attached to actual historical personages: those, for example, of Paršva, Māhavīra, Gautama, Jesus, Muhammed, Mani, Alexander, King Arthur, Charlemagne, Montezuma, Kṛṣṇa, Confucius. Did you really mean to say that Zoroaster, Moses, and

Jesus never lived? And finally, you failed to see that you pretty well knocked out your own ritual thesis with the very words—italicized—in which it was formulated at the bottom of p. 463, and which I have quoted supra. But these surprising blanks and lapses do not greatly mar your picture. It is vast and orderly (though a bit off the ground, I would say), and brings to focus the whole range of the problems that have to be faced. I don't know anyone who has done this job half as well—in fact, don't know anyone who has even recognized it. And you may rest easy about my personal feelings: I don't mind a bit losing feathers, or even a few good claws, to someone working the way you are. I think that you have done a really valuable service to everyone you've criticized in these pieces. I, for one, feel greatly helped by the fresh view. I didn't realize that the Jungian note came through so loudly in my work or that the style was so cheap: in the future I shall be more attentive to the voice of the censor. But most of all, I'm glad to see my work in relation to what's going on outside my shop. Working as I do, these days, practically exclusively with materials on remote times and places, lose touch with the current literary problems; and this helps hook me back. I like it; and I think it's just as well that the book should be a bit sharp.

What do you do, though, about the problem of the origin of ritual? Why is the imagery of dreams so much like that of rites? Are you satisfied with a cocktail of Frazer and Freud? Why is the story which the rite enacts or once enacted always the same?

May I keep these articles? They are too good to lose. I'd like to have them here as guy-ropes, and in return send you copies of the books they help me with. I'm trying to build courage for a new big effort, and a good steer before and after I shut my mind to the contemporary literary scene may make all the difference. This one's going to be big—or at least long—and I should like to direct it, if possible to the problems you've announced.

By the way, though, just for the record: my Oriental lore is not mostly German, though Zimmer has given me more than I can measure. Most of what I know comes from Coomaraswamy,

Suzuki, Nikhilananda, Vivekananda, and Ramaskrishna, on top of a long spell of trying to read Śankara's Vivekacudamani, the Gita and the Upanishads in Sanskrit. Zimmer entered my life in 1941, just after I had finished two years editing Nikhilananda's Gospel of Sri Ramakrishna.[7] He opened a great amount of new material to me, but I was already deep in the Milky Ocean before he came. In fact, he helped fill me out.

So much, then, for confessions and thanks and argument. You were good to send me these articles, and I should be delighted to talk with you some more about these things. Perhaps you will be in town, one of these fine days. If so, please let me know. And if you want the articles back, don't hesitate to ask. Best wishes to you both,

Yours,
Joe

Waverly Place
New York 14, N.Y.
Jan. 21, 1951

Dear Stanley—
Thanks for the letter with its very kind and attractive invitation. Jean and I, unfortunately, are involved so heavily in this season's karma that we cannot break away. However, a drink and good talk here in town would be wonderful. Do, please, give me a ring! My days in the city are Monday, Tuesday—Saturday, Sunday; and I'm usually right here at my work table.

It is good to hear that you are going to have a whole year of labors on the great book—also, to know that Shirley's novel is sliding down the ways.[8] I am looking forward to reading it.

Chez nous, and right now, it's Jean's big concert (Jan. 28, Sunday evening, Hunter Playhouse) that dominates the scene. Much to do! And just to add to the salt, the page proofs of Zimmer III

(Philosophies of India) have arrived. Zimmer IV (Indian Art) is the main job, however, and is rolling at a painfully slow rate. I hope to finish the MS this winter, and push on to something of my own.

I am pleased to say that I have never read a word of Richard Chase and have no thought of doing so. The Columbia paper was enough for me. Instead, I have been reading Zen: Suzuki, Blyth, and Watts; also read a superb introduction to the civilizations of the Far East, Ostasien denkt anders [East Asia believes otherwise], by Lily Abegg,[9] which is now, I think, translated into English and should supply a good counterweight to Whyte's *The Next Development in Man.*[10]

Jean joins me in thanks to you both for thinking of us and good wishes for the books. And I shall look forward to a call. How would you like to have dinner with me some Monday or Tuesday evening, or with us some Friday?

Yours ever,

Joe

Waverly Place
New York 14, N.Y.
Feb. 25, 1951

Dear Stanley—
Will this Friday still be O.K. for you and Shirley? If so, how would it be to arrive here some time between 6:30 and 7:00? We are both looking forward to seeing you, and send, meanwhile, our best, for the magnum opus.[11]

Yours,

Joe

Waverly Place
New York 14, N.Y.
March 4, 1951

Dear Stanley—
I find that the coming week is to be an extremely full one for Jean, and so propose the following, for our Friday. Friday, March 16. Who would have thought that life could be so full!

Our profound sympathies to your household, re: the measles. I thought that science had changed all that.

We are looking forward to seeing you and Shirley and hope that one of these proximate Fridays will be it!

Yours,

Joe

Waverly Place
New York 14, N.Y.
March 11, 1951

Dear Stanley—
I've written your name down in the date-pad for April 6, and Munsterbergers for March 30. Now it remains only to see what happens.

I'm a little surprised to learn of the anthropologists writing letters to the Kenyon Review; for I didn't know that these chaps read anything but the American Anthropologist. I don't think it matters much what they say. They'll probably contradict themselves in the course of their own letters and not even know it.

Hope the youngsters are well and that the work has begun to roll.

Yours—with hope

Joe

Waverly Place
New York 14, N.Y.
April 22, 1952

Dear Stanley—
Thank you for your kind note. I did not take your first comment on the Kerenyi volume badly, though my silence may have indicated otherwise.[12] It is not a perfect volume, but it seems to me a very good one, and I know that I like very much the way it runs.

Work advances slowly through my last Zimmer MS. Ten years of this, and one begins to get a bit tired.

Bennington again! You will be far far away. But we shall hope to see you when you can bring yourselves to town. Good wishes to you both—

Yours ever,
Joe

Waverly Place
New York 14, N.Y.
Oct. 12, 1959

Dear Stanley—
It was good to hear from you again and I appreciate greatly your comment on the new book. Arriving as it did on publication day, it set me up no end. For I am sure you know: you are the keenest and cruelest reader of them all, and to have your regard is immense encouragement. I am happy too that the book has brought me in touch with you again. Fat and bearded as a walrus? I should like to see! If you and Shirley reach New York some time, do let us know. Jean joins me in warm regards to you both—Many many thanks.

Sincerely
Joe

No he didn't make me jump: it was he who jumped around like a flea. He said he shoots athletes from below, authors from above. But that was long ago and perhaps his "philosophy" has changed.

Margaret Mead (December 16, 1901–November 15, 1978) was an American cultural anthropologist who was featured frequently as an author and speaker in the mass media during the 1960s and 1970s. She earned her bachelor's degree at Barnard College in New York City and her MA and PhD degrees from Columbia University. Mead was a respected and often controversial academic who popularized anthropology in modern American and Western culture. Her reports detailing the attitudes toward sex in South Pacific and Southeast Asian traditional cultures influenced the 1960s sexual revolution. She was a proponent of broadening sexual mores within a context of traditional Western religious life.

The American Museum of Natural History
West 77th Street
New York 24, N.Y.

November 11, 1957

Dr. Joseph Campbell
Sarah Lawrence College
Bronxville, New York

Dear Dr. Campbell:
I am delighted that you will be able to take part in the Conference on December 4. I enclose a background statement. In thinking over these points, perhaps you may be prepared to make a brief statement about one or all of them which can go directly into our record.

With deep appreciation,
Yours sincerely,
[signed] Margaret
Margaret Mead
For the Scientific Committee of the World
Federation for Mental Health

Campbell teaching, circa 1963

CHAPTER 4

The Masks of God

1959–1968

During the 1960s Campbell continued his vigorous regimen of teaching, traveling, and publishing. In 1963, he accompanied his wife, Jean, on a hugely successful tour of her dance production The Coach with Six Insides, *which was based on his* Skeleton Key to Finnegans Wake *and won the OBIE and Vernon Rice awards. There were shows at the Italian Spoleto Festival, the Paris International Theater Festival, and the Dublin Theater Institute, followed by two seasons in New York, three U.S. tours, and, in 1964, trips to Vancouver and Toronto. In the midst of the turmoil of the Vietnam war protests—and the death of his brother, Charlie—Campbell continued his lectures at the Foreign Service Institute in Washington, began taping extremely popular shows for channel 13,*[1] *and, in 1968, began his first of many seasons of lecturing at the Esalen Institute, alongside many friends, including Alan Watts.*

He was no less productive in his scholarship and publications, completing the last three volumes of the monumental Masks of God *tetralogy:* Oriental Mythology *in 1962,* Occidental Mythology *in 1964, and the final volume,* Creative Mythology, *in 1968. He also edited* The Portable Jung *for the Viking Press, published* The Flight of the Wild Gander *(a collection of his essays), and began work on* Myths to Live By, *based on his talks at the Cooper Union in New York over a fourteen-year period. All the while, he continued his long service as a trustee of the Bollingen Foundation in 1960.*

Among the longest sequences of correspondence from the 1960s are the letters to and from Ted Ray Spivey, a professor of English at Georgia State University in Atlanta. He was the author of Revival: Southern Writers in the Modern City *(1986);* Beyond Modernism *(1988);* The Writer as Shaman: The Pilgrimages of Conrad Aiken and Walker Percy *(1987);* Flannery O'Connor: The Woman, the Thinker, the Visionary *(1997); and* Time's Stop in Savannah: Conrad Aiken's Inner Journey *(1997). This section also includes letters from Signe Gartrell (later Lynn Gartrell Levins), whose book* Faulkner's Heroic Design: The Yoknapatawpha Novels *was published by the University of Georgia Press in 2008.*

Rock Springs Rd.
Atlanta, Ga.

May 1, 1961

Mr. Joseph Campbell
Sarah Lawrence College
Bronxville, N.Y.

Dear Mr. Campbell:

For several years now a group of us here in Atlanta have been reading your work, particularly <u>The Hero With A Thousand Faces</u>, and we have reached the conclusion that you are for us the most important American working in a philosophical tradition which is gradually toward some sort of new flow of psychic energy. Ever since 1959 we have been having some important dreams which indicate that new forces are at work in the psychic world. In all the reading we have done, particularly in Jung, we have found nothing quite like these dreams coming from psychological studies of the first half of the century, yet that all fit into the archetypal patterns discussed in your work and in the work of Jung and other depth psychologists.

To say the least, we are moved and awed by these dreams, and as time goes on we find more people having them. At thirty-three I am the oldest member of this group. The most interesting dreams are had by women and girls varying in age from twenty-eight to sixteen, but in our very loose-knit group there are also men who dream. We think it might be important for you and us if sometime we got together to discuss these matters in connection with your work in mythology. Four of us—two men and two women—will be in New York in late June, and we were wondering if we might see you either June 22 or June 23. We will sail for Europe on June 24 and will return around August 28. If it would be more convenient for you, we could come to see you at that time. I think there is no doubt that all people who have knowledge and experience of psychic conditions in the world today should help each other.

Let me again say how much your work has meant to us. I believe in the future it will even more profoundly affect than it does now the psychic activity of young people who will be the instruments used by God to remake the world.

Sincerely yours,
Ted R. Spivey

Wieuca Rd. NE
Atlanta 5, Ga.
June 26, 1962

Dear Mr. Campbell,

Your letter has meant a great deal to all of us. Everyone who has read it consider [*sic*] it an excellent statement by a greatly admired author. There is no doubt, as you say, that our adventure is a portion of yours, and this link between two generations is especially important to young people, who usually need a great deal of help to believe in their own souls.

I am particularly heartened by the fact that you agree with the interpretation of the dreams. What we do is based so much on dreams and their interpretation that we must constantly search ourselves to be sure that we are following a true light. In basic matters I believe that one should rely not on what he thinks, but on what he receives through dream or vision. If I had made that statement five years ago, I would have regarded myself as a candidate for the madhouse. I grew up with the usual rational approach to everything and quite recently I would have regarded such a statement as the above as typical of the fanatics the South particularly abounds in. However, so much has happened to my friends and me that we have to say that we are in a new period of history. Things are happening so fast and so mysteriously that we cannot possibly keep in touch with our souls without relying on dreams. Even many small events in our lives are tied up with dreams. More and more everything we do is directed by the soul. It would seem that only by this method can anyone survive in the new world of death and destruction that is upon us. No rational processes can possibly cope with what we have to face. Of course, the mind plays its necessary role, but once again the psyche becomes the center of our being.

In connection with your role, I believe what I said in the last letter is true. I myself have never wanted or expected to play much of a role in psychic adventures. Even I often am inclined to withdraw into myself and read works of English literature, which I have so long trained myself to do. But more and more I see that I have no choice but to become truly alive. It is a painful process but one is pushed on. Concerning you, I had this dream the night after I received your letter. You had come with your wife to visit me in my apartment in Atlanta. As you came in the door, I noticed that you were in your twenties and dressed in a beautiful coat. I did not see your wife very clearly. We talked for awhile, and then I suggested that we go somewhere to eat. As I walked out the door, the spirits of two of my best friends stood in the room unseen by you, and I said to them after you had gone out, "Well, he is not evil." Outside there was snow everywhere. We were about to get in your car when I suggested that we walk up to the Cherokee Motel to eat (this is actually a motel near where I live). As we walked up the street to the motel, I had a clear picture of your wife, who seemed not more than twenty years old, and this name came to my mind: Maud Begonne. I think the meaning of the dream is this. It is a continuation of Julie's dream, which I wrote you about. Before we had to go see you and prove ourselves. Now you came to us. This is important in becoming connected with anyone in the new epoch because today there are so many counterfeit psychic people and so many evil people who want to connect themselves with one who is on the right path, as I believe that you and I and those close to us are. Only dreams can tell who are the right ones for you. You are young and well dressed in the dream because this is your true psychic nature. The snow outside is a typical symbol of the winter period of our civilization, and eating together is the psychic experience shared together. The Cherokee Motel is important because much that we do is somehow tied up with the good Indian mana that is still present in America. I believe the Cherokees particularly felt much mana, and it is fitting that some of our best people have Cherokee blood in their veins. One of the deepest members of the group, if not indeed the deepest, had a Cherokee chief for his great-grandfather. In this dream your wife was not your wife, as in the other dream, but your soul. She recalled to my mind Maud Gonne, the woman who meant so much to Yeats. For a long time I have puzzled over the reason for Begonne instead of Gonne, and now I think I have it. It means either one or both of these ideas, probably both since the two ideas are often telescoped into one symbol. As all of us try to do, even as we accept the call to adventure, you are trying to push your soul away and say Maud be gone. Also you are trying to slough off the old soul so long ravished by the beauties of the old world, symbolized by the famous Irish beauty Yeats thought might become another Joan of Arc. Your work has always seemed to me to have a Celtic flavor, and of course it is filled with a richness and poetic beauty that we associate with the richness of the old world and particularly Ireland. Yet I remember that your first published work on mythology (at 15?) was about the American Indians. I would guess that you are in the process of leaving the old world and turning to the new world. There is something very important here. The old world (Africa, Asia, and Europe) must lie fallow, must have its beauties washed away by cleaning rains, and the new world must now receive on soil soon to be quickly cleansed (there is so little of the old to wipe away) the seeds for man's new life. All this emerges from the dreams we have had.

Well, it seems we have a closer connection with each other than I had thought and I suppose you had too. It seems that we will eventually meet. I have no idea when or under what circumstances. Possibly you can say.

I have recently finished your Oriental Mythology. There is a lot I would like to say about it, but I will save it until I write again. You mentioned certain problems in your letter, and of course in the book there is the problem of differences between East and West. We have had dreams about the problems, and it is possible some of them can be of value to you. Also we have done some group research on myth in certain writers from 1800 to the present and, without any system in mind, on recent movies and TV programs. Some modern writers that have been particularly helpful to us are Hesse, Eliot, Yeats, C. S. Lewis, Romain Gary, Flannery O'Connor, and a nineteenth century Hungarian poet Madach.[2] We have surveyed these and many more looking for material that might help us. If we can be of any help in writing your other volumes, we would be very happy to make any kind of contribution.

Again in closing let me say I look forward to the time when we can meet. I think we will have some important things to say to each other.

Sincerely,
Ted R. Spivey

Wieuca Rd. NE
Atlanta 5, Ga.
January 5, 1964

Dear Joe,
We have had several telephone conversations with Signe before and after Christmas and she tells us that you and Jean are doing well. People still continue to dream about you. Two dreams, which Signe might have mentioned, are these. A young man I am talking to dreamed that he had to be taught by Campbell but that I would be Campbell's substitute and teach him. The other was that you finally believed in the idea of Alaska. The dream that Signe told me you had about the box whose secret you could not yet see gave me a very good feeling indeed. In fact Signe's whole account of your get-together after Christmas had a very strong effect on both Julie and me. At the moment I am simply recording impressions. Later we will no doubt understand better our real relationship. The dream Signe had about the two of us being strongly masculine indicates that we both have even now important roles to play in the great movement of the Spirit that is now beginning. Our meeting in New York struck something deep in both of us and though we moved back into the orbit of our daily affairs we still were different in a most profound way from what we had been before. The part Signe plays in all this is most interesting and to me most amazing. You referred to her in your note on the Christmas card we received as being my lovely ambassador and in a sense she is, but it was by no conscious action of my own that she became this. Signe in some ways is way ahead of me, yet she remains our spiritual child. You who know so well the wisdom of paradox will understand this better than I do. The child saves the father as much as the father saves the child. Even as I write this I feel a great love for Signe, although it is a love mixed with pain because she has caused me pain. And now she tells me that dreams tell her to correspond with me, which she never has really done. You and I both are being involved with her at once in what can only be something very great. I want to see this from my view so that it will not seem

like some sort of generalship on my part to send her to New York. I am no general but I have had dreams of being a soldier and officer in the army of the intellect, which seems to be my particular role, to state truths for people who are having dreams and being sent here and there to do the work of God.

We are looking forward to seeing Jean in Milledgeville. As our plans stand now we will go down Feb. 21 and get a room for the night in a motel. If it suits her we could get together for as long as possible either before or after the performance, after I imagine being a better time for her. Or we could see her the following morning, anything that suits her convenience. Signe continues to urge us to come to New York this spring for a few days. I have not received a definite call in this matter. Do you think it is time for us to see each other again? I do not know yet, but we also need to see Signe and Julie's sister Paula, whom I would very much like for you to meet sometime. She has been having some excellent dreams lately and will eventually be one of the really great people in the movement.

Congratulations on your television show being a success. I really wish I could see it and would nearly come to New York just for that opportunity alone. We are seeing again this new year the series Alan Watts has done for TV, and we can say again that it is excellent. You and Watts are the men of the century for stating these matters. Signe told me some of the things you said to her about Watts and I have pondered them very carefully. This too is something we can talk about. The business of drugs is bad. Instant mysticism is the way of the Devil. Huxley's book Island is very important for stating certain truths. Do you know of the work of Velikovsky? We have been reading him lately and he puts certain matters important to all of us in proper perspective. I think he might one day be as important to us as Jung but of course it is too early to say yet. Signe wanted me to make some sort of comment on Jung's autobiography. I have only read parts of it, not being allowed to finish and give a complete statement. It is important to understand Jung's greatness; it is equally important to understand where he went wrong. To do so is to understand where all the

Europeans went wrong. With this knowledge it will be easier to accept the fact that the basis of the movement must be the Americans and others who have renounced the old world to join him. This is part of the difference between you and Watts. For all his outer efforts he has not become truly American yet. I know it is possible for some foreigners to make this transition and I pray he will too. Where Jung went wrong is in his failure to see the Devil at work in his own life and in the lives of all he knew. His knowledge of the Shadow archetype was only theoretical. Above all he did not understand vampirism, which goes finally back to the incest complex, which he too understood theoretically but not in fact, in for instance his own life. Dracula here is an important book, and Julie achieves some of her greatest moments in teaching with it. Jung did not get a hold of the right folklore. I can document in detail what I have to say here in conversation with reference to the book and to his dreams, some of which he did not interpret correctly by our patterns of meaning at least.

Well, we think of you two often and we wish you the best of everything in the new year. It will be an important year for everyone. If the spirit moves you write, but if not of course I will understand. We'll talk a lot of things out when we get together next, either this spring or at some later date.

Best regards,
Ted

M. Signe Gartrell
Rue de Seine
Paris VI, France
Sunday, February 9, 1964

Dear Joseph:

There is absolutely no reason to write to you tonight. That must be the reason of the beyondness that is making me type...

There is so little psychic energy here that dreams of great significance or insight are few and far between. So one seems to feel compelled to search and re-search the petty night myths in futile hopes that it isn't quite the sparcity of spirit seen and defined on the far off home shores. But it is; and even worse.

Last night, after reading Hero for a couple of hours I scribbled something on the back cover which I had been toying with, intermittently, for days. After ruminating this afternoon I decided that it is part of a revelation which shall take me to a plateau that even my fantasia does not yet perceive. Here it is—.

The worst of the old is yet the best of my new disciplinarian and parent. For the lion of the goddess is no longer a cub; but a vehement ferocious adult attacking and challenging me beyond my own infancy and escape.

(This Dear God, is my plight. How shall I ever cope with it?)

I have my volition—because it is God's will which is also my role—murdered something Eastern and intuitive. And through this massacre accepted the way of the West...which in the beginning was a conditioning against my inherent nature.

Thus my lion preceded me in death as in life he now chases and attacks me.

I wonder if in this dearth of energy in the world and within all, I shall ever be able to create anything. Especially since I am still so young and also a woman. People never seem to listen to women—except the men who love them and are inspired by them. But since females seem to vacillate between naiveté and vampirism it's understandable.

Even when "Ladies Home Journal" advocates and encourages "feminine creativity in the arts" it gets rather depressing to think that something which might be real within yourself will be taken over the mass participation of "Art for the Artist's sake" as society teaches that our group therapy is in the distortion of what little "Art for Art's sake," or "Art of the Soul," etc. is left today.

The more I am becoming Westernized the more I find myself relying (even living in a new way) on the teaching and experiences of the East. It still seems to be in a rudimentary state of balance rather than non-dualism. Everything appears to be so intense and peaceful at the same time that I don't know quite what to do. Therefore I am doing nothing and everything.

A few more comments about the East and West and my east and west. Forgive me if I have become redundant; but there seems to be some need to tell you these things...from a child's viewpoint. Two years ago I dreamed that I was in the midst of a forest whereupon I found myself near a scaffold. A hangman's rope was attached; but there was no victim—apparent or otherwise. A group of people were standing near the platform when suddenly a wild tiger appeared and they scampered into some bushes and huddled in a shivering frightened calm. Oddly enough I was not afraid. I began to ascend up the stairs but then turned around to confront the tiger. At that moment the tree of life entered my hands. It resembled a water stick so I could hold a branch in either hand. I pointed the base of the tree at the animal which not only calmed him but also hypnotized him. And so the people, the tiger, and I all were saved.

In esoteric ways the tiger could have been what was then the fullness of the panther and lion; but what since has had to be split...in a way different from the separation and union of opposites. But more than that it was the tiger of Buddhism which must meet with the eternal phallus of the west. Not in complete physical union have (or can I ever?) I joined them. But in their tête-a-tête there is a stillness which prevents the execution or suicide of either, and protects the people. Thus, I think that part of my role and my generation's is to not only go beyond your knowledge (if we can) but to further elucidate it. In both obscurity and detail. I think, too, that there is a strange insanity which prevails the East which none of us can fully understand.

My personal problem has taken on a new lease in that a cousin of mine who died last year with cancer and who played a rather large role, before and after then, in my dreams as the last of the giving up of my family, sickness, childlessness, the South, etc. came back last night to aid me. When I went to her funeral (in dreams) several months ago I married her rather than paying the customary homage. Now she is one of my guardian ghosts.

And childless as I am I have children of all types night after night. Some of whom I can be, and nurture; some of whom I try to hide from myself and the world; and some of whom I have no understanding.

Though you are many things, many persons in my dreams, you are yourself; you are your work, your wisdom, your truth; you are both a symbolic and real father; you are all of these things within me and beyond me from which I must learn. So it is that everyday I ask myself in all these facets and in their unrelatedness to me for strength and guidance. But I seem vaguely, to be asking us all something more.

Dear, Mr. Campbell, I wish that I could look out of your window tonight and see the world as it appears to me and then turn around and ask you how life really is that I cannot see or am not willing to see but by being told. It is good that I can't for awhile.

I am almost as patient as life. So I never look for a letter or expect it. When the time is right it shall be asked and fulfilled that you write to me and that I write to you again. No expectations. No demands. Only faith that all shall come to pass that should be.

Signe

Wieuca Rd. NE
Atlanta 5, Ga.
March 10, 1964

Dear Joe,

Julie and I want to thank you for the copy of volume three of The Masks of God. I would have written sooner thanking you, for receiving the book was a very welcome surprise indeed, but I wanted to have some time for the two of us to read it so that my remarks about it would be based on a careful reading. We are both extremely impressed with it. The image that comes to mind as I read it is that of a great river flowing along. We think it is the best of the three volumes. It is amazing how you can draw together so much material without seeming in the least strained or pedantic and the same time write in such a beautiful, flowing style. You show an awareness of the world's cultures, religions and myths that has about it a joy and a love that seems amazing to someone used to reading the sweeping prose of Toynbee and Spengler. These two and others take themselves so seriously, and you have in your view and in your style a lighthearted quality that the dull, serious ones could never understand. I think Nietzsche particularly would have appreciated your marvelous style. There were times when reading the book that Julie and I both just stopped and laughed. There were turns of phrase that had about them that comic quality that you noted in The Hero as being characteristic of myth. Your conclusion was the best thing I have read by you since The Hero, and leaves us waiting with more anticipation than ever for volume four.

There are many, many things that I would like to discuss with you about the book, but the time will come later. There is one overall matter that I would like to mention. I am in complete agreement with you when you speak of the greatness of Europe, which for both of us I think shines above that of any other civilization. But if this is true, then it must be that the religion which produced this great civilization shines above others, for what we are is a result of what we and our ancestors believed and the basis of this belief is Christianity. It seems to me that you do not sink yourself deeply enough into the greatness of Christianity. For instance, you do not make nearly enough of The City of God nor of the much greater sources of the history of histories that Augustine wrote—the Apocalypse of St. John, the teachings of Jesus, the Old Testament prophets. A statement like this bothers me: "Like the Christianity of Augustine, Manichaeism viewed nature as corrupt..." There is a vast difference between the way the two traditions viewed good and evil. Also the Christianity of Augustine is the Christianity of Catholicism and the main stream of Protestantism. As I say this,

I know you understand that I am not trying to view your work from any dogmatic viewpoint. What you say about the failures of Catholic Christianity is excellent, but I think you could have done more with the richness of the Christian myth, especially as stated by Augustine, John, Paul, and Christ. If Jerusalem were not the world navel, then how is it that Christian civilization has conquered the world? And why is America the last, best hope of man? The rational humanism that separated itself from the past has not made us great but only the mana given us by the culture heroes of our religion and our beliefs based on and derived from that religion. As you say at the end, that mana has run low and must be called forth again by finding new symbols. But this is not the work of the poet and artist, as you suggest, but of the seer, the mystic, the prophet, the philosopher. These are finally all words for what the sociologists call the culture hero that you wrote so well about in Primitive Mythology. You and I and the others having the dreams are the beginning of a new race of these people. The artist follows the seer, who literally sees the new symbols sent him by God and feels the new power which accompanies these symbols and visions.

Your book has helped me greatly in my writing of an essay. It is about what I call the prophets of knowledge—men who have erected a body of knowledge into the vision that is like that of a prophet's because they approached the knowledge with their whole beings and not simply as scholars and rationalists. The major prophets that I am considering are Einstein, Planck, Toynbee, Spengler, Freud, Jung, Campbell, Watts. I think you eight represent certain psychic impulses of man to work his way back to the full vision of God that we are moving toward now. The fields of physics, philosophical history, depth psychology, and mythology and comparative religion are the great fields of our time for pointing man back to the ground of his being. Right now my great labor is the pursuit of Jung. I had a dream last week that he was a friendly man of great psychic power but that he was a Rotarian and a racist. I am still pondering that one. I think I have got Jung's major dreams interpreted and they are very interesting. I don't think he understood them very well. If there is any help you can give me on this essay I would greatly appreciate it. Our one conversation greatly stimulated me and your book has helped much.

I have had some long letters from Signe and she is making that very deep plunge that is necessary to find truth and the pearl of great price. The great change of her life is now taking place and I pray for her because it is very dangerous. But I feel good about her. She mentions you often in her letters and I can tell that you two have meant a lot to each other.

The best of luck on all your projects. Julie's sister tells us that your TV programs are excellent. We look forward to seeing you before too long.

Cordially,
Ted

Wieuca Rd. NE
Atlanta 5, Ga.
April 15, 1964

Dear Joe,
Your letter of last month has caused me to think deeply about your work and the new psychic work that is now coming into full view for many to see. I had hoped to answer it much sooner, but the ending of one quarter of school work and the beginning of another has so far prevented that. However, I think it is just as well because Julie and I both have been led to some thinking and dreaming that we might not have known if I had written earlier. No one has ever written me letters that so provoke thought and so stimulate me to further explorations of my soul. And I have never seen such clarity and honesty about basic views as yours. Most authors seem to feel that they have to hide their deepest convictions from themselves, and these hidden views seem to come through the style and poison some or all of the work. What still gets me more than anything else about Volume III is the lightness of touch and the joyousness

that pervades the writing. Again it is not so much the individual views that matter as the poetry that is in the presentation of these views and the facts that go with them. The greatest thing about your book seems to be that it really does live up to the title of The Masks of God, which means that you are not enchanted by the various masks that God takes, as nearly everyone else who thinks about the matter seems to be. This means to me that your work points straight towards mysticism in the best sense of that word, which is where we are all headed, regardless of what we think about the Christian tradition or whether we can read Augustine or not. Within a few days after your letter arrived someone put in my hands the records of the meeting of the Joyce society in 1951. I had never before heard you read and comment on Joyce before, and I was struck as never before that the one universal power really is drawing us all together by different paths. When I listened to you speak the gnostic statement "Split the stick and there is Jesus," I was certain of the underlying unity of so many of us who are being drawn together. What amazed me most was your reading about Dublin, Georgia, in that section of Finnegans Wake. My father's mother's [kin] are from near Dublin and live today near the Oconee River, and my father, who is the nearest person I have ever known to the Mark Twain hero, played football at Dublin High School. In fact my father, who is about your age, is very vigorous and reams [*sic*], is in many ways that other side of you, the man of affairs. And so we have the two brothers of Finnegans Wake. Such ideas may once have seemed fanciful but now they don't at all because they strike the soul with such intensity. There is much more about this that I could tell you, but I will save it until later. Above all, I believe God is drawing together three generations—people from fifty on up, people between 25 and 50 and people under 25. We have had contact with all three generations and have seen the gradual convergence of all three groups with the particular problems and particular virtues. It will take the many virtues of all three groups to do what must be done. One thing I have noticed about people above 50 is that, unless they are fanatics, they must stay at some distance from the Christian thinkers, and in fact must be, even when they don't know it, pro-Greek and pro-Science. And yet they as much as anyone are drawn toward mystic revelation and even long for it.

Let me now tell you about two dreams. A third dream about you is enclosed in the letter I send along written by a friend named Jim Dahl who teaches in a college at Carrollton, Ga. Here is a dream I had about two weeks ago. I came to a forest clearing in the middle of New York City. I came and stood at the door of a small, white house where you lived. We had arranged to get together and I called your name. Receiving no answer, I went inside and you appeared with paint on you. You said you had been both painting and sleeping at the same time and that you were not quite ready to see me and would I come back. I said yes. In the next scene I was in the bedroom of your house changing into tennis shorts and looked up and saw Jean. I asked her if she wanted to talk and she said yes, with a smile. Then she pointed to the bed where the two of you slept and said, "You have changed around that bed and I told you not to." I said, "I didn't know I had." In the next scene Jean and I were talking together in New York. She asked me if I could talk about the dance. I said I had seen classical and modern dance but that I did not know any of the terminology. So she asked if we could talk about New York culture. I said that within twenty to forty years everything around us would be rubble. Then she wanted to talk about the quality of New York culture. I said that London culture was once superior to New York culture and was what New York culture was moving toward. She agreed. And I said that London culture was now uncreative. Then she asked me about Atlanta and said that the last time she was there it was so full of night clubs. I said that taken all in all Atlanta was the best place in the world to live. I said that it was not like other Southern cities because it was so high. It is, I said, the second highest large city in the country, second only to Denver. We then came to an apartment house where she lived and I left her and went to a hotel, where I took a shower. This dream was so vivid that it woke me up. I immediately told it to Julie. We both went back to sleep and she dreamed this. She and I were visiting you at a cottage where you lived in the mountains. There was a waterfall in the front of the cottage and it was very difficult to walk down it. Julie and I went down it to where it emptied into a great and turbulent sea. You yourself had not gone down it but I had come to show you how to walk down it to the sea. Julie and I returned to the cottage and with you was a lovely girl that I then embraced.

I will not comment on these dreams now except to say that I think they are fairly obvious in most part and that they point out the direction in which we are headed. Was it Signe who sent you the Alaskan News? It was not I; I did know there was such a publication. The night before the earthquake I had a dream about Alaska, indicating such a catastrophe would happen.[3] I like your statement in referring to Alaska as the "scene, the raw ground, of the next world age." I believe it to be just that more and more each day.

Give my best to Jean; I hope all is well with both of you.

Cordially,

Ted

Wieuca Rd. NE
Atlanta 5, Ga.
June 15, 1964

Dear Joe,

Now that the school year is over I'm beginning to get back some of the energy that flowed out of me this past year. Signe has been keeping me posted on how everything is with you, and I gather from what she says that you are very tired from a year of teaching and writing. I feel the same way and I have noticed this tiredness in others and have come to the conclusion that this is the beginning of a difficult transitional period for people like us who dream and are involved in the working of the world soul. Still in spite of the fact that we have not been able to correspond as much as we both would have liked to, I think Signe has served to bring us closer together. From her letters I feel I have gotten to know you much better, and I know that you have come to see Atlanta in a different light. Signe has made amazing progress since she left America in spite of the great dangers she has been subject to. Recently I had a dream in which she was sitting at a desk in a schoolroom and a girl who is a symbol to her of her soul came up and slapped her in the face and said it was time for her to wake up. I have no doubt that she is now awakening.

Since I last wrote I have had two dreams about you that indicate your roles in both the past and the present. In the spring I had a crisis with a close friend who doubted if we were really on the right track. I had a dream in which his wife came to me to find out, and I told her we were working in the way of truth and that truth had to come before love. Then she asked about the traditions of the intellect we were working in. I told her that there were several traditions but that we were in the right one. I said to her, "Campbell takes up where Jung leaves off and we take up where Campbell leaves off." I am now fully convinced that the Jung-Campbell tradition is the chief psychological and spiritual tradition of the twentieth century and that the work we are now doing is an extension of that tradition. But since I met you I have not doubted that the work you did as one of the two cornerstones of that tradition is but one part of your life work and is in fact the lesser of the two roles you will play. Last week I had a dream confirming this belief. In it you were lecturing at Emory University here in Atlanta and one of our best young men was travelling with you on this lecture tour you were on. He told me that everywhere you went you knew people and were very sociable at all times. I asked him if you could also remain alone for periods of time. He said you could and I said this was good because a great leader would have to spend time alone. I believe that this new movement will see you become one of the great leaders if not the greatest.

I think I have said enough for now. I hope this summer we recover some of our lost energy and can correspond about Jung and several other matters. If we don't get this far I feel it will be all right. We must go slowly now because the matters we deal with can only be approached slowly. Time will eventually bring us closer together and we will one day be cooperative in a very profound way to the benefit of many people. I have had some ideas about this but time will see if dreams confirm these ideas.

Give my very best to Jean. Julie sends her regards.

Cordially,

Ted

Wieuca Rd. NE
Atlanta 5, Ga.
July 16, 1964

Dear Joe,

I have wanted to write to you before now but something said wait. I am glad I did because a few nights ago I had a very vivid dream about Jean. I believe that the more vivid a dream is the more important it is. And this dream hit me very hard. Julie and I in the dream had gone to New York to visit Jean. She lived in the top of a building in the middle of a city and to get in touch with her we had to first go to a room in the middle of the building, where we found a little old woman who said she would get her for us. She went off and came back with Jean. I saw Jean's face very clearly, in fact it was radiant, and then I knew that I had known her not only at some previous time in my life but in some other life. She then took Julie and me to a building next door where she lived and this abode was on the ground floor. I don't think I have ever seen a more beautiful woman in my dreams. This dream contrasts interestingly with the other one I had of visiting with her in New York. One detail of this one I neglected to include and that was that in the first dream she had some bad teeth that had to come out, symbol of psychic change. I particularly wanted to tell both of you about this dream because of the deep effect it had on me. I will not now try to draw any conclusions about it except the one that we are all being drawn closer together, but I will for the time simply admire it as work of art. I had an involved dream about you and me doing something together, but I cannot remember the details of it. Julie dreamed that you wrote us a long letter which included some poems and we were surprised that you wrote poetry. Your prose is so very poetic that it should not surprise us if you did write very good poetry; but then maybe this is symbolic, I don't know.

The enclosed letter from Signe, written in London, will, I hope, reassure you about Signe's condition. We have had several others from her and they indicate psychic development. What you said about her in your last letter seems to me to be entirely true. Eroticism mistaken for mysticism and the search for one or both parents are possibly the chief forms that mania takes in young people these days who have great spirituality. Since you have been so closely drawn to Signe, I think I really should say something about the way Julie and I work with her and others like her. Like you we do not trust ourselves to probe the souls of other people, and I find that to try to do this arouses intense antagonism. One of our most difficult jobs in talking to people about psychic matters is to convince them that we are not psychiatrists. I think these learned gentlemen can be of some help to certain people, but they can not cure the deeper sicknesses of spiritual people like Signe. I am speaking of those I know about in this country anyway; some of these do some good but many do great harm. We do not try to be the friends of these people although we find that, as with Signe, real friendship begins to develop. We literally try to work with these people to examine together the meaning of dreams wherever we find them and to see how these dreams relate to the basic wisdom of man as it is found in the texts of the higher religions and in mythology and in literature. I see it as a task we all have in common. The fact that we know and talk to forty or fifty young men and women with souls as spiritually profound as Signe's is an indication to us that we are part of some very great movement of the spirit. Behind these are several hundred more people that we don't talk to with such intimacy and with such searching exploration of basic ideas, but these people too seem to have a part to play in this movement and will someday be as involved in it as we are now. And we find new people all the time. The fact of so many people of such high quality and the fact of dreams and visions by many people and the fact that there must be a spiritual revolution within the next hundred years if man is to go on existing—these facts make it plain that we are involved in something very big. With this in mind we let details take care of themselves and we let people probe their own souls. Of course Julie must be constantly probing our own souls and this is one of the big tasks. We notice that dreams tell many of the young people we work with to get married, and we have observed that the more advanced ones help each other when they are married to probe their souls. So all I can say about Signe is what Julie and I dream about her, what she dreams, and what we observe in general ways—such as that she is confusing eroticism and mysticism. Such confusion is a thorn in the side when it is viewed by a friend from a distance, but I don't know how young women can be helped over this hurdle except by the voice that speaks in dreams and in other ways that each individual must listen to for himself. There are other psychic aids similar to dreams. For instance, Julie can analyze handwriting and tell much about a person's weaknesses and strong points. She has been keeping up with Signe's psychic illness and says she has improved but that she is still in danger and that she must come home soon. The dreams she has had—Signe, that is—about Dr. Shepherd indicate that her career will be worked out with this lady psychologist who teaches at Ga. State and who works with dreams to counsel people in a way that is not so unlike ours. Well, there is more I could say, but I think this is the basic information.

I hope Volume IV is proceeding according to your plans. I liked Watts's review of Volume III in the New Republic. He could have gone a little deeper, but he rightly said it was the best of the volumes so far and he put his finger on some important points. The tone of the review sounded very friendly. I remember the

Times' (London) review of Volume II. It was extremely spiteful as one might expect from them, but it did say that you sounded like a man who wanted to found a new religion. I think all the best people since 1800 have been such people who wanted to found a new religion but for this reviewer it was a dirty, distasteful matter that he didn't want anything to do with. By the way, I wonder about Watts joining our conversations at some time in the future. A friend of ours from the Bay area was here in June and he dreamed of a purified Watts taking part in the new psychic work that is even now beginning on the West Coast. Signe herself said in a letter we received a day before this friend arrived that she had just dreamed there was a great flood and that a few people were saved and that these were thrown off a bridge and landed in California and South Carolina. The dreams of other people indicate that the Deep South and California will be centers of the new psychic activity. Again the best of luck on your summer work and our kindest regards to Jean. Congratulate her for us on her great success in Japan. It is a very good country to be well received in.

Cordially,
Ted

M. Signe Gartrell
Rue de Seine
Paris 6, France
November 5, 1964

Dear Joe:

Just as Prometheus was forced to call up a ghost to repeat his argument with Zeus so I have been dreaming all year of my cousin and my grandfather making peace with me and bringing me to insights into the horrible illusions and schizophrenia of our times which I have had to repress over and over again. Happily I have just about lost my value of "banal" reality and am about to return to the psychic sphere. It is surprising how much I learned on my visit to an old dimension.

I hope that the Fall has been kinder to you than the summer; and that you have had time to relax, concentrate on life, and regain your creative flow.

How is the book coming? I dreamed that I opened the cover of a book and found a new copy of the Hero with another title insignia on it. And so from your understanding of the cross, and circle and other truths beneath the images, has come the sign for the future. The book in progress will surely be as great or greater a "double-edged sword."

Many weeks have passed since our last communication. I have thought of you and Jean on several occasions...had a number of dreams concerning you both...and reread your work when visions did not come or when doubt pierced my soul.

There is truth in what your friend Mr. Watts says: that there is salvation in the "ending of the minds fascinated identification with the dead and unchanging image of what it was." We are all going to have to do this again.

I had a dream in which I was talking to you and Jean briefly before I gave the reading of an important paper and a music recital. I gave Jean two presents one of which was a book on witchcraft. The performance went very well. I saw the two of you backstage and you embraced me congratulatorally. As you did I saw the image of a rather elderly ill man in Dublin embracing me. Next we went to your apartment. You and Jean had separate beds. You and I spent a long time talking while Jean rushed around preparing a snack for dinner. Later we prepared a lot of food for a large dinner party.

I interpret this to have been an expression of something within me that has come forward as a projection of you. I feel that since there is evidently going to be some passage of energy between Jean and me that it predicts in a sense some of the secrets which I am bringing back. It is the beginning of my flow toward Jean rather than just her flow to me.

The recital represents the activity of the arts by which the final devil of Joyce which has burdened us all will be called out consciously. I find it a little ironical that I met you when you were performing Joyce. I wonder if the "Coach" had a cathartic effect on you and Jean since you had not worked with him for a while.

There appears to have been some holding back on Jean's part who is beginning to have her hearth opened so that she can, along with us, prepare the food for many. Love, the most precious of all "boons," is what we are calling out of each other. With this love are our three perilous devils: faith in the arts; Joyce's unresting spirit; and the scarcity of food. The following dreams show the steps to and fro.

I went to the home of friends where I found you and Jean and Ted and Julie. You were in a small house in the backyard. And I had to climb stairs and open many doors before I located you. Ted was in the background describing things to me and telling that though there were many steps between the lower and the upper I had made it in three. My friends said that I was a leader now; and then handed me some letters—two of which had already been opened. Then you said that you had many duties, presents, and mysteries for me. You began to introduce me to your wife and I said I remembered her. Suddenly I realized that I had only half of my clothes on. And this semi-nakedness was a little alarming though I felt very free about it.

You and I had many visits together during which we had long intimate conversations. You told me some movies to see. The following day I read in a newspaper that we had had an argument about forcing and willing life. Later I went to my aunt and uncle's apartment in Alaska. Then I had to flee from a group of people who wanted to take me somewhere. I ran to a theatre in Atlanta which always symbolizes my psyche. I couldn't get into the building because it was being rebuilt. So I hid under the cover of some canvass which the workmen were using.

The dream indicates a regression on my part for I have been possessed by a great fear of Alaska and psychic happenings. Alaska here seems to represent the highest state inwardly. I have not the strength to give myself up to the energies which beckon me and as a result I tried to return to my old ego and image where I found it impossible to see and depict certain things because I am truly changing. So I attempted to retreat into a womb of darkness. I have the distinct feeling that you as a god-symbol, and perhaps too in life, are tricking me without realizing it. For in some ways you still see me in the old life forms. I cannot see your movies in a theatre being renovated toward something new.

In the next dream you were talking about Alaska and everyone moving there. You named the city. But I did not understand you. You became irked and wouldn't repeat it. Perhaps as we begin to really speak of the supreme psychic states and about Alaska we are going to have to face the resentment that we feel about the situation. I don't want to really listen and you want to talk about it as little as possible.

Actually there is not too much else to say along the psychic path. I felt very close to you tonight and wanted to write to ask how you are and let you know how I am growing. Please let me hear from you when you feel moved to write.

My regards to your wife and the abundance of my love and my soul to you both,

Signe

P.S. My spirits are exhilarating and happy! You were the one to fill out the liquor form I think. Or did I not understand what you said in your last letter?

Wieuca Rd. NE
Atlanta 5, Ga.
December 4, 1964

Dear Joe,
Julie and I have had dreams about you and Jean that I think I should tell you about. I feel that though the four of us are not able

at the moment to communicate at great length, there is a deep current flowing between us. About the only thing I can say about this current is to echo what dreams say.

About a month ago I had a dream in which you came to visit me where I teach—Georgia State College here in Atlanta. We were sitting together drinking coffee and I had to reassure you that I really taught English there and that I was in fact a full professor, which in real life I am. It seemed to me that you could not really believe that I could be a part of an ordinary academic situation and at the same time have the dreams I have and serve as a kind of guru for certain people. I was showing you in the dream that this was true. Now about the same time Julie had a dream which clarifies this situation. She dreamed that you didn't want to believe that I could live in two worlds—the everyday world and the psychic world. You and Jean were in Atlanta and you wanted to go to a local club and have a party; you felt that we were too serious and that the psychic work interfered with parties—which by the way it does not. Also you didn't believe that anybody could really pray, and when I told you that I could and that I had prayed for you, you were incredulous. Then I said to you, "How do you think you have been able to go on living?" In another scene of the same dream Julie and Jean were talking and Julie was using a term called "psychic projection," a term she does not really use. She told Jean that she had the ability to project her thoughts onto other people, learn their thoughts, and then by rearranging the patterns of their minds, she could make them sane. Jean found this hard to believe. The general feeling both of you had in the dream was that it all seemed strange and hard to believe and that you were more interested in your own affairs than this sort of thing and that somehow it was interfering with a friendship that is gradually growing between us.

My comment on the above dreams would be this. I can certainly understand how you felt in the dreams. I know that it all seems too big and mysterious to be true. Julie and I and all others involved feel the same way quite often, yet it all keeps working out. Over and over we are all called to decide whether what we are doing psychically is so much insanity, but I have found that those who take it up can never really let it go, although they can and do walk off and leave it for a time. If one can once accept the idea that this is really the beginning of a new way of life for man, then he can begin to accept the many miracles that have to go along with the coming of a new era. It is always the way that new eras come into being, by people doing things that seem utterly impossible to people who believe in the old order. For instance, concerning yourself, it seems that after a long and full career as a philosopher and scholar you will, after sixty, begin a great psychic career that will make your previous activity, great though it has been, seem small in comparison. You will live what you have written. This is the kind of miracle I am talking about and I wouldn't believe it anymore than you except that dreams can come true in matters much bigger—and many of those dreams about the bigger matters have come not to one but to many people we know. In connection with the miracle of your own life, I might add this that also appeared in Julie's dream. You and Jean had the idea of a rather small house for your retirement and were driving around Atlanta looking for a house. But it was indicated that you should have a much bigger house than you had thought of. Whether this is a symbolic or a real Atlanta I am not sure, but since this dream was literal in many ways, it might be a real Atlanta. Anyway we hope and believe that you will one day want to visit us here in Atlanta. There have been several other dreams about your coming here and I look forward to the time when you will visit us in the flesh as well as in dreams.

Julie sends her best regards. We think about the two of you often and wish you the best of everything. The quarter's work will soon be over for me, and then Julie and I will go to the West Indies for two weeks in what dreams say will be a psychic trip. We still haven't heard from Signe but we feel that all will be well with her. Please write when you are so moved.

Cordially,
Ted

Wieuca Rd. NE
Atlanta 5, Ga.
April 26, 1965

Dear Joe,
I have put off writing you until I had something to report to you. Now I think I have something. Yesterday I visited Wilhelmus Bryan along with Julie and a good friend. For a reason I couldn't define I had put off seeing him, and then last week everyone heard that he had been dismissed from his position with the Atlanta Art Association. When I called him yesterday he was happy to hear from us, and immediately I knew he was a kindred spirit and someone who had a lot to talk about. On the phone he said that he had one foot in the grave, referring to his previous heart attack and, I gathered, to his present feelings. But after a long talk I got a view not only of what he was doing but a much larger view of the direction that psychic affairs were taking in Atlanta and throughout the country. First I am convinced that his feeling of death and the dream we had about yours had nothing to do with age at all, but in fact they point toward what we all feel, young and old, which is the death of an old way of life, the sensitive feeling it more keenly at first. Last night Signe called us from London and everything she said about herself and you and Jean confirmed all I had been thinking and saying to Dr. Bryan. He is ready to stay in Atlanta and work for the sort of grass-roots movement in art that he knows is springing up in spite of the opposition he has felt from members of the power structure both in Atlanta and Minneapolis. He believes, as we do, that if the right sort of movement gets launched here, where there is possibly more fertile soil than anywhere else, it will draw people like you and Jean and Watts and others he has in mind. His idea of linking together the intellectuals and the artists and working from the viewpoint of myth, symbol, and the hero is the great new idea that true workers in the arts and the humanities need at this time. For our part we brought him the news about dreams and the coming of the new psychic year and he heard us with true interest and

gave a few stories of his own to indicate that he had noticed some sort of possibility along these lines. He seems more than ready to accept the possibility of it all, and we left him about to go to a party where he said he would ask some psychiatrists who would be there about their ideas concerning dreams. Last night Julie and I both dreamed that some such school as he suggested (something like a Black Mountain in N.C.) would come about in Atlanta.

The other important news is a dream I had about you recently. You were here in Atlanta dressed in shirtsleeves and you were quite young and vigorous. This seems [an] adequate answer to me that you will pass beyond the barrier of death that I believe you are coming up against. I had the strongest feeling about Bryan that he was like you, a man who had done great things in the world but one who still had an enormous youth and energy waiting to be released for a new great activity. At the same time there was the feeling of dismay strong enough to produce a death wish which comes from facing the fact that the main current of society today is opposed to the true creative work you and he and others of us are capable of. But now we have received help from the collective unconscious and something new is even now beginning to work itself out. I still believe too that you and Jean will come to Atlanta in time. Bryan feels that you could be an enormous force here and indeed could get other scholars and thinkers who would work together with artists in a creative relationship. Anyway I hope you will write him soon if you have not already. His address is # Ridgewood Road, NW, Atlanta.

This is all I have time to write now. Signe is still struggling and I again urged her to return to Atlanta. Julie and I still have many dreams. The best of everything to you and Jean in all your activities.

Cordially,

Ted

Roswell Rd. NE
#A1
Atlanta, Georgia
August 7, 1965

My Dear Friend Joe:
Once again I greet you from the homeland. I arrived back in the States some six or seven weeks ago. I remained in New York the first week; and telephoned you several times but, alas, had no response. From there I ventured down South—to the most prolific yet barren place in the world.

I reached a peak in the month of January which lasted through a voyage around Europe, expedition to Ghana, and two months in London in the Spring.

While in England one night I had a series of four extremely interesting dreams about Jean. I then penned them to you and to her; but destroyed the letter. The following days left me with such a strong conscious sense of her presence that I expected to run into her on some London street as I turned the corner. Since I am certain to be back in your area shortly I prefer to withdraw the dreams still for a letter...

On my trip home I developed a psychosomatic illness during a gala dinner on board ship when the band struck up "Dixie." And became only released from it last week: after letting go of the vampire in my family and thus transforming my fear into a flow.

My grandmother refuses to see me or to relinquish my belongings. She has finally reached a state which Ted defines as "clinical insanity." After having been away for so long I feel that my return is a true home-coming. While being in Europe my view grew as if I had descended the mountain on which I lived; crossed a deep valley; and climbed another mountain from which I could see other parts of the circle as well as fully see my own pinnacle from afar.

Long ago I dreamed that there was a tremendous flood but that an uplifting tidal wave saved a chosen few and threw them either into the South or to California. These do, indeed, seem to be the two great psychic centers. Even this summer people from Atlanta of great depth have moved out West to take on new roles.

Despite my earnest belief in the cosmic order and the sperm within the Hero even I am amazed to discover how many persons have become involved in the psychic movement here while I was away. There seem to be hundreds here who are truly in the midst of the hero's journey; and who are all part of a tremendous spiritual procession toward Alaska.

I have had only one dream about you—after a long period of trivial night experiences. The dream occurred some weeks ago just before Ted and Julie moved into their new house. It was that you and Jean had come to Atlanta. You were both dressed in casual clothes; and both had grayed somewhat. Your face looked tired and worn as if you had been through many harrowing experiences; but there was also a look of relaxation as if many of your trials were over. We were driving around and I was pointing out to you houses where many psychic people lived: all in the area of the Spivey's home. I consider this dream to be very literal. In time you really must come down and be shocked by the magnitude of it all—so much of which has been started and held together by the god-flow through you. (Also we can be relieved of the recurrent dreams that you are coming and perhaps step up to another plateau!)

As soon as Ted and Julie are settled they intend to have your friend, Wilhelmus Bryan, over so that we can meet. Unless you have corresponded with him since his afternoon with Ted I doubt that you are cognizant of the task which he had proposed for Atlanta's new cultural center. (If you have communicated with him please pardon my reiteration.) He had planned a nucleus school which taught the ideas of the Hero: reinforced by the writings of Watts and others. From this focal point students and artists went on to technical schools; and then performing or exhibition areas; etc. I gather that he believes that he was fired because he was too near the truth and the power establishment became frightened of him, which is what we all tend to believe. However, Ted and Julie dreamed that a new school would be started here; and another friend dreamed that he and I would start a new school. I am certain that we will be given signs as to how to reinstate Bryan or to work further with his plan.

Meanwhile, I am quite busy with heading some political efforts of student organizations and publications here. Originally, I had planned to come back to New York in September and resume some studies at Columbia. But events, thus far, have unfolded a plan for me here temporarily.

This evening I re-read parts of Volume II and Volume III and again they took on new meaning. I hope you have found peace from the tragedies of this past year. And, too, that the book is at long last finding its due place in your schedule.

I send you love from my soul and kind hopes from my heart,

Signe

The following letter is from Agnes (Mrs. Eugene) Meyer. For more on her, see chapter 5, "Political Matters," p. 230.

Seven Springs Farm
Mount Kisco
New York
October 8, 1959

Dear Joe:

I have been able so far to read only the introduction to your book and Chapter 1. I can't tell you what a relief it is from housing statistics in which I am buried because I soon have to make another one of those addresses on subjects about which everybody knows more than I do.

I am really overwhelmed by the progress you have made, Joe, in knowledge, insight, and breadth of vision. Nobody but you could undertake this important task of writing the history of the myth. You are that rare person—I regret to say especially rare in America—a scholar who is also a poet. I am proud that I discerned your unique qualities and urged you to write long ago when we met as a result of a common interest in Thomas Mann. In the beginning chapter I can see his influence on you was profound.

With admiration, and with unfailing love for you and Jean,

Yours devotedly,

Agnes

The following letters were exchanged by Campbell and Alan Watts. Watts (January 6, 1915–November 16, 1973) was a British philosopher, writer, and speaker, best known as an interpreter and popularizer of Eastern philosophy for a Western audience. Born in Chislehurst, England, he moved to the United States in 1938 and began Zen training in New York. He attended Seabury-Western Theological Seminary, where he received a master's degree in theology. He became an Episcopal priest in 1945, then left the ministry in 1950 and moved to California, where he joined the faculty of the American Academy of Asian Studies (today the California Institute of Integral Studies).

Watts gained a large following in the San Francisco Bay Area while working as a volunteer programmer at KPFA, a radio station in Berkeley. He wrote more than twenty-five books and articles on Eastern and Western religion, including The Way of Zen *(1957), one of the first bestsellers on Buddhism. In* Psychotherapy East and West *(1961), he proposed that Buddhism could be thought of as a form of psychotherapy rather than as a religion. He considered his book* Nature, Man, and Woman *(1958) to be "from a literary point of view—the best book I have ever written." He also explored human consciousness in the essay "The New Alchemy" (1958) and in the book* The Joyous Cosmology *(1962). Mary Jane ("Jano"), mentioned below, was his third wife, whom he married in 1964.*

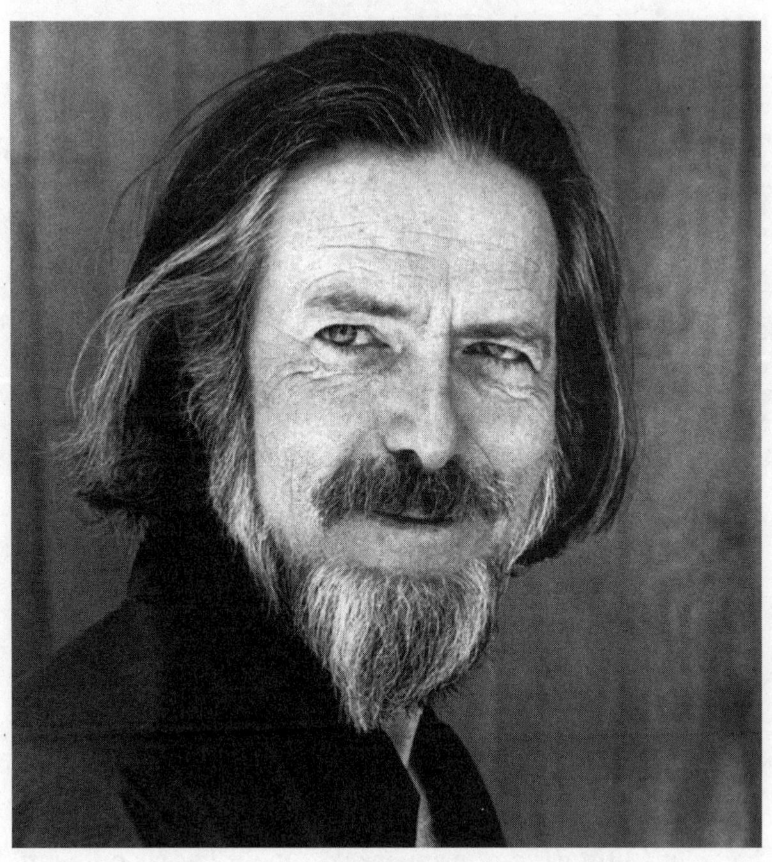

Alan Watts

March 23, 1958

Dear Alan:

Thank you for the lively letter. The speaking and teaching tour reads like a dream. And I'm delighted to learn that the book is finished. Shall be looking forward to its publication.

You ask for the address of Pupul Jayakar. Oyez! # Sundar Nagar, New Delhi; also: Himmat Nivas, # Dungersey Rd., Malabar Hill, Bombay.

Too bad Jean missed you in San Francisco—but how wonderful that you are in Hawaii! If you find yourself with time on your hands and would like to look up some people who would be delighted to meet you, I can recommend Jean's sister Bargie and her husband: Mr. and Mrs. T.N. Fairbanks, Jr., # Papai Street; also, my mother: Mrs. Charles W. Campbell, # Puuhonua St. They would be pleased, I know to help you see something of Honolulu as they see it. But I'm sure you'll have little time for socializing.

I'm looking forward eagerly to your visit to New York and hope indeed that I can arrange to have you and Eliade meet each other. I'm keeping the week as clear as possible, to take care of whatever moments you may have to spare.

Aloha nui oe

Anata no tomodachi

Joe

January 12, 1959

Dear Alan—

For your Christmas card many thanks. And it was good to learn that you will be in New York again the middle of April.

The Minneapolis man:—

Dr. Wilhelmus B. Bryan, Director

The Minneapolis School of Art

East 25th Street

Minneapolis 4, Minnesota

And I wonder if you could send me, meanwhile, that little Piaget volume (The Child's Conception of the World).[4] I have started work on Vol. II of my large opus and find that I am going to meet Piaget again.—Also, did I ask you whether you know anyone who might be able to give me the dates of the mystical sandal-maker Saichi, whom Suzuki quotes extensively in his Mysticism:

Christian and Buddhist? Nobody—but nobody—seems to be able to place him within 3 centuries!

Hope you make the Minneapolis connection—and am looking forward to your visit. We must try to have another session at the King Cole Bar.

Love and New Year Greetings to Dorothy and the youngsters—

Yours

Joe

December 30, 1960

Dear Alan—

Many thanks for the card—and the invitation to participate in your program. I should like to; but, as you guessed, the pressure right now is just too great. College, my four long sessions a year in Washington, Bollingen meetings and chores, a string of unavoidable occasional lectures for this and that, and the grim battle with this big book project, make up the limit of my capacity.—No can do!

The Open Sesame to the matter of my book has, at last, been found, and I can at last look forward to getting through it—perhaps by early spring, some six months late: after which Vol. 3 will have to be started immediately, lest the way close again. These two volumes, 2 and 3, are to be a sort of matched pair.

From Bollingen I have received for judgement a fascinating book in German on Zen—by Wilhelm Gundert (do you know him?): Bi-Yän-lu, Master Yüan-wu's transcription of the Emerald Rock Wall (have you ever heard of it?).[5] I'll perhaps be able to tell you all about it when I see you next.

Jean says hello, and sends her love along with mine. We are already looking forward to our next view of you. Best for the New Year

Yours ever

Joe

Alan Watts
The Gate Five Gallery
P.O. Box #
Sausalito, CA
January 4th, 1962

Dear Joe:
Many, many thanks to you for two feasts: that fabulous mince-pie, and now the proofs of Volume 2 [of *The Masks of God*]. I have spent three hours giving the latter a fairly thorough skim, and returning three galleys to you which may perhaps belong to the set which you were correcting.

I am really flabbergasted by the scope and detail of your knowledge, combined with a flair for writing that makes such a learned work positively poetic. I have specially enjoyed the wealth of historical and archeological background, which makes tremendous sense out of things that are otherwise confused and puzzling.

I have two comments that may be useful. I may not have skimmed thoroughly enough, but have you given adequate treatment to the dramatic aspect of Hindu mythology—the theme of Brahman-atman as the player of all the parts in the world? There are, indeed, lots of references to the theme, but I think the book would be enriched by more substantial quotation from the appropriate sources.

Galley 40. Haven't you put the precession of the equinoxes backwards? The sun is now rising at the vernal equinox in Pisces, and is on the verge of moving into Aquarius. Or rather, I should ask whether your version is up-to-date, not backwards. You are putting it now in Aries, but this is where it was when astrology was invented. Anyhow, I think you might check on this. Astrologers today make a lot of the fact that the vernal equinox was moving into Pisces at the time of the birth of Christ, and that we are now entering the Aquarian Age.

I think you did a great job with the Egyptian materials, usually so out-of-this-worldly confusing. I've also been working on the Horus-Set polarity. I've turned up in Mercer's Religion of Ancient Egypt (p. 55) a marvelous figure of two heads on one body.

So—all good things and a most happy New Year to you both. When I've been through the galleys more carefully I'll write you again.

Love from us both—

Alan

February 6, 1962

Dear Alan—

Your letter gave me great heart—and saved me from one fell blunder besides. Pisces is correct—and I had an interesting time checking on it. Apparently two systems are in operation: one based on a conventional zodiac of signs, according to which the spring equinox is always in Aries; the other based on the actual constellations. So that although the sun, according to the first, is in the "sign" of Aries at the time of the equinox, it is in the constellation Pisces!!—A kind of Sothic cycle, you might say, of conventional vs. astronomical naming.[6] Many many thanks for this fine work of rescue of a friend in deeper water than he knew.

I appreciated, also, your suggestion about the dramatic aspect of Hindu mythology: Brahman-ātman as the player of all the parts. I think this comes out in my text, though not as strongly as it should—and the lack is due to the fact that in my final draft I cut three sections out of my Hinduism chapter. I realize now that I should have found some way to render at least this of their main themes. But the next time I come around to these matters—in a book that I shall be doing, one of these days, for the Bollingen Series—I shall bear this suggestion in mind. The galleys are for me too late a phase for insertions or adjustments of the magnitude that the introduction of this theme would have required. And I am glad to have it as a platform for my next production.

The page proofs have gone back to press and I'm simply waiting for the book itself, which is scheduled for next month. And meanwhile, I have already launched myself into Volume III: Occidental Mythology—which is going to be a lark. I am already feeling a new delight in this whole vast subject, as I tease along through Genesis, etc. Furthermore, it is nice to be writing about people and books that do not have to be explained to the reader from scratch. To refer to Aeschylus, without giving a thumbnail biography, for example, or to the Bible, without presenting a brief summary in 10 lines, is a luxury not permitted to anyone working with, say, Nagarjuna or the Puranas. I think I've gotten off to a promising start—and Volume II is already far behind me.

It was good of you to write to me so promptly and helpfully. How I would have felt had this Pisces / Aries bloomer been called to my attention shortly after, instead of before, publication, I hate to think. And I caught a couple of other nifties myself: for example, the Hebrew alphabet has 22 letters, not 23.

Well, anyhow: I'm now safely under the sheltering roof of my absorption in Volume III—so let it rain now if it likes on Volume II.

Jean and I are hoping that you and Mary Jane will be heading this direction again, pretty soon. And meanwhile, our love—and my particular thanks.

Yours ever,

Joe

July 27, 1963

Dear Alan—

A wild wild two months have elapsed since last our ways did cross. Jean's event in Spoleto, Italy, was marvelous. It went over as soon as I had finished my book, and found her and her group installed in a beautiful little town, performing in a delicious little 17th/18th century theater, and even speaking a sort of pigeon [*sic*] Italian.

Paris, on the other hand, was madness. Firstly, her costumes failed to arrive from Italy. The opening night had to be cancelled, as a result of which there were no reviews or proper notices. The performances, the rest of the week, were rendered in makeshift costumes and although rapturously applauded they were played to rather small audiences, with a consequent economic calamity that was greatly furthered by the shameless behavior of the directorship of the Théâtre des Nations. Two California groups followed Jean, and I dare say they got the same Shylock treatment. If you know anyone planning to accept an invitation for next year to gay Paree's Théâtre des Nations, warn him off.

To add to the unpleasant side of Jean's Paris episode, she learned while she was there that her Japanese engagement had been arbitrarily changed from November 1963 to late April 1964. The extent of damage, economic and otherwise, that this little change of terms involves, we have not yet even begun to know; but time will tell.

The first and most important consequence of the Japanese turn is that Jean's whole American tour now has to be rearranged, and I have decided to take a hand in the large task. She has a sheaf of really great Italian reviews and I think these should help convince our American college communities that the play is really worth the attention. The chief problem, as I see it, is to fill out Jean's schedule for the West Coast and Middle West, to keep her group together until time comes to leave for Japan. She has a date at U.C.L.A. for Feb. 28, a Saturday, and a completely open calendar from then to March 20, Friday, when she is to perform in Ames, Iowa—March 21 at Rockford, Ill. The hop to Honolulu and Japan would take place about April 3. And so the problem looks like this: Phase A [West Coast], Feb. 28 to March 16, is the phase that I am most eager to see settled soon, and I wonder whether you could suggest to me any people in the San Francisco area to whom it would make sense to write. The best period for a San Francisco, Stanford, or San Jose performance would be between March 4 and 11, and I think that if something could be settled there pretty soon the rest would build out around it. What do you think? If there is any possibility of half a week at the Encore theater, or some similar place, that would be just great. Jean also wonders whether James Broughton would be interested, or of any help. Actually, a whole week in San Francisco would seem to make great sense, and would easily solve the whole question of that area. In fact, the more I think of it, the better I like the idea of a S.F. limited run. What do you think? Can it be done?

New York is in the grip, right now, of an absolutely brutal hot spell: five days, so far, over 90°, with two, so far, over 100. Thank God (or rather Western science) for my air-conditioner. Peace! Peace! Peace!

Best wishes, peace, and love to you both, dear buddha-beings, from

Jean and Joe

July 30, 1963

Dear Joe:

Just a quickie in answer to yours. I talked this morning with Jim Broughton,[7] and he has the following suggestions for San Francisco:

The Contemporary Dancers Theater. (Seats about 200/250)
The Playhouse (Seats about 140.)
Mills College and/or Stanford.

He is making inquiries, and quite possibly Playhouse would sponsor several nights' run. Let me know, though, if you feel that its capacity is too small. Jim is a very good friend of the manager, but he also knows the Contemporary Dancers people, and it may be that they, too, would like to take it on. It's quite a pleasant theater, and bigger. Playhouse is very gemütlich.

Am hard at work on my new book. Volkening does splendidly as an agent, but Pantheon's Random House association leads to some pretty nutty things. They inadvertently let "The Joyous Cosmology" go out of print for almost a year, even to the extent of advertising it when they had no copies!

Our love to you both,
As ever
[Alan Watts]

August 4, 1963

Dear Alan—
Our hero!
Jean is dealing with the suggestions that you very kindly—and quickly—sent, and I expect she will have made contact with something promising by the time she takes off next month for Dublin. I have just finished translating a set of Italian reviews of her Spoleto performances, and I don't see how anyone in the world could read these and not wish to produce the play right away.—The contrast in quality, by the way, of these reviews with those of our New York brood of critics is almost more than my patriotic hopes for the civilization of the U.S.A. can support. One of the horrors of the century, it seems to me, is the role played by the journalists of this country in determining the course, not of politics only (which is bad enough) but even of literature and the arts.

I was glad to learn of your having commenced work on book next. My own first step toward a new volume was taken just six hours ago. Ship ahoy! Good sailing! And let's see what they will do with these!

Yours ever
Joe

September 17, 1963

Dear Mary Jane and Alan—
Before you take off for Japan I must tell you what has come of Jean's San Francisco plans. As of now, it looks like a five day run: March 1, matinee and evening at Berkeley, March 2, 3, 4, 5, performances for Contemporary Dancers. March 8, they play in Seattle, March 12 or so, they start back East. All are at present in Dublin, and the spring tour of the USA seems to be developing nicely.

I was happy to receive your note and am delighted to know that you are going to have another spell of Japan. Best wishes and love to you both

Yours
Joe

April 12, 1964

Dear Alan—
Is this any good?

> This witty little book is a large theological event—an Olympian laugh. Its felicitous prose, wisdom of the serpent, and learning carried as lightly as a jester's cap and bells, make elegant reading, as well as modern sense of the troublesome old myth of the Fall of Man. The secret is also whispered of Salvation—for those with ears to hear. O felix culpa—at last! (that will set "Kings to cutting capers and priests to picking flowers")

Jean is not here to tell me. If so, please say so. If only fair, likewise. The main point is, not to save my little offering, but to get the right words on your jacket. So, do cut, transform, or reject—as you see fit.

It was very good to see you: disappointing to miss Mary Jane. All best to her, and to thee,

Yours
Joe

July 1, 1964

Dear Alan—

This is simply to thank you for the fine review of Masks III that you wrote for the New Republic. I can't tell you what a pleasure it was to me to find the whole scope of my project appreciated in terms that were precisely appropriate to what I had imagined I was doing. And I shall try to meet the invitation of the last lines.

Jean has just returned from a Tokyo triumph, in great spirits, and now that she has come back, my own work begins to move forward again. Vol. IV is going to be an exciting book to write.

When do we see you again?

Best luck—which we all need; and love to you both from us both.

Bowing thanks—arigato gozaimasu—bowing-bowing-and-bowing. I am

Yours,

Joe

June 12, 1969

Dear Alan—

Miss Fabrizio phoned, but I was unable to see her. Both her letter and yours had been addressed to # Waverly, and had arrived only the morning of her call. I had already booked my whole week full: but since Jean and I shall be in S.F. the middle of August, I promised to see her then. I shall be delighted to meet the young lady and am extremely sorry for the postponement. This is the first week after the closing of College, and one that I do not look forward to having to endure again an infinite number of times in the unending course of the rounds of Eternal Return.

My dear colleague, you find enclosed one sheet of Xeroxed MS, from your piece for the ARC volume that I am supposed to be editing. It asks for a bit of handling and should be returned (at your leisure) to

Mr. Walter Arnold
E.P. Dutton and Co., Inc.
Park Avenue South
New York, NY 10003

Do I learn from your letter that you have written a review of my Masks IV for the Virginia Quarterly? If true, let me thank you, sincerely. If not, let me tell you that I feel that you have already done so very much to further the cause of my writing that I would hardly ask or expect you to do more—and especially when, as you say, it is the Grail this time, with Joyce to boot, on which delicacies you have not feasted. My book, besides (and I knew it even while writing it) is far too heavily packed.

It was a delight for both Jean and me to be with you and Jano again, of an evening: and again, I appreciated your remarks about that transformed voice of mine. Hearing myself, I felt like a sort of cross between a social scientist and YMCA secretary. But then, who was I to judge?

I've been working hard on my new Bollingen book, enjoying enormously all this fooling around with pictures.[8] Have they sent you The Mystic Vision? It came out a couple of weeks ago. And I expect you will be receiving my Flight of the Wild Gander before the month is out. N.B.—These volumes come to you, not with hopes, expectations, or petitions for reviews, but with my hope, simply, that you and Jano will like them—and with love to you both—

Ever,
Joe

July 28, 1969

Dear Alan—

Our plans for California have at last begun to shape up. At least, we now have a confirmed flight reservation for August 8; United

Flight 132, to arrive in San Francisco 4:15 p.m. Dick Roberts has invited us to occupy his apartment during the time of our San Francisco stay and if he can still manage such an arrangement that will be our station for the two nights of the 8th and 9th—after which we are to roll away to Big Sur for what promises to be an amusing dual bill.—Dick, as you probably know, has a kind of ancestral home at "The Castle," that fabulous Scottish ale house; and I have suggested that it would be fun if we could all have an evening there together. Could you and Jano make it for such an event?—There will be lots to talk about, and no place better than a place with an inexhaustible tap in which to bring the gifts of the gods to be heard!

In any case—we'll be getting in touch with you on arrival—looking forward to whatever time with you chance may grant us. And meanwhile, to you both, all best—

Ever
Joe

May 11, 1971

Dear Alan—
With a free evening (miraculously), I gave myself the pleasure of reading your richly informed and highly instructive piece on Oriental Erotics, and full of the spirit of love, reviewed a number of my lists of friends, to see what I might contribute in the way of suggestions for that incredible project that you named to me [see below]. As you see, it is quite a catalogue that unrolled.—I think you need hunt no further!

It was a very great pleasure to be with you and Mary Jano again, and particularly, since you both looked blooming—as I haven't seen you for some time. Jean was unhappy to have had to miss the occasions: but she is now dropping that NYU job, and expects to be present, next time you pay this Boddhisattva-town the honor of a darshan.

We both send love—"house to house"—and I, a special load of thanks of all kinds for all kinds of things—

Sincerely,

Joe

Professor Dr. Hermann Goetz (Hinduism)
Mr. Anthony Burgess (Novelist, Finnegans Wake)
Mr. Gerald Sykes (Art & Lit Critic)
Professor Antony Alpers (Polynesian Mythology)
Professor John Hutchinson (Religion)
Professor Wilfred Cantwell Smith
Professor Alex Wayman
Professor Donald Keene
Professor James Luther Adams
Dr. Rollo May (Psych)
Dr. Werner Muensterberger (Psych)
Dr. Jacques Barzun
Professor Stanley Hoffer
Mr. Demer Lindley
Mr. Ralph Ellison (Novelist)
Mr. Winthrop Sargeant (Music & Lit Criticism)
Professor Maurice Valency (Lit & Theater)
Mrs. Nancy Ross Young
Miss Maud Oakes
Mrs. John (Olivia) Vlakos
Professor Annemarie Schimmel (Islam)
Mrs. Dorothy Norman
Mrs. Adela Bozeman
Professor Mircea Eliade
Professor Joseph Kitagawa
Professor Charles H. Long
Professor Herbert Schneider
Professor Huston Smith
Mr. Michael Murphy
Dr. John Perry (Psych)
Professor Schuyler Cammann
Mr. Horace Gregory
Dr. Mortimer Ostrow
Professor T. R. Spivey (Lit Criticism)
Professor David Miller
Professor Richard Underwood
Professor William Paden
Mr. Sam Keen
Mr. Glenway Westcott
Mr. E. M. Wright

November 4, 1971

Dear Alan—

Just a word, to let you know how pleased I was to receive a copy of the new edition of Behold the Spirit.[9] I thought your new Introduction marvelously forthright, clear and firm, and I am finding the text extremely interesting now as "A Portrait of the Author as a Young Man."

I was sorry not to see you last month, but perhaps I shall have the pleasure in March. I am due to conduct a little seminar in San Francisco (Extension Branch of University of California), March 24–26 (Fri–Sun), and to be doing something with Dick Price at Big Sur the following weekend (Good Friday–Easter). If I have the luck to catch you and Jano at home this time, it will be a good and auspicious start for my 68th year of life on this earth. Two more years, and I enter the period that Dante names "decrepitude," the virtues of which are a) to look back upon the life lived with gratitude, and b) to look forward to death as to returning home.

Om. Shanti Shanti Shanti—

Yours,

Joe

March 1, 1972

Dear Alan—

Thank you for the delightful little taste of Dionysius the Aereopagite [*sic*] that surprised me the other day, coming out of its envelope. It was dear and generous of you to send this lovely wakener to your friends, and I want you to know of my appreciation.

I see by your brochure that you will again be away from home when I visit San Francisco, end of this month. I shall be sorry to miss you.

Take care—and blessings

Yours ever,

Joe

March 14, 1972

Dear Jano—
Thank you so much for the lovely note and gorgeous card (which is now in my treasury). It is not clear to me yet what free moments I shall have in San Francisco, but I shall certainly give you a ring and arrange for a hello. I want very much to meet the whole family and to see you again. My annual spring visit always crosses Alan's: but it will be a compensation for this time to be with Joan, Mark, and yourself.

Again, best thanks—
My love to you all—ever
Joe

October 28, 1972

Dear Alan—
I have just finished the reading of your lively (and delightfully fascinating) autobiography, with its rogues' gallery of oddballs, including myself. You were marvelously generous to us all—and amusingly tough on the squares. I enjoyed the reading immensely, and was particularly impressed by the way you let the mood of the work illuminate the philosophy. Also: I found the flowers, spices, odors and tastes wonderfully vivid throughout; the sketches of people, too. And the final chapter, I thought superb. It is a book that should enjoy a fine career, as I hope it may.

You have heard, I am sure, of the passing of our little friend, Henry. God rest him merry! He was very very frail, there, at the end; deeply melancholy too, I think. When Natalie died, his whole world fell apart.

I'm planning to be out your way in March, and hope I may

have the luck to find you aboard your good ship "P.O. Box #." All best to Jano—

Ever, (and thanks for your "life"),

Joe

Alan Watts died on December 16, 1973.

June 19, 1974

Dear Jano—

Mr. Harold Kramer, of Celestial Arts, asked me to write an introduction to the series he is publishing of Alan's TV talks. Here, for your approval or disapproval and suggestions, is the piece that I have sent him.

I was sorry to have missed you when I was in California last time, but I shall be out there again next week, and perhaps we can get together. I'll phone.

Meanwhile, my love, to which Jean joins hers.

Yours

Joe

Alan Watts

by Joseph Campbell

The essence of Alan Watts was wit, the courage to live in a witty way, and delight in the greening of life that was thus, through his whole career, disclosed. And I use the word <u>wit</u> here carefully, not only in the sense of its current meanings, of (to quote from the Webster's Dictionary on my table) "Mental sharpness and alertness; intellectual quickness and penetration acumen... Felicitous perception or expression of associations between ideas or words not usually connected, such as to produce an amusing surprise"; but also in its earlier, archaic denotation (also given in the Dictionary) of

"A person of extraordinary intellectual powers or constructive genius; a person of learning, knowledge, esp. of human life and nature. A person keen and quick in perception of felicitous and amusing associations of ideas or words or the intellectually entertaining congruities and incongruities of life; more esp. one who has marked aptness for brilliant and happy expression of such impingement of incongruous ideas upon each other." The word is of the same Anglo-Saxon family as *wisdom*, *vision*, and *wizard*; also, *guide*. I see Alan in all of these. And finally, in the larger Indo-European language context, it is related to the Latin *videre*, "to see," and to the Sanskrit *vid*, "to know, in the way of transcendental insight." The word *Veda* is from this verbal root. And the great thing about the wit, witting, (or watting) of Alan Watts was that it was itself rooted in this *vidya*, "knowledge of the void that is the ground of being." And he could play it all the way, right up and down the line, from bright repartee to the flinging—with an Olympian laugh—of Indra's thunderbolt.

But it takes courage to live, not only with, but also according to, such knowledge—to live wittily, or wittingly, that is to say. For, as all the wisdom books of the ages tell, this thunderbolt (Sanskrit, *vajra*; Tibetan *dorje*) of the knowledge of the voidness of phenomenality, which Alan could fling about with such wizardry, is no philosophical game piece, but the terrible destroyer of illusions: all the lies—the big lies and the little lies—by which we generally live out our years. Indra's thunderbolt, according to Vedic legend, blew to pieces a giant serpent that had gathered into its scaly folds all the waters of the earth, and so, had turned the world into a desert. Its name was Vritra, the "Encloser," "Hold Fast," the "Enveloper," the "Obscurer." By analogy, the scaly habits of belief and custom by which most of us safely measure out the expectable three-score-and-ten of our unadventurous lives—and so, turn our world into the Waste Land of T.S. Eliot's poem—can be only exploded by such a knowledge of the voidness of phenomenality as motivated and inspired Alan's living. It is one thing to hear and think about such things and then to go on living as before, holding fast to one's own lies as truths, or as the values or meanings without which one's life would be a vacuum. It is an altogether different thing, on the other hand to let the vacuum take over in one's life; and that is what Alan allowed to happen in his. When I think of his finest qualities, the first that comes to my mind has always been, therefore, his courage. He would not buckle down to any god, church, or institution that drained the joy out of life. And in fact, it was in one of his most endangered moments—when he had thrown to the devil a career of ensured respectability toward which he had long labored—that he wrote his most personal statement of faith in the creative power of life's joy, The Wisdom of Insecurity.

For the wonder had been, that, when the vacuum-bolt exploded, annihilating all the scrags and scales of the phenomenality that up to that time had been his support, the true greening of his life as a creative, free-lancing teaching-philosopher began. And it was his puckish delight in the wonder of this continuing confirmation of a certain saying from one of his favorite books of quotations—"Whosoever shall lose his life for my sake and the good tidings shall find it" (Mark 8:35)—that then became, along with his wit and his courage, the culminating jewel of his philosophical crown.

Alan Watts was perhaps the first of a new breed of teaching philosophers now to come, in whose lives the wisdom of the Orient and Occident will equally participate, each world annihilating with its thunderbolts the encumbering proprieties of the other, to release the waters of an ever renewed and renewing life joy and courage in us all. Not many, however will share his personal charm or be able to match the wizardry of his extraordinarily witful wordplay. The pomposities of prodigious learning could be undone by him with a turn of phrase. One stood before him, disarmed—and laughed at what had just been oneself. It is delightful and appropriate, now, that a series of sensitively illustrated jewel-books of his jewel-thoughts should be published for those whom he loved to teach—the youthful, searching spirits of this century of transitions, when a world of collapsing civilizations, all outlived, is removing itself from around us, opening a vista into the void, where there is no marked way. Toward the venture into such an unbounded field there is no better guide than Alan Watts.

Henry Alexander Murray (May 13, 1893–June 23, 1988) was an American psychologist who taught for over thirty years at Harvard University. He was director of the Harvard Psychological Clinic in the Graduate School of Arts and Sciences after 1930. Campbell invited him to review the first volume of The Masks of God, *sparking a relationship that would last years.*

Henry A. Murray, M.D.
Professor of Clinical Psychology
Harvard University
Department of Social Relations
Divinity Avenue
Cambridge 38, Massachusetts

The Viking Press, Inc.
Madison Avenue
New York 22, N.Y.

October 21, 1959

Dear Sirs:

I was very pleased to receive a copy of [volume 1 of] THE MASKS OF GOD. I am not enough of an expert in the field of mythology to be invited to write a review, but if you are so disposed you may quote the following paragraph, or any part of it.

THE MASKS OF GOD is the first volume of an epic history of myths—graphic apperceptions and prospections of existence—that have shaped, for ancient and more recent centuries, the feelings, thoughts, and acts of men, an immense chronicle and commentary which, in temporal span and spatial scope and in relevance to the needs of its own day, is unexampled. The book is a monument of learning, wonder, and wisdom, daringly conceived and brilliantly written by a man who is at home in the Eastern and Western universe of spirit. Here already is sufficient nourishment, if thoroughly digested, to fill the crying existential emptiness of orphans of a deceased faith, who know that materialism is not enough; and, if the succeeding volumes fulfill the promise of this first, the whole great work may prove to be the Archimedean lever that, with necessity as fulcrum and the aid of chance, will move the world of mind to a new orbit, a new vista of its potential creative powers.

You can see from this that I am a great enthusiast for this book.

Sincerely yours,
Henry A. Murray, M.D.
Professor of Clinical Psychology
Harvard University

June 30, 1959

Mr. Joseph Campbell
Waverly Place
New York 14, N.Y.

Dear Joe

I am in the midst of your marvelous first volume. There is nothing that compares with it in the world's literature. Already it has fulfilled the high expectations I had for it after reading the piece that was published in Daedalus. It is very learned, but your immense store of knowledge does not interfere with the flow of your animated language, and your reader is carried along like a full-rigged barque sailing before the wind. My own knowledge is not sufficient to make any judgments as to whether or not in this or that instance you are justified in your interpretations. As far as I am concerned there are no defects in it, and I am captivated by the chronology of your garnerings from various mythologies and numerous illustrations that you bring to elucidate your points. It is a stupendous piece of work, and I hope your energies will keep bubbling as they did in this first volume. I shall have more to say after I finish it.

I am in the midst of various scribblings myself and do not have much leisure for reading outside my immediate sphere of concern. I am sending you a copy of a Phi Betta [*sic*] Kappa address I was asked to give this spring because I believe it is pertinent to the task you have set yourself. If it appeals to you, perhaps you can suggest a place for its publication.

I have had difficulty in getting the right fourth speaker for the Conference on Myth. We wanted a scientist but could not find one with interests congenial to the proposed topic. Alan Watts suggested that he might speak on certain mythic elements in the ideology of modern science, and so we decided to abandon the search for a physicist and I have invited Northrop Frye of Toronto to be the fourth speaker. I have not heard from him, and this means—since the committee have dispersed for the summer—that we cannot do much in the way of preparations, inviting other participants, etc., etc., until September. As this would be rather late it has recently occurred to me that April would be a better date than November. How would Saturday and Sunday, April 23 and 24, suit you? I hate to keep changing the date, but I think we would have a better conference if there were plenty of time to prepare for it.

Thanks so much for relaying the message from Mircea Eliade. Do you happen to know whether he will be in the United States in April, 1960?

Best regards to you,

Cordially yours,

Henry A. Murray

Swami Nikhilananda first came to New York City in 1931, sent by his monastic order in India, the Ramakrishna Mission, to negotiate changes at the Vedanta Society. Eventually he broke away to lead the Ramakrishna-Vivekananda Center. Campbell helped with the translating and editing of the definitive version of The Gospel of Sri Ramakrishna *and remained close friends with Nikhilananda, visiting him in the Adirondacks in the summer of 1940 and traveling with him to India in 1954.*[10] *Nikhilananda was renowned as a brilliant speaker, and his admirers included J. D. Salinger and Woodrow Wilson's daughter Margaret.*

Ramakrishna-Vivekananda Center
East 94th Street
New York 28, N.Y.

October 22, 1959

Mr. Joseph Campbell
Waverly Place
New York 14, New York

Dear Mr. Campbell,
The Viking Press has kindly sent me a copy of The Masks of God. As I was away last week in San Francisco I could not write to you earlier. I have read several chapters of your book. What a broad sweep of mind and tremendous scholarship you have shown! The language is powerful. Certainly you have opened up new avenues to the scientific study of mythology. It is an entirely new book of its kind. For those who are dissatisfied with dogmatic religions and the mechanistic interpretation of life and the universe given by the physical sciences, The Masks of God will be of great interest for the understanding of deeper realities.

Whether one agrees, or not, with all your conclusions, one cannot but be swept away by your scholarship and deep convictions. Please hurry up with the next three volumes, so that I can add new truths to my little storehouse of knowledge before I quit the world. Thank you for sending me a copy.

Yours affectionately,
[signed] Nikhilananda
Swami Nikhilananda

Lewis Gannett (1891–1966) was the author of The Living One, Magazine Beach, *and* The Siege, *as well as the two Millennium novels,* Gehenna *and* Force Majeure.

Cream Hill Road
West Cornwall, Conn.
October 25, 1959

Dear Pat
You sent me some weeks ago with no release date in it, Joseph Campbell's "The Masks of God: Primitive Mythology." It looked heavy, and I laid it aside. But at last I have at least dabbled in it, and with growing excitement.

It is, of course, an impossibly ambitious synthesis and projection. As neither Spengler nor Toynbee seemed to me to do, it opens rather than closes horizons. It has depth. It is written with a sense of wonder rare in those who piece together the mosaic fragments of knowledge. I tend to question much of it, but am obviously incompetent to judge. Much of it, of course, will be superseded, but you may have on your hands one of those history-making syntheses of science and imagination, comparable in its way to "The Origin of Species" and "The Golden Bough." It makes me wish I were younger, to watch horizons expand further still.

I'd better seal this letter before I can sleep on it and begin to qualify.

Yours for the joy of publishing—and reading—
Lewis Gannett

Mircea Eliade (1907–1986) spent four years at the University of Calcutta and in an ashram before completing his PhD in yoga, after which he moved to Paris, lecturing occasionally at the Sorbonne, and corresponding with A. K. Coomaraswamy and Henry Corbin. After a recommendation from Corbin, Eliade spoke at the Eranos Conference in 1950 and would return to lecture at Eranos nearly every year until 1963. Bollingen's publication of the Myth of Eternal Return *in 1954 launched his American career. It was followed by well-known books on yoga and shamanism. In addition, he was the author of several novels and was the editor in chief of the* Encyclopedia of Religion. *His* History of Religious Ideas *was published by the University of Chicago in 1978.*

This letter from Mircea Eliade has been translated from the French by Evans Lansing Smith, with the consultation of Dr. Ginette Paris.

Chicago, December 5, [1959?]

My dear Joe,

It is already two months that I have wanted to write you, and to thank you for your beautiful and rich volume The Masks of God. I have started to read the book around October 10, and postponed the letter in the hope of writing you after having finished. But your book is a summa, and the program in Chicago is terrible—and instead of two weeks it took me six weeks to read it. But I don't regret having proceeded slowly in the reading of your book. For two weeks The Masks of God has been my bedside reading: I read an hour every night, before going to sleep, and I slumber in my dreams with Far-li-mas, Houshken, or Our Lady of the Mammoths—Dear Joe, your book is very beautiful, extremely stimulating, audacious, personal, and carries new views even when you present well-known theories (such as Frazer or Frobenius). You have a unique talent of "saving" hypotheses considered (perhaps wrongly) outdated or unfounded. In any case your book provides the occasion for prolonged discussions between (I hope!) intelligent researchers. In what concerns me, I have already presented the book in my Fall seminar (Psychology and History of Religion) and I am going to use it in my Winter course (Mediterranean Religions).

Evidently there are points of view that I would love to discuss with you. I would not agree with all of your conclusions; not because I consider that they are not justified, but because I sometimes approach the subject from a different perspective. I hope to continue this dialogue in a couple of weeks, in New York. Once again, thanks with all my heart—and my sincere congratulations. (Don't forget that we are awaiting—for now with impatience!—the second volume!).

My regards to Jean—and goodbye for now. Christine sends her affectionate thoughts.

Amicably, your
Mircea

This letter, from reporter Larry Glen, discusses the cycles of Venus. Campbell's preoccupation with this subject would perhaps reach its climax in the masterful analysis of the mythologies of Inanna and ritual regicide associated with the Royal Cemetery of Ur in his Historical Atlas of World Mythology: The Way of the Seeded Earth, Part 1: The Sacrifice, *79–83.*

April 15, 1961

Dear Mr. Campbell,

Recently I was collecting myths concerning the planet Venus for an article—I am a reporter—and stumbled into something which has me intrigued. I doubt that I'll ever have time to pursue it so I'll ease my conscience by passing it on to you.

In your "The Masks of God: Primitive Mythology" (p. 430–31) you state "...one day in eight years (or, at least, so the local story goes), the morning star may be seen to rise and cast its beam precisely to the place of the stone of the two worn sockets. The tale may be true or not, but the coincidence of eight years with the period assigned by Frazer to the reigning kings of Crete gave me a shock when I heard it..."

G.C. Vaillant, in his "The Aztecs of Mexico," said that priests in the Mixteca-Puebla area "...observed the planet Venus and took note of a Venus Year of 584 days. At the end of two cycles (104 years) there was a tremendous ceremony of great ritualistic significance, for at the same time as the beginning of the Venus count, a solar count, a fifty-two year cycle, and a tonalpohualli all coincided."

I read many references in many books but never found scholarly reference to the eight-year rhythm of the planet Venus. It occurred to me that this rhythm may have been overlooked.

It's simply this: five synodic periods of Venus exactly equal eight 365-day years; that is, each equals 2,920 days.

Venus waxes and wanes over a 584-day period, roughly 19 months. Put another way, any given phase—let's say greatest brilliancy—recurs every 584 days. But it will recur on the same date only once in eight years, using the pre-Gregorian calendar.

For example, in 1961 Venus will be at its greatest brilliancy on May 16. It will be 1969 before it will again be at its greatest brilliancy during the month of May. It is scheduled to appear in that phase on May 14, 1969, and on May 12, 1977, and so on. But the two-day difference in dates is the result of the two leap-year periods in each eight years. Otherwise—as it was in the era of the 365-day calendar—the planet would always return to its greatest brilliancy on the same date every eight years; i.e., it would reach the same point in the ecliptic, while at greatest brilliancy, once every eight years. Astrologers would say it returns every eight years to the same point in the Zodiac, while at greatest brilliancy.

If I knew a tame astronomer I'd get him to plot an ephemeris for Venus over the past three or four thousand years. I wonder for instance whether Venus was touching the constellation Libra at the time the Spartan king's life "flew up and hit the beam," overweighted by a falling star. Could it be that Venus was the original signal for a king's death? As astronomy became more sophisticated, Venus would not serve as a signal since its phases did not mark exact time with the sun's passage through the ecliptic, Zodiac. But in the epoch of the 365-day year, its regularity must have been astounding—every eight years, at least.

Do you know of any works which contrast astronomical data with anthropological and mythological data? As a hobby I'd like to continue a ways into this question. But since I am not a serious scholar I thought I should draw your attention to Venus's eight-year rhythm. I can't help but feel that it was once of paramount importance.

Yours truly,
Larry Glen

The Asia Society (founded in 1956) focuses on educating the world about Asia. It has several centers in the United States and around the world. The Society's headquarters in New York City includes a museum that exhibits the John D. Rockefeller collection of Asian art and rotating exhibits with pieces from throughout Asia.

The Asia Society
East 64th Street
New York 21, New York
July 6, 1961

Dear Professor Campbell:
At the annual meeting of the Asia Society Board of Trustees last month, you were unanimously elected a Trustee, subject to your acceptance. As President of the Society I am writing to say that I sincerely hope that it will be possible for you to serve. Your participation as an active member of the Board would mean much to us.

The Society was founded in 1956 by a group of us here in New York who felt the importance of bringing the people of the United States and Asia closer together in their understanding and appreciation of each other and their respective ways of life. With the opening of Asia House on East 64th Street a year and a half ago the demands upon the Society as well as its opportunities have grown rapidly. The budget has grown from roughly $100,000 the first year to $593,000 approved at the meeting last month for the year 1961–1962.

I am enclosing herewith a booklet just published which outlines our progress to date as well as our program and objectives.

If there are any further facts or information which would be helpful to you, I will count on your letting me know.

Looking forward to the possibility of working with you, I am

Sincerely,

John D. Rockefeller 3rd

Benjamin Kimpel was a professor of philosophy at Drew University from 1938 to 1972. Campbell had given a talk to a graduate colloquium titled "Theological Meaning and Eastern Religion" in the fall of 1962.

Drew University
College of Liberal Arts
Madison, New Jersey

February 25, 1963

Professor Joseph Campbell
Sarah Lawrence College
Bronxville, New York

Dear Professor Campbell: This note to you is certainly altogether too late. I wanted to write immediately after your wonderful lecture on this campus, but I had this ugly old flu, and this took the last erg of my vitality. Now that I have a little power at the finger tips, I should like to tell you how much it meant to me to have you come. The entire series before your coming was at a low ebb. I can't believe that any group of lectures could have been weaker. I was almost inclined to give up. Then you came with your vast gift to make a lecture so delightful and so uplifting that I have regained my confidence in the entire academic program! I hate to admit now often this confidence gets to a frightfully thin thread that can hardly bind me to the job. But whenever I get discouraged, I shall see and hear you the evening on this campus. I must refer to the "seeing" because your hands are eloquent, and convey such a graceful way of generalizing a point, and at other times, such a delightful way of announcing the humor of it all. I can image very well how your students must carry you on their hands.

I apologize for cluttering up the evening you spoke with the mimeographed material I handed out on Zen. But after what we had on the field of Buddhism, I thought that it was time for a little something to be said that had some bearing on the topic.

With all my heart, I hope you can be persuaded to return.

Always my good wishes,

Ben Kimpel, Professor of Philosophy

Barbara Morgan (July 8, 1900–August 17, 1992) was an American photographer best known for her depictions of modern dancers. She was a cofounder of the photography magazine Aperture. *Morgan is known in the visual art and dance worlds for her penetrating studies of American modern dancers Martha Graham, Merce Cunningham, Erick Hawkins, José Limón, Doris Humphrey, Charles Weidman, and others, including Jean Erdman. Morgan's drawings, prints, watercolors, and paintings were exhibited widely in California in the 1920s and in New York and Philadelphia in the 1930s. For some examples of her work, see Campbell,* The Ecstasy of Being.

Barbara Morgan Studio
High Point Road
Scarsdale, New York
Post-Valentine's Day, 1968

Dear Jean & Joe:
Since I had to vanish from the Van Waveren's party for you—in order to get my Volkswagen over the tundra to Scarsdale before the werewolves entered my empty house—I didn't get to finally say what a superb totality it was in all its complexity made understandable—your lecture series.

And I also wanted to tell you—partly for fun and partly for real—the following—my photographer reflexes make me always both consciously and unconsciously watch other people's gestures (even when I have no intention of doing so), reflexes, shifts of mood, etc.—and so by the next-to-last-evening I suddenly realized that your "gestural aggregate" (so to speak) meant for me—at least two things—

1. That you are first of all a reincarnated Bard and/or Shaman—and that only—
2. Secondly, you are a contemporary scholar. When you would pause in your discussion to quote or chant—an entirely different psyche took over. There was an inner glee—a magnetic something—your own individuality happily slid into another collective—ancient—embracing—psyche. It was like a snake casting off old skin and you glowed anew with security of speaking for the Eternal. (And there was a special gleam for the demonic).

Then—chanting over—you took up the duties of logical thought as a 20th Century man, inheritor of our rat race traumas & trajectories from the past—seeking inner logic & harmony for mankind's future.

But then here came the next realization—these two phases were "integrated" and slid back & forth like gears in a Cadillac. But, for me, that more primordial element will henceforth be "there," the genuine Joe, from which all springs no matter how many PHD'S. If we were together I would laugh at this point—so you can take it or leave it.

Jean, it was so good to see you—and I wish you well for the difficult and important work you are doing. No doubt you have seen that new magazine from U.C.L.A. that has considerable on dance in it: "AFRICAN ARTS / ARTS d'AFRIQUE"—Vol 1—no. 1, Autumn. Looks very promising.

The two of you have such potentials. I can't help sharing crazy ideas such as the following: a TV series (myth relived)—Each program would be a dramatization of the story telling around a campfire (or whatever): at caravanseries on the SILK ROUTES—AMBER—SPICE ROUTES—Joe could be the teller of tales—and Jean would be the dancing girl to enchant the listeners (have camels in the shadowy distance). One evening it might be an encampment near Banion—just after the destruction of Buddha's face (was it Genghis Khan?). Another night it could be Homer at Troy, etc. Maybe Marco Polo could drop in too, from Cathay. Another episode—Troubadours—Taliessin—Navajo Sand Painting & Chant—An Eskimo Shaman or African Negro medicine man—live today with interpreter if they couldn't speak English.

The Series would be loved by high school students in audio-visual series.

Well—I'll leave you in peace—I'm in bed with this flu "bug"—hence these flights of fancy—

Again—thanks—

Love—

Barbara

The following is a letter of appreciation to Campbell from an admirer of whom we have no other record.

Joyce Marie Slade
Exposition Boulevard
Los Angeles, California, 90064
June 21, 1971

Dear Joseph Campbell,
I first met with you in an English class at UCLA in 1966 when I was assigned to "skim for the main ideas" in your work Hero With a Thousand Faces. Instead I devoured it from cover to cover amazed at the wealth of imagery and the ideas in the myths of the peoples of the world. You turned me on to the breadth & depth of the unconscious life that exists within myself. I look upon your work as the prime catalyst in my own (just beginning) lifelong growth process. Your work reached my soul & unlocked it so that I have been able to transcend the rigid structure of my past Catholic religious experience and enjoy a psychic life of exploration into the wealth of the unconscious without fear or guilt. As you say in Psychology Today, each of us must create our own mythology, and you are part of mine.

Sincerely,
Joyce Marie Slade

American theater director Joseph Chaikin (September 16, 1935–June 22, 2003) is best known for founding the Open Theater in 1963. Originally a closed theatrical laboratory, it evolved into a performing troupe.

West Street
Apt. G359
New York, N.Y. 10014
August 5, 1971

Dear Joseph Campbell,
I just finished reading your part in the collection "Dream, Myth, and Religion."[11] I can't tell you how moving it was and significant for me. It is a poem full of visceral and subjective information.

My impulse after it is to reassess the whole of my direction in the theatre. That impulse will have to change into action. All that has to wait around 8 months when I finish the responsibilities I've taken on. It will give me time to incubate a new direction. If this seems an extreme response, it's because I found your thoughts extremely inspiring and lucid in this time where most things are scattered and confused.

It is [as] enlarging to come across your writing as it has been your talks to us. Wisdom is a precious quality that I forget still exists, until I come across it again.

Also, I hope you will enjoy your meeting with Rinpoche Trungpa. I think it will be worthwhile.

I hope you and Jean have a good rest of the summer. We are now on our way to the mid-east.

Joe Chaikin

Hermann Goetz is principally remembered for his work on the history of Indian art. In 1953, he became director of the National Gallery of Modern Art in New Delhi. In 1961 he became honorary professor at the newly founded South Asia Institute of the University of Heidelberg, where he taught until his death in 1976. Goetz's work on Wolfram von Eschenbach's Parzival *was very important to Campbell, who wove the information into his discussion of the Grail romances in* The Masks of God: Creative Mythology *and his article "Indian Reflections in the Castle of the Grail" in* The Celtic Consciousness, *edited by Robert O'Driscoll (George Braziller, 1985).*

Heidelberg, 15.1.1968
Hausackerweg 14

Dear Professor Campbell,
Thank you very much for your pleasant letter of January 7. Indeed, it had been a great pleasure to meet you again in New York after so many years since we had made your acquaintance in India.[12] I am

glad that you received my two papers on Wolfram's Parzival and on Mira Bai:[13] I had already been afraid that they might likewise have been destroyed in the great post office fire like apparently some other parcels we had sent to the U.S.A. And I am especially glad that they could be of immediate use to you.

Nevertheless we regret to some degree that our meeting had offered no opportunity to talk about your wife's art and activities. For both my wife and I are highly interested in stage dance and ballet, though merely as an appreciative public who in the course of the years have seen and enjoyed innumerable performances by dancers of many countries—and known also a few personally—from the Karsavina, Sent Mahesa, the Wiesenthals, Mary Wigman, Palucca, Kurt Joos, the Argentina and Argentinita, most famous Indian dancers, up to the present day—except Martha Graham whom to see we never had an opportunity (only through the insufficient medium of stills). In New York we had thus also consulted the Library of the Performing Arts at the Lincoln Center. A short time ago the German dancer Dore Hoyer has died by suicide at the age of 56; she was a pupil of the Palucca. We regard her as the greatest dancer West Germany has had. Her severe style, most beautiful and expressive, had made never any concessions to cheap popularity, and thus she could appear only seldom in public. Just before her death she got at last the news of an award which was then given her posthumously, too late and too little. A shame!

Unfortunately we had to cut short our stay in New York because my only sister had been killed in a motor accident. Shortly afterwards we learnt that another friend of us, Xenia Zarina, a former dancer and then dance teacher in Mexico, had died, just before her book on Oriental dances (Crown Publishers) came out. She had worked also on a book on Persian dances. I wonder if this manuscript can be salvaged because the subject is practically unexplored.

I would like to take this opportunity to raise a question which probably might find your professional interest. When still in India, I hit on what I feel to be a grand poem, the Assumpta Maria by

Francis Thompson. But what intrigued me likewise, were first its Greek refrains as if it had been inspired by a Byzantine hymn, and then its theology which reminded me so much of Indian Śākta concepts that I wondered how far it is compatible with Orthodox Mariology, and from where those ideas had come. However, Francis Thompson is regarded as the greatest Roman Catholic poet of England of the ending 19th century. But here I am helpless. The poet is in Germany hardly known, his works are not in the university library, and those references I could discover, proved useless. For me this is just a personal issue in the search for the primary experience underlying all religious symbolism; for you it might be more.

With our best wishes for the New Year and forever, and with our kindest greetings from house to house,

Yours sincerely
Hermann Goetz

Heidelberg 29.6.1968.
Gutenbergstr. 8.

Dear Professor Campbell,

Since quite a time your last volume of The Masks of God is lying on my desk, and I am reading it time and again, as circumstances permit. I am simply fascinated. And it is a shame that I have not yet thanked you for this wonderful present. But as you will already have seen from a printed information, we have in April moved to another house, in the plains and nearer to the town center, though likewise a villa. The former, up the slopes of the Neckar Valley, though it had commanded a lovely view, had become too strenuous to reach. You are surely aware how much time and work such a move involves. For some time also my health had been rather indifferent, so that my work had badly fallen in arrears. But to return to your book! This is indeed the coronation of the whole set. For here you touch on our actual life. And is this not the real value of a book that it not merely enriches our knowledge and judgment, but opens to us an approach to the basic problems of life? It is one of the greatest dangers of our time that, with a horizon widening every day, we become satisfied with cataloguing and classifying our experiences, and thus debasing and devaluating them to insignificance by squeezing them into shadow categories. Whereas we should rather try to rediscover the underlying experience beyond words with the help of so many approaches from the most different angles, geographical, social, psychological and philosophical view points and scales of values, embodied in symbols and myths, in all the imagery of our subconscious and its rationalization, but also falsification in dogmatic systems. Those changing view points had been the fascination of your previous volumes, and now you are coming to a sort of synthesis. Especially I enjoy your chapters on the ideas underlying our mediaeval epics, Parzival, Tristan and Iseult, etc. My own studies in this line had been very much tête à terre, though this may have created a foundation for explorations in a wider context. But you deal with the underlying experiences which are familiar to us through Wagner's operas which I know practically by heart. And notwithstanding all changes they seem to me to have rather intensified the basic experience. I am quite aware of all that might be objected, and yet they emerge the more sublime the more I immerse myself into their world. I did not find mentioned by you a beautiful book on somewhat related lines which perhaps may not be known to you (alas, today it has become impossible to keep track of all, even important books): Denis de Rougemont, L'amour et l'occident, Paris (Plon) 1939, reprinted in the paperback series: Le Monde en 10/18, Union Générale d'Éditions, 8, rue Garancière, Paris 6e.[14]

We hope very much to meet you and your wife again earlier or later, in Europe or in the States, and in the meantime to keep in contact. With many thanks for your last letter of 5th April, and with our best wishes and kindest regards,

Yours Sincerely.
Hermann Goetz

Heidelberg 26.12.1969.
Gutenbergstr. 8.

Dear Professor Campbell,
Thank you most heartily for your letter of Sept. 20. I am sorry I had to postpone this letter until the Christmas vacations because I am badly in arrears with all my work.

Partly it is my own fault, because in August we had spent some weeks in Istanbul and surroundings, studying the Greek and Roman, Byzantine and Turkish monuments of art there. Though not in the main line of my researches, I felt it desirable to become better acquainted not only with that branch of Islamic art, but with this whole transition area between Orient and Occident.

The other reason is the rather chaotic situation here. Our South Asia Institute, hitherto scattered over the whole town of Heidelberg, was to move into a new building common to all its sections in the new university campus in the N.W. of the town by the end of the summer term, and all our equipment was packed away, but it was not before the beginning of the winter term that we could—or rather had to—move into it, not yet ready, without approach road, without lift, still hardly furnished, the library just now being unpacked. Thus the maintaining of the lectures and seminaries has become most precarious. And at the same time we have most unpleasant students' troubles (even an incendiary bomb in our new institute), a new, rather confused university constitution and elections, as well as the polls which brought the present socialist government to power, and now a bad flue [*sic*] epidemic.

I am glad that you have liked my book. Of course, for me it is old stuff, though in many cases endless work and heartbreaking difficulties had once been involved. Since I am in Europe, I am more preoccupied with broader issues, which is also one reason why we have visited the Near East as well as South East Asia.

However, I hope to bring out more of my scattered articles in further volumes. The illustration pl. 37 of my book you can probably not obtain from the Bhuri Singh Museum, but as soon as my photo collection which I had deposited in our institute will be accessible again, I shall make the necessary arrangements.

What really impels me to write to you, is however your wonderful book: The Flight of the Wild Gander. I feel that what you have to say is more than careful professional research. It is a vocation which inspires you, i.e., how to overcome the very crisis of our industrial society, of our art, our research. For there we are: Like Beckford's megalomaniac caliph, Vathek, we have entered Salomo's palace, with all its glittering treasures, we have occupied his throne to rule over the forces of nature—and discover that we are in hell and our pride has turned into desperation. We have conquered a world of abstract formulas but the creative, warm life, the love behind them, has escaped us. But just this experience is all the difference between the glory of God and the absurdity of hell.

We have forgotten what prayer really means, i.e., meditation and contemplation which are quite compatible with and even intensified by modern critical methods; and likewise its conceptual abstraction in symbolic personifications, be they God, Lucifer, angels, devils, or whatsoever else. E.g., Dionysius Areopagita is quite explicit in this respect, and therefore this terminology can also be changed into symbolism of other religious systems (cp. Aldous Huxley), in my opinion also coordinated (but not equated) with those of modern natural science.

However, our churches have done so much to discredit this approach, that even a great scholar like C. G. Jung is not taken seriously by more pedestrian scholars. Although most of our greatest scientists today, Einstein, Oppenheimer, Heisenberg, Planck, agree with Schroedinger, or you. I remember a passage in Jas. Jeans' Mysterious Universe, which, without being aware of it, formulates something identical with the Vedanta approach.

Though I believe, also Jesus had been a paramahamsa, and that his real passion had been that he was never understood. The

"Prayer of the Lord," not being recited collectively, but interpreted as a meditation text as closely knit as any mathematical or physical formula, if correctly interpreted, is Vedantic, though not inspired by the Upanishads. Only here we find "our father in heaven," i.e., the paramātman. Later Jesus felt his utter isolation and addresses "my father," identifying himself with the innocently suffering "Just Man" of Isaiah. The Passion, then, was merely the climax of a desperate struggle against misinterpretation. But for this very reason doctrines, scientific, religious or philosophical, are just words if they are not understood, not experienced, and therefore they have to be different in different civilizations, times, and human individuals.

Unfortunately it is impossible to find the time to discuss all the issues to which your book is inspiring me. I have been most interested in the interpretation of the mandala as the mental symbol of an authoritarian agrarian society. Will it really be overcome? Or has it often been overcome, though merely by an intellectual elite who soon discovered that it could not be divulged to the masses. Only the form of authority is changing in our time, the disintegration of former authority now leading mostly to licentiousness and nihilism.

Do you know: Hartmut Schmökel, "Heilige Hochzeit und Hohes Lied" (Abhandlungen für die Kunde des Morgenlandes, 32, 1), Wiesbaden (Fr. Steiner) 1956 which interprets the Song of Songs as an Ashtharot ritual dissected and disarranged, because it had been too popular to be suppressed by the priests of Jehova?

By the way, have you observed that the story of the Fall in the Bible is a typical Indian dryad or dakini story (of course only a parallel) being set into the context of a patriarchal deity and then reversed in its meaning?

There are many more questions. But this letter is becoming too long, and this is Christmas time. Let me therefore break off and tell you again how much thought-inspiring pleasure your book has offered to me.

With our best wishes for a Happy New Year and kindest Chrismas-greetings to you and your wife,

Yours sincerely,
Hermann Goetz

P.S. I have mentioned your name to the trustee of a small foundation who will probably forward to you a book "Cosmobiology" by Harmut Pieper. The author has been a private scholar completely dedicated to his scientific vision. I believe this book would be worthy of being published in the USA, though some of his apodictive statements may arouse outright resistance by many scholars. I believe this could be mitigated if some sympathetic scholar could write an introduction explaining the deductive process of the author's concepts. I believe it would be worth the trouble.
H. Goetz

Heidelberg, 15-12-70

Dear Professor Campbell,
May I use the opportunity of the present festival to retain contact with you and your wife. For I am again and again reading your interesting volume on Creative Mythology which is a real pleasure in all the dearth and dirt of an Occident where self-styled "progressive" people misinterpret the poisons of a disintegrating European civilization as the forebodings of a future culture. Fortunately we have been twice in S.E. Asia from Bali and Khymer Penh to Chiengmai and Rangdoon, and we have seen also a lot of fine dancing. On the other hand I am by and by returning from the now well established art seminary in the South Asia Institute of the university, though I intend to continue lectures and research, and also editing my former writings. We still hope that in the next years there may be another opportunity of coming to New York. Many hearty greetings, H. and A. Goetz

Joseph Campbell's passport photo, 1954

CHAPTER 5

Political Matters—Thomas Mann to the Vietnam War

1939–1970

Politics was Joseph Campbell's "inferior function," full of contradictions—staunch right-wing conservatism alongside anger against the nation's shameful treatment of Native Americans, rage toward the demonstrations protesting the war in Vietnam, and bewildering animosities.

This attitude is exemplified by a lecture Campbell delivered at Sarah Lawrence in December 1940, while the United States was still trying to decide whether to enter World War II. The lecture, entitled "Permanent Human Values," advocated a studied neutrality toward current events: "My theme forbids me to be partial to the war-cries of the day," he said. While this isolationism was far from unusual at the time, Campbell made some statements that are in retrospect quite shocking, such as "We are all groping in this valley of tears, and if a Mr. Hitler collides with a Mr. Churchill, we are not in conscience bound to believe that a devil had collided with a saint." (The entire speech is reproduced in Larsen and Larsen, A Fire in the Mind, *287–90.)*

One man who reacted strongly against this speech was Thomas Mann (June 6, 1875–August 12, 1955), the German novelist, short-story writer, social critic, philanthropist, essayist, and 1929 Nobel Prize in

Literature laureate. Mann was a member of the Hanseatic Mann family and portrayed his family and class in his first novel, Buddenbrooks. *His older brother was the radical writer Heinrich Mann, and three of his six children, Erika, Klaus, and Golo, also became important German writers.*

After Hitler came to power in 1933, Mann fled to Switzerland. When World War II broke out in 1939, he moved to the United States, returning to Switzerland in 1952. He is one of the best-known exponents of the so-called Exilliteratur, *literature written in German by those who opposed or fled the Hitler regime.*

Mann had been introduced to Campbell by Agnes Meyer, wife of the publisher of the Washington Post, *and their initial relations were cordial: in December 1939 they even attended an opera together (see letter on next page). But after Campbell's Sarah Lawrence address a year later, Mann wrote a powerful rebuttal. Campbell's angry reaction is illustrated by an excerpt from his "War Journal" on page 235.*

This unfortunate situation is all the more baffling given the centrality of Mann's novels in Campbell's writings, as demonstrated in The Masks of God: Creative Mythology. *His animosity persisted until nearly the end of his life. In the early 1980s I attended a weeklong series of lectures on James Joyce and Thomas Mann sponsored by the C. G. Jung Institute of San Francisco, and was astonished by Campbell's fury when I suggested that* Doctor Faustus *(a novel which casts the rise of Nazi Germany as a deal with the Devil) of 1946 was a great book—contrary to Campbell's assertion that Mann wrote nothing of significance after* Joseph and His Brothers. *His objections began while reading the final volumes of that tetralogy, which suggest positive analogies between Joseph and Franklin Delano Roosevelt.*

Crescent Place, N.W.
Washington, D.C.
December 14, 1939

Dear Mr. Campbell:
Unless the heavens fall out of sheer excitement, it appears we are going to hear TRISTAN with the Thomas Manns on the twenty-first!

I imagine the matinee will begin at one-thirty o'clock.

If it is not too much trouble, will you meet me at the Plaza Hotel at one o'clock sharp so that we can go down together? I refuse to take any chance of missing the opportunity to say "Dr. Mann, here is Joseph."

With kindest regards, and looking forward to the great occasion,

Yours sincerely,
Agnes E. Meyer
(Mrs. Eugene Meyer)

The following is from Campbell's "War Journal" (excerpted in Larsen and Larsen, A Fire in the Mind, *296–97).*

The fall of 1939 there appeared in my office at Sarah Lawrence College, Mrs. Eugene Meyer, who discovered that I was giving a course on Thomas Mann. She sat in on my class. The first day of the Christmas holiday she invited me to hear *Tristan and Isolde* with the Manns, and to have dinner at the Plaza. It was a fairly dreamlike afternoon and evening. Mrs. Meyer and I arrived first at the opera. When the Manns came down the aisle we stood up and Mrs. Meyer introduced me: "Dr. Mann, this is Joseph." We sat down. Gene Tunney [the boxer] was in the seat just in front; he turned around to greet Mrs. Meyer, and was introduced to Mann. Everybody was charming.

During intermission we crowded up to the room where people mill against each other and try to drink their tea. We found a table in the midst of the turmoil and I pushed quietly up to the bar to fetch tea and cakes for us all. When I returned, the Master said with grace, but with, of course, deep undermeaning, humanly ambiguous and rich with a sense of the already present future: "Thank you so much! You are a hero."

Thomas Mann, early 1950s

Thomas Mann
Stockton Street
Princeton, N.J.
29th February, 1940

Dear Mr. Campbell,
Your gracious and friendly letter about LOTTE IN WEIMAR gave me very great pleasure, all the more so as I know that you

read the book in its original German. No matter how excellent a translation may be, a writer likes best to earn his readers' approval with his own untranslated work.

My wife and I have the happiest recollections of our meeting with you, and we feel most grateful that you should have written to tell us that you remembered us.

With many thanks for your letter and with kindest regards in which my wife joins.

Yours very sincerely,
Thomas Mann.

The following is taken from Letters of Thomas Mann: 1889–1955, *edited and translated by Richard and Clara Winston, abridged ed. (Berkeley: University of California Press, 1975), 277.*

Princeton, January 6, 1941

Dear Mr. Campbell:
Thank you for sending me your lecture, "Permanent Human Values." Naturally I read it with close attention. I should like to make the following comments.

As an American you must be better able to judge than I whether it is appropriate to recommend political indifference to young people in this country—which is beginning slowly, slowly, against ponderous resistance (and, let us hope, not yet too late) to come to an understanding of the situation and the pressing necessities of the times.

The question as I see it is this: What will become of the five good things which you are defending, or think you are defending; what will become of the sociologist's critical objectivity, of the scientist's and historian's freedom, of the poet's and artist's independence; what will become of religion and humanistic education, in case Hitler wins? I know from experience exactly what would become of all these things everywhere in the world for the next generation, but a good many Americans do not know it yet, and therefore they believe that they must defend these good things by the method and in the spirit that you do.

It is curious: Since you are a friend of my books, you must think that they have something to do with "permanent human values." Now these books are banned in Germany and in all the countries Germany at present dominates, and anyone who wants to read them, anyone who offers them for sale, anyone who even speaks well of me in public, would end in a concentration camp, and his teeth would be knocked out, his kidneys bashed. You maintain that we must not allow ourselves to be excited by this, we must rather see to the preservation of the lasting human values. Once more, that is strange.

I do not doubt that your lecture has won you great applause. You should not, I think, be deceived by this applause. You have wittingly or unwittingly told young people already inclined toward moral indifference what they would like to hear; but that is not always what they need.

I know you mean well and desire the best. But whether you are right, and whether you may not be serving the cause of evil by such speeches, is a matter we had best not dispute further.

Once again, my thanks and sincere good wishes.

Below is Campbell's response (excerpted from Larsen and Larsen, A Fire in the Mind*, 298–99).*

Dear Dr. Mann,

Thank you for your letter of Jan. 6. I am sorry that my paper on "Permanent Human Values" seemed to you untimely. In defense of myself I can only say (and it is very difficult for me to say anything whatsoever in the face of disappointment from the author of the great works which for the past twelve years have been my guardians and guides) that, having been invited to speak from the standpoint of the speculative order, I strove to distinguish the virtues of this order from those of the practical. That seemed to me a distinction conducive to sanity, and I did not think sanity an evil, even from the political point of view....

That Americans must now learn to play their rôle in history *consciously* I do not deny. All the more reason for reminding young people that the confusion and hatred of the hour are not precisely the truth and love that are called eternal!

That is all I can say in defense of myself; and I should have been incapable of saying even this, had Mrs. Meyer not discovered something in my talk which she thought worthy of the eyes of Dr. Thomas Mann. I have re-examined myself carefully, both in the light of her pleasure and in the light of your disapproval.

Thank you again, from the bottom of my heart, for the minutes which you devoted to the letter of Jan. 6.

I beg to remain,
Most respectfully yours,
Joseph Campbell

Campbell's private reflections on this exchange, from his "War Journal," appear in Larsen and Larsen, A Fire in the Mind, *297. The bracketed comment at the end is the Larsens'.*

The letter which I received from Thomas Mann in reply was one of the most astonishing revelations to me: it signified for me the man's practical retraction of all his beautiful phrases about the timelessly human which no force can destroy, and about the power of love over death and about the Eternal altogether. It exhibited a finally temporal-political orientation, and not only that, but a fairly trivial and personal view of even the temporal-political. Christ would not have Peter draw his sword to defend the Word Incarnate from crucifixion, but behold the invitation of Thomas Mann to the hero who is to defend the Collected Works from going out of print! [Mann had asked Joseph, his "hero," for help with the latter project.]

The next two letters are from Erika Mann. Erika Julia Hedwig Mann (November 9, 1905–August 27, 1969), an actress and writer, was Thomas Mann's eldest daughter. In 1952, because of the anticommunist Red Scare, the Mann family left the United States, and she moved back to Switzerland with her parents. After her father's death, she became the caretaker of his works.

Kilchberg am Zurichsee
Alte Landstrasse 39
March 11, 1963
Prof. Joseph Campbell
Waverly Place
New York City 14

Dear Professor Campbell,—
As you may—or may not—have heard, I am engaged in editing three volumes of selected letters by my father. Of course, there is a great deal of correspondence between him and Mrs. Agnes E. Meyer to be considered and your name figures repeatedly in that correspondence. What I do not know, however, is whether a letter addressed to Mr. Campbell (with no Christian name mentioned) was ever received by yourself. The letter is dated January 6, 1941 and concerns a lecture entitled "Permanent Human Values" which "Mr. Campbell" had delivered and subsequently sent to T.M.

Somehow I feel fairly certain that you are the "Mr. Campbell" concerned. But I should have to be entirely sure and hence should be much obliged if you'd let me know whether you were the recipient of the communication in question. Also I'd be glad to learn if the lecture was delivered at Sarah Lawrence's—and if not, where else.

Thanking you in advance for your kind cooperation,
I am yours very sincerely,
Erika Mann

Following is a reply to a letter from Campbell that was evidently destroyed at his request. It is translated from the German by Evans Lansing Smith.

Quellenhof Kur-und Golfhotel
Bad-Ragaz
Switzerland

Esteemed Professor Campbell,
Thank you very much for your kind letter of April 9th, and be assured that I will, according to your wish, destroy your letter, so that from then on it will not be found with us. Today I have a request: Since you are not only a "recipient" in Collected Letters II, but are repeatedly mentioned in TM's letters to Mrs. Meyer, I need urgently for the "notes" your curriculum vitae,—year of birth, most important positions in your career, the most important publications with data (possibly books). Unfortunately, the time is urgent, so I would be most grateful to you for a speedy completion of my request.

With the best wishes for your personal well-being,
Your very devoted Erika Mann

P.S. I can still be reached at the above address.

Arthur Miller (1915–2005) was an American playwright, best known for such plays as The Death of a Salesman, The Crucible *(an allegory for the anti-Communist "witch hunts" of the early 1950s, during which he was blacklisted), and* All My Sons. *He served as the first president of the American branch of PEN International, an organization for writers. In 1965, Miller turned down an invitation to witness President Lyndon Johnson signing the Arts and Humanities Act. In his telegram to Johnson, Miller wrote, "The signing of the Arts and Humanities bill surely begins new and fruitful relationship between American artists and their government. But the occasion is so darkened by the Viet Nam tragedy that I could not join it with clear conscience. When the guns boom, the arts die."*[1]

Waverly Place
New York City—10014

October 11, 1965

Mr. Lewis Galantière, President
P.E.N. American Center
c/o IIE, Room 925
United Nations Plaza
New York City—10017

Dear Mr. Galantière:
Thank you very much indeed for your kind and cordial reply to my note of resignation. It is of course true, as you say, that Mr. [Arthur] Miller has a right to say what he likes in this country, and I would agree, as well, that the International P.E.N. Clubs have a right to have Mr. Miller for their president. However, his public statement was not merely a fool's remark in "bad taste"; nor was it (as he seems to have pretended at the Club dinner in his honor) a mere protest against the bombing of civilians. It was a clearly worded charge, by a man who knows not only how to write but also how to gain a world audience for what he writes, stating that the President and State Department of the United States had dishonestly disregarded an honest Communist bid for negotiations in

the interest of peace. Furthermore, the idiotic additional observation that "when the guns go boom the arts die" [*sic*] implied—or at least, it did to me—that responsibility for this ugly war in Viet Nam was to be assigned to the U.S.A. as aggressor—neither of which thoughts can be said either to have originated in the mind of Mr. Miller, or to have been blundered forth by him in sophomoric ignorance of what he was saying.

I was kindly touch[ed], Mr. Galantière, by your personal, open-hearted plea to give P.E.N. and Mr. Miller a second chance. But Mr. Miller has had his second chance: on second thought, he could have publicly apologized. Besides: second chances are for beginners. Shall we consider the argument, then, that the value of P.E.N. as a bridge between the Free and Communist worlds is so great that it must be supported by Americans of good will even at the cost of acquiescing in such disparagement of the motives of their own national effort, to give comfort to the Iron Curtain lot? I am sorry (and I mean it, I am sorry), but the P.E.N. Club symbol has now acquired for me such ambiguous connotations that I no longer wish to be a member.

With cordial personal regards, I beg to remain,

Very sincerely yours,

Joseph Campbell

Gary Snyder (born May 8, 1930) is an American man of letters. Perhaps best known as a poet (often associated with the Beat Generation and the San Francisco Renaissance), he is also an essayist, lecturer, and environmental activist. His work reflects an immersion in both Buddhist spirituality and nature. Snyder has translated literature from ancient Chinese and modern Japanese into English. The following letter from Snyder addresses Campbell's response to Snyder's article "Buddhism and the Coming Revolution."

3.11.68

Nishinoyama-cho
Shichiku, Kita-ku
Kyoto, Nippon

Dear Mr. Campbell,
At risk of annoying you further, I'd like to respond to your response to my little essay in Alan Watts' bulletin. Alan told me what you said.

First, I'm enclosing a later and revised version of it. The version Alan reprinted was issued in 1961 I believe. The "violence" is somewhat toned down.

Second, let me say I respect and admire the work you've done—when I first read Hero, in 1950, I couldn't put it down, and read until dawn and it was finished. I can't help but feel I've learned from your books.

Now: first of all I'm not clergy, I'm a Buddhist layman who was brought up by Socialist parents to feel very keenly the problems of society and the responsibility of the individual to address himself to them. If Buddhist laymen have no interest in politics, then we have the spectacle of the Japanese Buddhist public silently cooperating with Japanese militarism prior to World War II; the Zen monks from the monasteries enthusiastically going to the war as soldiers. One Roshi is reported to have encouraged the departing monks to concentrate on MU as they fought. Not one monk was left behind in the sodos.

I'm sure you will agree that the time has come for people who have faith in spiritual truths to apply that faith and energy—however little good it may do—toward the overwhelming problem facing the globe: the ecological and population problems being actually far more serious than Viet Nam or urban rioting. If Buddhists believe in Ahimsa, in the Buddha nature inherent in all beings, let them speak out for the Desert Kit Fox, the Blue Whale; for no one else will.

As for disagreeing with the concrete proposals I make; let other Buddhists—or Christians—or Hindus—speak up. I hope they will. Let the Jungians speak up. You are doing no one a favor by retreating into white, middle-class, Christian sensibilities. I base my views on what I've read and studied of anthropology and history, what I've experienced as a merchant seaman and logger, and—God help me—as a student of Rinzai Zen.

As for violence, I am only being honest. I would do violence to a man to stop him from killing a third person; I would apply moral and intellectual "violence" to American society to stop it from continuing its murderous course in Viet Nam. As the Buddhists teach, sometimes one will do violence; even kill. Only let one not deceive himself about it: he bears the karma and must work that karma through.

If we today must still take on the karma of violence, it is because the white imperialistic Christian consciousness before us was too irresponsible, too flawed, to keep from exploiting and making slaves of men.

I read recently about a famous Yankee slavetrading captain, who piously read his Bible while the slaves stifled in the hold. That's keeping religion out of politics, for sure.

Someone recently (I forget who now) made a remarkably intuitive note on the eruption of the working-class / peasant / non-white world into history as an outward, social, equivalent of the entrance of the Unconscious into the reckoning of modern man. There is indeed a complementary outer & inner revolution taking place in the world.

So—I say—save your disgust and revulsion for men who are peddling death and pollution, for large sums of money, all around you—within blocks of Waverly. From the Zen standpoint one does his meditation, and sweeps his garden. The size of the garden doesn't matter. That essay is part of my trying to keep my garden swept.

My best regards to you,
Gary Snyder

The following letter, addressed to Richard Nixon, is a response to a letter to Nixon sent by Charles DeCarlo, president of Sarah Lawrence, protesting the bombing of Cambodia.

May 11, 1970

My Dear Mr. President:
As a member of the faculty of this college, on duty here since 1934, I wish to dissociate myself absolutely from the impudent letter you have lately received from our president, Charles DeCarlo. It is obvious to me and to a few others on our faculty that the action you have taken in Cambodia is both necessary and courageous. I, for one, was thrilled to hear of it, proud again (at last!) of my country and its President.

You must know as well as I what forces for subversion have been at work these years on our campuses. In the building in which I have my office, which is occupied also by the student leaders of the SDS [Students for a Democratic Society, a leftist student organization], I have seen a Viet Cong flag in a room above mine, a portrait of Mao Tse-tung on the stairwell, a Black Panther poster posted on the outer wall. Moreover, I have this year lectured at some dozen other campuses, east and west, and have found on every faculty the same unholy combination as the one we have here, of young bewhiskered Maoists and old, long-seasoned CP [Communist Party] leftovers from the thirties, teaching communism as "democracy," denigrating the United States and everything it has ever stood for, substituting clichés for thought and picket signs for books. It would be a cosmic calamity if the trumped-up cries from our dangerously subverted campuses should ever succeed in baffling your noble effort to return this country to its course.

Respectfully and sincerely,
Joseph Campbell
Professor of Literature

The President
The White House
Washington. D.C.

This letter is in regard to Campbell's membership in John Jay Associates, a fundraising organization for Columbia alumni.

Waverly Place
New York City—10014

July 10, 1970

Mr. Jerome A. Newman, Chairman
John Jay Associates
West 43rd Street
New York City—10036

Dear Mr. Newman—

I have your letter, asking to know why I have not renewed my membership in the John Jay Associates, pointing out to me that financial support for our colleges has "fallen off disastrously," and that the educational process needs my help. As one who has been teaching in a college for the past 36 years, I know all this as well as anybody; and I also know—perhaps better than the editors of The New York Times, whom you cite—why this disaster has befallen us. I have watched the gradual but relentless conversion of our campuses into institutions of revolutionary propaganda, with activist sectors of their faculties not only supporting but actually teaching and inspiring the outrageous programs that have converted the term "academic freedom" into a screen for deliberate vandalism, arson, and infringement of the rights of non-Marxist students to make use of the buildings, libraries, R.O.T.C. facilities, etc., for which their fees have paid. Moreover, I hold the disgraceful affairs precisely at Berkeley and Columbia as largely responsible for what has been going on since on the lesser campuses of this country. The shameful, spineless capitulations of the administrations of these two once noble institutions to violence and the obscenities of "students" celebrating and waving Viet Cong flags, red flags, black flags, and wiping their asses with the American flag, I regard as simply beyond toleration. Why were these ruffians not immediately expelled? Why were the faculty members not dismissed who presented their chests, like a bunch of St. Sebastians, to the police in defence of their "children"—Rundel (?), etc., and this idiot Herb Gold who recently blew himself and few colleagues to smithereens on 11th Street, within view of my own library window?—doing his graduate work on homemade bombs! And as for Columbia lately: the consummate gall of the so-called University Senate, sending rebukes and instructions on political matters to the President of the United States! I have former students now working for advanced degrees at Columbia who were actually barred from use of the library this spring by gangs of activist thugs "on strike" against the U.S.A.—with permission of the present Administration.—Is it an educational or a political institution for which you are soliciting my support?—Indeed, I know personally a good many of the faculty up there on Morningside, and am pretty well aware of what they stand for.

In short: the basic situation has not changed; and if you are wondering why our colleges are facing financial disaster, it is because I am not the only alumnus who thinks about these things. Who wants to give his money for the repair of buildings, computers, equipment of all kinds, deliberately vandalized by "students" (freshman 27 years old, for example), or to pay the salaries of faculties fostering and protecting such "students"; or for the scholarships of such "students"; or for the "academic freedom" of campuses to become sanctuaries of subversion, dope peddling, and political advertisements. When I feel that Columbia has returned to what used to be regarded as the work of education, you may hear from me again; but meanwhile, please accept this letter as my answer to the question that may again arise from a consideration of your membership files, as to why my gift for the year will not have been received.

And please know, also, that my respect and affection, as well as gratitude, for the Columbia that I once knew are as great as ever they were.

Cordially and sincerely,

Joseph Campbell, '25—M.A. '27

Joseph Campbell in his Waverly Place apartment, circa 1970

CHAPTER 6

The Mythic Image

The 1970s

Shortly after the publication of The Mythic Image, *my revered dissertation director, Albert Friedman, criticized the book for having no theory about myth. It has taken me many years to recognize that in fact this is one of its main strengths. Theories about myth are a dime a dozen, and many of them are worth considerably less. When such speculation descends into the morass of algebraic equations to track the migration of folk tale motifs—as it does in Lévi-Strauss—it achieves the kind of philosophical absurdity Samuel Beckett parodies in* Waiting for Godot. *What we need rather—and what Campbell offered in this spectacular publication—is not another theory of myth, but a direct, visual experience of the deep, creative energies myth activates, through image, ritual, poetry, dance, and dream.*

The correspondence during this period of the 1970s, when the Bollingen Series moved from Pantheon to Princeton University Press, allows us a unique glimpse into Campbell's commitment to this agenda and the difficulties he overcame in negotiating the printing of this remarkable book. Shortly after the publication, Campbell was awarded an honorary doctorate by Pratt Institute in 1976. The letters recommending him for that award are included here, along with his address to the institute's graduating class.

Princeton University Press
March 15, 1971

Dear Joe:
As you know we are getting into production with MYTHIC THEMES, which is intended to be Volume 1 of a two-volume work entitled THE MYTHIC IMAGE. The manuscript seems to be exceedingly carefully prepared, and we are in the process of getting estimates and working out detailed plans. In this regard, we expect to ask Miss Abadie to work with you on the layout, since she is already so familiar with the volume. She will of course have to consult with our designers in that regard.

I find that neither we nor the Bollingen Foundation ever made a formal agreement with you for the publication of the book. Accordingly I am enclosing a proposed agreement for Volume 1, which I hope will be satisfactory. You will see that for the most part it follows the practices of Bollingen in years past, though with some modest changes. In particular, we have provided a fund of up to $250 to pay for the line drawings which I believe must still be made. Of course we have already taken care of the illustrations and paid Miss Abadie to work as your assistant in that regard, as well as in other ways.

With respect to Volume 1, we should like to urge you very strongly to prepare a short preface stating the purpose of the book, and clarifying its relationship to the volumes that you did for Viking. This would also be a place to put appropriate acknowledgments. I believe that Ben Houston has also sent you some other suggestions for minor revisions, including some suggestions from an outside reader; we hope that you will take these suggestions seriously and will at least consider changes along the lines suggested.

We are of course planning to follow the general format worked out between you and P. J. Conkwright a couple of years ago. P. J. has retired from the Press, and we shall assign the book to another staff designer, who will perhaps make some minor modifications in the design, though the same double-spread approach will be used, and we will maintain the same characters-per-line relationship so that your planning for layouts will hold good. Ben mentioned to me that you had planned when necessary to cut the text to fit the space when the material is in proof. This might be possible in a few cases, but in general we are working on the assumption that you have written your material to fit the space, in accordance with the layout and sample pages that we provided, so that there will be a minimum of changes in proof. Of course a good deal of flexibility is provided by the option of adjusting the size of the illustrations. That is, if the text appears to be too long, the illustration can be made smaller. We very much want to avoid extensive changes in proof, and I thought I should bring this problem to your attention at this point.

As I said above, the enclosed agreement for Volume 1 is very much along the lines of the traditional Bollingen agreements. I think we must now address ourselves to the question of Volume 2, which was not envisioned at the time the Bollingen program was transferred to Princeton, and which, if we are going to do it, we must somehow work into our budget. Consequently I think that the arrangements for Volume 2 will have to be considerably different. In particular, we shall have to put some limitations on the amount of help we can give you in the way of editorial assistance, payment for permissions and illustrations, preparation of the index, and the like. My idea is that we should make a round sum available to you for these purposes, as a maximum, and that anything beyond that maximum would have to be charged to royalties. We should expect to pay royalties on Volume 2 at the same rate as for Volume 1. In this regard, we are asking Miss Abadie not to do any work on Volume 2 until arrangements for Volume 2 can be settled. As soon as such arrangements can be settled, she can pick up from there, assuming that you want her to continue.

Also, I find that we do not have any very clear idea of what is going into Volume 2, and what it will be like. I think we need more information about that, and about when you would expect to complete it. I should hope, for example, to specify a delivery date not later than January 1, 1973, which would give you nearly two years from now. It would be fine if the book could be ready earlier. It is always a handicap if there is too much time between volumes in a two-volume work.

I am sure you realize that changes are necessary on account of the change in status of the Bollingen program, since we are now working with a fund that is definitely limited, and within which we must carry out the various projects. In this regard I should note that I understand that you have asked for 36 color plates in Volume 1, and it seems most unlikely to me that we will be able to afford this many. We shall certainly be in touch with you about that as soon as we have some estimates.

Although we don't yet know very much about Volume 2, it seems clear that Volume 1 will be an interesting book, and we are going to do our best to make it a handsome and successful one. We are looking forward to working with you on the second volume and to completing this capstone of the Bollingen Series.

With very best wishes,
Sincerely,
[signed] Herb
Herbert S. Bailey, Jr.

Princeton University Press
16 March 1971

Dear Joe:
Lin Peterson, one of our best editors, is even now working on your manuscript, and we are definitely under way. I am very pleased that Herb has agreed to retain M. J. Abadie: you and I both know how valuable she is.

Herb's letter to you states our feeling that the book needs a preface or introduction that would state the general intention of THE MYTHIC IMAGE and orient the reader in relation to The

Masks of God. Beyond that, as I told you earlier on the telephone, there are some passages toward the end of the volume that involve quoted material that seems excessive. Specifically, MS pp. 675–80 are one long quote from Plato, Phaedo; 682–702 seems a too-long section of the Tibetan Book of the Dead; and 760–782 is one continuous quote from Captain Cook's journal.

Our reader, who was (naturally) very pleased with the book and enthusiastically approved it, made one comment that you may wish to consider. He feels that "section 5 of Chapter IV doesn't seem to tie in too well with what has gone before. The reader has the feeling that the preceding theme has been abandoned for an excursion into Yoga."

Other than that, the reader appended a list of "possible errors," a copy of which is enclosed. As you will quickly see, there is nothing here that you cannot dispose of readily. As for the diacriticals, we have already decided that they will be used only when certain key terms are given in parentheses. We will have to be careful, however, about the transliteration of non-diacritical words in the text. The copyeditor will be looking out for these.

Mark Hasselriis, who has done excellent work for Bollingen in the past, largely Egyptological, was once proposed by Bill as a good man to do the line drawings in your book. He lives, I think, in Forest Hills. We can put you in touch if you like.

With every good wish,
Sincerely
[signed] Ben
Benjamin F. Houston

April 1, 1971

Dear Joe:
Thank you for your understanding letter of March 26. I quite understand your feelings of concern, your disappointment that we cannot have as many color plates as you would like, and your hesitations regarding Volume II. I still believe that we shall be able to produce a

very handsome volume, and that Cinderella's carriage will hardly be considered a pumpkin, with sixteen color plates. Compared to our regular program, in which we are hardly ever able to afford any color plates at all, your volume will appear quite lavish.

Your immediate reaction, I am sure, is that Bollingen funds ought to be used to pay for these things, and my reply must be that of course they are, but the funds are now limited, and we have already exceeded the total pre-editorial budget (for editorial assistance, permissions, and the like) for the project, with nothing left over for Volume II. Of course at the time we were making plans, and when the Bollingen program was transferred to Princeton, it was still very difficult to see how this project would turn out, and obviously we didn't allow enough for the rather elaborate project you have in mind, and apparently we did not envision it properly. Perhaps it would have been better if at that time we had given you a maximum budget to work on, but at that time I don't think any of us could see well enough what would be required. We have proceeded in good faith, trying to work things out as well as possible. In addition to the support you received from Bollingen, we have continued to pay for the pre-editorial expenses, and full royalties are provided, so I don't think it could be said that we are skimping the project.

But how shall we proceed? I am very much attracted to your suggestion that we should recast the project into a single volume. As I said in my letter of March 15, we do not have a very clear idea of what the proposed Volume II would contain, and at this point I have no idea what would be needed to round out the present volume to make it complete and self sufficient. Could you give me some idea of how you would want to go about that? Or does the present volume, perhaps with the new conclusion, constitute a self-sufficient entity? I would be glad to know how you think this might be worked out, and I agree entirely that it would be desirable to work out arrangements so that we could stop worrying about how things would turn out, what the book would include, what it would cost, when it would be finished, and so forth. No doubt we should have pinned this down earlier, though it seems to me that we at Princeton have only recently been able to get a full understanding of the project, if indeed we have that now. At any rate, we do want to produce a handsome book that will be the capstone of the Bollingen Series, and I have no doubt that out of this discussion we will be able to do just that.

With very best wishes,
Sincerely,
[signed] Herb
Herbert S. Bailey, Jr.

P.S. Since dictating the above I have had chance to talk again with Ben Houston about the manuscript presently designated MYTHIC THEMES, Volume I. Ben feels that, except for a few references to a projected Volume II, Volume I is very much a self-contained unit and could easily stand by itself. He also said that he thought that the proposed MYTHIC HORIZONS would be more historical, having to do with the spread of mythic images, and would thus be closer to THE MASKS OF GOD. I wonder, then, whether we couldn't consider MYTHIC THEMES to be "the volume," though I think it would probably be better to return to the original title, THE MYTHIC IMAGE. It seems to me that this might be a good solution.

HSB Jr.

Waverly Place
New York City—10014

May 10, 1971

Mr. Herbert S. Bailey, Jr.
The Princeton University Press
Princeton, N.J. 08540

Dear Herb—

I dare say the estimate of costs has been about completed by now and we can begin to settle our affairs. I have gone through our whole set of pictures with Miss Abadie, and have decided to settle definitely on the prospect of one volume. "The Mythic Image" would be the title. And as far as I can now see, the only outstanding questions have to do with a) the number of color prints to be published, and b) who is to pay for the line drawings. Miss Abadie and I figured that a sum of $1500 would likely be sufficient for the latter; and in going through our picture file we found that we had planned for no more than 29 color prints. I now wonder whether it would be possible to estimate the difference in cost between the publications of 29 and of 16 color prints and discover thus precisely what our argument is about. Does the reduction of our project from two to one volumes not make a difference?

In any case, I think that before drawing up our next contract we should be certain of where we stand in relation to these two questions. I might add, furthermore, in relation to the contract offered, that, in view of the fact that an introduction is to be written and certain adjustments made in the text, line drawings are to be made, and certain charts composed, October 1 would be a safer date than July 1, for final delivery. Also, I do not like your [section] 9, Revised Editions. There will be no revisions necessary in this work, and I want no other "person or persons" than myself to be fooling around with it after publication. Finally, let us delete that Reduced Rate-of-Sale paragraph. I think Princeton is going to make money enough on this work to survive its seasons of reduced sales.

Best regards, and my thanks, sincerely for your patience through the long weeks that have elapsed since your letter of April 1.

Yours cordially,

[signed] Joe

June 4, 1971

Dear Joe:

I have delayed in replying to your good letter of May 10 until I had a chance to review plans for THE MYTHIC IMAGE again. I have now reviewed the project and it appears that we can go along with you on almost every point in your letter. I think we have already agreed to make this a one-volume project, and partly in view of that I have decided to go back to the larger 9-1/8" x 12-1/4" trim size that we originally talked about. This will provide a better display of the pictures, and I think it will be a stunning book, not a poor Cinderella. We can also provide an allowance of $1,500 toward the cost of drawings, though I would hope that it wouldn't come to that much. We shall cancel the revised edition clause (Paragraph 9) and the reduced rate of sale paragraph. I think that takes us through your various points, except for the question of the color photos, which I think we must hold to 16 pages. Moreover there is a problem of the positioning of the color photos, which will have to be worked out with the editor. The text of the book itself, along with the black and white photos, will be printed by offset, whereas the color photos will be done by letterpress, probably by a Swiss printer. This means that the color plates will have to be tipped-in to the book at the proper location, and presumably the versos of the color plates will be blank, unless you should want two of them back to back. This sounds a bit awkward, but a clever editor will be able to work it out, I am sure.

I have an alternative suggestion with regard to the color plates, which I think might work out even better. That is, if the color plates were planned as 4-page inserts and wraps, we could include 24 color plates instead of 16. This would mean, for example, that you could have 24 double-spread color plates, inserted in the middle of the signatures. This would again take some planning, but Ben Houston thinks it could be worked out with inserts and wraps, and double-spread inserts would be very effective.

The problem over the color plates comes, of course, because they are so very expensive. It is impractical to print the color plates at the same time as the rest of the book, on the same press, because that would mean that all the parts of the book containing color plates would have to go through the press at least four times. I am not sure how familiar you are with printing, but I hope this is clear.

In sum, I think we are agreed on just about everything except the color plates, and I think we can work out the problem of the color plates with either 16 pages of tips or 24 pages of inserts and wraps. I rather hope you will choose inserts and wraps, since glued tips have a tendency to come loose eventually. In any case, if this seems all right, I'll draw up another contract. I'm sorry you felt that my proposed contract was premature; I always think of a contract as being in draft until it is signed. Sometimes it is easier to talk about a proposed contract if one has a draft in hand.

Obviously the July 1 delivery date is now out of the question, and if you like I would be glad to put January, 1972 as the delivery date in the contract, with the understanding that we would be glad to have the manuscript whenever you have it ready for us. Also, as soon as we have agreed on a contract, we'll make new arrangements with Abadie for her remaining part of the work. I'll look forward to hearing from you. With very best wishes,

Sincerely,
[signed] Herb
Herbert S. Bailey, Jr.

P.S. As I think you know, Lin Peterson is doing the copyediting and is well along in the work. But I suppose she should return the manuscript now for revision. Is that correct?

June 18, 1971

Dear Joe:
Many thanks for your very nice note of June 14 in response to my most recent letter about arrangements for your book. I am glad that the new proposals seem good to you, and I shall look forward to hearing from you when you have had a chance to talk with Miss Abadie. Actually, I will be on leave during July and August, but Carol Orr, whom you probably remember from your visit to Princeton, is thoroughly aware of our discussions, and she can do

whatever is needed. Actually, since you won't be delivering the final manuscript until some time in the fall, it isn't terribly urgent to get the contract signed, so long as we agree on what we are doing. And I think we may as well put January 1 in the contract as a delivery date, and then if you deliver the manuscript sooner, it would be all to the good.

With best wishes for a pleasant summer,
Sincerely,
[signed] Herb
Herbert S. Bailey, Jr.

Below is an in-house memo from Princeton University Press regarding the editing of The Mythic Image.

To: Carol
From: Lin
Subject: Campbell MS
6/29

I edited the first chapter and part of the second, planning to show the first hundred pages to him before going on—but then with the uncertain state of things just held on to the whole.

So—you should mention:

1. That queries accompany the first part of the MS, and that he might want to consider them in revising.
2. An important design problem that should be considered: the regular footnotes will go at the end of the book, because of the extremely complicated layout. But the captions also have footnotes, and I thought of minimizing clutter by placing these in parens at the end of the captions. Say this is tentative, and that other possibilities are two sets of notes at the back (more trouble for the reader than it's worth); or a short bibliography of works cited, so that all refs. in parens

would be very short and inconspicuous (lots of work for him).

3. If either of the first two systems is used, he should know or be reminded that each work will have to be cited in full on first use in <u>both</u> sets of notes—since in most cases the refs. aren't at all coordinated and the reader will reach the full cite in the regular notes <u>after</u> the same work is mentioned in the caption notes, etc.
4. And so say that I would be glad to talk to him about any of this—would save me a great deal of work in the long run. My phone numbers are # here, # home.

---

30 June 1971

Dear Professor Campbell:

The manuscript is on its way to you under separate cover. I hope you will not mind the informality of my enclosing a memo written to me by Lin Peterson, who is the copyeditor of your manuscript. It seems simpler to enclose the memo than to repeat its contents in this letter. Lin is a fine editor, as you will learn, and I am sure you will be pleased with her handling of the manuscript.

As soon as I have heard from you about Herb's suggestions about the color illustrations, I ought to be able to draw up a Memorandum of Agreement for your signature.

Best wishes to you and Miss Abadie,

Sincerely,

[signed] Carol

(Mrs.) Carol Orr

Executive Assistant to the Director

Waverly Place
NYC 10014
July 31, 1971

Dear Mrs. Orr—
I have been going through the MS very carefully, mainly to reach a decision about the pictures, but also to review the editorial suggestions, etc. There are two or three large revisions that have been suggested and an introduction to be written. Miss Peterson's careful editing and questioning has given me a lot to think about, too. Yesterday I had a long conference with Miss Abadie, to go through all of this with her advice and suggestions, and to make sure that we were in agreement on all points.

In your very kind letter of July 14, you ask for an outline of Miss Abadie's responsibilities and an estimate of the approximate amount of time likely to be involved. As we understand our project, her responsibilities will be exactly those that formerly were to have been Mr. Sauerlander's, namely, of designing the book, page by page. Centuries ago, in a large conference at the Bollingen Foundation building here in New York, Mr. Conkwright, Ben Houston, Mr. Sauerlander and I preferred a model for Chapter 1, which was to have been set up in different styles of type, etc. as a test, so that we might reach some decisions about the rest of the volume(s). Nothing ever came of this, and so, the whole question of type, etc., is still rather vague. I should like Miss Abadie to take over now in Mr. Sauerlander's place, and participate in our decisions in these matters. She will be at work with me here, as my advisor and collaborator in the delicate job of relating pictures to texts, page by page. And in addition to all this (in addition, that is to say, to the task that Mr. Sauerlander would have undertaken), she will prepare the captions and front-matter list of illustrations with all the information for which Miss Peterson is asking. This, in other words, is a large and important role to play.

Next week Mrs. Campbell and I are leaving town for a month in the West and Hawaii, and I think it would make sense for the understanding of the Press with Miss Abadie to be worked out during those weeks, so that when I return, Miss Abadie and I may be able to send in our signed agreements together. For my own part, I should not wish (or even be able) to go ahead with the shaping of this book without her, and, before signing and sending in my own contract therefore, I should like to know, quite securely, that I am going to be able to depend upon her support.

In short: her task is to be exactly that which was to have been Mr. Sauerlander's <u>plus</u> that (which she is well prepared to fulfill) of researching and preparing all the front-matter information relating to the pictures.

I hope that this now is clear and that by the time I return (Sept. 6), the Press will have settled matters with her in a manner satisfactory to all, so that the work that has been so long delayed may at last get under weigh [*sic*]. I want very much to be able to finish this job by next spring.

All best, and my thanks for your kind letters.

Sincerely

Joseph Campbell

William McGuire (1917–2009) began his career as a newspaper reporter in his home town of St. Augustine, Florida. In 1948, he accepted an offer from Kurt and Helen Wolff to work as an editor at Pantheon Books. At the time, Pantheon happened to share a cramped walk-up office at 41 Washington Square in New York City with a new publishing organization founded by philanthropists Paul and Mary Mellon, to which they had given the name of "Bollingen." Soon after, McGuire was recruited by the Bollingen group to edit the first titles in the Mellons' ambitious publishing plan, and a few months later he found himself on the subway ride home with the manuscript for Joseph Campbell's Hero with a Thousand Faces *under his arm.*

In 1967, when the Bollingen group found its new home at Princeton University Press, McGuire joined the staff as executive editor of the

Bollingen list, which at that point had as many unpublished projects as published titles. In 1982 he announced his retirement, to take effect that December, following the publication of his history of the Bollingen enterprise, Bollingen: An Adventure in Collecting the Past.

15 September 1971

Dear Joe:
I enclose a memo from our printing estimator, showing the relative cost of printing 16 and 32 color plates, by either of two processes. "C & H" = the Swiss firm of Conzett & Huber, who do high-quality work by letterpress (i.e., regular halftones), but indeterminate shipping costs and time would be involved. The estimate is based on printing one subject to a plate, 2,000 copies. The procedure of tipping in, costing about 64 cents per copy (i.e., book), has been included.

For 16 plates not tipped in but wrapped around text signatures, the cost is about $560 less per 2,000. Using the figures at the bottom of the memo as a base, therefore, it appears that about $12,000 extra would be involved in doing 32 plates, tipped.

I hope this is helpful.
Yours ever,
[signed] Bill
William McGuire

cc: Jack Barrett[1]

September 16, 1971

Dear Joe:
As you already know from Mrs. Orr, I was away from the Press during the summer, and I am only now able to reply to your letter of July 31. I hope that meanwhile you and Mrs. Campbell had a

good trip to the West and to Hawaii, and I suppose you are now very much caught up in the beginning of the fall term. Nevertheless, I hope we can make progress on THE MYTHIC IMAGE, and this letter is intended to push the project along a step or two further.

It seems entirely reasonable to me that Miss Abadie should finish up the frontmatter, especially the material relating to the illustrations with which she is so familiar. I also think that she could help greatly by dummying the volume, and we would like very much to have her do that. At the same time, I don't feel that she should assume the role that Mr. Sauerlander presumably would have assumed if the Bollingen had stayed in New York. We have a design staff here, and we have assigned Mrs. Peterson to the book as staff editor. Consequently I think the design and normal editorial roles should be assumed by our designer and by Mrs. Peterson, and we should not ask Miss Abadie to duplicate that work. As you know, Mrs. Peterson has already gone carefully through the first two chapters, raising questions and pointing out inconsistencies and I would suppose that Miss Abadie could take advantage of that in her preparation of the frontmatter and illustration material in their final form. But when the manuscript is returned, Mrs. Peterson will finish her editorial work.

With respect to the design and layout, I want to correct some statements in your letter of July 31. I do indeed remember vividly your visit to Princeton back in the early days of the transfer of the Bollingen Series, and consultations on typography, layout, and so forth. As a result of those consultations we did page layouts, with samples in various type sizes, and so forth, in the hope that in preparing the volume you would use those layouts, preparing copy to fit. Apparently that has not been the case, and I will immediately add that it doesn't worry me very much, since the main thing is that the book should say what ought to be said. It does, however, mean that we must be absolutely clear on the procedures to be followed in putting the book through.

Our designer will review the original layouts and perhaps make some modifications, and we will give Miss Abadie general instructions for dummying. Mrs. Peterson, as you could tell from her queries, was not always sure where different illustrations should go, since not every one is referred to in the text. Miss Abadie, I am sure, understands this completely, and so the dummying would be easier for her, using a format that we would determine. Thus, after the text with captions, etc., is in final form, it will be set in type, using various sizes for the main text and for the picture and display text. Then, using the galley proof, it would be Miss Abadie's task to do a dummy, scaling the pictures to fit, and pasting up the galleys. The thing that worries me about all this is that you may be tempted to rewrite the text to make it fit with the pictures. I think this should be avoided at all costs, and it should be a clear understanding that, barring a few minor changes, the text and pictures will be fitted together in the format determined. In this process it may be necessary or desirable to discard or add a few pictures, but I think those are details that can be worked out in the actual process.

In short, I have attempted to define more clearly what Miss Abadie is expected to do, and if this is agreeable to you, we will make arrangements with her accordingly. I really believe that this will work out well for everyone concerned.

I shall hope to hear from you soon. Meanwhile, best wishes,

Sincerely,

Herbert S. Bailey, Jr.

Copies: Miss M. J. Abadie, Mrs. Peterson

P.S. This letter was dictated before your letter of September 13 arrived. I am sorry not to have been able to write sooner but I think what I have said above should put us on the right track.

[No date or heading]

Dear Herb:

You will have been relieved and pleased, I am sure, as myself, to learn of additional funding of our project, to the tune of $25,000. Having already reduced the work to be published from two volumes to one, and having received this considerable gift, we shall be able without further ado to carry through with all sails unfurled: 32 color plates, instead of 16; and Miss Abadie to assume the task originally to have been Mr. Sauerlander's. I recall that in that first meeting, some years ago, of Wolf, Sauerlander, Ben Houston. P. J. Conkwright, you and me, there was no sense of any threatened duplication of functions, but rather of cooperation; and I have worked now for two years with the idea in mind that between Miss Abadie and the present personnel of the Press, a like spirit of cooperation would be in play.

I have just had a long conference with Miss Abadie, and she—like you—is particularly concerned that there should be little or no rewriting of texts after the type has been set and the galleys pulled. She has told me, therefore, that if she could be sent samples of the type faces to be used, she would be able to begin, right away, to lay out the entire book to suit the order and placement of the pictures even while Mrs. Peterson's editing of the manuscript is in progress. Any necessary revisions could then be made before the typesetter's work began. This seems to me an excellent suggestion. It would give us a chance to see and to know what we were doing before any big outlays of money would have been ventured, and greatly speed the production of the book.

As we all agreed, back there in the prehistoric period, this book is to be designed chapter by chapter, page by page, not pre-designed and then put together according to a pre-set plan. I have worked on it, all these months and years, with that in view—and that, let me say, is exactly why Mrs. Peterson found if difficult to know just where the various pictures were to go. None of us shall know until the work of designing begins and we see how the pictures look on the pages, how they balance to the text, etc. My aim is a visual book, and for this I require the help and advice of someone close at hand, every step (or rather page) of the way.

And so, now that we have our money, I am returning to you our contract for one more revision, as follows: 1. Miss Abadie is to be our designer, for which she will receive a fee of 12,000; and 2. we are now to have 32 color plates, tipped in.

There are three little tasks to which I must myself attend meanwhile. First, as suggested by your reader, I shall write an Introduction. Next, again as suggested, I shall cut the text of Chapter IV. And finally, there are parts of V that I find I want to revise. This work can be done while Mrs. Peterson is editing and Miss Abadie—as suggested—designing our pages.—O.K.?

I hope you feel, as I do, that we have crossed the last barrier reef and are now, at last, under weigh. Ship ahoy and good cheer.

Sincerely and truly yours
Joseph Campbell

Waverly Place
New York, New York 10014
November 1, 1971

Dear Herb:

Jack Barrett phoned me the other day, to let me know that you had refused the large sum of money that he so kindly and loyally procured for me from the generosity of Mr. Melon [*sic*], to enable us to bring out my book in the manner originally planned. I am going to assume, therefore, that unless I hear from you to the contrary, that this means that you now believe it possible to do this job as I meant to have it done, with the funds already on hand: in one volume now, of course, instead of two, but with 32 color plates tipped in, and Miss Abadie to assume the task originally to have been Mr. Sauerlander's.

[The remainder of this version repeats the preceding letter

(page 264) beginning with the second paragraph: "I have just had a long conference with Miss Abadie."]

November 22, 1971

Dear Joe:

It was good to see you in New York on Thursday. I just wish we had got together last spring, so some of our misunderstandings and difficulties could have been avoided. At any rate, I think we are on the track now. I am enclosing two copies of the agreement, revised to indicate that there will be 32 color illustrations. We shall place these where they need to go in the text, as tips wherever necessary, though I hope that when we put the book together you will keep it in mind to use wraps or inserts if it appears to be possible.

We are writing separately to Miss Abadie to make arrangements for her to do the layout, and I don't anticipate any difficulty about that. However I realize that you may not want to sign the agreement until we can inform you that definite arrangements have been made with Miss Abadie.

We'll be in touch with you again soon. Meanwhile I want to say again that I think our meeting was productive, and we are looking forward to working with you on the book.

With best wishes,
Sincerely
[signed] Herb
Herbert S. Bailey, Jr.

Copy: Mr. John Barrett

December 7, 1971

Dear Mr. Campbell—

Well, here it is: THE END. It gave me enormous pleasure to tuck those pictures away in the safe deposit box. I think in some way

I needed to protect that material—let a psychologist make of that what he might—and I am glad you didn't think I was crazy!

Your magnificent letter to H. B. came today. I'll bet that really spoiled his serve! The analogy to the typist's rate was nothing short of brilliant. I stand in awe and admiration, as usual.

Here's an amusing note: after finishing up the billing, I reconciled it with the estimate I had made for them in March—the one Carol Orr never acknowledged. My projections for work then undone amounted to a minimum of 350 hours, or $1,565. After subtracting the hours for work not included in the estimate (such as work on the line drawings, the trip to PUP, etc.) total billed was $1,547. Even Herb Bailey's unimaginative soul should appreciate the finesse in that!

I am sending this Special Delivery, with postage for Special Delivery to PUP also, as I want them to pay me before the end of 1971 for income tax purposes. I've enclosed a note to Carol to that effect.

With love and thanks for the superlative letter to Herb,
MJ [Abadie]

P.S. Note 3 invoices plus one expenses to sign.

December 13, 1971

Dear Joe:
I think I have agreed to pretty much what you asked for in the book itself, including all 32 pages of color illustrations, tipped if necessary, and it will be an enormous and expensive book, with its 400 illustrations plus a complex arrangement of text.

It seems to me that the putting together of the book is really the publisher's job, and although we want to put it together according to your conception of the plan, we must be the ones to control that and to arrange for it to be done. Miss Abadie, if she takes the job, will report to Mr. Conkwright, who will be the designer in control.

As I told you in New York, I am not willing to turn the design responsibility over to Miss Abadie, nor am I willing to pay what I regard as a completely outlandish fee of $12,000 for the work. We have offered Miss Abadie $5.50 an hour, which on a full-time basis would be approximately $11,000 a year, so I can hardly think it is an inadequate offer. It is possible that her working from the manuscript will make a substantial saving in the typesetting, but I have serious doubts as to whether that will actually work well, or whether there will actually be a saving. We have agreed to have her do Chapter 3 from the manuscript, and we will then set it up and see how it goes—but we have our doubts. I am more inclined to believe that we will have to set the book in type and then dummy it in the normal way.

I am glad you raised the question whether a flat fee would not be better, since it is hard to tell how much time will be required. I will meet you part way by agreeing to offer a flat fee of $8,000, to be paid in parts as the work is completed. I think this is reasonable and even generous. In fact, if Miss Abadie were unwilling to do the job for this fee, I do not think she should be engaged.

It should be pointed out that the book is estimated to make 200 pages of printed text plus 417 black and white illustrations, or a total of between 400 and 500 pages, which makes 200 to 250 double-spread layouts. Thus a fee of $8,000 would mean $32 to $40 per layout, considerably more than we have ever paid for this kind of work. Since there are so many pictures, they will have to be scaled to go with the 200-page text, which means that they must average something like ½ page each, and an average layout will include two pictures, or one per page. We shall expect Miss Abadie to work along those lines.

If Miss Abadie does not want to do the book, I think that Mrs. Peterson and Mr. Conkwright, working together here, could do it very well. We would not be able to work as closely with you as Miss Abadie apparently will, but I am quite confident that we could produce an exceedingly fine result. P. J. is away right now, and I am not really sure that he would be willing to do the detailed layout, but if it were necessary we could find someone else here to do the layout under his supervision.

I am reluctant to propose it, but one possible alternative occurs to me, and I am suggesting it only against the possibility that Miss Abadie will refuse the $8,000 fee. At one point you agreed to the proposal for 24 color illustrations. Increasing the number to 32 added something like the additional cost asked for Miss Abadie's fee. If you want to go back to 24, I shall simply transfer the money in the budget, and Miss Abadie can go ahead on the $12,000 flat fee basis. I am suggesting this, even though I don't think it is really the right thing to do. It is a possibility, however.

In short, having met virtually all your requests regarding the book itself, I think you ought to leave the arrangements for the production of the book to us, within the general conception of a picture-text arrangement.

Since you raised the question earlier with Jack Barrett, I am sending him a copy of this letter. I think this is clearly a question of our management of the program, not a question like that of the number of color plates. I am sorry to have to be so unyielding, but unless we manage such matters we are not managing the program.

Sincerely,
[signed] Herb
Herbert S. Bailey, Jr.

Copy: Mr. John Barrett

Following is an excerpt from an interview with M. J. Abadie in Larsen and Larsen, A Fire in the Mind, *481.*

Herb Bailey offered to pay me six dollars an hour for the design work. I looked at him as if he'd gone off his rocker and said I couldn't consider it. He said, "Miss Abadie, we aren't obligated to publish this book."

"Mr. Bailey," I said, "that is a matter you should be discussing with Professor Campbell."

When I returned to New York, I called Joe and told him what had transpired. A couple of days later I got a copy of the letter he wrote—two pages that would blister the paint off the walls. It said in no uncertain terms that if PUP could not "pay Miss Abadie properly," he would as of then forfeit publication of the book. I was so touched I was flooded with tears, and I called to thank him for his defense of my worth.

Miss M. J. Abadie
East 70th Street
New York, New York 10021
December 30, 1971

Dear Miss Abadie
This is a revision of my letter of December 7 on our plans for the design and layout of Joseph Campbell's THE MYTHIC IMAGE. I think we, you, and Professor Campbell are now basically in agreement about how we should proceed with the design and production of the book to achieve an effective "visual presentation," and I would like now to confirm our arrangements with you.

Collaborating with Professor Campbell, Mrs. Peterson (the editor), and Mr. Conkwright (the designer), and working with the text manuscript and illustrations, you will lay out one chapter at a time according to the general format we discussed in our meeting of December 2, 1971. Beginning with Chapter 3, you will submit each layout to the Press for approval. This approach to Chapter 3 is a trial, to see whether it is possible to lay out the book accurately enough from the manuscript. We hope that this will be the case. If not, we shall have to adopt another approach.

We agree to pay you a total fee of $8,000 for the complete work, including layout from the manuscript (if that proves possible) and/or dummying the proofs and sizing the illustrations exactly in final form. We shall pay an advance of $1,000 on the countersigning of this letter and then $1,000 per month until a total of $6,000 has been paid. A final payment of $2,000 will be made when the final dummy is turned in so that the book can go to press.

You are acting under this agreement as an independent contractor and not as an employee of Princeton University Press. The work produced by you under this arrangement will be the property of the Press, which shall be the sole owner and proprietor thereof, with the exclusive right to take copyright thereon in its own name or the name of its designee.

The Press shall have the right to assign this agreement and its rights and privileges in whole or in part. Either party may terminate this agreement by giving the other party at least thirty days' written notice.

If this arrangement is satisfactory to you, please indicate your agreement by signing and returning to us the enclosed carbon copy of this letter.

Sincerely yours,
Herbert S. Bailey Jr.
Director

January 4, 1972

Dear Joe:

You are absolutely right on the two points in our contract, and I am embarrassed that I didn't notice them earlier, when I corrected the number of color plates. Paragraph 15 should have been deleted, and in fact we delete it more often than not nowadays. And of course the proposed delivery date has already passed by. I'm enclosing two copies of the revised contract, in which I have inserted July 1, 1973 as a delivery date. That is still a year and a half away, which should allow plenty of time. Actually I suppose the revised manuscript will be in long before that, and I would even hope that we can publish the book in early fall 1973. But it is a big complicated book, and that is cutting it pretty fine. At any rate I am glad that work is going ahead now, and I hope it will all go smoothly.

With best wishes for the New Year,

Sincerely,

[signed] Herb

Herbert S. Bailey, Jr.

January 28, 1974

Dear Joe:

Many thanks for your generous note about M. J. Abadie. I certainly understand and sympathize with your desire to give her credit for the extraordinary amount of help she provided. I remember discussing with someone, perhaps Carol, the question whether M. J. should be listed as "designer" on the title page, and I said that (as is true) that this is against our policy and I did not think it was appropriate, partly because the word "designer" is not exactly descriptive. Normally a design is acknowledged either on the copyright page or in a colophon at the end of the book. Also, in this case, a lot of the basic design was done by P. J., and from the Press' point of view he has supervised it, though she has done an enormous amount on the layout. In short, it is not a "pure" situation. Moreover, M. J. has really done a great deal of editorial work, though Press editors have been assigned to the book, and so to acknowledge her simply as "designer" doesn't fully take account of what she did.

Accordingly, may I suggest that the title page read "by Joseph Campbell" (in large type) to be followed in somewhat smaller type by "with the editorial and visual assistance of M. J. Abadie." Or if you like, simply, "with the assistance of M. J. Abadie." I like the first formulation better, or perhaps you will want to provide different wording. Anyway, I am in favor of giving M. J. proper credit on the title page, and I'm glad that you want to do it. It seems to me that the title page is primarily for the title and author (with the publisher at the bottom so people will know where to order). But

I do agree that this book is "special," and so will the suggestion above suffice?

With very best wishes,
Sincerely,
[signed] Herb
Herbert S. Bailey, Jr.

The following appears to be addressed to Carol Orr, executive assistant to the director at Princeton University Press.

Joseph Campbell
Waverly Place
New York, N.Y. 10014
Feb. 15, 1975

Dear Carol:
I've spent the weekend reading, and for the first time experiencing, page by page, with picture and text, the whole of our production, for the most part greatly pleased, but happening every now and then upon mistakes that will have to be corrected in the second printing, if we have one. Of my findings the list is enclosed.

The most important (and unfortunately, conspicuous) mishap is that of page 396, where twenty-two words, quite critical, have dropped out. How I, or anyone else, could have missed this in the proofs, I can't imagine; but here it is. And it was the first thing I hit upon when I opened the book for the first time. Rather a jolt!

But I suppose that in a work of this kind, with all its complicated matchings of this to that and that to this, twenty-odd slip-ups are not too terrible. In any case, they do not wipe out, by any means, the glory of the book; nor my appreciation of all that was done to bring about the realization of my project. My thanks, once again, to you and to all.

Cordially
[Joseph Campbell]

The Mythic Image—Errata

Page xi, line 8 from bottom: IV should be V

Pages 109 / 114: last line of page 109 reappears as first page of 114

Page 116: last margin note, cf. Figs. 123ff. should be cf. Fig. 123

Page 119: caption to Fig. 105, second line, should read:

> A.D. 13th century Java. Reverse of a

Page 140: Fig. 122: The Sanskrit captions have been cropped from the picture; my translations of them are consequently superfluous. My text should now read as follows:

> The style is of the popular 19th century mass-produced Anglo-Indian colored prints. Below are Vishnu and Lakshmi on the cosmic serpent Ananta. Four-headed Brahma, above, the lotus of Vishnu's dream, holds in one hand a lustral spoon and in the others books of the Veda.

Page 148: supply for the second line a marginal reference: cf. Fig. 330

Page 149: footnote missing under column 1: *Above, p. 142

Page 152/153: details of pictures are invisible

Page 166, bottom line, column 2, of picture caption:

Figures 111–112 should be Figures 116–117

Page 167: second line from bottom should read:

> ceasingly revolves. Above, Quetzalcoatl is seen ...etc.

marginal note, Fig. 148, should be brought down to match this line

Pages 168/171: if possible, text of p. 171 should be transferred to conclude that of page 168;

Caption of Fig. 151 should then appear below, not above, picture.

Page 175: fig. 155, details are not clear

Page 176: second marginal note, Fig. 157, should be moved down one line, to start of paragraph

Page 199: details of Fig. 187 are invisible

last line of page, column two, should read:

> Olmec jaguar-man of Figure 102

Page 200: fifteenth line from bottom, (8) should be (7)

following this numerative line, another should be added, as follows:

> man holding a bird eating a grape (8)

seventh line from bottom, (11) should be (3)

Page 204: Opposite, the curtains of the sanctuary, etc. should be:

> Above Helios, the curtains of the sanctuary part…

The marginal note, Fig. 191, should be moved up, to line 3 of text

Page 207: marginal note, cf. Fig. 151, should be cf. Fig. 150

Page 209: Figure 195: Pharaoh's form invisible

Page 388, column two, lines 2 and 3:

Figures 161, 173, and 174; also 244 and 245 should be

Figures 102, 175 and 187, 253, 256, and 258

Page 389: Figure 353: lower part very dark, forms not clear

Page 396: line six from bottom—twenty-two words omitted between endures & only!

text should read as follows:

> endures for a long time. But in those who have led an evil life and in those of unsound nerves, this state endures *only*…etc.

Page 400, caption to Figure 358, fourth line: round should be rounds

Page 404: caption to Figure 361:

> Chakra-Samvaraja should be Chakra-Samvararaja

Page 408: line ten from bottom: Figure 362 should be Figure 358

Page 429: add marginal note to match line 14 of column two: Figs. 277, 278

Pages 439/441: the type styles for the dates (Sept. 1 and Sept. 2) do not match

Page 469: caption to Figure 405: omit Greece

Page 504: note 60, line 6: Mexica should be Mexico

The following letter was written by Rudolf Ritsema (1918–2006), who served as director of the Eranos Foundation for more than thirty years.

Casa Eranos
CH-6612 ASCONA Switzerland

March 28, 1975

Mr. William McGuire
Princeton University Press
Princeton, N.J. 08540
USA

Dear Mr. McGuire:
I have just received the beautiful book by Joseph Campbell THE MYTHIC IMAGE. Our warmest thanks for this splendid present. Let me congratulate you upon this monumental publication. I opened the book on page 338 and was struck by the Serpent Stone with the inscription Genio Huius Loci. This has certainly been one of the sources of inspirations for the stone in the ERANOS GARDEN that bears C. G. Jung's and Gerardus van der Leeuw's inscription Genio Loci Ignoto. I had forgotten all about Leisegang's article in ERANOS 1939, where it is mentioned. Probably I read the article before I knew about the ERANOS STONE. We shall display the book at this year's Tagung.

Yours sincerely,
Rudolf Ritsema

Joseph Mitsuo Kitagawa (March 8, 1915–October 7, 1992) was a Japanese American scholar of religious studies. Considered one of the founders of the field of the history of religions, he would later serve as an editor of the first edition of The Encyclopedia of Religion *(1987).*

The University of Chicago
Chicago 37 Illinois
The Divinity School
Office of the Dean

April 1, 1975

Professor Joseph Campbell
The American Society for the Study of Religions[2]
Waverly Place
New York, New York 10014

Dear Joe:
Thank you for the magnificent book The Mythic Image. It is indeed a work of art. I am particularly interested that the picture of the great Sun Buddha is displayed so prominently in the book.

See you in Toronto soon. All the best to Jean.

Sincerely yours,
Joseph M. Kitagawa
Dean

Aniela Jaffé (1903–1991) was a Swiss analyst who worked with C. G. Jung, editing his book Memories, Dreams, Reflections. *"Bill" in the following letter is, naturally, William McGuire, who had published the English edition.*

25.3. 1975

Dear Bill,
Thanks a lot for the exciting book by Campbell—I enjoy it!
Ever,
Aniela [Jaffé]

David Miller (born 1936) is the Watson-Ledden Professor of Religion, Emeritus, at Syracuse University. Miller is the author of many books exploring the intersection of mythology and religion, including Gods and Games: Toward a Theology of Play *(1970),* The New Polytheism: Rebirth of the Gods and Goddesses *(1974), and* Christs: Meditations on Archetypal Images in Christian Theology *(1981). He served as a board member of Joseph Campbell Foundation (2004–2015).*

Syracuse University
Department of Religion
H.B. Crouse Hall
Syracuse, New York 13210

Feb. 25

Dear Joe—
I have just received The Mythic Image. Congratulations on this most fantastic work! What an appropriate way to climax the Bollingen Series! Luxuria befitting the Hare of Aphrodite and textual insight worthy of the White Raven of Apollo. Lovely and Brilliant—
Thank you for another fine labor—
David [Miller]

March 13, 1975

Dear Joe,
I understand from Carol that your schedule is free on April 15, and so we have set that date for the publication party for THE

MYTHIC IMAGE. It will be a private celebration, a dinner party at the Algonquin, and we are inviting people who had something to do with the book. The list of invited guests is enclosed. I have left M. J. Abadie off the list only because I know that she will not be in the country. Incidentally, I have checked the date also with Jack Barrett and Vaun Gillmor; since the book is dedicated to them, they certainly ought to be at the party! The party is to include spouses, and I hope very much that Mrs. Campbell can come with you. We won't have any elaborate ceremonies, but I think it would be nice if you would be prepared to say something about the history of the book, the Bollingen Foundation, Jack and Vaun, or whatever seems appropriate to you.

The party will be in a private room at the Algonquin Hotel on 44th Street, beginning with cocktails at 6:30 p.m. I shall be looking forward to seeing you there. Meanwhile, best wishes,

Sincerely,
[signed] Herb
Herbert S. Bailey, Jr.

P.S. The party is definitely not a publicity affair; our Marketing Department wants to plan some special publicity activities, probably on the same day, but separate from the party. Abbot Friedland and Dan Harvey will be in touch with you about that.

April 15, 6:30 p.m., Algonquin

Mr. and Mrs. Joseph Campbell
Mr. and Mrs. Paul Mellon
Mr. and Mrs. Stoddard Stevens
Mr. and Mrs. Donald Osborn
Mr. and Mrs. David Johnson (Polychrome)
Mr. John D. Barrett
Miss Vaun Gillmor

PUP Staff

Mr. and Mrs. Bailey
Mr. and Mrs. McGuire
Mr. and Mrs. Conkwright
Mr. and Mrs. Becker
Miss Miriam Brokaw
Ms. Carol Orr
Mr. and Mrs. Evenchik
Mr. Abbot Friedland
Mr. Dan Harvey
Miss Jan Lilly

January 28, 1981

Dear Mr. Campbell:
I am pleased to inform you that we have finally decided to issue a paperback edition of THE MYTHIC IMAGE and plan to have finished copies available in late October or early November of 1981. We plan to have an initial printing of 5,000 copies, and the list price will be $15. As you know, we have been making plans for a paperback for some time now, and have decided that the only way we can issue a paperback is to convert all of the color illustrations to black and white and to reduce the trim size to 5⅛ x 9¼. Maintaining all the color for a paperback edition is not financially possible. For the paperback edition, we will pay royalties on the following scale: 5% of the list price on the first 10,000 copies sold and 7½% thereafter. One half of the stipulated percentage will be applied to sales outside the continental limits of the United States. On sales at special discounts of 50% or more from the list price, the regular domestic royalty will be calculated on the net amount received by us.

These terms are included in our original contract with you for the publication of the cloth edition. In many cases, we will use the original photograph, and in cases where the color illustrations cannot be converted adequately to black and white, we will make every attempt to locate a black and white photograph. We will pay permissions and fees in those cases. Another matter, since it is apparent that we cannot issue a paperback reprint in full color, it is also apparent that we cannot reprint the full color cloth edition. We have approximately a six-month supply of the cloth edition and a few copies of the deluxe edition. We will not be issuing a cloth edition of the black and white paperback, for it is Mr. Bailey's opinion that the color cloth edition should be remembered as a major achievement in hardcover book-making.

I am enclosing a form requesting information that will help us in the promotion and production of the paperback edition. Please return the form to me at an early convenience. If you have any questions or comments, please call me as soon as possible. We will need your help in this rather complicated and extensive project.

Sincerely
Loren Hoekzema
Reprints & Paperbacks Manager
(#)

JOSEPH CAMPBELL
WAVERLY PLACE
NEW YORK, NEW YORK 10014
Feb. 7, 1981

Dear Mr. Hoekzeme [*sic*]:

I don't know why you had to add insult to injury enclosing your form, Information for Sales Promotion, to the letter telling me of Mr. Bailey's intentions to scrap The Mythic Image. The Princeton University Press has already published thirteen works over my signature. (Or rather, it did have thirteen before Mr. Bailey began disregarding his understanding with the Bollingen Foundation by letting some of the volumes that we committed to his charge go out of print before their time—for instance, Heinrich Zimmer, The Art of Indian Asia, 2 vols., edited and completed by Joseph Campbell, which is still the best and most useful introduction to Indian art in English.)

The idea of a 5⅛ x 9¼ black-and-white parody of my book is ridiculous. And why should it be apparent to me that Princeton University Press cannot reprint the full color cloth edition before dismembering that "major achievement in hardcover book making" (as you called it)?

In re: the color plates by the way. Not a few were made especially for The Mythic Image and no black-and-white counterparts exist. The originals of others were mislaid at the Press and cannot be found. More were returned to the good people who had kindly supplied them. Please do not now start writing to me for help in these matters. I gave eight years of my life to the fashioning of that book and cannot now go to work to reconstruct it in miniature black-and-white.—And as for Information for Sales Promotion: you might ask someone to read the reviews and jackets of my books already published.

Sincerely,
Joseph Campbell

February 11, 1981

Dear Joe

Loren Hoekzema has shown me your letter of February 7 with regard to our plan to do a paperback of THE MYTHIC IMAGE, and I am naturally very disturbed at your reaction. Perhaps it will help if I explain further.

We would also like to reprint THE MYTHIC IMAGE in its present form and have studied the matter very seriously, but the very great increases in printing prices since the book was originally published, taken together with its unusually complex format, along with the regrettable fact of its greatly reduced rate of sale, make that prohibitive. Apparently you feel that we have an obligation to keep Bollingen books in print forever, regardless of cost, but I must say here that that is a mistaken idea. I believe that we have acted responsibly with respect to the Bollingen Series and have even enhanced it in various ways, including especially the development of the Bollingen paperbacks, and I am quite sure that Paul Mellon would agree. I am proud of the way that we have pushed the Bollingen program forward in the past thirteen years, and we have increased the distribution of Bollingen books far beyond anything that was ever achieved under Pantheon. The availability of the Bollingen fund has made it possible to do all this, but I do not believe that a responsible administration of that fund includes keeping books in print regardless of cost.

On the other hand, we are anxious not to let THE MYTHIC IMAGE go out of print. For that reason we considered a number of alternatives, finally deciding that the best choice would be to issue a black-and-white paperback edition in a 6⅛ x 9¼ format. (I am sorry that there was a typographical error with respect to the trim size in Mr. Hoekzema's letter). We feel that such a paperback edition is desirable for several reasons. In the first place, it would make it possible for many people who could not afford the large hardbound edition to purchase the book for their personal libraries. Secondly, we chose the black-and-white edition in a smaller format rather than the size of the original hardback in order to avoid making the reprint look like a second-rate reissue of the original book; for the same reason we decided not to do the paperback with a hardback overrun, even though some libraries would undoubtedly like to have such an edition. This project is very much like our paperback reissue of Malraux's THE VOICES OF SILENCE, in which the color illustrations of the hardback were converted to black-and-white for the paperback, and which has been a highly praised and widely distributed book. Consequently we feel that the proposal to issue a paperback of THE MYTHIC IMAGE is a step forward rather than backward, and we hope that on further thought you will agree, regrettable though it is that we will not be keeping the original hardback in print.

We shall not have to trouble you about photographs or anything else with respect to the production of the paperback edition. Also, unless you wish to do so, there is no need to return the "Information for Promotion" form; we sent that to you only to get updated information. Obviously we have earlier biographical information and plenty of fine reviews.

Nevertheless we would not want to issue a black-and-white paperback edition without your approval. The choice, however, is to do a black-and-white paperback edition or none at all. Consequently I hope that you will, however reluctantly go along with us in our proposal to keep THE MYTHIC IMAGE in print in paperback, if not in hardback, and I shall look forward to hearing from you about this. We want to begin production quickly in order to avoid a hiatus between the time when the hardback edition is no longer available and the publication of the paperback edition. We also need a quick decision in order to get the book into our fall catalogue. I therefore hope that you will let me know at least by March 1 whether you agree to go ahead along this line.

I shall look forward to hearing from you, and I even hope that when a paperback edition is issued that you will be pleased with it.

With very best wishes,

Sincerely

[signed] Herb

Herbert S. Bailey, Jr.

February 15, 1980

Dear Mr. Campbell:

I am responding to your letter to me of February 8, which in turn was a response to my letter of February 4.

Your recollection that you never received one cent of royalties from either of the two Spanish translations of HERO OF A

THOUSAND FACES, or from the French and German translations as well is, I'm afraid, totally inaccurate.

Our records indicate that we paid you a total of $2,042.87 for the Spanish translation (100% of the royalty); $1,464.42 for the French translation (85% of the royalty); and $575.00 for the German translation (86% of the royalty). In addition, we paid you the sum of $920.12 for the British edition brought out by Sphere. Details on these payments are appended to this letter.

It is true that for many years payments were not forthcoming from the Spanish translation. After extensive correspondence in 1971—which was helped considerably, I think, by a personal contact I had at Fondo De Cultura Economica—we finally collected the amounts owed on the Spanish translation. Further correspondence with Fondo then led, either directly or indirectly, to their bringing out a new edition. Copies of this correspondence are enclosed wherewith.

I don't blame you for forgetting all this, particularly since you were conditioned over so many years to not receiving the Spanish royalties. I trust this clears matters up, and explains why I instructed Fondo De Cultura Economica to pay you directly for any royalties owing to you for HERO OF A THOUSAND FACES.

Sincerely yours,
William C. Becker
Associate Director and Controller

P.S. I might add that I do recall writing to you back in 1971 informing you of the breakthrough on the Spanish translation. I probably wrote to you when the check was transmitted to you. I also recall receiving a reply from you. Ironically, I can find all of the correspondence on this subject, except those two letters.

Pratt Institute is a private, nonsectarian, nonprofit institution of higher learning located in the Clinton Hill neighborhood of Brooklyn, New York, United States, with a satellite campus located on 14th

Street in Manhattan. It originated in 1887 with programs primarily in engineering, architecture, and fine arts. Princeton Review *recognizes Pratt as one of the best colleges in the Northeast, placing it among the top 25 percent of all four-year colleges and universities in the United States. In 1976 Pratt awarded Campbell an honorary doctorate. Below is a collection of endorsements he received for the award.*

Joseph Campbell receiving his honorary doctorate from Pratt Institute, 1977

Written to Ms. Marion Lillard
Croton Ave.
Hastings-on-Hudson
New York, 10706

1. Conrad Hyers, Associate Professor of Comparative Mythology and History of Religions
   Beloit College, Wisconsin
   March 26, 1975

"As a scholar of literature and comparative mythology Professor Campbell is so well-known and respected that it hardly seems necessary to emphasize his professional stature and merits. His Hero With a Thousand Faces and his four-volume Masks of God are in themselves enough for a place in the sun." He then goes on to pay tribute to the ten years Campbell devoted to the editing and publication of Heinrich Zimmer's posthumous papers, during "a potentially very productive period of his life."

2. Michael Murphy, Chairman of the Board, Center for Theoretical Studies, Esalen Institute, March 28, 1975

"Mr. Campbell is, as you probably know, one of the two or three most authoritative people in the world today in the fields of comparative mythology and the history of mythology. His Hero With a Thousand Faces and The Masks of God are modern classics of comparative world mythology. They give us a magnificent comprehensive view of the evolution of myth and are the best systematic works of their kind. There are fertile connections in his work with other fields of inquiry, such as the study of symbol and archetype in dreaming, art, shamanism and schizophrenic experience." He concludes by saying that "he is the only person in the twelve year history of Esalen Institute who has brought the entire audience to their feet for a standing ovation after every talk he has given. Other speakers—and there have been some great ones—have aroused such enthusiasm upon occasion, but with Mr. Campbell it happens every time." The others Murphy refers to include such luminaries as Aldous Huxley, Gregory Bateson, and Alan Watts.

3. Ted Spivey, Professor of English, Georgia State University, Atlanta, March 26, 1975

Professor Campbell is, quite simply, the greatest living mythologist and has been so recognized by authorities all over the world [....] In The Hero With a Thousand Faces Professor Campbell has written the finest book of its kind relating depth psychology to the work of modern mythologists and to the great myths of many cultures. In his four-volume work entitled The Masks of God Professor Campbell has created a systematic survey of the world's mythology that is the greatest work of its kind since Sir James Frazer's Golden Bough. The Masks of God is one of the very few scholarly works by an American in any discipline which can be discussed seriously in connection with a work like The Golden Bough." He concludes by saying that Campbell "has had a powerful effect on scholars, creative thinkers, and artists all over the world. I know that this is a continuing effort and that it will be important in helping to shape a new age of creative endeavor in the arts and humanities." [Echoing Paglia's concerns]

4. R. Panikkar, Professor of Religious Studies, The University of California at Santa Barbara, April 3, 1975

"When a man has reached 70 there is no doubt whether what shines is pure or false gold; when a mortal has passed the test of time, there is no hesitating in affirming that he is authentic. Joseph Campbell was not considered a scholar by those who had a narrow idea of scholarship. Today the harmonious blend between the Man and his Work proves that he is one of the few whose knowledge is life and he is recognized as a real Master."

5. John D. Barrett, President of the Bollingen Foundation (1949–1969)

"A distinguished writer, an accomplished lecturer in the modern academic work—both here in this country as well as in the more rarefied atmosphere of European cultural centers."

6. Claude W. Faulkner, Professor of English, University of Arkansas, April 5, 1975

"The English Department at the University of Arkansas has an extensive program of visiting lecturers, and we have been fortunate to have had many nationally and internationally known scholars on our campus. Of all these outstanding men, Joseph Campbell was by far the most stimulating and enjoyable. In fact, he is the only person whom we have invited to appear more than once in our series."

7. Adda Bozeman, Professor of International Relations, Sarah Lawrence College, April 7, 1975

Notes that "from 1956 to 1973 [Campbell] was a lecturer at the Foreign Service Institute, U.S. Department of State, where he received a special award for his contribution to the nation's cause," and concludes that The Masks of God have "received general critical acclaim in the world as the first comprehensive history of mythology written in our time. Mr. Campbell's contributions to the field of comparative world mythology are of the highest, indeed of unequaled significance."

8. O. W. Markley, Ph.D, Project Director, Center for the Study of Social Policy, Stanford Research Institute

"When we here at SRI undertook the very difficult task of trying to discern the societal implications of changing images of man (a recent major research effort), we found that of all the anthropologists and mythologists that have tried to deal with these issues, it was Professor Campbell's work that stood out head and shoulders above the rest[....] I believe that Joseph Campbell is one of the more important intellectual figures of our time, and <u>the</u> most important in his own chosen field of work."

9. Stanley Hopper, Department of Religion, Syracuse University, April 2, 1975

"Joseph Campbell is perhaps the foremost mythologist writing in our time. He has achieved this primacy not only through indefatigable research, a keen critical intelligence and an impressive creative elan, but through his mastery of the several fields essential to competence in the mythological field: namely, anthropology, depth psychology, literature, philosophy, and the religions. His mastery of the methodologies and data of these several fields is not impressive merely on its own account; but it provides that manifold of critical perspectives essential to any adequate interpretation of culture at the present time. With critical equipment of this kind, Joseph Campbell has written with courage and imagination, and with an independence of mind and judgment that is the watermark of greatness in any field."

10. Lynne Kaufman, Program Coordinator, Arts and Humanities, The University of California at Berkeley, Extension Center

"University of California Extension has had the honor of presenting an annual lecture program with Joseph Campbell for the past four years. Each of the programs has been a special blend of scholarship, unique insight into the major themes of human life, and artful and articulate delivery."

11. Jean Houston, Ph.D., Director, The Foundation for Mind Research, March 25, 1975

"There is so much one can say about this extraordinary man. In a time of so much international dissension and fragmentation, he has done more than anyone I can think of to reveal the psychodynamic threads which suggest deep and abiding unities within the human condition. In a time when too many scholars have opted for facile generalizations and shallow perspectives, he has probed and presented in his luminous books the complexity and the profound implications of the psycho-cultural weave. It is my deepest conviction that Joseph Campbell is more than scholar, more than teacher, more than Renaissance man. He is one of our great national resources."

12. Joseph M. Kitagawa, Dean, The Divinity School, University of Chicago, July 31, 1974

"Professor Campbell is a unique scholar-teacher in American academia. Early in his life he made up his mind not to be a bookish scholar, but rather an effective teacher for undergraduate college. Thus even though he was very well trained in Sanskrit and

Indology both here and in Germany, and had done extensive field research in India, he applied his knowledge primarily for undergraduate teaching on the one hand and the edification of intelligent lay people through his publications on the other[....] I have met Professor Campbell a number of times at international conferences both here, in Europe and in Asia. I can testify that he is highly respected by scholars in the Field of Comparative Mythology and Religion throughout the world. For me personally, it gives me a great deal of pleasure because Professor Campbell succeeded me two years ago as the President of the American Society for the Study of Religions, a group of leading scholars in the field of History and Phenomenology of Religion.

13. Jacques Barzun, Columbia University

"Joseph Campbell is without question the leading American interpreter of myth in its relation to literature and religion. Scholarly but not system-ridden, his works have opened the minds of many critics to the legitimate use of mythic analysis for understanding the great works of the past and present, as well as artistic activity itself[....] What is more remarkable still, his own writing is free of jargon, lucid and strong, and as worthy of being called literature as any critical and expository prose since Sir James Frazer himself."

14. Ira Progoff, Director, Dialogue House Associates, March 19, 1975

"It is a great pleasure to recommend Joseph Campbell for an honorary doctorate degree. He has conducted pioneer studies in the areas of myth, symbolism and literature which have opened major new areas of investigation. His writings over a period of four decades have been distinguished by their scholarly competence and their creative imagination. While his main researches were conducted during a period when the importance of inner experience was not highly valued, his writings have become a significant resource for the spiritual and artistic searching of the present day.

His books are certain to have a seminal and inspiring effect in the generations to come."

15. Stephen Larsen, Ph.D., Psychology Department, Ulster County Community College, March 21, 1975

"The field of mythology is a vast labyrinth of symbolism, which because of its complexity, has lent itself to a variety of interpretations. There are few men who have mastered the almost inexhaustible detail necessary to create a meaningful and coherent overview of myth. Anthropologists, literary scholars, psychologists each have a vested academic interest, pertaining to their several disciplines. As often as not this segregation leads to a partial view of things, relevant only to a specialized audience. Joseph Campbell's work, on the other hand, seems to me of a more universal scope; offering to both the specialist and the general reader an access to the world of mythology that is at once scholarly and fascinating; highly structured, yet open to the mystery dimension that is at the core of myth[....] His collected work functions as a resource for creative artists, psychologists and anthropologists, historians of religion."

16. Robert L. Payton, Office of the President, Hofstra University, March 25, 1975

"Joseph Campbell is a person of great accomplishment, in our eyes, and we were proud to include him in 1973 among the first Distinguished Scholars to receive the Faculty Medal from Hofstra."

17. Eugene C. Kennedy, Professor of Psychology, Loyola University of Chicago, March 26, 1975

"I can think of no scholar more worthy of an honorary degree than Joseph Campbell. His work in mythology has earned him an international reputation of the highest order. It would be difficult, it seems to me, to overestimate the contributions which Joseph Campbell has made to our understanding of ourselves through his careful and thorough unraveling of the mythic language spoken across the world and throughout history. He has illuminated the arts, literature, and theology through his quite remarkable achievements. His books are an example of scholarship at its humane best."

18. Harold Taylor, United States Committee for the United Nations University, March 21, 1975

"I am writing to say in the strongest terms I can find that Joseph Campbell is one of the cherished few in the entire field of scholarship who should be given all honors, praises and forms of tangible recognition for his lifelong work as a scholar, teacher and source of creative energy in the field of literature and mythology. I have known Joseph Campbell for 30 years as a colleague and dear friend and can speak from first hand experience of his extraordinary gift as a teacher of the young and of whomever has had the advantage of coming into his presence[....] It can also be said that Joseph Campbell's approach to the study of myth, literature, cultural history and the arts is one which takes full account of the relation between the creative artist and the fundamental ideas which artists in every field have struggled to express. He writes with the insight of a poet and the language of an artist and puts life into every idea he touches."

19. William E. Paden, Chairman, Department of Religion, The University of Vermont, March 24, 1975

"It is a pleasure and privilege to write in recommendation of the achievements of Joseph Campbell, who is so clearly one of the most important men in his field and in his culture. As a writer Campbell was able to overcome the provincialism of traditional guidelines on the subject and opened up the world of myth and symbol along truly cross-disciplinary lines. In doing this he has brought the humanistic and global nature of the subject 'home' to moderns. He has accomplished this in a way that is free of pedanticism on the one hand, and of mindless, naïve romanticism on the other[....] In saying that his writings have been important for our culture I mean that they constitute part of the process of deliverance from our own restraints and of re-orientation to the larger human community. His works help Westerners to recognize their roots in the world of symbols and to understand the relationships of East and West, literature and myth, past and present. He invested his energies in building up a global understanding of the mythic impulse when the subject was not yet popular, and at considerable sacrifice of external vocational rewards."

20. Rollo May, Ph.D.

"I am honored to recommend to you Joseph Campbell. In my judgment he is the authority in the entire country on myths and their history. His writings are unique for their scholarliness and their imaginativeness. Great numbers of us are indebted to Joseph Campbell for crucial portions of our education. He brings to his work an aesthetic sense which gives it a vitality, which partially accounts for his vast influence around the country."

PRATT INSTITUTE
June 4, 1976

REMARKS OF DR. JOSEPH CAMPBELL,
PRINCIPAL SPEAKER

DR. CAMPBELL: President Pratt, members of the faculty, graduating students, parents, friends of Pratt Institute. It's an enormous pleasure to me to be receiving the honors of an Institute devoted to the arts, to the professional practice of the arts, as is the case with Pratt, because the field of my own interest which has been of mythology and ritual is very intimately connected with that of the practical arts. Each supports the other.

And this has struck me in a very pleasant way the past three years attending the fashion shows at the Hilton of Mrs. Lillard's group of students in the field of design. The sense that both mythology and art have to do with the glorification of life and the amusement of life, struck me particularly strongly when I saw those fantastic young women who exhibit the clothes come in a rather finicky way down the line, heads turning this way and that way, as much as to say, Am I not glorious to see? And they were. And so were the garments. And so were the quality of the cloth.

I remember when I was a student in Paris, the great sculptor, Antoine Bonel [*sic*], used to say, Art brings out the main lines of nature. This brings out the main lines of nature. And I was thinking what I would talk about today to a graduating class in the arts, I thought of making this point. The grand lines of nature as recognized in this, not only in the way of what you behold when you regard the world, but also in the way of what you discover when you turn within yourself. And what you will discover during the course of the unfoldment of your life.

Because there are many aspects of the grand lines of nature. One, the world without. Two, the world within. And two aspects of the world within: that which is put upon you by the society as to the mode and field of your life in existence, and that to which you undoubtedly, at this stage in your life, have already become gradually aware. Namely, the peculiar talents, the peculiar possibilities, of your lives, your individual lives. Different from all other lives. And yet, walking along the same grand road with others, so that you will find when you have come to the end of your course, that although you may have lived a life completely yours, looking back you will see that it has been a normal, beautiful standard life of the sort you share with many.

Now this whole mystery of the two aspects of a lifetime is brought out beautifully by the poet, Yeats, in that extraordinary book of his, "A Vision." He takes in that work the course of the moon, the 28 days of the moon cycle, as analogous to the course of a lifetime, and he counts the years of our lives by analogy with the stages in the crises of the moon's cycle. Now the first stage of the moon is dark, and then at the 8th day, which is the day almost precisely corresponding to this time in your lives, the darkness is half and the light is the other half of the moon.

So that there is a movement now into a new moon situation of light dominant over darkness. And Yeats calls the period of our lives that is represented by the first eight days of the moon, the period of the primary mask—m-a-s-k. This is the system of ideals and principles and order for life that has been put upon you by your society, by your family, by your training. Just at this time, one begins to have the realization there are potentialities within me that are also value judgments that I make, that were not of those of the world that I was brought up in.

That is to say, a new day has dawned for the world. The old systems are a little bit archaic. Moreover, I am unique, as each person is. I am told that there is something like 15 million cells in the brain, or more than that. No two hands are alike; no two brains are alike. You are never anticipated in your uniqueness. And then at this eighth day of the moon, where the moon begins to be lighter than dark, we come to this realization gradually, and Yeats uses a very interesting term to describe this moment in a life. He calls it the moment of the awakening of the antithetical mask. That mask, that form of life into which you are going to move and through which you are going to meet the world, which is drawn away and must be drawn away, from the primary mask, so that there is a moment of struggle. There is a line of conflict that comes into a life at that time.

Now in a strictly traditional society, the individual is not allowed to follow the impulse of that individual way. The society has put upon the individual what in India is called his dharma, his duty. The quality of the antithetical mask at first seems to be one of temptation following temptation, disobedience and all. But the individual in our society is urged even, to follow that temptation. It's the temptation of your life style, and to follow it requires renunciation as well as conflict. Renunciation of the assured values of the assured support, of the society in which you were born.

And there comes a crisis of decision at that moment. Are you going to opt for the assured, the well established and security or are you going to move uniquely along your own path in the forest of adventure?

In my own teaching of 38 years at Sarah Lawrence, I saw this moment in many lives as I looked into those lovely young faces—new possibilities dawning for them—the decision. And then ten years later at alumni reunion, 20 years later, 30 years later, I would meet again these people beautiful who had been my students.

And it was not difficult to recognize who were the ones who had dared the adventure, and who were the ones who had not. If you do not dare the adventure you will enjoy a respectable, a very fine and noble life. If you do opt the adventure, you experience an interesting life. It will be full of danger, full of surprises, full of shocks and disappointments, but somehow as I saw in those eyes, a freshness, a vitality has somehow gone out of the others.

The next thing is the full moon, the 15th night. This is a moment that Yeats and others have identified with the middle of life, approximately the 35th year. At that time the vehicle of your consciousness is at its fullness and it is at this moment that the great mystical crisis comes. Because from that moment on the moon is growing dark again. This is the moment of your high, this is the moment of your fullness.

The question comes at that time, who am I? With what do I identify myself? I have reached the fullness of my individual career, my possibilities—I know what they are. And now it's going to fade. This is the moment, the 35th year that Dante identified with his vision in the "Divine Comedy." Where he passed from the identification with the body in this world of time and space, coming to birth, maturing, and passing in death. He transferred the identification of his consciousness from that body to the consciousness that was aware of it.

In mythology there are two great symbols of eternal consciousness and eternal life. One is the moon, which waxes and wanes, and throws off its shadow as life throws off death to be born again. This is the way of the engagement of consciousness in the field of time and space. Courageous in its passage through the darkness, in the way of the cycle of the moon.

But there is another heavenly sphere, the sun namely, which is never shadowed except in eclipse time. It does not carry its death within it as the moon does, as we do in our bondage. And the sun symbolizes that aspect of life and consciousness which is transcendent at times, which is the eternal consciousness. And now on the 15th night of the moon, if you've ever been out on a great plain, like the plains of Kansas or Nebraska, or out on the sea at night—at the sunset time of the 15th night of the moon—in the west the sun is going down on the horizon; in the east the moon is rising on the horizon, and they look at each other across the world, and they are the same brightness. And they are essentially the same size. So that actually—I've seen this a couple of times—you hardly know whether you are looking at the sun or the moon.

Now the image that Yeats gives for this moment of life, the 35th year or so, and the 15th night of the moon, is this. The shift of the order of your consciousness from identification with the reflected light in the moon, to identification with the solar orb—this is the moment when you are in full consciousness and you can ask yourself—Who am I? Am I this body which is the vehicle of the consciousness, or am I consciousness?

If you can make that shift, it's a subtle shift, you nevertheless, gradually feel at peace with the mortality of your body. You can watch the body then go, grateful to it for it's having brought you to this moment of relief from it. And yet at the same time, attachment to it. It's a beautiful dual play. This is the theme of all the mystery cults. This is the theme of all the great high myths of vision and realization. All rests well in God. All rests well in consciousness, depending on what kind of mythology you use for interpreting to yourself these great mysteries.

And I rest well in my consciousness. I am that. And then the moon begins to decline again, until the 22nd night darkness begins to take over. The primary is coming back again. You are no longer taking care of people; people are taking care of you. If you have been able to dissociate yourself from the body in its mortality, and identify yourself with consciousness in its glory, you can let the body go. If you haven't made that change, you die like an old dog. Resisting death. Afraid of death.

The great vehicle today for initiating us to this mystical crisis is art. The method of art is the method of disengaging yourself in your consciousness and observation from the personal desires and fears, achieving what we call objectivity. James Joyce, in "Portrait of the Artist as a Young Man," gives an extraordinarily clear, precise, definition of the nature and vehicle of art. He distinguishes between what he calls proper, and improper art. Art that is truly art, and art that is in the service of something else.

Art that is truly art, he says is static. You have what we call the moment of aesthetic arrest. Just rapture in the viewing of an object. Not that object in relation to this, that or the other thing. Not that object in relation to philosophical problems and mysteries, but just sheerly that object—thus there, thus come. And against that is the art that attempts to excite desire for the object. This kind of art he calls pornographic.

For example, when you look at an advertisement and see a refrigerator advertised, and a beautiful smiling girl beside it, you say—I would like to have a refrigerator like that. This is the pornographic motif, or even if you see a picture of a lovely, dear old lady, sitting down in her living room or something like that, you think, Oh what a lovely dear soul that is. I'd love to have tea with that old lady. That's pornography. You are relating to the object in a way that is not that of aesthetic arrest. Aesthetic means sensual, having to do with vision.

And contrary to the desire motif of pornography, you have the instructing motif of didactic art, telling you what kind of person is good, what kind of person is bad; what kind of society is good, what kind of society is bad. Now you recognize that a great deal of what's passing as art today and has forever been either pornography or didactic. I would say that the novel since Zola's time has been largely the work of didactic pornographers, where you have the didactic coming through all about society and then the sugar-or-chocolate-coated pornography.

Turning from that, a lot of you will be working in advertising. But the actual work as you do it, as artists, in your hands must be proper art and then somebody else can put it to the advertising use. And if you can in your own work make the distinction between the pull by desire, or by intellectual criticism, to the work, the decision between those views and that of just sheer delight in the rapture of contemplation, bringing out the main lines, you will find your own heart clarified.

Now the next thing that's so interesting to me, and with this I want to conclude, is this dismissal of pornography and didactic, of desire and fear or loathing, is exactly what the Buddha achieved seated under the tree of the world axis. The immovable spot. There is a direct line from the aesthetic experience to the experience of the mystical moment. And what I'm telling you is, and I know that this is true—the art that you now master to a certain degree is the greatest vehicle given to us today for the achievement of this fulfillment [of all] the possibilities of human consciousness.

And so in conclusion now, let me just give you a word from Nietzsche, this great opening gun you might say, of the twentieth century. At the opening of Zarathustra, he speaks of what he calls the three transformations of the spirit. First the spirit is a camel. The camel gets down on its knees and says, "Put a load on me." You have up to the present moment been camels. The camel is the student. Put a load on me. Put a heavy load on me. Give me something to do. Give me something to carry.

And when the load has been put on, the camel struggles to its feet and trots out into the desert. And in the desert the camel becomes a lion. The heavier the load, the stronger the lion has come of it. And what is the function of the lion? The lion is to kill a dragon, and what is the name of the dragon? The dragon's name is Thou Shalt. It is a glorious dragon, with scales of many scintillating hues, and on each scale is written, Thou Shalt. Some dating back to 5000 B.C., some from yesterday morning's "New York Times."

The lion must kill the dragon, Thou Shalt. That is the work of this moment, my friends, the 8th night of the moon. And when that lion has been killed there takes place the next transformation. One becomes the wise eternal child. As Nietzsche says, moving out of himself, "I am a wheel moving out of its own center."

And this is the life then of the truly creative artist, who knows that within his movement are the energies of fulfilling consciousness and it's with that thought then, that I would leave you today, with my good wishes to you all for the life of beautiful, wise, released innocence that is the fruit of a life in art.

My thanks and good wishes to you all.

END OF REMARKS

Dr. Joseph Campbell, in recognition of his work as the leading American interpreter of myth in literature and religion; of his own strong, lucid prose, which has been described as "literature" itself; and of his some 40 years as one of the unique scholar/teachers in academia, was presented with an Honorary Degree of Doctor of Humane Letters at Pratt's Commencement.

Joseph Campbell, 1985

CHAPTER 7

The Last Decade

THE 1980S

IT IS ASTONISHING that a septuagenarian nearing the end of a long and prolific career would embark upon the monumental task of producing his magnum opus, the Historical Atlas of World Mythology. *It is equally sad that he left more than half of this monumental work unfinished at his death on October 30, 1987.*

We begin the correspondence during this period with an important letter to Professor Vernon Gras, which articulates Campbell's rejection of the theories of Claude Lévi-Strauss with eloquence and equanimity. We then proceed to the fascinating letters from the Icelandic mythologist Einar Pálsson.

These conversations and the information in the letters below found expression as a frequent theme in Campbell's lectures in the late 1970s and early '80s, and in the posthumously published "Mystery Number of the Goddess," his contribution to In All Her Names: Explorations of the Feminine in Divinity, *edited by Campbell and Charles Musès and published in 1991 by HarperSanFrancisco.*

Joseph Campbell
Waverly Place
New York, N.Y. 10014

Professor Vernon Gras

Feb. 11, 1980

Dear Professor Gras—

Thank you very much indeed for the fine paper on Jung, Lévi-Strauss, and the post-structuralists, which I have read with care and admiration.[1] Since I have never been able to read more than a few pages of Lévi-Strauss at a time, this paper of yours has given me my first clue to the reason for my indifference to his arguments. "Myths are narratives made out of language... a mytheme is constituted out of sentence bundles..." That is the clue. In my view, myths are more like dreams and visions, constituted, rather, out of images; grounded not in the culture, but in the psyche; which, in turn, is of the human nervous system and the body; these, in turn, being of nature, not of a culture (like language). The mythemes, of which Lévi-Strauss treats, are, in this view, secondary, in the way of culturally conditioned interpretations of the given images. And your sentence on page 18, "The gap between Nature (the Other) and culture cannot be bridged," would from my point of view have been better written: "The gap between nature and culture (the Other) can be bridged, and the bridge is by way of myth and dream."

I have been lecturing, lately, in collaboration with a biologist, and if I had needed confirmation of my belief that the imagery of myth is grounded in nature, this collaboration would have convinced me.

I must confess that I did not understand at all, however, the Oedipus-Parsifal argument on p. 16. Parsifal was not chaste, but married; nor did his failure to speak at the Grail Castle have anything to do with a riddle; it had to do with his suppression of the impulse of his nature (namely, to ask, "What ails you, Uncle?"), in order to conform to the ideals of his culture ("A knight does not ask questions")—the Chrêtien question was different, but the sense of the silence was the same. Furthermore, the adventure did <u>not</u> fail, finally, since Parsifal returned to the Castle and did, then, ask the question (Chrêtien's account breaks off and is incomplete). And still further, the incest motif does not always appear "in myths invariably accompanied by the solving of a riddle." One thinks immediately of the house of Aeolus in the Odyssey, who married his daughters to his sons: there was no problem there (that I can find, at any rate) of the solving of a riddle. I have always had a sense of Lévi-Strauss pushing things around to contrive his arguments, and I find him here doing it again.

You were <u>very</u> kind to send me this paper. It has helped me to clear up many points of my own, as well as to understand something of the problems of the structuralist position.

My thanks,
Sincerely,
Joseph Campbell

Einar Pálsson (1925–1996) is best known for his theories about the origin of the Icelandic saga literature as the relict mythology of pagan ritual landscapes. In 1969 he put forward his theories in a series of eleven books in Icelandic and three in English. In 1995 he was awarded the Knight's Cross of the Order of the Falcon by the president of Iceland as recognition of his research into Old Icelandic literature.

Joseph Campbell met Pálsson at the International Association for Transpersonal Psychology meeting in Iceland in 1972, during which Stanislav Grof and Joan Halifax were married, Campbell presiding. The story is memorably told by Grof: during the festivities, "a giant, unbelievably rich double rainbow" appeared and disappeared three times."[2] *Grof noted:*

> Einar Pálsson had spent more than twenty years studying Viking mythology, but you know, it didn't take more than ten minutes and Joseph was telling him things about [Buddhist parallels to] Scandinavian and Nordic mythology that

he didn't know. For me it was an amazing example of the immense knowledge that Joe had. They really got involved in this idea that the Icelandic mythology was linked very much to the landscape, every rock had meaning: and Joe said the religion was like that of the Australian Aborigines.[3]

Einar Pálsson and Joseph Campbell

Dr. Einar Pálsson
Sálvallagata #
Reykjavík, ICELAND

Joseph Campbell
Waverley [*sic*] Place
New York, N.Y. 10014, U.S.A.

June 2, 1973

Dear Joseph Campbell,
Many thanks for your last letter. No procrastination on your side of the ocean. Having read most of your Occidental Mythology I

marvel at the ease with which you state the position of the Western European heritage—in spite of religious opposition and Germanicists. Your insight is unerring. One of the major discoveries I made up here in Iceland was precisely "the ultimate accord that was reached between the older mysteries of the fairy forts and the new of the Roman Catholic Church" (p. 463). In fact it was the very basis of Icelandic PAGAN society ca. 930–1000 A.D. This will explain to you the interest shown by Catholic medievalists in my studies. Yes, you may well ask "the meaning of such a mass conversion as takes place when a pagan king submits to baptism and all his people follow." People have been asking up here for nearly a thousand years. The answer now before them has staggered everybody in Germanic studies, as you presumably know. Obviously none of these people ever read your stuff.

Don't think you are not appreciated though. This winter I met an American novelist here. He intends to write about Iceland it seems. His name is James Michener, he writes popular although good books I am told and is very well known in the States. Mr. Michener told me he had written about Hawaii so I asked him if he knew you. Indeed he knew OF you; he said, "Campbell is one of the truly great Americans ever."

How about that from a popular writer?

On the other hand a curious article appeared in the left socialist/communist paper here last summer. It stated no respectable scholar had heard of you—you were not even mentioned in books on mythology etc. Needless to say this was an oblique attack on me—referring to your interview in Morgunblaðið without mentioning that fact nor my name. So it seems we are in the same solar boat for better or worse!

Arthur Gibson arrived here yesterday. Many others are fleeing to Iceland from the heat of civilized countries. Gibson told me on the phone that he had been in touch with you this winter and would tell me about it later. It occurred to me that you are now free and master of your own time. Do you realize we are only five hours apart by plane? And cheap too for Americans. In case you ever decide to cool off a bit Iceland will stay in its place. It would be fun to see you again. I could drive you around and we could discuss many things. Next spring I should like to take a trip to Greece. I have never been there and will probably have time off as from 1st April. How about joining me in that pilgrimage?

Today—2nd June—it is precisely a year since we met. Several things have happened since then. You have been busy you tell me, so have I. The material for my fourth volume has now been collected. This volume deals with the Vinland-sagas—the ancestry, settlement and mythical connotations of those Norsemen who settled the western part of Iceland, some of them later Greenland, and on to America. As astonishing amount of material can be uncovered here. Even you would be surprised, although the solution will hardly surprise you.

Recently I had a pleasant surprise—a letter arrived from the landstyrimaþur of the Faroes (landstyrimaþur: "land-steering-man" isn't it a beautiful title?) saying they wanted to invite me down there this summer. Why? Because they found a system there precisely as predicted in my second book in precisely the correct place. Something new has been added, however, in the Faroes a plan of the system has been found actually hewn into the rock—a clear plan of a circle with 16 spokes, a Centre and a directing sign SW-NE. They have already published a picture of this Wheel along with other markings found in situ in their scientific publication Fróðskaparrit 1972.

This was a missing link, now only Norway eludes us. All the others are there: þingvellir (Iceland)—Tinganes (Faroes)—Tara (Ireland)—Tingvold (Isle of Man)—Stone Circles (Hebrides)—Uppsala (Sweden)—Jelling (Denmark). All based on the same mythological principles. You know what this means. The great wealth of material found in Iceland can now be used to explain the intermediaries.

As you have heard your Icelandic friend has been anathema to Germanicists for some time. At long last they have now grudgingly given me permission to submit a paper for discussion at the

2nd International Saga Congress to be held in Reykjavík 2nd–8th August next. It so happens that two of their big guns, Peter Hallberg of the Univ. Of Göteborg and Steblin-Kamenskij of the Univ. of Leningrad seem to have given up their opposition to my work, or at least modified their positions greatly. What will happen at the congress is anyone's guess. I shall certainly not spare them my conclusions. The Germanicists will be a tough nut to crack—you wouldn't believe the weapons they have used against me—biting attacks can be expected at the conference. But then, well, I shall cite Mircea Eliade and Joseph Campbell—and who can harm me? I shall send you a copy of my paper when it is finished. I must hurry, only a week left, all papers will be sent to all universities in question for scrutiny before the congress convenes.

Goodbye for now, thanks for everything. Bessie and I send your good Erdman, Jean our very best regards. We hope you are really enjoying your otium, having a fine time in your new-found freedom.[4]

Yours ever,
Einar

Reykjavík, June 7, 1974

Dear Joseph Campbell,
I almost said Dear Joe, I feel I know you so well after reading so much of your wisdom and erudition. Your greatness stays my fingers.

This is just to tell you that a breakthrough has been made which I had not dared hope for. In actual fact it is a corollary of the previous discovery tying a specific place to a certain portion of the sky. That fix made it possible to define the abodes of the gods of our pagan Nordic heritage as set out in Grímnismál. I know this interests you as few others as we are dealing with the components of the 432000. Hence this letter. Grímnismál (a plural word) are along with two other lays the foundation of Snorri's

Edda. The other two are Völuspá and Vafþfrúðnismál. You yourself have pondered str. 23 and 24 dealing with Einherjar, the doors. Valhöll and Bilsskirnir. What no one has hitherto been able to make out is the enumeration of the abodes of the gods as set out in str. 4–16. The Norwegian Magnus Olsen (Edda-og Skaldekvad, VII Oslo 1964) tried hard but got nowhere, nor did Jan de Vries (Die Götterwohnungen in den Grímnismál, APS XXI, 1952, p. 172–80). Their mutual conclusion: the text is corrupt, the ordering wrong, Die Götterwohnungen in den Grímnismál are based on faulty preservation of the sources. Most scholars have taken this view at face value; you might say it became a dogma with Sijmons & Gehrings Kommentar zu den Liedern der Edda (Halle 1927, p. 181–216). This view is now seen to be wrong. The writer of Grímnismál knew what he was doing. The abodes are correctly set out.

No one will understand the significance of this as well as you. This simply means we have a potential yardstick of great promise. It could be made precise and a wealth of material could be compared through its usage. We are dealing with the known universe of our ancestors—by comparing each portion of, say, Breiðablik in Iceland with known counterparts in Greece, Rome, Egypt, Sumer, India, etc. we might be able to forge a fabulous instrument. Relationships could be studied, ideologies of the various cultures, even philological implications. The material has already given me an entirely new understanding of the actual MEANING of each god, his place in the universe and his/her function. Suddenly myths make sense which were completely obscure previously. Such major dilemmas as Heimdallur, Skaði, þjazi, their parts in the total scheme and their roots, reveal themselves through their specific places within the context. If only I had another hundred years and one less school to run.

I shall probably not be able to publish this material for some years. That is why I feel you should know right now. The greatest difficulty will probably be man's inability to understand how important it is to work scientifically on myths and lore connected with the night sky as well as other places of nature. Astrology has such a bad name that scholars don't realize its importance in the lives of bygone generations. I myself did not suspect how important the stars had been in Icelandic paganism.

Arthur Gibson arrived here yesterday. He urged me to tell you of this new development. I didn't need the exhortation, but it made me sit down. I hear you also partook in the CBC series on Rituals. As you possibly know I did a lecture called Rituals of Nordic Paganism on the 2nd of May. I feel very proud of having been allowed to speak in such distinguished company.

I shall be showing some medievalists the abodes of the gods and their terrestrial counterparts 17th–27th July. Perhaps there will only be two aside from Gibson, Archbishop Pocock and Cardinal Flahiff. They head the Pontifical Institute of Medieval Studies in Toronto. As you know rank does not impress me. But these two are great and humble men. And they sound genuinely interested.

Gibson told me you spoke of the Icelandic system of Alþingi, the 432000 feet etc. in Montreal. He thinks you have already published a paper about this. Is he mistaken? If not I should very much appreciate hearing about it. Could you possibly send a copy to Iceland? Gibson said you had spoken extremely generously of my modest contribution for which I hereby send you my warmest thanks.

The new development makes one pause. We can now work on—not only the number 432000—but WHICH universe, WHOSE universe composed of WHICH abodes that number was part. I felt I had to tell you. Goodbye dear Joe, best regards from Bessie and myself to you and Jean,

Yours sincerely,

Einar

Reykjavík, June 5, 1975

Dear Joseph Campbell,

Thank you very much for "The Mythic Image" which I received a couple of weeks ago. It is a beautiful book. My sincere congratulations. Your text brings to the mind the saying of our late Grandmaster Sigurður Nordal: "Only he who masters his subject can write simply about it." It is a happy gift to be able to write intelligibly for the public.

The battle for free speech rages here in Iceland. I asked permission to give lectures on the historicity of our sources at the University of Iceland and to debate the question with the university people. I was turned down, once more. The government gave all sorts of prizes—poetry prize, music prize, even a ballet prize. And for the study of our sources? None whatsoever. And certainly no discussion. What baffles me is the attitude of the papers: not one of them has called for free speech at the university. They don't even partake in the debate. It does not take a major religion to see that whoever seeks truth in a small community with only one major seat of learning, is utterly lost. There is only one set of elders who hold all power in their hands. That set of elders is concerned with nothing so much as the propagation of its species. Their ideas and views must prevail. Disinterested search is just not their cup of tea.

I have been lucky in being allowed to give lectures on the radio. That way you reach a great many people. This winter I at long last gave a withering attack on the philosophical faculty of our university in a 40-minute broadcast. Until then I had hardly attacked them directly. I am glad to say the attack hit the target.

Last month, SAGA, the official organ of the Icelandic historians, printed an article about my studies. It is the strangest thing, composed of scathing comments on my poor self as well as the trump of doom over all who will defend the practices of such as me. The author of the article, Kolbeinn Þorleifsson, is actually a clergyman. My major fault? CREDULITY. A simpleton, that's what I am. The strange part of the article is actually the credits bestowed: my quotations are always very precise. Then they go on to say that people must be rid of the assumption that E. P. can be dismissed as a solitary eccentric. In point of fact, the article goes on, you simply MUST shoot down the theories of Mircea Eliade before you can shoot down E. P. Unless that is done, the work of E. P. stands.

I am sure you will agree with me that such a proposition is not overly dangerous for anyone, although, what Eliade has to do with my research remains a mystery. And what does this Icelandic clergyman do about it? He shoots down Eliade. That, as you know, is easy: the ideas of Eliade are "nothing but a castle of playing cards, put together from sources which in no way belong together, and in complete lack of understanding of the disciplines which he calls on for help. The scientific work of Eliade is in fact nothing but a simplistic collection of odds and ends (the word used: "sheep's manure") from all over the place, where the ignorance of the Indian Ananda K. Coomaraswamy of the Icelandic language is made to account for the end result of the concoction" (SAGA 1974, p. 152, the publication is a year late).

You will recall my astonishment on hearing what the people at the University of Rochester (Colgate Divinity School) had to say about Eliade. The way you can dismiss the greatest thinkers of the age seems the way of the almighty to judge by the connection of Eliade's critics with the church. You yourself have the honor of being mentioned in the above article. You and Eliade are not people I should have "believed in." If I had been a real scholar I would have corrected the two of you somewhat as one corrects naughty schoolboys. What the three of us write (please forgive me for placing myself in this illustrious company, not my fault, you know, it's the idea of the Icelandic historians) is "pure nonsense," "a scientific concoction which no true scholar can admit in earnest" (p. 151), we show an "incredible lack of knowledge." As for Coomaraswamy, he "makes manifest his ignorance"—and as for me I "take the theories of Eliade as proven fact, and (he) does not try to check whether they are based on truth or misrepresentation." What I should have done is to "correct the absurdities of Eliade and Campbell instead of swallowing them raw" (p. 155).

That, I hope, is enough samples for you, Mr. Campbell. All our work is "superficial" (p. 162), and, as for your own specific brand of superficiality you do "not make the slightest effort whatever to dive into the depths (of your subject) and feel the heart beating underneath" (p. 161). The work referred to: The Hero with a Thousand Faces.

All this will, I presume, make you and Eliade feel extremely sad. You completely forgot to think about your subject before writing about it. So now you must promise to be good boys. The thing which will be all but unintelligible to you is that you are not here dealing with irresponsible journalists. You are dealing with that organ of Germanic learning which sets the standard of the debate. And while you and Eliade write in English, and so get through to the world, my books were written in Icelandic and are at the mercy of these people—academically speaking. As far as I can see the above article is their justification: after all, you can't allow a person to speak and defend himself who has not better qualifications than those here stated. Campbell and Eliade! Don't be ridiculous. How deep can one sink?

I can't remember what I have sent you before. I am sending you my broadcast this winter and an article in Lesbók (Literary Supplement of Morgunblaðið) which I may have sent you before. Then you can have your copy of that ignorance which is bliss and belongs in particular to Campbell and Eliade. I have not published a book since 1972, but am sending you a little textbook on Icelandic prepared for foreign housewifes, embassies etc. in Iceland.

As for serious matters: I have just returned from Vienna. There is a Hans-Kayser-Institute für harmonikale Grundlagenforschung there, Vorstand Prof. Dr. Rudolf Haase. These people have been studying Pythagoras, his music-theories and the origin of musical notation, ancient music, etc. They tell me my work on the Music of the Spheres in Iceland—connected with our creation myths—coincides with what they have found down south—down to the most singular detail. This means that the Icelandic—"Nordic" heritage is directly connected with that of the Greeks/Egyptians/Babylonians even down to our musical remnants.

As for other items: I have had the singular lack lately of being upheld by British and American scholars in my major theses. I found that þingvellir in Iceland—seat of our GODAR and our court of law—was erected in direct connection with the sign of Capricorn in the sky (which has more than one name in Icelandic). Now the British have given out that this was indeed the custom during the time in question: law courts were tied to that sign to such an extent that "Anyone wishing to erect a court of law would choose Capricorn" (Warren Kenton, Astrology, Thames and Hudson, London, 1974, p. 21). Then professor Livio Catullo Stecchini of the M.I.T. has published results monumental in their implications. You will recall that according to my findings Icelanders, Swedes and Danes constructed a Cosmos which you call Mesocosmos, a replica of the Macrocosmos, on the scale 1:432000 at þingvellir, Uppsala and Jelling respectively. (By the way, where did you get that word?). I even published maps showing this (Baksvið Njál p. 207), Trú og landnám p. 43, and p. 110). In my first book I pointed out that this numerology was known by Indians, Egyptians and Babylonians, but in Trú og landnám and Tíminn og Eldurinn I showed that this whole construction corresponded in every major way to the Egyptian worship of Osiris. In other words: our pagan religion of kingship—that of Freyr/Freyja was in actual fact a parallel to Osiris/Isis. Ergo: this geometry will be found in connection with Osiris—a prototype of the Icelandic Cosmos will be found—in these measures 1:432—in Egypt. As far as I know nobody has found this before as geometry, as the measurement of space/land. And in 1971—two year [*sic*] after Baksvið Njál—Stecchini states the conclusions of 20 years of research with precise instruments on the spot in Egypt: "The Great Pyramid represents the northern hemisphere in a scale 1:43.200"!!! My results were in thousands, his in hundreds. But what if we accept H. Waton's explanation: "I call attention to the following. When a number ends with a zero or zeros, the zero or zeros are counted in computation but not always in interpretation. Take the number 3. 30 is only ten times 3; 300 is only 100 times 3; 3000 is only 1000 times 3. In all cases is it only three?" (Key to the Bible, Spinoza Institute of America 1952 p. 27).

Waton is here discussing the numerology of the Cabala which he considers under Egyptian influence. In other words: you can almost say that what I predicted was found precisely as predicted—even in direct connection with Osiris—if you stipulate the Great Pyramid to be connected with the death of Farao and Osiris worship. I have only just had this information. Stecchini's monumental article is published in a popular but very well written and intelligent book by Peter Tompkins: Secrets of the Great Pyramid, Harper and Row, New York, 1971, as an appendix (p. 378).

To come back for one minute to the article in SAGA: not one of my theories, not one of my hypotheses is attacked by its author. To this brilliant scholarship it is enough to state that whoever is against their pet theories is a simpleton, an ass, somebody not to be taken seriously. The frightening aspect of the whole thing is that you are powerless against such scholarship in a Lilliput community. Nobody—and I mean NOBODY—will stand up and defend your rights. You have no rights. After all you have only WRONGS—all you say is wrong anyhow—that's why you will not be allowed to defend your results.

Best regards, it would be nice to see you soon. Bessie sends you her regards, give all the best to Jean,

Yours sincerely

Einar Pálsson

Reykjavík, June 20, 1977

Dear Joe,

Thank you for your warm and encouraging letter. It is great to hear that you are so busy and that McGraw-Hill have the sense to make use of a genius when they see one.

As to your questions: I have had such a heavy workload—been so engrossed in my research—that I have had no time to write in foreign languages. But I do feel the time has now come for an effort in that direction.

Your 432.000 order is a tall one, you might say all four volumes so far published in Rītur íslenzkrar menningar (The Roots of Icelandic Culture) relate to that problem some way or another. However, here are some points to start with:

Baksvið Vjálu 1969 (The Background of Njáls Saga) had two World Pictures. The first one: Hringur Rangárhverfis (The Circle of Rangárhverfi). This world picture was basic to Icelandic paganism. It was created by the Icelandic settler Ketill hīngr ca. 900 A.D. The Goðaveldi (Priest-Chieftainship) was based on it, so was the layout of Alþingi at ðingvellir (216.000 feet from its centre). The diameter of this circle was 216.000 feet. Ideologically it would seem to have corresponded to 216 diametres of the sun, that being the accepted size of the great circle of the Universe. (B.Nj. p.205)

The second World Picture: Hringur Jalangurs (The Circle of Jelling, the seat of Danish Kings in Jutland until ca. 980 A.D.). This circle was found to be 432.000 feet in diameter. (B.Nj. p. 207)

To summarize: the whole of Baksvið Vjálu deals with those two World Pictures. They are found to be the same except for the difference between 216 and 432. Sixty-four hypotheses as to the nature of the symbolism used in both instances are set forth in Baksvið Vjálu (all the major ones have already proved correct, strange as that might seem after only eight years!).

Perhaps the most exciting confirmation was the following: At the archaeological centre of the University of Ārhus, Denmark, I predicted that the world picture of ancient Egypt would be found to be based on the ratio 1:432.000. I made the same remark at the U. of Toronto in 1969. This prediction was printed as a hypothesis in Baksvið Vjálu p. 206–213. Needless to say this prediction was ridiculed by some people. In 1971 Livio Catullo Stecchini published his results in Peter Tompkins's book "Secrets of the Great Pyramid" on the measurements of ancient Egypt, stating that they were the result of 20 years of research. There he comes to the following conclusion: "The Great Pyramid represents the northern hemisphere in a scale 1:43,200; this scale was chosen because there are 86,400 seconds in 24 hours" (p. 378). The World Picture found by Stecchini corresponds to what I had predicted some years previously and published two years prior to his written account. This was presumably one of the reasons Buckminster Fuller was quoted in the newspaper with a 5-column headline that the research of your poor friend was the most interesting thing about Iceland along with a certain way of building houses in a country lacking wood. I know you will forgive me for telling you this, I sent you the clipping. For a person still banned in his own university, utterly excluded from any help or even communion with university circles, this was most helpful. The Zero—the 10—the thing called "involution" in ancient ideology, making 43200 equal to 432000 is explained in my last book Steinkross ch. 7. The extraordinary correspondence does not stop there: I had also predicted this ratio would be found to be based on the idea of 9 feet. And that is what the scholars find. (Steinkross ch. 11) As you yourself note without being able to read the Icelandic, the most varied details in Iceland are seen to correspond to counterparts in Egypt—in precisely the same places, within the same framework.

How could I predict this? That is a long story, I still have about 10 unpublished volumes in Icelandic—I kept silent for years. But you will readily understand the following: Freyr/Freyja in Iceland were found to be parallels to Osiris/Isis in Egypt. And the Icelandic Primeval Hill was found to correspond to the two counterparts in Memphis and Heliopolis. The detail is astounding, making it possible for us to reverse the usual procedure: from the decipherment of the Icelandic material one can predict with accuracy the most curious details of Middle-Eastern cosmology. And—MOST IMPORTANT OF ALL—one can EXPLAIN what those details mean, how they fit into the picture and why. You have many of these explanations in the four published volumes on your shelves—in Icelandic.

In the book <u>Trú og landnám</u> 1970 (Religion and the Settlement of Iceland) two further World Pictures are added to the original ones: þingvellir in Iceland (chart p. 43) and Uppsalir in Sweden (chart p. 110). These are explained and found to be based on the same ideas as those of Rangárhverfi and Jalangur. Both are based on the number 432.000 (feet). It is now almost certain that those feet were thought of as the feet of the 432.000 Einherjar in Valhöll. (Would it interest you to know that my name Einar, actually means Ein-harr, i.e. Einherji—one of the 432000 in Valhöll!).

Otherwise, Trú og landnám deals with Icelandic and Indian numerology (ch 49); Great cycles and ekpyrosis (ch 50–51), Time and Law (ch 58), all dealing with this theme. In the conclusion on p. 353 it is noted how seats of kings and priest-chieftains were measured—and how Mediterranean kingships will presumably be found to correspond to northern kingships, i.e. as being in geographical centres based on the ratio 1:432.000. The nordic king WAS Freyr—the Egyptian counterpart WAS Osiris—the Great Pyramid was in all probability the spiritual abode of Osiris. That can be inferred from the Icelandic counterparts—the Holy Fells (Helgafell)—again based on the number 432.000 as well as many other remarkably complex mathematical patterns.

In this conclusion, section 14, it is stated that time-space was connected with the vault of heaven. The segment of the sky called Capricorn by you was a PLACE ON EARTH as well as a place in the sky. Thus whole areas of the country were bound up with the stars in our heaven. The place of Capricorn in Iceland was called Bergþórshvoll. That is why the allegory of Njáls Saga is tied to that knoll. Bergþórshvoll was the Primeval Hill, it is situated near the mouth of the rivers in Landeyjar, i.e. the "islands of land"—the Delta region of Iceland. It was the beginning and the end of the great circle. Section 17: the number 432.000 was bound up with ekpyrosis (world cataclysm), three rocks and the SW-direction. On p. 368 there are ten theories; nr. 3: "þingvellir was an ideological centre tied to the number 432000. The same applies to Jalangur, Uppsalir and Tara (in Ireland). The numerology which relates to these sites is in full conformity with ancient teachings of Mesopotamia and India" (which are quoted in the book). Nr. 9: There is no basis for considering Icelandic paganism as divorced from or as cut off from, the mainstreams of Greek-Roman paganism.

Tíminn og Eldurinn 1972: In this book the World Picture is further explained. Runes as numbers and ideas. Ideology of the Ancients and the Middle Ages. Man as Microcosm. Hellenism. Correspondence between measurements, heaven and earth. Man as the Zodiac. The Stoics. Human society as Mesocosm (your word). Ancient materialism.

Ch 40: Niall and the Primeval Hill.
Ch 46: The idea of Man and the Einherjar.
Ch 47: The idea of Feet and kingship.

Further: Icelandic correspondence with Time as the Phoenix, man as the number 5, ancient usage of the 36 chieftains. The Celts and their knowledge. Frey-Feyja. The combination 16 and 5.

Steinkross 1976 (Stone Cross)

Ch 3: Holy measurements
Ch 4: Seat of Danish king at Hróarskelda as the centre of the circle.
Ch 5: The number 432.000 and the Nordic Cosmos.
Ch 6: The Icelandic Primeval Hill corresponds with the Egyptian one. Both intimately bound up with 432.000
Ch 8: King Aethelstan in England measured his seat precisely. His good friend in Iceland was Egill Skallagrímsson who owned Myrar, the place from which Alþingi was measured in the west. King Aethelstan and Icelandic law are interconnected.
Ch 23: Freyr and Nordic measurements. Correspondence with Egyptian measures and mythology.
Ch 27: Doors of Valhöll, the number 432.000
Ch 42 and 55: The Holy Grail as explained within the Icelandic context. It was the same as the Icel. SKAPKER which belonged to the goat Heiðrún—intimately bound up with the number 432.000
Ch 43: Jewish usage of the 216.
Ch 58–61: The lines which I have found in the Icelandic

> countryside correspond in a great many details to lines ("leys") found in Britain. I found these lines through myths and their connection with certain places in nature, the English found theirs through actual landmarks, stones, cumuli, paths etc.

Steinkross also discusses the ideas of the Ash and Time, nine heavens, nine gods of the primeval hill, mathematical ideas which are intertwined with myth, among them the PI and the PHI, the Tetractys, the triangle 3,4,5, the idea of the six fifths, the pagan oath, Freyr as a unit of measurement—the interconnection of all weights and measures and their place within Icelandic pagan mythology. The Helgafells (Holy Fells) in Iceland and in Hörðaland in Norway prove to be based on ideas which you also find in the most intricate parts of the Kabbalah and in the legends of Osiris. The pentagon and the pentalpha also seem inseparable from this web.

I hope this will suffice for the time being. I must go to work—I teach for a living as you know. Please forgive me for not writing this properly, I simply haven't the stamina right now. On second thought: Would you like me to come over and answer your questions one of these days, explaining the salient points, looking over your chapter dealing with Germanic paganism etc? All books on Germanic paganism are based on Icelandic material. Most of them are worthless now. It takes an Icelander to sort out such complicated webs. It isn't fair on others. You must know the land as well as a great wealth of detail which simply cannot be learnt by a foreigner in a lifetime—in addition to the language which is very difficult. I am the only Icelander since Snorri's day to devote a lifetime to the study of Icelandic mythology. And I fear I have broken far too many bridges for far too many people.

If I could find a way to come to New York—would that be agreeable to you? If so—when would it be convenient? Is there a reasonable Hotel not far from your apartment? It is clear to me that I ought to start working in English. The question is when and how. Perhaps you could give me hints if I had a couple of chats. Having published the four volumes I feel free as I never did before. Who is interested in such material? What universities might be induced to hear a lecture or two? Is there any way in which one could earn a dollar or two to defray expenses while doing a tour of the U.S.? I was once in New York—for the period of one solid day. One really ought to get acquainted with that great country of yours.

Best regards to Jean and Joan. You are a mighty lucky fellow. Bessie sends her regards. Thanks for everything,

From your friend,
Einar

Dr. Einar Pálsson
Sálvallagata #
Reykjavík, ICELAND

Joseph Campbell
Kalakaua Avenue
Honolulu, Hawaii 96815

November 30, 1984

Dear Joe,
How wonderful to have your letter of June 18! Your gentleness, consideration and human qualities must have made you a legend in America. I owe you at least three or four letters, I presume you will have guessed what was wrong, I have been in very bad health for many years, just managing to crawl up to my little school, to run it, teach, deal with students and teachers, try to keep track of accounts, advertisements, staff, taxes and the like, then back home to do research and write in whatever spare time I could wrangle out of existence. This horrid schedule finally caught up with me, it is not just my colon et al which have been afflicted but also my eyes and nervous system. I have thus been incapable of dealing with mail for many years. The mail of the school had to come first, even that was beyond me.

When I returned from my lectures in Norway last spring I finally gave in and resigned my post as director of Mímir. They will give me a pension for six years, from then on I shall be on my own. As from January 1, 1985, research and writing will be my main occupation, that is, if I can work up some strength again.

Your publication The Mythic Image was a beautiful piece of work. And how much of all your books fits exactly with what I myself have discovered in this country and expounded in my books and articles. It is a wonder we live so far apart and base our works on such different premises.

I was very happy to hear your comments on Hypothesis as a Tool in Mythology, my lecture at the U. of Oslo. However, so heretical is my work considered in Germanic circles that the invitation to account for my working methods sounded almost as a rude challenge made to a schoolboy. I later spoke at the U. of Bergen on the allegory of Njáls saga; that U. was polite enough to tell me—in writing—a week before I was due to give the lecture, that they had "received information that (my) work could not be relied on scientifically." This was an astounding letter to receive but I was treated accordingly. A scholar in a great country can have no idea what a student of religion and mythology has to go through in the Liliput environment. You can have little understanding of the fate of Socrates and Jesus until you realize that they belonged to precisely the same atmosphere, the local specialists and the preservers of fixed interpretations. Needless to say I am inclined to agree with you: had it ever occurred to me that I would still be forbidden to speak at the philosophical faculty of my own university and my own country in my sixtieth year, I would in all probability have learned English properly and written in that tongue. At Oslo I simply had to show up to be shot at, but, to my great surprise nothing of the kind happened. All those present received a copy similar to the one I sent you, so they could study the manuscript and follow my words while I spoke. Mirabile dictu there was not an archaeologist, nor, for that matter, a scholar in religion or any other field, who contradicted me. They just sat there, silent like Christmas Night. However, neither has any of them commented upon the lecture, adversely or otherwise, and not one of them has sent me a letter about it. I did receive two letters, highly prized you may be sure, from you and from the anthropologist Claude Lévi-Strauss at the Collège de France. So who is complaining, two jewels instead of a heap of slag.

I have been wishing for your return to Iceland for a long time. There is so much to discuss with you. In some ways I am very rich, sitting here all alone studying the mythology and the ideology of medieval Europe—and being the only native Icelander so to employ his time. The so-called Germanic specialists are simply not competent to judge and decipher the mythological language. I have learnt to my amazement that they can not even read my books. Each of us inherits his own place in life and has to be content therewith. It must be wonderful for you to work in Hawaii, the question for me now is: will we ever meet again?

Much of my present work concerns Celtic Christianity, The Holy Grail, the Icelandic version of the Arthurian legends, and, especially the meaning connected with all this material. It gives one great satisfaction to have so much stuff to work on known by no other scholar. Numerology and Geometry are part of the whole complex of ideas. The Icelandic material binds together such diverse subjects as Pythagoras, Homer, Roman law. Gothic cathedrals and Germanic pagan societies. Amazing? Like your president says: You aint seen nothin' yet. (What a line!)

From now on I shall try to lead a sober life, not travelling extensively as I did before. I shall go slow and sit at my desk at Sálvallagata. If you and Jean decide to have a look at this strange place once more, you know that we should welcome you like Aloha Royalty or as one volcano rumbles to another. Our kids have grown up and left, we even have a guest room for you if you should so desire.

Please find enclosed a photo-copy of relevant material sent to Mircea Eliade during a brief exchange of notes in 1978. This photocopy has lain in my drawer in an envelope addressed to you for six years! This, perhaps, tells you more about my utter exhaustion than any words.

Your great admirer James Michener never came back to write that book on Iceland. It seems he wrote a book on Poland instead. So he never needed my help. In Time Magazine I read that Michener recently donated two million dollars to his old university, with the provision that it should be used for speakers and not for buildings. One almost wishes he had mentioned as one of the crowd a specific speaker who is forbidden to speak elsewhere. But daydreams are a thing of the past now.

While doing my work in Florence a Headmistress (?) from Hawaii lived in the same Pensione, perhaps not one of the deeper natures of this world but a very nice and jovial person named Mary Ray Pohl, # Paiko Dr. Honolulu 96821. If you know her or should bump into her give her our best regards.

I send you, as ever, my best regards, and thank you for your great friendship over the years. Bessie joins me in greetings to you and Jean!

All the best, I do hope we shall meet again one day,

Yours Sincerely,

Einar

Einar Pálsson
Solvallagata #
Reykjavík, Iceland

Joseph Campbell
Kalakaua Avenue
Honolulu, Hawaii 96815, U.S.A.

April 30, 1985

Dear Joe,

Thank you for your wonderful letter of April 22 received yesterday. The planes must be flying faster than usual! Perhaps they are starting to feel how much your letters mean to me. This is just a quick reply to your question: You will find all the necessary information about my published books on page 24 (References) in my latest paper "Celtic Christianity in Pagan Iceland." To make certain they are: Einar Pálsson, Rītur íslenzkrar mennigar (RṢM) (The Roots of Icelandic Culture) 6 volumes in Icelandic, untranslated, Mímir, Reykjavík 1969–1981.

I have actually written two more volumes which are lying on my desk waiting to be published. I hope to publish nr 7 this year (named Hvolfþak himins, i.e., "The Dome of Heaven." It is a big book, however, about 500 pages. The way things fall into place nowadays is a marvel. The eighth volume deals with Sicily, Pythagoras and the subject of Troy—all part and parcel of the Icelandic heritage. Snorri knew this, but nobody believed him. The prologue to his Edda dealing with the connection with Troy is generally regarded as pure nonsense NOT Snorri's work. I have found it to be Snorri's work and that basically Snorri was right, although, needless to say, his word etymology and the legendary character of his account are not exactly in accordance with the science of etymology or factual history as we understand those terms.

Your vigour is astonishing, when I met Dumezil some years ago he was 79 and seemed to have given up, his apartment in Paris was a sea of books stacked all over the floors.[5] He could not find anything so I am astonished that you can locate my two papers in English on the Dome of Heaven and Hypothesis. Surprisingly enough Dumezil did not want me to read any of his works, he had sorely needed information on certain Icelandic subjects. He kept asking me why I had not arrived ten years earlier. I would certainly have liked to. But how was I to know that HE would have liked to discuss things with me. I understand it better now after I have seen the childish nonsense still being printed in France as Icelandic Mythology! But, needless to say, the birds of Saga-studies have no droppings for such sleeping beauties. Once again thank you for your wonderful and stimulating letter. Best regards from Bessie and me to you and Jean, Yours ever,

Einar

Dr. Einar Pálsson
Sálvallagata #
Reykjavík, ICELAND

Joseph Campbell
Kalakaua Avenue
Honolulu, Hawaii 96815

August 7, 1985

Dear Joe,
Many, many thanks for your letter of 29th July received last night. What injections of spirit. One senses a battle cry in every line.

Tomorrow I shall be reading proofs of two articles which I have written and which are to appear in Morgunblaðið two consecutive Sundays, 11th and 19th August. I will send them to you when they appear. As for the recent extraordinary archaeological excavation, I am for the time being leaving it out of my main arguments. The excavation is a good subject for debate, so you would do well not to introduce it at this moment in spite of its implications. It will cause stir, and, hopefully, some dissenting articles. However, your questions can be readily answered:

The archaeological discovery. Place: Dagverðarnes in Breiðafjörður, i.e. in western Iceland (It is NOT in southern Iceland, NOT in the Bergðóshvoll/Hof Circle.[6] The place is intimately connected with Celtic settlers and Celtic culture in general as from ca 890 A.D. (Landnámabók S95-111) (Formerly named Dögurðarnes). Most famous settler Auður djúpúðga, formerly queen of Dyflinnarskíði, wife of king Óleiff the white. This ness is close to the Western Circle (illustration: Trú og landnám 1970 p. 43). I actually declared in my lecture on the Allegory of Njáls Saga at the U. of Bergen 2nd May 1984 that in order to understand the symbolism of Njáls Saga and its cultural sites, you were well advised to start in the west—in precisely this part of Iceland, as the Sagas connected therewith could not be explained by a "literary loan"—they could only be understood if their symbolism was a living ideology in those settlements. Part of that living ideology was, of course, the idea of the Tetrahedron, the "three-sided" pyramid plus bottom, hence its name "four planes" or four sides. That form had then never been found in Iceland as an actual object; I had worked it out as an IDEA. Now it suddenly emerges from the earth as a major symbol of a demonstrably Celtic Christian settlement—IN STONE. It is an extraordinary verification, but then again I was not all that surprised after my experience in Florence: I had worked out the CUBE at Hof as an IDEA, an actual object in the form of a cube had never been found. But that missing link was certainly discovered in Florence. Why? Because it had been worked out as a whole combination of ideas, i.e., whereof the cube was part and how it stood in relation to the rest.

The harbor at Dagverðarnes was used until the 13th century. The name of the archaeologist: Thorvaldur Fridiksson. He has NOT published a scientific paper on his discovery, in fact he might be said to be just beginning his work. He is doing a doctoral thesis on Celtic Christianity in the light of Archaeology at the U. of Gothenburgh. So far he has found about thirty buildings (ruins) from different periods. Of these two are of overriding importance, they are typically Celtic and hardly known in Norse lands. Norsemen never used them, they have typical Celtic fireplaces which the archaeologists name "ovens." In addition several "remarkable stones" are to be found in the vicinity, some apparently with pictures or illustrations or even scratches reminiscent of some type of script. Thorvaldur also tells us he has found the remains of a Stone Cross. Remarkable wells done in stone are among the finds. The archaeologist thinks what he has found is a "papyl," i.e. the remains of a Celtic Christian monastery. All the instruments used by Thorvaldur and his assistants are from the U. of Gothenburgh, but a sample of birch-coal was dated by the C-14 method at the U. of Trondhjem in Norway. The dating gives the year 680 A.D. plus or minus a hundred years. Only one dating has been effected [*sic*] so far, but the archaeologists say birch-tree is particularly suitable for such dating and that results are therefore unlikely to change much. The Celtic-type houses are described as being of "borghlaðinni gerð" (erected like castles or battlements) i.e. stone laid on to form a vault. Such clearly Celtic remains have not been discovered in Iceland before by archaeologists.

My hypothesis concerning the Cube and the Tetrahedron were, naturally, ridiculed, when they saw the light of day (I wrote at length about their purport in Steinkross 1976 ch. 44–47). They dig and what do they find? Their precious ridicule. It is like a play of Molière's!

Next week I hope to visit the site. The Tetrahedron has not been measured precisely, but to judge by pictures the height would seem to be about four feet.

Icelandic scholars have been quick to react: the dating can not be correct. It contradicts Landnámabók. Iceland can not have been settled before 870 or so. Hence my two forthcoming articles.

My first article, due Morgunblaðið 11th August, HISTORY. Our scholars are making a mistake when they declare that the date 680 "stretches the history of Iceland beyond credibility. I mention Dicuil and Bede on the island of Thule six days' sail from Britain. Ṣslendingabók and Landnámabók both mention "papar" Celtic Christians who were here before the formal settlement of Norse people. Bede died in 735; if the people he mentions—the ones who travelled to Thule—ca 25–50 years after 680, that dating would tend to confirm that the Thule of our Venerable Bede was indeed Iceland. The funny thing is that we already have four archaeological datings by four different universities, one gives 610 and another 810 to early settlement in Reykjavík (Arch. Mus. of Copenhagine and U. of Uppsala) and one gives 580, hitherto unconfirmed or withdrawn because found too wild (U. of Gothenburgh, Margrét Hermannsdóttir) and now this fourth dating by Trondhjem—680. The reply of our university people and the Curator of our Archaeological Museum: As those datings must be wrong, according to other sources, the C-14 method can not be valid in Iceland. Volcanic eruptions or the sea may affect the outcome. (This you can even read in the articles I sent you.) My reply: By all means let us do further studies, but why MUST these datings be wrong? There is no reason to reject them a priori. They have withdrawn a little.

Second article: the TETRAHEDRON, named Ferhyrna in my writings ("of four horns, angles and sides"). It had been predicted that this form would prove to have been used by the settlers of Iceland, in particular by Celts. The archaeologists find just that in demonstrably Celtic surroundings, connected with Celtic Christianity and Celtic kingship. My hitherto published conclusion pertained to Bergþórshvoll in Landeyjar (the Primeval Hill, major site of Njáls Saga, the burning of Niall, beginning the end of the world). I went so far as to mark that site with a Tetrahedron (see Rammislagur 1978 p. 19). It signified Fire, creation by Fire, destruction by Fire, the end of one era, the beginning of another era. It also signified the hallowing of land which was done by Fire, this particular Fire being the most important of all in Iceland, that Fire which also measured the State, the holy distances and Alþingi, our seat of sacred assembly at Þingvellir where we once stood together. In actual fact these particular forms have been implicit in my books from the beginning as corrollaries [*sic*]of the Four Elements, being introduced as such in Steinkross 1976 p. 316 with a translation of their meaning in our heritage. Needless to say nobody understood what I was talking about. In Rammislagur 1978 ch. 1–16 I linked the Five Regular Solids, whereof the Cube and the Tetrahedron are a part, to the Directions, the Elements, the Allegory of Njáls Saga, the myth of Ingólfr and Leifr (Ari's Settlement Myth). All were further connected with their respective signs of the Zodiac, Tempers and certain Colours. On page 124 in Rammislgur you will find a table correlating the aspects of this complicated web.

Already at the age of twenty, when told that we boys could hardly learn more about the religion of our ancestors than we had learned already, I understood that if we were supposed to be the selected few who understood these things then nobody understood them at all. There was a tremendous gap in our knowledge; the symbolic language of our literature had not been deciphered. Our university disagreed and I left for London where I did some studies in the Ancient Greeks and Shakespeare. When I returned I slowly started my mental gymnastics which have made me so notorious.

You ask a question which it would take a long book to answer: How did I come to understand that there was an idea of a Cube inherent in Hof and that it was based on the number 6 x 6 x 6 = 216. You must remember that I have been at this game more or less during all my adult life. When I was offered a professorship at the U. of Toronto (St. Michael's College) I had on their insistence hastily done a translation of all my unpublished studies, then 1140 in number. I am sending you a copy of that somewhat unusual manuscript. It was prepared in 1968. Not one of the studies there enumerated has been published, nor was I allowed to read, explain, or otherwise tell of any of them at the U. of Iceland. If you leaf through the Roots of Icelandic Culture as it stood in 1968, i.e. those studies which had actually been written and catalogued, I believe you will understand from how many angles the studies were pursued. One thing I can tell you, however: I slowly became aware of number not as a cipher but as an idea. This was totally unexpected and took years. There used to be an intangible something always eluding me behind number, it had to be explained. With time I came to the following conclusion: Fire is probably connected with a Triangle, Wind with the number 8, Earth (and its creation) with the number 6 and the Cube (length, width and breadth)—the third power playing an immensely important role in the whole complex. The World as a whole was connected with the number 12, Water with the number 20. It was years later that I learned that my conclusions actually tallied with the Five Regular Solids of Plato.

Today I am writing the seventh volume of RṢM. It will be entitled Hvolfþak Himins (The Dome of Heaven). There the ideas in our shorter English account are deepened and added to. There is now a great deal of information which I have on the Cube alone. I have even found it mentioned in a manuscript (Hauksbók) which contains Völuspá and Landnámabók (source of both major versions)—no scholar ever mentioning this—or the connection—because they thought Algorismus had been placed in Hauksbók fortuitously—it was a freak which did not concern its subject matter—and hence did not merit study in that context. Can you imagine that? All the rest of Hauksbók was published in pieces, this one being left out! When I discovered the link between Landnámabók, Völuspá, the Cube and the number 216 I had no idea the best sources on the subject—actually mentions the Cube and other related material. But as it had no bearing on the manuscript otherwise, this information was confined to a handful of people who certainly would not bother to give it to others. It was an "innskot"—an inn-shot, something which had been added to make use of unused parchment.

Poetically minded people will probably swoon if you tell them the idea of the Perfect Cube was directly connected with Völuspá and Landnámabók; to the "literature" scholar such a thing is absurd. But even Snorri knew about the Cube in his Edda; it is implicit in his very words, it has just not occurred to anyone to look for it or to interpret his symbolism—within its context.

As for Hof, it was the first abode of the first settler of Rangárhverfi in southwest Iceland, Ketill hīngr (male salmon). His Vestmenn, almost certainly from the Hebrides, Hildir, Hallgeirr and Liot, presumably marked the area. Ketill's son, Hrafn Hīngsson, became the first law-speaker when Alþingi was established at þingvellir.[7]

Meaning: the CUBE was the immovable point, to which everything else was fixed. Everything, in other words, directions, ideas, religion, law etcetera was directly centered on the first abode of that first settler of the area in question. The TETRAHEDRON: it stood for FIRE. Land was hallowed through Fire. Fire denoted a limit, a beginning and an end. From Bergþórshvoll Time started his wanderings, from there you started counting when measuring space. It was the point of Yule, of the SW-axis, the fixed point on the fixed perimeter of a circle signifying the universe. If you look at RṢM in 1968 you will observe that already 20–25 years ago I had understood through the symbolism of my material that

Dagverðarnes was connected with the Yule-child, and hence, with the symbol now discovered there, the Tetrahedron (Book 18, study 38. "The Yule-Child and Dagverðarnes"). So, perhaps, I am not so surprised as some others. I stopped writing RSM when I discovered the "leys" in Iceland. Lines across the land that nobody had suspected for centuries—what were they? They were evidently bound up with myth and allegory. Why did certain things in our Sagas pertain to certain leys? After having discovered the Circle of Rangárhverfi surrounding this amazing blend of landscape, number, direction, myth and allegory, I measured it. I was at that time preoccupied with understanding the usage of runes: If my hypothesis was right, the circle would measure "something." I tried. When I came to the Sacred Foot now called the Roman Foot of 29.69 cm (used in Denmark in those days) the measurement clinched. It got 216000 feet. Later I found many other clues; I now have a whole network of interrelationships of which I have never written. The whole web seems to come from Iona in the Hebrides, Glastonbury in Somerset plus our sacred places in Scandinavia. Celtic Christian kingship was not basically different from Norse kingship to judge by my sources.

I am mailing this letter tonight and shall send you the other material by separate cover. To conclude: almost all the material I have studied pertains to not only the Nibelungen cycles etc. In Europe but also to Arthur, the Round Table and the Holy Grail. Through the Icelandic material you can now check and compare meanings in those works.

Best regards to you and Jean. I start feeling optimistically about the world when I think of you and your generous nature. You could have been an idea in a Saga like Skarphedinn and Niall. Do you know why King Arthur was killed precisely 960? The Dome of Heaven has a hunch, Best regards, ever Yours,

Einar

Bessie also sends her warmest regards to both of you.

Einar Pálsson
Solvallagata #
Reykjavík, Iceland
Feb 17, 1986

Dear Joe,
Just a little Hello to let you know I am still on the surface of the earth. I have just come home from an examination at the hospital, they tell me recovery is fair and that I stand a good chance of getting over my somewhat unsavory experience. In six weeks time there will be another examination and they then will decide if they will give their client the pleasure of a little surgery.

God not only knows the number of hairs on your head or the providence of each sparrow, he also knows every letter in the mail. Through some incredible bungling up here ten days actually elapsed from my first heart attack until I got into the hospital. You can reason this out for yourself, someone out there knew your letter plus your Marija Gimbutas manuscript were due in a week's time and hence did not admit me to the morose coma of three weeks until after I had had a look at them. Having corrected those few items and sent them back to you gave me a piece of mind I would not have enjoyed otherwise. So you are partly responsible for my recovery. The instructions doctors give you are somewhat in the line of the Delphic oracle: under no circumstances must you do anything you really like to do. So, needless to say, I decided your manuscript was something I really liked to do. To which no one has objected to this day.

When I wrote you the letter of 29 Jan. I was drowsy and half asleep. Now my body is starting to function again, hopefully also the brain. I am certain it will be good to read your finished paper on the Mystery Number of the Goddess. Right now I feel a bit too weak to read your manuscript properly.

Hvolþak himins was not exactly a bestseller, but there are compensations: Halldór Laxness, our Nobel Prize laureate in literature, has finally come over on my side, all the way, in the strongest terms possible. So have some others. An interview on the book was printed in a survey of the books of 1985, front page, literary supplement of Morgunblaðið, Reykjavík. Just yesterday, one of our best known writers, Guðmundur Daníelsson (who thoroughly knows our medieval Sagas), wrote an extremely strong article in Morgunblaðið, stating without reservation: "Einar has now proved with incontestable arguments the 64 hypotheses which he published in the first volume of the series in 1969, besides a great many others which he did not there set down" (Morgunblaðið 16. Feb. 1986, p. 10C).[8] As a matter of fact I am experiencing a shower of adjectives these days decidedly healthy for us poor miserables.

Halldór Laxness invited me to his noble place and gave me his latest publication (this was in December) as well as record which is a collector's item, done in Switzerland. As you are putting your reputation on the line with your statement on RṢM, it seems to me correct that you hear Laxness's own words, he thanks me "for theories and positions in Icelandic historical studies which are destined to open up a new era in Icelandic history." There have been more comments of the same nature by him and others, although somewhat unorthodox I feel you should know about them. They might be relevant, even come in handy, should someone chance to question your judgment in the Gimbutas Festschrift. To my great pleasure architects have come out strongly in favour of Hvolfþak himins, so has the most distinguished director of building affairs in Iceland, the engineer Haraldur Ásgeirsson, who is familiar with town planning and writes a fine article about the book in Morgunblaðið 12. Feb. 1986, p. 18. I will try and send you copies of these by separate cover.

This is all for now. Once again I thank you for your spirited letters and your brave thoughts. Best regards from Bessie and me to Jean and yourself,

Yours ever,

Einar

P.S. You once mentioned the letters þ and ð: the reason why we have to use them and can not simply write th instead, like þór: Thor, is, that we ALSO have TH, we have both names þór and Thor, they are not the same etc. It may sound like a dilemma, but it need not concern you. All TH-names are late, most after 1550 AD, so we never confuse them with others.

Einar Pálsson
Solvallagata #
Reykjavík, Iceland
March 3, 1986

Dear Joe,
Things are happening fast now. Some ten days ago I received a letter from the University of Ārhus in Denmark inviting me to a conference on 5–6 May.[9] The circular sent out is nothing you have ever seen. Some of the people who had read my papers had intimated to me that a change in the position of Germanic Studies might be expected. The letter, however, goes far beyond anything I ever expected. It declares flatly that although methods of Germanicists in judging and evaluating the history of the Viking period and the Middle Ages had served their purpose after the turn of the century, and then given important results, they, the universities, are now, all the same, confronted by a "radical revision" of all their tenets and working methods, in the light of the results and views established by the study of texts and anthropology in the meanwhile. The direct aim of the conference is to advance and collect the beginning new evaluation of our literary sources concerning the Viking period and the Middle Ages. A central problem discussed will be the relationship between text and historical "reality," the letter specifically states that under that heading is also meant material which has not been preserved in written records. Although RṢM is not mentioned translation is hardly needed. The enemy camp

is capitulating and violent storms are likely to occur. Perhaps the people concerned aim at making traditional Germanicists a myopic sect within the fold.

Note that the letter does not say that they intend to discuss WHETHER their former position is in ruins. They state without any reservation THAT their position is untenable and that the universities of Scandinavia will have to revise their procedures radically. Some letter. Leading authorities in Odense, Copenhagen, Oslo, Ārhus and Gothenburgh will state their cases, also my hitherto prime antagonist Peter Foote from the U. of London. The State Antiquarian of Denmark, dr. phil. Olaf Olsen, whose specialty is measures, temples, churches et al is in charge. There can hardly be any fleeing away now, they presumably intend to face the issues squarely, although, naturally, in their own time. The whole structure of Germanic studies seems to be crumbling. Best regards, send me your Mystery Number as soon as possible, when printed,

Yours ever,
Einar

Einar Pálsson
Solvallagata #
Reykjavík, Iceland

Joseph Campbell
Kalakaua Avenue
Honolulu, Hawaii 96815
U.S.A.

7 May 1986

Dear Joe,
Just a brief note to tell you I am still afloat. I have told our minister of culture about the Mystery Number of the Goddess, and he was interested in seeing a copy. Then I suddenly realized that

I did not know when or where the "little volume" was to appear. Two bookshops have asked me if they may quote your p. 94 in your manuscript (which I have shown them). I hereby pass on the request. The point is you can not quote something which has not been published.

If you have a minute kindly send me the following information (you need not bother with a letter): Who is publishing the Mystery Number of the Goddess, where and when?[10] It is rather important for me to know as soon as possible as I have spoken about it and recommended it to a couple of people.

As for your information that you would like to give an outline of the major findings of RṢM in your great Historical Atlas of World Mythology—it occurred to me whether you would like me to help you from the start? If you, for instance, do the layout—an approximation—I should be more than happy to fill in details which you could then present in accordance with your own wishes. Do not hesitate to ask (NB my health permitting).

I found your comparison between Berossos and Genesis of extraordinary interest. I have written about Berossos, but the Genesis-analogy was unknown to me, i.e., this part. What a piece of work was Noah!

I have finished a short book of ca 60 pages plus 30 illustrations for our children's schools on our numbers and the Icelandic Holy Circle. The authorities concerned are now considering whether to take the plunge.

My warmest regards to you and Jean,

Yours sincerely,

Einar

Einar Pálsson
Solvallagata #
Reykjavík, Iceland

To Claude Lévi-Strauss
Copy to Joseph Campbell

July 5, 1986

Dear Sir,

Re. the foundations of ancient Rome as worked out by the architect Piero Maria Lugli:

The hypothesis of the Roots of Icelandic Culture had predicted the following:

1. Ancient Rome will be found to have been based on a circle.
2. That circle will be found to be a world picture, a replica of the horizon, i.e. the cosmos.
3. The circle will simultaneously be a Wheel divided into eight segments (and spokes).
4. The main axis will be aligned on the summer and winter solstices.

This is what Piero Maria Lugli discovers and exhibits in the Campidoglio (21 April 1986). The Icelandic parallel to the foundation of Rome was worked out through symbolic material connected with the Icelandic landscape, the Rome hypothesis was based thereon and presumed to date from Numa Pompilius.

If architect Lugli's plan is proved to be correct we have an extraordinary chance of comparing cultural items in Rome, Greece, Britain and Scandinavia. This is not to mention all such parallels and semi-parallels which you have found elsewhere. As the Icelandic Wheel has been deciphered in many ways we actually have at hand about four hundred hypotheses which can be applied instantly to all the above cultures as well as those of the Middle

East, Sumer and Egypt. Needless to say there will be differences and divergences, but these will prove equally important as the similarities, they will reveal the course of historical and linguistic developments. The myths will prove particularly important as we now know how and in what fashion many of the most important "Germanic" myths were connected with the Icelandic Wheel. The Icelandic Wheel can be used as a common denominator, a yardstick whereby we can compare the abovementioned cultures.

This issue is engendering animosities, especially among "Saga-scholars" in Germanic studies, but, hopefully, it is also arousing interest.

I hope all is well with you, Yours sincerely,
Einar

Einar Pálsson
Solvallagata #
Reykjavík, Iceland
December 3, 1986

Dear Joe,
I am sending you clippings from Icelandic papers. First: thank you very much for your book: The Inner Reaches of Outer Space. As you will see I told about it in Morgunblaðið, mentioning our common adventure in sacred space, i.e. the wedding [of Stanislav Grof and Joan Halifax] at Bifröst. The gist of the article is that you are giving Americans a raison d'etre with your book and paving the way for the idea of a unified religious experience in our world. The end runs somewhat as follows: "Leifur was ahead (of him) but Campbell follows in his wake: at least one American settles the mental world of the West in the 20th century with the hindsight of the knowledge of Icelanders in (our) era of Settlement." Translation: sacred space. Name of the article: The Discovery of America. Leifur, of course, is Leifur heppni (Leif the lucky) your own Leifur Eiríksson.

The U. of Oslo have published my paper Hypothesis as a Tool in Mythology. I thought their preface might interest you.

At present I am doing a 4-article examination in Lesbók, Morgunblaðið's literary supplement. Its conclusion: some of the major ideas which have hitherto been considered "Icelandic" are in actual fact ancient and can be seen to have Latin origins. Among them is the major myth behind Njáls saga. I am sending you the two articles which have already appeared. Some people may not wish me a Merry Christmas.

Dear Joe, Bessie and I send you and Jean our very best wishes for Christmas and the New Year,

Yours sincerely,

Einar

Jamake Highwater (center), with Angeles Arrien (left) and Bette Andresen, Esalen, 1982

Jamake Highwater (February 14, 1931–June 3, 2001), born Jackie Marks, was an American writer and journalist. He was the author of over thirty fiction and nonfiction books of music, art, poetry, and history. His children's novel, Anpao: An American Indian Odyssey

(1973), received a Newberry Honor. His book The Primal Mind: Vision and Reality in Indian America *(1981) was the basis of a film documentary. Highwater assumed a false identity as a Cherokee in the 1960s. Although it was exposed by the mid-1980s, confusion about his life remains widespread. In spite of this dubious heritage, the letters to him show that Highwater stimulated important aspects of Campbell's creative energies during the time of his work on the* Historical Atlas. *Highwater also appears in the film* Joseph Campbell: The Hero's Journey.

Kalakaua Avenue
Honolulu, Hawaii 96815
Aug. 11, 1982

Dear Jamake—
Good to hear from you and to learn how well things are going in your camp. I have been on the point of writing to thank you for that fantastic article by Jett on Transoceanic Contacts. I have been at work on a couple of chapters dealing with what they are now calling the Formative Period of Ecuador, and this piece together with <u>Man across the Sea</u>, helped me through some pretty rough water.

As for that film: I am told that Stuart Brown will be flying out here to show me what they have done with it, about the middle of August.

And as for Seznec on mythology: ideas that he cites are from late, Hellenistic authors. The notion that myths are but distorted accounts of historical events and personalities is known as Euhemerism, after Euhemerus, a third century B.C. mythographer who had found that Alexander the Great was already deified. Snorri Sturleson makes use of the same idea in his interpretation of the Eddas. Myths do, indeed, tell of historical personages (Moses, Jesus, and the Buddha, for example), but also of divinities that never walked the earth (Indra, Kwan Yin, Zeus, and the Holy Ghost, for example). Myths indeed tell of the powers of nature, as well: solar, lunar, mountain, and water gods. But what makes them myths is not that they simply relate stories about all these. What makes them mythological is that they relate the mind, through these, to an experience of the mysterium tremendum et fascinans that is the ground of being of us all. The images are local. The social applications that are given them are local. But unless all these local, historically conditioned matters open at the back to transcendence, we do not have myth, but anecdote. In every early period of mythological creativity the mythologized phenomena have been experienced this way: the buffalo and eagles, for example, of the Plains mythologies; or, in the period of the Old Sumerian temples, the wonder of the order of the heavens. For one reason or another, the focus of wonder will shift and then the old mythology loses force: but prosaically, as mere facts, and it is then that Euhemerists and Jean Seznec come along.

Fables, also, are late, either late or playful. They may deal with figures (animals, for example) that formerly had mythological power, or may still have some mythological force when regarded in a sacred manner. But in the fable their adventures are applied to moral or practical instruction: as in Aesop or in the Jatakas, the earlier lives of the Buddha as a monkey, a turtle, or a deer. Fables are not myths.

And finally, as for a term to replace "pre-literate": as a chapter or section heading, I have thought of using "shamanic and folk mythologies"; but for a simple adjective, I am still in search.

Jean and I are enjoying our new Hawaiian home enormously. She is at present on Maui, visiting one of her sisters, but will be back Aug. 22. Why don't you drop her a line to the above address? That will be much better than my trying to explain to her what it is I think you are wanting. And meanwhile, my dear friend, hang on in there. What you are doing is of high importance.

All best—

Sincerely, Joe

Waverly Place
New York, New York 10014
Feb. 10, 1982

Dear Jamake—
Have tried twice to phone you my thanks for the Xeroxes and for the delightful luncheon hour. The articles are exactly what I need, and our noon conversation left me with a lot to think about. I have enjoyed John's piece on the unicorn. It is full of absolutely necessary information, of which I had had no knowledge whatsoever. My thanks to him—and to you for having invited him to our meeting.

I am leaving Friday for a lecture tour in the West and shall be returning March 4th. Meanwhile, I shall have read "The Primal Mind" and will probably want to talk about it. Perhaps we can have another meeting and conversation before I again set off, March 25th, for California.

It's a privilege and pleasure to know you, Jamake.
All best
Sincerely
Joe

Kalakaua Avenue
Honolulu, Hawaii 96815
Feb. 20, 1983

Dear Jamake—
My short dip into New York in December resulted in a fine new contract for the book on which I have been working, these past ten years; but I was so caught up in all the meetings, preparations, and so on, that the chance of getting in touch with you, to which I had been looking forward, never occurred. I'll be back briefly end of April (around the 21st), and shall hope to see you then.

I have to tell you, that, as I work now on this volume (which is going to be the first of four) I have your critical eye continually in mind and am hoping that when you see what I have done, you will find it acceptable. The last third, or so, of this volume deals with North American materials, with particular attention to what has been learned of their historical background, from 10,000 B.C. to the Ghost Dance years. I am calling the tetralogy "A Historical Atlas of World Mythology," and there will be maps and charts and all kinds of archeological information.

Hawaii is being a delight, and I am finding our apartment a wonderful place in which to do my writing. The pressures of New York were becoming a bit more than I could tolerate—though, of course, there is a great deal that I very much miss out here: mostly moments with my friends.

I was delighted to learn of the progress of your own career, and am looking forward to our next occasion.

Warm regards and all good wishes,

Ever yours

Joe

Kalakaua Avenue
Honolulu, Hawaii 96815
Jan. 27, 1984

Dear Jamake—
Now that the task has been accomplished of adding 20 carton-loads of books to the content of the Honolulu apartment, I am able to sit down with the beautiful volume that you so generously inscribed and sent to me just before our departure from New York; and I find it entirely wonderful: not only packed with essential information much of which is new to me, but also alive with that quality of spirit that I know and have long revered as American Indian. I am still at work on the American chapters of my own second volume (The Way of the Seeded Earth), and am fortunate to have your "Leaves from the Sacred Tree" at hand, to steady me

Rubbing from the Raimondi Monolith, mentioned in Campbell's letter of January 27, 1984, to Jamake Highwater. It is from the Chavín de Huántar site in Peru.

in my course. I am just now at work on my pages on Chavín de Huántar and find myself in very deep water indeed.

Have you ever (for example) studied the rubbing from the Raimondi Monolith, upside down?!!?[11] I don't know whether I dare even suggest what I think I see there. Look at it, first, one way, then, the other! The date of the piece, c. 200 B.C. (Highwater, 1983, p. 227), is seven or eight hundred years earlier than the Hindu/Buddhist Tantric development; and yet, if anything like what I think I see is actually what was intended by the artists fashioning this monolith, we have here the most sophisticated slab of engraved stone in the history of art. Esoteric it surely is, in any case—and very deep.

Jean and I are in a heavenly environment here, perfect for the concentration that I now shall need to get on with the large operation at hand. I have already recovered entirely from the numerous excitements of the fall and, looking back now, in quiet retrospect, upon the wonder of that big event, December 4th, I find myself rich in the friends and friendships of my lifetime. Your own words at that time touched me deeply, and I shall be thanking you for them, the rest of my years.

Jean joins me in warm good wishes; and again, my thanks for your beautiful book.

Sincerely
Joe

Kalakaua Avenue
Honolulu, Hawaii 96815
April 13, 1985

Dear Jamake—
Your kind greeting at the National Arts Club event; review in "Commonweal" of <u>The Way of the Animal Powers</u>; and words of friendly caution concerning Jomon-Valdivia sent to me via Bob Walter, lie here spread before me on my New York work table. Last week I arrived, principally to see Jean's production at The Open Eye of Philip Gotanda's <u>Dreams of Kitamura</u>, but also to consult with Fred van der Marck about an unexpected book that I have just written which he hopes to bring out in a couple of months. In two days, I shall be leaving with Jean for Honolulu; so that my only chance to visit with you this time has to be by way of these generous tokens of your friendship and concern for my welfare, which I deeply appreciate.

My second Atlas volume, <u>The Way of the Seeded Earth</u>, has split into two. Part I, which is almost ready, will treat of the Native Planting Cultures of the Americas, and Part II, of Oceania and Africa. The contrast with the hunting-and-gathering mythologies is dramatic, and the parallels over the whole earth are, of course, amazing. I am going to have to find some way to present these parallels simply as facts, without getting myself embroiled in the endless argument of "convergence" vs "diffusion." I find that if I suggest that anything may have been carried from one place to another, I am a "diffusionist," whereas if I suggest that certain other things may have appeared in two places independently, I am a "Jungian." Actually, what I am trying to be is a historian, reporting what appear to be documented facts, and where literally thousands of practically identical parallels have been reported of the New World and the Old, I find it difficult simply to settle for the anthropological cop-out of "convergence"—as though "man" had nothing to do with the matter, only mechanical circumstance. If I were dealing only with the Americas, or only with Oceania and Africa, I should be able to ignore the problem, in the usual way of local specialists. But my interest is global and psychological. Moreover, I have chanced upon a couple of real tough ones to call to people's attention, which, if I had any care for my scholarly reputation, I would suppress and not even mention. For example: Have you ever turned a line drawing of the Peruvian Raimondi Panel upside down and tried to explain to yourself what you see there?

Following your timely suggestion, I am getting hold of Lathrap's Upper Amazon and Ancient Ecuador.[12] Does he have a date for the earliest ceramic figures in America? I hope that during my next visit to these parts, I may be able to talk with you about these things. I was really sorry that you could not participate in the National Arts Club evening.[13] It was a grand affair, and I would have been proud to have had you at my side.—Jean joins me in warm greetings and affection.

Aloha

—Joe

Kalakaua Avenue
Honolulu, Hawaii 96815
May 22, 1985

Dear Jamake—
I shall, of course, be delighted and regard it as an honor to lend my name to the project described in the Proposal just received. I am also delighted to see that you have already become an influential citizen of the state of Connecticut. The Project is well presented, timely, and very nicely coincides with what now seems to me to have been the leading interest of my life.—Which life, by the way, has just now become transformed by the introduction of a computer to its worktable. A truly monstrous substitute for a pen! The brute arrived last week and I have not been able to persuade it to do my will instead of its own. But the lesson of Bruce's Spider is giving me heart.

All good wishes to your project and your work. And best thanks for this invitation.

Aloha
Joe

Kalakaua Avenue
Honolulu, Hawaii 96815
August 25, 1985

Dear Jamake—
Little River Farm, I assume, is affording you the hermetic space required for the living of your own life. The heavy lecture schedule, however, suggests something more. Unfortunately (for me) you will be in Ecuador and Peru when I return to New York, briefly this fall. Jean is taking her dance company to Athens the end of September, and I shall be landing in the City September 20 to go along with them. She has prepared a program for Greek mythic themes for the occasion, which will be then shown in New York in

December. Presenting Greek myths to Athenians (daisies to Florida! Owls to Athens!) is really exciting.

My IBM computer, of which you

[lacuna here: page missing]

the Bill Moyers event, which took place at George Lucas's fabulous Skywalker Ranch, about 20 miles drive north of San Francisco. Three days, with 9 hours of interview! Everybody was enormously pleased with what happened, and for me it was a really marvelous occasion. The man is tops.[14]

On the last line of your lecture schedule I see scratched out visit to Hawaii. Perhaps there will be in the not too distant future another such line, but not scratched out, when I may have the very great pleasure of sitting down with you here in this lovely apartment and exchanging refreshing ideas. All best, meanwhile for the fine career that I see shaping up around you. Jean is in New York, right now, working with her company. I am sure she would be delighted to tell you of her plans; sure, also, that if she were here, she would be adding to this letter with mine, her admiring and sincere aloha.

Ever

Joe

Kalakaua Avenue
Honolulu, Hawaii 96815
Nov. 10, 1985

Dear Jamake—
The trip to Athens was a great success and real adventure. Jean's company performed in the big Roman theater beneath the Acropolis, two full-moon nights, to two audiences of 3,000, and I gave an illustrated lecture on Greek mythology to the Greeks. Looking forward now to further adventures to come, I find a couple of letters before me from one Jamake Highwater, proposing a Native

Arts Festival to be held some time in May (is that correct?), in Storr, Connecticut, as well as a second festival of the kind to be held in Texas, in late October (correct?). I shall be delighted to participate in both and await whatever news may be forthcoming of these important events.

And thank you for the news from Peru and the interesting piece by Doig. That Raimondi figure is to me one of the most mysterious works of art in this world. The view from the side is certainly a surprise—visualizada, I take it, by some artist: I have been thinking of the stela as a work in low relief. But all I can find are line drawings—no photographs. How large it is, or where it was originally, or what it really looks like, I cannot imagine. Nor can I tell whether the line-drawings are accurate. The impression gained from Doig's perspectiva de frente is rather different in detail from that which I find in J. Alden Mason, The Ancient Civilizations of Peru (a Pelican Book), p. 43—which is the only other representation of the work that I have yet found. No one seems to want to say very much about the monument. I finally may have to fly to Lima to have a look at it myself.

And about this computer! One day I'm greatly pleased with it; the next, I could sell it for junk. Now that I'm back in Hawaii for a spell, I am going to arrange for a session or two with my IBM advisor, to iron out a few nasty quirks or quarks. "Invalid codes found. Job cancelled," is a piece of news that I regard as downright mean. With all the marvelous things this machine can do, why did they have to add a bug like that? Or is this something peculiar to my software: Display Write 3? My printer is ripping along gloriously, then suddenly stops and this notice appears. And the work is lost.

Ah well! [doodle face] and try again! I do not yet [doodle heart] my computer.

Aloha nui & mahalo:
Yours ever
Joe

The Native Land Foundation
Room 1007
Lafayette Street
New York, N.Y. 10012
May 26, 1986

Dear Joe:
Hope all is well with you, and that Jean continues to recover her full, marvelous power!

I just got back from Minnesota, where the very fine people at the Minneapolis College of Art and Design gave me an Honorary Doctor of Fine Arts Degree after I gave their commencement talk. One of the Deans had read my interview with you in Quadrant, and therefore told me that a group with which he is associated very much hopes to lure you to Minneapolis as its keynote speaker. I explained that you were dedicated to finishing the series of books you are now producing, and that you were getting involved in many lectures. They asked if I might give them your address anyway, and so I suggested, instead, that I pass along their letter to you with a kind word in their behalf. They are good people, but I insisted that your work has to be considered before any other activities, and therefore I could do nothing more in their behalf except transmit their good wishes.

In the meantime, let me tell you that all of my airport time has allowed me to complete the fifth reading since 1965 of your OCCIDENTAL MYTHOLOGY. I could write a great deal of praise with ease, but let me simply say that part I "The Marriage of East and West" and part II "Syncretistic and Ethnic Monotheism" and part III "Mystery Cult and Apocalypse" of Chapter 6 on Hellenism have to be the most brilliant and precise summary of the very core of East/West mentality that I have ever encountered. The range of your research in these sections, the profundity of your grasp of the issues, and the ease with which you deal with elaborate and complex issues in a language that is at once specific and poetic is astounding. Simply marvelous!

I send you and Jean all good wishes,
Fondly,
Jamake

Kalakaua Avenue
Honolulu, Hawaii 96815
7/86

Dear Jamake—
Thank you for your very kind letter. I am pleased to be able to report that Jean is now pretty nearly back to her pre-1986 state of good health and vigor. We are both making a big deal of taking care of ourselves, and it begins to look as though we may be winning the game.

In relation to games: I have been having some thoughts of my own about the Mexican ballgame. In Anthony F. Aventi's Archaeoastronomy in Pre-Columbian America (Univ of Texas Press, 1975), there is an article by Carmen Cook de Leonard, "A New Astronomical Interpretation of the Four Ballcourt Panels at Tajín, Mexico," which I think you will find very helpful. Panel 2 is delightful and the main clue to the sense of the Tajín series. It shows the bird quetzalcoxcoxli (= Xochipilli, the god of lust and music, games and play) dancing over the genitalia of a reclining Quetzalcoatl. Two musicians are standing by, beating a wood-block and shaking a rattle. The message (according to de Leonard's reading) is of Quetzalcoatl squandering his manly strength in nights of sharing the sky with the moon. Next panel, he confronts the sun-god as challenger to a ball game (Quetzalcoatl and Tezcatlipoca). But his manly strength has already been squandered, and so, in the next panel, he has lost the game and is being sacrificed on an altar. In this reading, it would be the loser of the game who was sacrificed)—at least at Tajín.

However, browsing about in Seler's huge analysis of the symbols of the Codex Borgia, I find that Xochipilli has been described by Sahagun as related to, or in some way identified with, Xolotl, Quetzalcoatl's grotesque little brother ("the Dog"), who is the particular god of the ball game and of monstrosities. He it was who was the first sacrifice to the sun, from which immolation he tried to escape by running away and changing form several times. Caught, however, he was thrown into the solar fire, and is in this role identified with the down-going phase and aspect of the planet Venus as Evening Star. Now, since the bird quetzalcoxoctli = Xochipilli = Xalótl = Quetzalcoatl as Evening Star, it may be that the meaning of Panel 2 may not be that Quetzalcoatl is spending his strength, but simply that he is here in his character as Evening Star, who is about to be challenged by Tezcatlipoca (as in the standard myth) and descend into the underworld, as though following the sun. And here, now, is my question: Might it not be that the passage of the ball through the ring for a winning score can have been taken as equivalent to a passage of the one who sent the ball (namely, the winner) along the way of the sun, through the narrow gate, to such a glorious death and resurrection as was that of Quetzalcoatl, first as Evening, then as Morning Star? I do not think it accords with the Mexican concept of the sacrifice that a loser, instead of a winner, should be identified with the symbolized god. On the other hand, of course, it was Tezcatlipoca who brought about the abdication, departure, and self-immolation of Quetzalcoatl. Perhaps the aim of the ballgame was to identify the winner with Tezcatlipoca, who then would have become the sacrificing priest—which seems to me a bit too banal.

Anyhow, the ballgame was almost certainly associated with the confrontation of Quetzalcoatl and Tezcatlipoca, as represented in the well-known legend.

We can perhaps talk about all this and bring forth a few more ideas when we see each other in the Fall.

Meanwhile, all best and fond aloha from us both—

Yours ever

Joe

P.S. Am still waiting to see an acceptable copy of my book. Perhaps next month!

Kalakaua Avenue
Honolulu, Hawaii 96815
August 31, 1986

Dear Jamake—
Returning yesterday from a 3-day session with Bill Moyers at George Lucas' Skywalker Ranch, I find here your very kind and interesting letter about 1. Our Houston, Texas, event, and 2. Your Athletes of the Gods. The news of the book is super, and I am looking forward to its publication. The Houston event will be a very special affair indeed, and that, too, is something to which I am looking forward with great interest. Jean will be with me, and I have just written to Sue [undecipherable] to let her know about that.

Fred tells me that The Inner Reaches etc. has at last arrived in Manhattan. I am preparing a list of people to whom copies are to be sent, and your name is high among them. After all the noise and delay, the little book itself will come as something of an anticlimax. I have myself lost all interest in it, and have only unfriendly feelings toward Fred's shop, for what they did to my little offering. Work on Vol. 2 of the Atlas now has all of my attention, and I am only hoping that they can get this one into print without again blowing my mind.

I have just received from Marija Gimbutas a copy of her manuscript for a volume on the symbolism of her Great Goddess, 7000 to 3500 BC. It makes an enormous statement. In my own work on Northeast Woodland myths (specifically a Mohawk version of The Woman Who Fell from the Sky) I have detected what I think must be a connection with Central Asian themes; and with the Goddess already at Lake Baikal in late Magdalenian times, I am now wondering whether parallels of some kind may be discernable. A long shot, but it just might be.

September 24th I'll be watching for your Native Land—if we are in touch, out here, with your Public Television station. Meanwhile, dear Jamake, all good wishes for your important undertakings. Jean joins in warm Aloha.

Ever

Joe

Kalakaua Avenue
Honolulu, Hawaii 96815
Dec. 27, 1986

Dear Jamake—

Jean and I spent an elegant afternoon, last week, viewing in her studio your two television creations, The Primal Mind and Native Land, which returned me to a reading of your two books—the latter bearing a very kind inscription and a warmly appreciated dedication to myself. On top of all this, I have just finished writing my piece, for the Guggenheim people, and am consequently very full today of thoughts about you and your work. I think it is important: the work that you are doing! And I take great satisfaction in the knowledge that my own work has in some way contributed to its realization. I want to start the New Year by thanking you for letting me know of this connection and by letting you know in return, that in my work, now, on Vol. II of the Atlas, I shall be making use of your books and ideas to help me along. As I think I have told you, I am at work on my Native American volume, commencing in the Northeast, with the Iroquois and Algonquin tribes; next, the Southeast and the "Trail of Tears" . . . etc. The Olmec-to-Aztec development belongs properly to the culture stage of <u>The Way of the Celestial Lights</u>, along with the Old World archaic high cultures, and so, will be only noticed in this volume. On the other hand (perhaps inconsistently), I am going to try to handle the South American development, Chavín to Inca, and the coming of Pizarro, in the concluding chapters of this volume. The next volume of my series (Part II, of The Way of the Seeded Earth) will deal with Oceania and Africa, and the following two volumes (Parts I and II of The Way of the Celestial Lights) with Sumer and Egypt, Early Greece, China, and Mexico. The Classical, Indian, and Chinese chapters will conclude at the date-line of c. 500 BC, of Pythagoras, the Buddha, and Confucius, which is where the last volume of my series will begin, The Way of Man, and which is where the Mythos-to-Logos transformation occurs, from mythic imagery to rational discourse and the "Perennial Philosophy"; also, the transformation that I have called "The Great Reversal," where something like the Jainism comes along, "All life is sorrowful—and evil" etc., so "let's pull out." The first break, we might say, from the way of the "Primal Mind." Am I correct in thinking that we do not find any development of a tradition of this critical, negative kind in the Americas?

The big thing for me this Christmas was a gift from Jean of an IBM

[apparent lacuna]

and I hope that we may have another visit together at that time. Meanwhile, our love and warm good wishes to you for the year and years ahead. All success to your important project, to the reawakening of the spirit of our Native Land:—

Aloha
Joe

Phil Cousineau (born November 26, 1952) is an American author, lecturer, and filmmaker, as well as an expert on mythology and film and the hero's journey structure of screenplays. Campbell was a mentor and major influence. Cousineau wrote narration for the documentary film about Campbell's life, The Hero's Journey, *and edited the companion book of the same title.*

Phil Cousineau
10th Ave. #5
San Francisco, CA 94118

Joseph Campbell
c/o The Clift Hotel
Geary and Taylor
San Francisco, CA

April 5, 1986

Dear Joseph,
Welcome back to San Francisco once more. I trust you are in fine fettle and that Jean is well. Since I am not sure that we will be able to meet this trip I want to be sure that I get a copy of this interview to you.

As you can see, my attempt to synthesize your work in comparative mythology with Robert Bly's in poetry, James Hillman's in psychology, and George Lucas' (and others) in film is finally getting some attention. I do hope, Joseph, I have represented your work well. It is with respect that I am doing this Myth and Movie work at all.

The response to the interview has been overwhelmingly positive. There is a hunger for this work, for this attempt to synthesize the classics and the modern. Because of this I have been approached for several more workshops, including Esalen, the Hermes Project and the Edinburgh Film Festival. Thank you for paving this Royal Road, to paraphrase Freud.

As far as the film goes, much has happened since we spoke last at the Grateful Dead concert and party. (Incidentally, I thoroughly enjoyed seeing the rock and roll phenomena through your eyes and Jean's. It was remarkable to consider my generation's music as "mythical"). I have completed my "paper cut" of the film but the financing for post-production has fallen through on Stuart a couple of times. It is exasperating for everyone involved. Yet he persists and in the last week has found commitments from two other sources.

This protracted process has given me a chance to outline several of the videotaped lectures for the new market of "home education," as I briefed Jean at Bob Weir's party. "The Grail Romances" lecture has been chosen as the first to go on the market. It is a brilliant, lucid presentation, I might add.

The downside of this long wait has been a stalemate for "The Companion Book." The stipulation all along was a simultaneous release date for book and film. But without even a post-production schedule until this week it has been impossible for me to ask writers of stature to commit themselves to the essays we had in mind for the book. I am terrifically disappointed in the lost work but am consoling myself in this unexpected work on the videotape series. Watching these 52 hours of lectures a few times has been worthy of a Master's Degree.

Another source of satisfaction has been getting the Dead and Betsy involved in the film. It was unforgettable for me to take all this footage over to Bob and Mickey's and watch long passages of it with them. Their asides are worthy of a short story. Believe me, I have been doing all that is humanly possible to push for the completion of the film at a time when they are available to compose a score for it. Let's pray for some synchronicity!

I realize you are pushed for time on these lecture swings through town, but if you have the inclination for a late-night brandy tonight (Saturday) or breakfast tomorrow please feel free to call me here at home (#). Perhaps I can bring you more up to date about the film, the videotapes, or even my plans for the future concerning this "Myth, Dream, and Movies" scenario of mine.

Once again, Joe. I thank you for the inspiration in my work. I have been moved and given the courage of my convictions because of men like yourself, Robert, Jim Hillman, and the splendid artists I've known because of all your work.

Sincerely,
Phil Cousineau

Emilios Bouratinos is the Greek author of Homeopathy of the Mind: How the Greeks Defeated Rationality *(1993) and* Science, Objectivity, and Consciousness *(2018).*

August 27, 1987

Dear Joe,
It was good of you to write such a long letter. I never expected more than a line or two, so you can imagine my elation at receiving such a communication from you. Thanks for taking the time to read my piece. But thanks even more for taking the trouble to commit your thoughts about it on paper. Your words of praise are encouraging and give me hopes that I will perhaps find a magazine willing to publish the article. The only magazine I can think of is PARABOLA and I will give it a try. As to the English, please do not concern yourself. Steve is here and he promised to correct my poor English. I think he will do it well, because he writes excellently. It was very kind of you to even think of correcting the text your self.

The mystical insight and the mythical outlook are very closely connected. But myth performs a different function. It takes us into the models, energies, relationships and hidden laws of the world of phenomena. Mystical insight takes us through it—to the region beyond phenomena. Myth of course touches on that aspect as well, as you yourself never tire of repeating in your books. But myth will point that way, it will pose the problems, it will elucidate the dangers. What you will do with what myth tells you is your own responsibility—and to the extent that you perform as in fact myth intends, you approach the mystical. Myth experienced is mystical. But to the extent that the mystical takes you beyond the region of phenomena, beyond the even hidden interpenetration of them, means that the mystical experience is capable of transcending the mythical. That is why Capra and the others who connect modern physics to the mystical insights of the East or West tend to confuse, to some extent, the deeper issues involved. The material world and the world of form which permeates it correspond more to the mythical approach than to the mystical. Lewis Carroll is far more pertinent than Lao-Tzu or Meister Eckhart.

My reference to the world of form is not accidental. Lately there has been some very interesting finds by biochemists, biologists and zoologists indicating that the platonic "ideas" do in fact imprint themselves on the material dimension in a very striking and organizing way. This too has mythical repercussions of great importance. I am reading just now a book by Rupert Sheldrake called *A New Science of Life* which deals with this subject in an extremely enlightened way. The book is absolutely fascinating and I will try to draw the mythical connection and write a second article along the lines of *Myth, Physics and Consciousness*.

I am very happy that you keep on working so much. The Atlas would be of enormous value. So please put all your energies into that: It is too precious a job to leave undone. The very idea of it tickles me. I have just finished reading your Way of the Animal Powers and cannot tell you how much it has inspired me. The task you have accomplished there is truly herculean. I now realize not only the mystique of animals themselves but of the human relationship with them in so-called primitive societies. In other words, I see how and in what sense animals are in fact wiser and more knowledgeable than man and why there is so much divine power in them. The totem approach doesn't even touch the surface of the subject, with its sociological and psychological overtones and its total naivety. No author has brought out what you have in this book—and I can only express my unending thanks to you for having sent it to me.

With best wishes for the successful outcome of your new herculean task,

Emilios [Bouratinos]

Joseph Campbell's tombstone

CODA

Testimonials and Condolences

In August 1987, Campbell was diagnosed with cancer of the esophagus. He died at his home in Hawaii, the land beyond the waves, on October 30, 1987. Following are some tributes and letters of condolence.

Betty Sue Flowers is the former director of the Lyndon Baines Johnson Library and Museum and an emeritus professor of English at the University of Texas at Austin. She is the author of a number of texts, particularly about the nineteenth-century poet Christina Rossetti. She also acted as a consultant to Bill Moyers's 1988 documentary series, Joseph Campbell and the Power of Myth, *and edited the book derived from it.*

31 Oct 1987

Dear Jean,

I just heard of Joe's death and feel—as so many others, who considered him to be one of their special teachers—that I have lost a valued friend, and that the world has lost a treasure. Please do let me know if there is anything at all that I can do for you and

Joe. With all that he did in the past year, he went forth in a blaze of light, giving us many gifts. I know from so much that he said that while giving these gifts to the world, he received a major gift himself—you!

With deepest sympathy,

Betty Sue [Flowers]

Joseph Lewis Henderson (August 31, 1903–November 17, 2007) was an American physician and a Jungian psychologist. Henderson founded the Jung Institute of San Francisco, of which he was the president.

Box #
Ross, California 94957
11/1/87

Dear Jean,

I have just learned from Barbara of Joe's death and I want you to know how strongly I feel for you and have been feeling for you both during this ordeal. I would have written sooner but initially I was told to wait until you were more ready for Joe's illness to be known and I was just going to write today when I got Barbara's news.

Helena and Liz are here with me this weekend and they join me in sending love and hope to see you whenever you come through S.F.

I appreciated your kind letter to me last year and your appreciation of my paper on Morris Graves. It really pleased me what you said.

Again, our love and greetings in harmony with memory of all the wonderful times we had with you and Joe.

Yours,

Joe [Henderson]

Little River Farm
Route 1, Box #
Hampton, Connecticut 06247

Jean Erdman
Kalakaua Avenue #208
Honolulu, Hawaii, 96815

Nov. 2, 1987

Dear Jean,
What can possibly be said about such a loss?

No matter how many vivid years he lived

No matter how many of us he touched with his brilliant ideas and marvelous persona.

No matter how many great books he left for us

No matter how much we loved him

And no matter the joy his wild spirit brought to a spiritless world

Still, there is nothing...absolutely nothing that can lessen the pain of losing him.

We can only take some slight comfort in knowing that he went out upon the eve of the feast of Samhain, when the white ravens of the ancient Celts are sent from the Glass Castle to summon the dead to a celebration with the living.

In our hearts and memories, if nowhere else, he persists as vivid and as fresh and as sunny bright and full of wonderment as he was on the best day of his shining!

Love,
Jamake

Martha Graham (May 11, 1894–April 1, 1991) was an acclaimed American modern dancer and choreographer. Jean Erdman was one of her students at the Bennington Summer School of the Dance and performed with the Martha Graham Dance Company in the 1930s and 1940s, before leaving to create her own troupe.

Martha Graham Center of Contemporary Dance Inc.
November 3, 1987

Dear Jean,

I have just received the tragic news. This is one of the great losses of the world. Joseph, whom I first came to know in Bennington days, has given me things for my mind and soul through his writings and beliefs that no one else has ever given me.

What Joseph has done for the world is to have opened gates to the mysterious past through his treatment of myths and legends; his intuitive soul and spirit have guided him and us through these gates, and nothing will ever be quite the same without him, just as nothing today would be the same without his power to influence us so profoundly.

By his knowledge, his love of life, his recognition of the blood memories that move us all, Joseph has contributed immeasurably to the great moments in my life, both personally and in my work.

Jean, to you who shared his glory and contributed to it by your companionship, your love, your encouragement, and your own animation of spirit, I send my love and blessings; I think of you now when you first danced with me reciting words of Emily Dickinson in Letter to the World:

After great pain, a formal feeling comes,
The nerves sit ceremonious like tombs,
The mechanical go round a wooden way
This hour of lead.

You were so young when you spoke those lines, and yet no one has ever given that special meaning to the word "lead" that you did.

As a tribute to Joseph and to his eternal quality I would like to plant trees in Israel in his name, and I will ask Teddy Kollek to do this on my behalf.

And I would like to plan a tribute to Joseph here at the School during the period of the Affirmations Lectures. It is to my deepest sorrow that last year Joseph's schedule would not permit him to speak to our students, to share with them, the young, the essence of a life well spent.

Please call me at any hour if you need to talk. My private number is #.

With love and blessings,
Martha [Graham]

Judith Davidson Moyers is an award-winning television producer and the wife of Bill Moyers.

November 3, 1987

Dear Jean
I am thinking of you every day. How I wish Bill and I could come to see you!

Thinking of Joe I was reminded of this bit of Robert Burns:

"If there's another world,
he lives in bliss:
If there is none, he
made the best of this."

I will always remember Joe with great affection.
Love to you,
Judith Moyers

Robert J. Griffin (July 8, 1921–July 4, 2008) taught comparative literature and foreign languages in institutions including San Francisco State University, University of California, Berkeley, and the University of California, Riverside.

Department of Literatures and Languages
University of California
Riverside, CA 92521
November 4, 1987

Dear Miss Erdman,
I have just read of the passing of your husband, and want to express my sense of personal loss to you. I honestly cannot say, however, that my current shock is a sorrowful one. A celebration of his life, it seems to me, is the order of the day. Joe Campbell was without any doubt the most important presence I have encountered in nearly thirty years of academic life. I couldn't possibly begin to measure his vast contribution to the world of letters, let alone his impact on creative life in the U.S. in this century.

Please excuse the official letterhead (since it's the only thing I have at hand). My message is a personal one because the man simply transformed my life in a way that has isolated me from workaday academic life and has led me to revere what I used to teach with a false sense of understanding. An American Indian student of mine once gave me a used copy of The Hero and asked me to read it. I dutifully took it with me to a Pizza Hut on a cold, raw, windy night. As a packed house of irritable people waited for their pizzas, I huddled by the juke box and began reading the book that would transform my intellectual life. I distinctly remember telling myself that THIS is the promised land, a perspective that I had been seeking for most of my life. My bookshelf is now crammed with all of his well-worn books and editions. I will sorely miss not being able to read The Seeded Earth. My best students continue to read him and thus to discover something valuable in themselves. I have had many occasions to cite him and have just completed a book in which I express my gratitude for his deep courage and splendid example of knowledge leading to wisdom. Right above the desk in my study is a gold framed note he once wrote me, which ends with "Having a ball, lecturing, and working on the biggest and toughest book yet"; can you imagine how those words will encourage me for the remainder of my professional life? The lecture he once gave at my campus was easily the best public lecture I have ever heard. And since my department was virtually out of funds at the time, he gave us his masterful talk for a song.

I have periodically taken the liberty to bug him with postcards from some of the far-flung places, principally because the beauty and energy of his mind at work drove me there. The Skeleton Key led me to a sunlit day in Piazza San Marco, the Mythic Image came to my mind as I surveyed the Mayan ruins at Uxmal and further led me to learn Mayan hieroglyphs; the Animal Powers placed me atop Ayers Rock this past spring. Each time I whispered a prayer of thanks to Professor Campbell, while realizing that I would never be able to thank him for what he showed me. I will miss him very much.

With heartfelt sympathy,
Bob Griffin

Playwright Rosemary Foley's Punch With Judy, *mentioned in the letter below, was performed at Jean Erdman's Theatre of the Open Eye in New York in March of 1982.*

Rosemary Foley
Manor Lane
Pelham, New York 10803
11/6/87

Dear Jean,
Bill and I were most saddened when we saw the notice in last week's newspaper. We're numbered among so very many people who admired Joseph. What an amazing mind and heart; a fascinating and complex man.

We had always promised ourselves that someday we were going to invite you both to our home or ask if it were possible to meet in the city for dinner. I think we felt as though it might be misconstrued or maybe we didn't want to intrude, you were both involved in dozens of cultural and academic pursuits.

I keep getting a picture of the two of you at one of the early rehearsals of Punch With Judy. You were radiant, encouraging, positive about the play's worth but Joseph sat and looked a little puzzled...he wasn't quite sure but he wished us all the best luck and meant it.

You were really two of a kind except information travelled different paths...you from your heart to your head and he from his head to his heart.

I'm sure the loss is inestimable. You have our love,

Rosemary and Bill Foley

Peter Donat (1928–2018) was a Canadian American actor. He narrated Campbell's film biography, The Hero's Journey: A Biographical Portrait *(1987), and moderated the multivolume video series* The World of Joseph Campbell: Transformation of Myths through Time *(1989).*

Broderick Street
San Francisco, CA 94115
November 7, 1987

Dear Jean—
A brilliant light has gone out. Along with millions of others we will miss Joe, but very especially because we came to know him. That, and knowing <u>you</u>, has been very meaningful & important to us.

We are thinking of you, sending our love, & look forward to seeing you again soon.

Do let us know when you are coming to San Francisco.

Very sincerely yours—

Peter and Marijke [Donat]

John ("Jan") N.H. Perkins is a Jungian psychoanalyst who studied with Campbell in 1971–72, the final year of Campbell's teaching tenure at Sarah Lawrence.

November 8, 1987

Dear Jean Erdmann [*sic*],
"...that is a rare and fine thing," writes Thomas Mann, "to gaze unflinchingly through tears." As the mild afternoon light of Autumn falls across my desk, illuminating Joe's excellent photograph in THE NEW YORK TIMES, I am painfully and abruptly reminded how bright and richly inspiring a presence it is which has slipped away.

By private arrangement, Joe allowed me to audit his final year's lecture series in "Folklore and Literature" at SLC. The ever-recurring message throughout was that the richly varying resonances of mythological fiction from the Stone-Age European caveman and the Australian Aborigines to Thomas Mann and James Joyce reveal to us the structural elements of human nature, both socially and individually. "Facts of the mind made manifest in a fiction of matter." Those "lies," "tricks," and "delusions" of which Thomas Mann was so fond of speaking do sustain life, and with convincing eloquence. Mythology is the Truth, we learned. What a high and exciting irony of appreciation Joe touched off in us. It truly left us in a state of profound and nearly helpless giddiness!

And if that weren't enough, his humor was devastating:

"There is essentially no difference between a Roman orgy and a church supper. In each instance, the quality of love is entirely indiscriminate!"

And then, if my memory serves me well, the story of the girl student who had been demonstrating in the streets for some left-wing cause, and as Joe raked her over the coals for cutting the class, he spied what looked suspiciously like lapis lazuli beads peeping out from around the frayed and dirty collar of her sweatshirt. After questioning her, he learned they were a gift from her wealthy father, and were, in fact, valuable artifacts from Egyptian antiquity. At the hands of so skilled a raconteur as Joe, even this charmingly naïve young revolutionary, in her somewhat ludicrous circumstances, was transmuted to become for us a living mythologem, demonstrating the confusing paradox of so much contemporary life.

During that year and the ones following when Joe lectured in New York, I came to realize that he was more than a prodigious scholar and intellectual. A vital spiritual energy had come to reside in him, which he was able to radiate to others. As you certainly know, this is the finest and most excellent gift which a teacher can bestow upon his students, and which they may take with them all their lives. It is primarily for this reason that I feel indeed so fortunate to have known Joe and to have learned so much from his books and lectures. He made a deep and indelible mark upon my life!

I find it deplorable that the great east-coast universities paid so little attention to him. It was certainly their loss! I have always hoped that this did not pain or discourage Joe inordinately. He was far too <u>inconvenient</u> for the boxed-in academic establishment. What an excellent example and tribute this man was to the philosophy and integrity of Sarah Lawrence!

I am a practicing (Jungian) analyst in this part of Fairfield County, where I live in close contact with Joe's metaphorical and mythological world in my daily life. It will be a comfort to have him always with me in my library, but more importantly in my so vivid inner memory, ever as bright and alive for me as in those days at SLC nearly fifteen years ago.

On a warm and sunny midday in May, 1972, the students arranged to have a little champagne luncheon picnic on the back terrace of Andrews, immediately following Joe's final lecture. There he stood, with those bushy eyebrows and radiant eyes, talking away in his inimitably enthusiastic manner with characteristic youthfulness, as if the theme or motif at hand were a priceless ore, mined only this very day! I was thirty-three then, and teaching related subjects at the Master's School up in Dobbs Ferry. I recall so well standing there as I took in the scene, thinking to myself, "Perkins, you nearly arrived too late!"

I occasionally wrote letters to Joe after his speaking engagements, and he was careful to answer each one in some detail. I did not take this respectful treatment for granted, knowing full well how busy he was and how much mail he generally received.

In his study, there may be an unopened file-folder taped around the edges to form an envelope, which I sent to Joe a month ago. It contains a photocopy of a 1939 LIFE article on Thomas Mann in America, together with a letter from me asking advice regarding the study of Joyce, and some comments from me on passages from Mann and Joyce, which I knew Joe loved. I don't suppose he was well enough to have read it.

When he lectured at the east side Open Eye, some of us used to eat at the same little corner restaurant as you two did. I often spied the two of you holding hands as you walked back to the theater. I hold the image in my mind's eye during the last moment of this writing.

My wife Margery Cuyler, SLC '70, joins me in this expression of sympathy and appreciation.

I am most sincerely yours,
John ("Jan") N. H. Perkins

Fillow Street
West Norwalk, CT 06850

Leon Edel (September 9, 1907–September 5, 1997) is regarded as the twentieth century's foremost authority on the novelist Henry James.

Leon Edel
Lurline Drive
Honolulu, Hawaii 96316
9 November 87

Dear Jean Erdman
We read of Joe's death in New York last week but I could not bring myself then to speak to you of the sorrow we felt. Now, back home, I wish simply to say how difficult we find it to think of him as gone—that we will no longer have our little encounters at the Club and elsewhere: encounters I've had with him during some forty years in various times and places—not least in a little vivid study group in which we participated long ago in New York. He was a wondrous illuminator and told so well his feelings, enthusiasms, discoveries.

If I find it painful to write these words it enables me to imagine the depths of your loss and sorrow.

Please accept all our sympathies. He remains in all he wrote and in his expression of the enduring depths of the human imagination.

Sincerely,
Leon and Marjorie Edel

Paul Mellon (June 11, 1907–February 1, 1999) was an American philanthropist. He was co-heir to one of America's greatest business fortunes, the Mellon Bank fortune. He and his wife, Mary, established the Bollingen Foundation in 1945.

Paul Mellon
Oak Spring
Upperville, Virginia 22176
9 Nov. 87

Dear Jean—
Bunny and I send you our deepest sympathy. Joe was a really extraordinary person, a wonderfully positive force in the worlds

of the mind, of our religion, and of history—a really universal man. But also a very human and understanding man. The world of scholarship will miss him greatly. And I know how deeply you will.

Love from us both,

Paul

Bill Moyers (born June 5, 1934) is an American journalist and political commentator. Perhaps his most famous achievement is his 1988 series Joseph Campbell and the Power of Myth with Bill Moyers, *consisting of interviews with Campbell, which aired on PBS after Campbell's death.*

Public Affairs Television, Inc.
Bill Moyers
12 November, 1987

Dear Jean:

I have been trying all these days to come to grips with Joe's death. But there he is, day after day on the screen in my editing room, as vibrant and inspiring and as generous with himself as he was in person. And I am struck by the realization that this man will live as all great teachers live—in the hearts and minds of those he touched and the eternal ripples that go forth in them. I am so deeply grateful that we were able to capture so much of him as we did, and I am sure the series will be a legacy that will enrich his legions of students and millions of others who never met him personally.

Of all that I shall remember about Joe, the most endearing is the relationship between the two of you. There was a radiance which must have been like the glow described by the troubadours, one that lasts.

We shall be in touch about the premiere of the series and hope you can be present.

Affectionately,

Bill Moyers

Emil Mihelich is the author of Around the Horn, The Purple Bow, Running Clear, Eden and the Individual: Christianity for the Twenty-First Century, *and* The Serpent of Eden.

North 28th
Tacoma, Washington 98407

November 12, 1987

Mrs. Joseph Campbell
Kalakaua Avenue #208
Honolulu, Hawaii, 96815

Dear Mrs. Campbell:
I would like to take this opportunity to thank you, once again, for your gracious telephone call of last Saturday, November 7, and to acknowledge receipt of my essay entitled "Mythological Illiteracy: Western Man's Folly." To communicate what I can only refer to as "the salvatory significance" of Mr. Campbell's discoveries has become both the professional and practical purpose of my life, and it is to this end that I have written my "creative mythology" in four novelistic segments and my initial collection of essays culminating in the one on Western man's "folly." I have discovered that to pursue such a purpose is not convenient; but with Mr. Campbell's inspiration to guide me, I will, to refer to William Faulkner, "endure and prevail." I only hope that my own life can be as creative and as sacrificial and, therefore, as inspirational as was Mr. Campbell's.

I will be forever grateful for your telephone communication because it allowed me the privilege of being a part of something that otherwise I was separate from. To make that communication meant everything to me because I felt that at last my being allowed to share in the anguish of Mr. Campbell's death, I had touched the rapture of his life as well. Of the many highlights of my life thus far, I can assure you that none surpass receiving your telephone call and talking to you. I hope my life and my work both affirms and builds on that which Mr. Campbell lived and produced before me; and I thank you, once again, for providing me with that "one, brief, shining moment" that allowed me to connect with a life I so authentically admired.

With warmest regards,
Emil Mihelich

Roger Lipsey is the editor of Coomaraswamy: Selected Papers, Volume 1: Traditional Art and Symbolism *(1977);* Selected Papers, Volume 2: Metaphysics *(1978); and* Volume 3: Life and Work *(1978).*

A Member of Arthur Young International
Third Avenue
New York, New York 10017
November 17, 1987

Dear Mrs. Campbell,
The world is so much richer for Joe having been here and done the work he did. To me personally he was an unfailing benefactor in things large and small, but I am thinking now of "the seventh generation" not myself. In this technological age he regrouped and redisseminated myth and tale so winningly that even "the seventh generation" will be in touch with that precious heritage. This is no small accomplishment.

Susan joins me in wishing you well and in confidence that your life will continue on its richly creative course.

Yours sincerely,
Roger Lipsey

The following is a letter of condolence to Erdman from an admirer of whom we have no other record.

Nov. 21st, 1987

Dear Jean,
I wrote you a long, ponderous attempt at expressing my grief and condolences for you at the physical loss of Joe. It is now in the wastebasket as part of the inexpressible.

Now, at 32,000 feet, on my way to Joe's Memorial Service in San Francisco, I think I can say it in a few words.

Basically, all us Joe Campbell devotees—from Bette and Bob down to those who only read one book—carry a deep sense of his Shakti, of you. I could not have imagined this strong, loving, often stern man without the effects of his wonderful, tenderizing woman (He often spoke of Odysseus's and Parzival's need to be "tenderized." Who but woman could do it? Who but the woman? he would ask.)

And we loved you in your own right. Everyone whose husband after so many years refers to her as "My darling Jean" or "my beloved wife," and who was the only critic he trusted, was special. After seeing "Gauguin in Tahiti," and watching you dance, I wondered if Joe was living with a mystic.

Since I first met Joe in 1974, having made him my mentor thirty years ago, he spoke of the Alchemical marriage, using himself and you as manifestations, as the only way one could get more than a glimpse of the Mystery into which he has now entered.

I am the mythologist who so nervously introduced you and Joe at UBC in October 1979. You were utterly gracious towards me and greatly lessened my sense of being engulfed in mana power.

If, as Joe's committed student, I am so sad, I can imagine your grief. And though I am sure he is still with us, he must have felt unbearably stricken at leaving his beloved soul-mate in that form.

By the time you receive this I'll have seen the flyer on Joe which I've undertaken to distribute in Canada, beginning with UBC's Extension department. Because he was the most important person in my spiritual and intellectual life, and because I am so grateful to him and you, I'll help keep his presence and ideas alive.

No one else said the unspeakable—no world ever needed to hear him more.

My tenderest memory out of many was the vision of you, beautiful and poised like a goddess, on stage at the Palace of Fine Arts on Joe's 80th birthday. You broke us all down with your magical statement that you were so proud to be Mrs. Joseph Campbell.

We know how proud he was to be Mr. Jean Erdman.

With love and fondest memories,

Linda MacDougall

Richard Tarnas (born February 21, 1950) is a cultural historian known for his books The Passion of the Western Mind: Understanding the Ideas That Have Shaped Our World View *and* Cosmos and Psyche: Intimations of a New World View. *Tarnas is professor of philosophy and psychology at the California Institute of Integral Studies, and is the founding director of its graduate program in philosophy, cosmology, and consciousness.*

Vineyard Canyon
Big Sur, CA 93920
November 22, 1987

Jean Campbell
Kalakaua
Honolulu, Hawaii 93815

Dear Jean,
Heather and I wanted to let you know of our sorrow upon hearing the news of Joe's death. Somehow it almost seemed as if he'd go on forever. And in some deep sense, he certainly will. He was a genuinely great man, and the world has been made richer by his presence in it.

We will always remember our sunlit lunch here in Big Sur with you and him last March, the day after his last birthday. As it happens, that month was the first month of Heather's pregnancy, and we are today expecting the birth of a baby quite literally at the moment. It has been a happy and healthy pregnancy these nine months. On the night of October 30, however, Heather suddenly began to bleed and went into premature labor, and we spent a tense night at the hospital in Carmel. As the night progressed, her contractions and bleeding gradually stopped, and the crisis passed. Since then she's been resting and the baby has now gone to full-term.

Jean, if there's anything we can do for you ever, let us know. If you're passing through Big Sur, we would be very happy to have you visit. In this difficult time, our thoughts are with you.

Sincerely
Rick and Heather Tarnas

James Merrill (March 3, 1926–February 6, 1995) was an American poet whose awards include the National Book Critics Circle Award for The Changing Light at Sandover. *In this work he mentions a dinner discussing Maya Deren's film* Divine Horsemen, *during which:*

Joe Campbell spoke
Authoritatively of your amazement
At being overwhelmed quite simply by
Gusts of material so violent
As to put out the candle held to them
By mere imagination. Such a theme,
He said, took all one's powers to "document".[1]

The crucial role Campbell played in the writing of the book version of Divine Horsemen *is well documented by Stephen and Robin Larsen in* A Fire in the Mind.

Water Street
Stonington, Connecticut 06378
24.xi.87

Dear Jean—
What a wrench to hear that we've lost your wonderful Joe—yours and everyone's. This is only to press your hand in sympathy, and in ongoing wonder at his achievement.

Dina gave me your address when I went to Bard on Sunday for her celebratory lunch. It was a wonderful occasion. We wished you were there.

Ever affectionately,
James Merrill

Carolyn Kizer was an American poet of the Pacific Northwest whose works reflect her feminism. She won the Pulitzer Prize in 1985.

8th St East
Sonoma, CA 95476
30 November '87

My dear Jean,
Of course you are, and will be, inundated with mail from all those who loved Joe and were influenced by him—but I'm unable to spare you one more letter. The deepest shock is that all of us, whether 20 or 60, thought that Joe would outlive us all, with the strong possibility that he would outlast the rest of the human race when we succeed in blowing ourselves up. I can't believe he's gone, and of course in the deepest sense he never will be.

I can't imagine what my life or my work would have been like without him. Not worth so much, I suspect. But there he was! That radiant presence. I'm especially grateful that I was around as he moved from chapter to chapter in his early book—and all his girl disciples panted to keep up with him! And how blessed he was to have you, and you him, for so long. I hope his physical suffering was not intolerable, & that you are not worn to the bone. Or if you are, that you will spring back to life and hope, in his memory.

I hope also to learn of memorial service plans in San Francisco, as I would dearly wish to take part.

Always love, dear Jean,

Carolyn Kizer

Betsy Kagan (January 16, 1942–June 7, 2017) was a dancer from the San Francisco Bay Area.

B. Kagan
Plaza Dr.
Berkeley, CA 94705
12/7/87

Dearest Jean,

I just heard that Joe had died in October, and was deeply saddened by the news. I was about to write to you that I had seen "A Hero's Journey" and was very moved and delighted to see such a beautiful portrait of you both. It was a wonderful tribute to Joe, and the shots of you were lovely, and very special to me.

This must be a sad and difficult time for you, and I wish I could be of help. I will be in New York in June, and will certainly try to see you then.

Meanwhile I send my sincere sympathy, and hopes that you can gain some comfort from the incredible legacy of creativity, brilliance, and beauty that came from your mutual inspiration.

Much love,

Betsy [Kagan]

Jon Berg is a film producer and production manager, known for such films as Wonder Woman *(2017),* Out of Time *(2003), and* Justice League *(2017).*

Elizabeth and Jon Berg
Falcon Way
Hercules, CA 94547
12/1/87

Dear Ms. Erdman
I've carried this card with me for weeks, wanting to write something so beautiful, so communicable of my feelings for your husband, and how much he has added to my life. I just don't have the words, but I want to say in the way I have, that I feel such gratefulness, such a sigh of relief, for his presence in the world and the light he sheds.

We've brought out his books again, and will spend a lifetime going over from time to time. He will always be part of our lives and that gives comfort to us.

I have been to over a dozen lectures, conferences, have tapes, the books, and have always loved, been inspired & awed by his vision—of which more has opened to us as a result.

I know of his great love for you and your work. I only hope all the love and help he's given to other people is a comfort to you now and the memories of your lives together.

With warmest regards,
Elizabeth and Jon Berg

If we could ever be of help to you in any way, what an honor it would be. If there's anyway we can participate in some aspect of?, [*sic*] please keep us in mind. (I'm a Physician Assistant, my husband Jon works in Special Effects in Film (George Lucas of Star Wars, Chris Wala Inc, etc.)

Namasté

William Schuman (August 4, 1910–February 15, 1992) was an American composer who left a substantial body of work. His career included stints as president of the Juilliard School and of the Lincoln Center for the Performing Arts.

William Schuman
Park Avenue
New York, N.Y. 10021

December 10, 1987

Mrs. Joseph Campbell
Waverly Place
New York, NY 10014

Dear Jean:
I just want you to know how much you have been in my thoughts since I read your sad news. Joe was fortunate indeed that you were his life companion. What a remarkable duo—you two! You have my affectionate sympathy.

Faithfully,
Will [Schuman]

December 19, 1987

Dear Mrs. Campbell—
It was with sadness we heard of Joseph Campbell's illness and death.

Oregon Friends of Jung was so fortunate that he was willing to come to Portland. Always it was the highlight of our year. Not only are we grateful for the insights he offered, but the large attendance he attracted started us on the way to a secure financial basis.

As recognition of Joseph Campbell's gifts, Oregon Friends has made a donation to ARAS [Archive for Research in Archetypal

Symbolism], with the request it be used to prepare his slides for use in that collection. The amount of $1,000 was approved at our November board meeting.

> "The manifestations of the spirit are truly wondrous, and as varied as Creation itself. The living spirit grows and even outgrows its earlier forms of expression; it freely chooses the men who proclaim it and in whom it lives. This living spirit is eternally renewed and pursues its goal in manifold and inconceivable ways throughout the history of mankind. Measured against it, the names and forms which men have given it mean very little; they are only the changing leaves and blossoms on the stem of the eternal tree."
>
> C. G. Jung

There are so many lives he touched. We will always be grateful for his kindnesses—and as grateful, too, we had the opportunity of meeting you.

Appreciatively
Oregon Friends of C. G. Jung

Charles Arthur Musès (April 28, 1919–August 26, 2000), was an esoteric philosopher who wrote articles and books under various pseudonyms. He founded the Lion Path, a shamanistic movement. He held unusual and controversial views relating to mathematics, physics, philosophy, and many other fields.

In 1991, In All Her Names: Explorations of the Feminine in Divinity, *edited by Campbell and Musès, was published by Harper-SanFrancisco. Each contributed a chapter to the book, along with Riane Eisler and Marija Gimbutas. Musès wrote the following tribute to Campbell after his death.*

Last Friday in his home, Dr. Joseph Campbell, in a too weakened state, tried gallantly to rise from his chair and walk into another room. At that moment of his 84th year of extraordinary mental and physical activity his bodily heart sank, and he walked into a room larger than life here on earth. It was a transition without suffering and in the midst of living.

Actually, that is always how one tends to think of Joseph Campbell—for he was ever on the creative go, never resting on his abundant laurels, always striding from where he was towards an ever more creative place, towards another room, another space.

His spirit is like a lambent flame that will light coming generations to evermore creative awareness of that inner world which in the end determines all our external acts—as the consciousness of a true dancer dictates the movements and stance of the body: the vibrantly feeling idea moulding limb and muscle like clay. Perhaps that is why Joe's and Jean's marriage was so wonderful. He designed his words to dance as she, her choreography. Together they engaged graciously in the greatest art of all—the dance of life itself—and in their shared and interflowing creativity, entrained their audiences in exaltations of uplifting experience.

That was what we felt around Joe—a sense of enormous "lift." His presence transformed what otherwise would be ordinary evanescent events into shining symbols—shining through time as through a curtain.

Joe's presence pulled aside the curtain of time for many, letting them glimpse the timeless flame through living words and that benevolent élan vital he fairly emanated wherever he was and went.

It would be selfish grasping to try to hold him back from his own experience of the eternal, the thirst for and satisfaction of which he so generously awakened in so many. He, like a cosmic program of light and music, passing beyond all terrestrial receivers out to the limitless stars, has left on his greatest hero journey of all. The least we, still here, can do is wish Bon Voyage to a great captain of the soul—for he is gone to his own spirit, and as Coleridge wrote, "the soul itself is of all sweet sounds, the life and element."

So let it be with Joseph Campbell—mourned by his beloved Jean, his relatives, his friends, and the many who merely knew his name and his logos. Ave atque vale, Greetings and Farewell, Aloha, dearly-loved guide and friend!

Charles [Musès]

Richard Adams (May 9, 1920–December 24, 2016) was the author of Watership Down, *among other books.*

Richard Adams
Benwell's
Church Street
Whitchurch, Hants RG28 7AR
31st January, 1989

Dear Jean,
I was so glad to receive your letter of 9th January, together with the In Memoriam brochure about Joseph. This is something which I shall keep carefully and resort to from time to time for spiritual comfort.

It is no more than honest truth that nobody, except the Baroness von der Heydt, has had more influence upon my life and done more to develop my true personality than Joseph. Thank goodness I had the opportunity to say as much, and to thank him, at that splendid 80th birthday party in New York.

It's pleasing to read that you think the T.V. interviews have communicated Joseph's message far and near: but I am sure that in point of fact his message is universal, and will affect people—as do the work of Darwin and the work of Freud—who may not even have read "The Hero" and "The Masks of God." What has actually come into my head as I write this is a verse from the Psalms—which I have now identified as Psalm XIX, verse 4. "Their sound is gone out into all lands and their words into the ends of the world." That's Joseph, wouldn't you agree?

Love from
Richard Adams

Stephen Larsen is a graduate of Columbia University (BA, MA), and the Union Institute and University (PhD). He is Professor

Emeritus in Psychology at the Ulster Community College (SUNY). He trained with Edward Whitmont, MD, Jungian training analyst, and Stanislav Grof, as well as Joseph Campbell. His wife, Robin Larsen, is an artist and art historian, and editor of the biography and anthology Emmanuel Swedenborg: A Continuing Vision. *Together, the Larsens codirect the Center for Symbolic Studies in New Paltz, New York, and are coauthors of* A Fire in the Mind: The Life of Joseph Campbell *(later subtitled "The Authorized Biography").*

The following letter mentions scholar Wendy Doniger's negative review of A Fire in the Mind *in the* New York Times Book Review.[2] *The letter's writer, a former student of Campbell's, refutes the review's attacks on Campbell's character.*

Poughkeepsie, NY 12601

Stephen and Robin Larsen
Springtown Road
Tillison, NY 12486

Dear Dr. [and] Mrs. Larsen
I had read Wendy Doniger's extremely vituperative review of your book in the NY Times Book Review and was incensed by it. I did not know, until reading today's Woodstock Times that you were local people, or I should have written earlier, although your book is finished and my comments wouldn't have changed it except to back up your conclusions.

I was a student at Sarah Lawrence College from 1950 to 1953 and a student in Joe Campbell's classes which were enormously popular then. It must be remembered that the entire student body at that time was about 380, so being in a Campbell class was a great deal more meaningful than it would have been at any other school. Also, the teaching system included weekly conferences at which we sat nose to nose with the professor, in a very small room. All of the teacher's offices were small.

If Joe had been a womanizer, he would have had every opportunity to make passes at his students. There were many who were extremely beautiful. I never heard a word about him although we did know of other teachers who indulged in romances with the students.

At the time I attended SLC, about 60% of the student body, including myself, were Jewish. I counted my graduating class of about 100. I believe more than 60 members were Jewish. I think this was because they took so many students from the New York area. If Joe were anti-Semitic, it was the worst place in the world to be so. I never heard a word about it, and would have since we also had a system of "Dons" (student advisors). Mine was a European who loved the campus gossip. We certainly gossiped about everything else.

With respect to Brendan Gill's accusations, he liked to frequent the Bronxville station bar and pick up SLC students. I think his comments are sour grapes, as he got turned down a lot. Everyone drank a lot then, so it wasn't unusual to allude to it. The President of SLC was a notable drinker but his job wasn't jeopardized by that.

I think Doniger's comments are sour grapes as well. It may be noted that none of this criticism came up until Campbell became so enormously popular after the TV series. He was certainly very well known academically for many years before that but until he achieved popular success, neither Gill nor Doniger felt it worthwhile to comment on what they perceived as his failings.

It was a unique and wonderful experience to have classes with Campbell. After almost 40 years, I still have my class notes. I am sorry that academia has to be so small minded.

Sincerely,
Helene Reiner

Campbell had a long connection with the rock band the Grateful Dead (see Phil Cousineau's letter of April 5, 1986, on page 358). Band member Bob Weir had him as a dinner guest, and Weir and fellow band member Mickey Hart attended a luncheon for Campbell that included Bob Dylan and Governor Jerry Brown, hosted by Barbara McClintock, the director of public programs at the C. G. Jung Institute in San Francisco. Campbell appeared with Hart and the Dead's lead guitarist, Jerry Garcia, on a panel called "From Ritual to Rapture: Dionysus to the Grateful Dead," held at the Palace Theater in San Francisco, November 1, 1986.

For one performance, the band invited Campbell and his wife to sit onstage. Campbell was delighted by the experience and later described the Dead's concerts as modern-day equivalents of the ancient Dionysian rituals. Mickey Hart's book Planet Drum *is laced with quotations from Campbell's work.*

Following is an excerpt from David Browne's interview with Bob Weir, which appeared in Rolling Stone, *October 25, 2016.*[3]

DAVID BROWNE: Who are your heroes?

BOB WEIR: Joseph Campbell, for his true openness and sensitivity to...I don't know what you'd call it—the profound fabric of the universe. He was a great guy. Drank me under the table a few times.

APPENDIX

The Works of Joseph Campbell

Chapter 1. Wanderings—Paris to Pacific Grove: 1927–1939

During this period, Campbell had one story ("Strictly Platonic") published and worked on a number of other pieces of short fiction. Those stories were published posthumously in the collection below.

Joseph Campbell. *Mythic Imagination: Collected Short Fiction.* Edited by Robert Walter and David Kudler. Novato, CA: New World Library, 2012.

Chapter 2. Decade *Mirabilis*: The 1940s

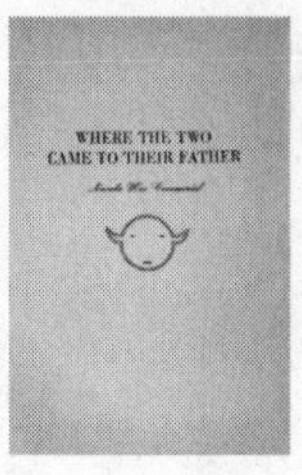

Jeff King and Maud Oakes. *Where the Two Came to Their Father: A Navaho War Ceremonial.* Commentary by Joseph Campbell. Bollingen Series I. Richmond, VA: Pantheon, 1943.

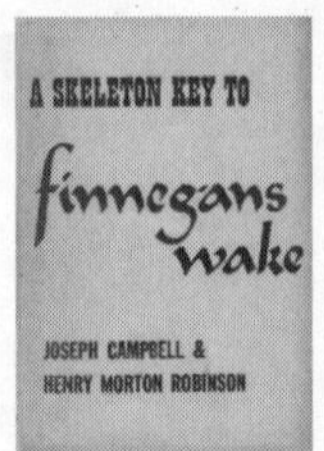

Joseph Campbell and Henry Morton Robinson. *A Skeleton Key to Finnegans Wake.* New York: Harcourt, Brace, 1944.

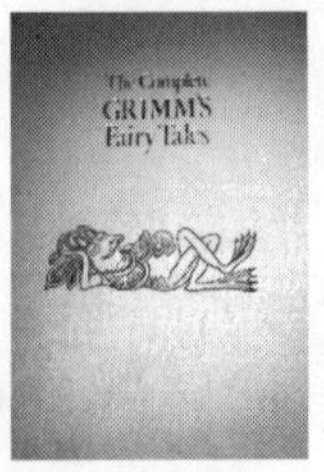

Joseph Campbell. "Folkloristic Commentary." *The Complete Grimm's Fairy Tales.* New York: Pantheon, 1944.

Heinrich Zimmer. *Myths and Symbols in Indian Art and Civilization.* Edited by Joseph Campbell. Bollingen Series VI. New York: Pantheon, 1946.

Heinrich Zimmer. *The King and the Corpse: Tales of the Soul's Conquest of Evil.* Edited by Joseph Campbell. Bollingen Series XI. New York: Pantheon, 1948.

Joseph Campbell. *The Hero with a Thousand Faces.* Bollingen Series XVII. New York: Pantheon, 1949.

Chapter 3. The Banquet Years: The 1950s

Heinrich Zimmer. *Philosophies of India.* Edited by Joseph Campbell. Bollingen Series XXVI. New York: Pantheon, 1951.

Heinrich Zimmer. *The Art of Indian Asia: Its Mythology and Transformations.* Edited by Joseph Campbell. 2 vols. Bollingen Series XXXIX. New York: Pantheon, 1955.

Joseph Campbell, editor. *Papers from the Eranos Yearbooks.* Translated by Ralph Manheim and R. F. C. Hull. Bollingen Series XXX. Princeton, NJ: Princeton University Press.

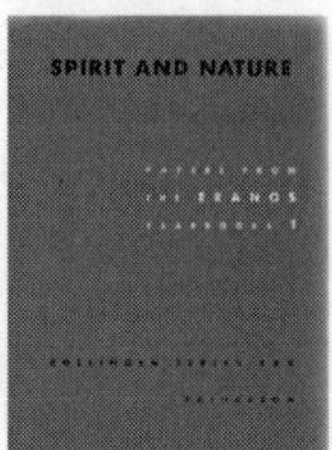

Papers from the Eranos Yearbooks, Volume 1: Spirit and Nature, 1954.

Papers from the Eranos Yearbooks, Volume 2: The Mysteries, 1955.

Papers from the Eranos Yearbooks, Volume 3: Man and Time, 1957.

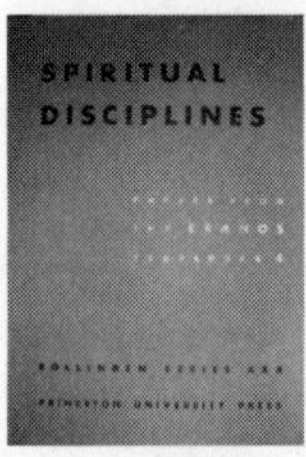

Papers from the Eranos Yearbooks, Volume 4: Spiritual Disciplines, 1960.

Papers from the Eranos Yearbooks, Volume 5: Man and Transformation, 1964.

Papers from the Eranos Yearbooks, Volume 6: The Mystic Vision, 1968.

Chapter 4. *The Masks of God*: 1959–1968

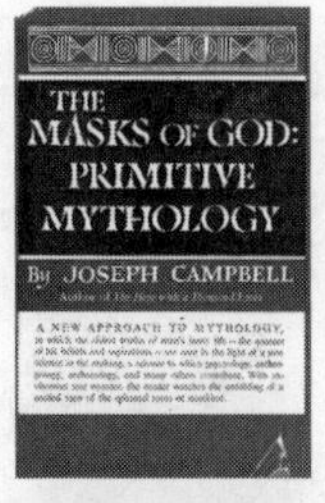

Joseph Campbell. *The Masks of God, Volume 1: Primitive Mythology*. New York: Viking, 1959.

The Masks of God, Volume 2: Oriental Mythology. New York: Viking, 1962.

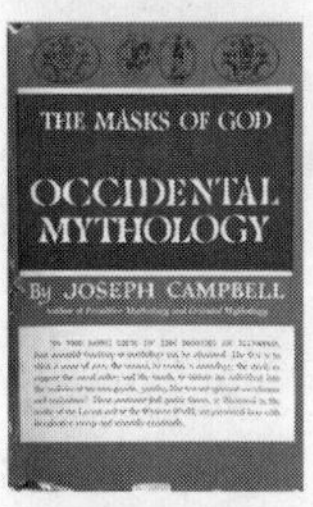

The Masks of God, Volume 3: Occidental Mythology. New York: Viking, 1964.

The Masks of God, Volume 4: Creative Mythology. New York: Viking, 1968.

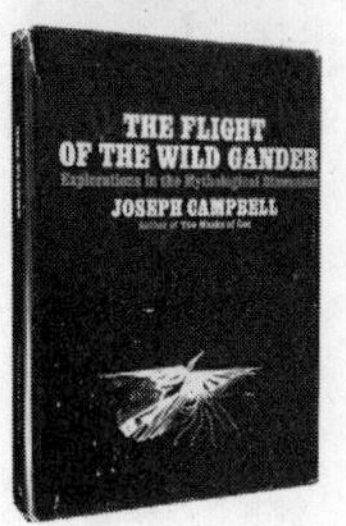

Joseph Campbell. *The Flight of the Wild Gander: Explorations in the Mythological Dimension*. New York: Viking, 1969.

Chapter 6. *The Mythic Image*: The 1970s

Joseph Campbell, editor. *Myths, Dreams, and Religion: Eleven Visions of Connection.* New York: E. P. Dutton, 1970.

C. G. Jung. *The Portable Jung.* Edited by Joseph Campbell. Translated by R. F. C. Hull. New York: E. P. Dutton, 1970.

Joseph Campbell. *Myths to Live By.* New York: Viking, 1972.

Joseph Campbell. *The Mythic Image.* Assisted by M. J. Abadie. Bollingen Series C. Princeton, NJ: Princeton University Press, 1975.

Chapter 7. The Last Decade: The 1980s

Joseph Campbell. *Historical Atlas of World Mythology, Volume 1: The Way of the Animal Powers.* London: Summerfield Press, 1983.

Joseph Campbell. *The Inner Reaches of Outer Space: Metaphor as Myth and as Religion.* New York: Alfred van der Marck, 1985.

Joseph Campbell. *Historical Atlas of World Mythology, Volume 2: The Way of the Seeded Earth. Part 1: The Sacrifice.* New York: Harper & Row, 1988.

Joseph Campbell. *Historical Atlas of World Mythology, Volume 2: The Way of the Seeded Earth. Part 2: Mythologies of the Primitive Planters: The Northern Americas.* New York: Harper & Row, 1989.

Joseph Campbell. *Historical Atlas of World Mythology, Volume 2: The Way of the Seeded Earth. Part 3: Mythologies of the Primitive Planters: The Middle and Southern Americas.* New York: Harper & Row, 1989.

Joseph Campbell and Charles Musès, editors. *In All Her Names: Explorations of the Feminine in Divinity.* San Francisco: HarperSanFrancisco, 1991.

NOTES

Foreword. Letter Writing: The Imagination's Personal Genre

1. For Jung, *mana* is a form of psychic energy. He cites a number of writers on this power, which approaches the supernatural, the numinous. "Much that was taken by investigators animistically as spirit, demon, or numen really belongs to the primitive concept of energy," which is a more involved definition of *mana.* C.G. Jung, *The Structure and Dynamics of the Psyche* (vol. 8 of *The Collected Works of C. G. Jung*), Bollingen Series XX, trans. R.F.C. Hull (New York: Pantheon Books, 1960), para. 127. Later in the same volume, Jung writes in a footnote, "Like the now obsolete concept of ether, energy and the atom are primitive intuitions. A primitive form of the one is *mana*, and of the other the atom of Democritus and the 'soul-sparks' of the Australian aborigines" (para. 280, fn. 11).

Introduction. Joseph Campbell's Correspondence: A Portrait of an Epoch

1. Camille Paglia, "Erich Neumann: Theorist of the Great Mother," *Arion* 13, no. 3 (winter 2006). This is a slightly expanded version of a lecture delivered on November 10, 2005, for the Otto and Ilse Mainzer Lecture Series sponsored by Deutsches Haus at New York University.
2. Andrea Wulf, *The Invention of Nature: Alexander von Humboldt's New World* (New York: Knopf, 2015), 335.
3. See Charlene Spretnak, "Anatomy of a Backlash: Concerning the Work of Marija Gimbutas," *Journal of Archaeomythology* 7 (2011). Marija Gimbutas (January 23, 1921–February 2, 1994) was a Lithuanian American archaeologist known for her research into the Neolithic and

Bronze Age cultures of Old Europe. "Her volume *Gods and Goddesses of Old Europe, 7000 to 3500 B.C.*, contained some daring hypotheses about the Neolithic goddess cultures, which Campbell embraced and which he often cited in his work": Stephen Larsen and Robin Larsen, *A Fire in the Mind: The Life of Joseph Campbell* (New York: Doubleday, 1991), 536. See, for example, his August 31, 1986, letter to Jamake Highwater on page 355.

4. Alan Dundes, ed., *Sacred Narrative: Readings in the Theory of Myth* (Berkeley: University of California Press, 1984).
5. One would do better by consulting John Vickery's edited volume, *Myth and Literature: Contemporary Theory and Practice* (Lincoln: University of Nebraska Press, 1966), which includes a fine selection from Campbell called "Bios and Ethos."
6. Brendan Gill, "The Faces of Joseph Campbell," *New York Review of Books*, September 28, 1989.
7. Joseph Campbell, *Creative Mythology* (vol. 4 of *Masks of God*) (New York: Viking, 1968), 650 and passim.
8. Joseph Campbell, *The Hero with a Thousand Faces*, "Preface to the 1949 Edition" (1949; reprint, Novato, CA: New World Library, 2008), xii and passim.
9. Gill, "The Faces of Joseph Campbell," September 28, 1989.
10. Jeff Sharlet, "Comparing Myths: A Scholar Uncovers the 'Bare Bones of Human Experience,'" *Chronicle of Higher Education*, March 26, 1989.
11. Ibid.

Overture. About Joseph Campbell: On the Occasion of His Centennial

1. Stephen Larsen and Robin Larsen, *A Fire in the Mind: The Life of Joseph Campbell* (New York: Doubleday, 1991), 3.
2. Arthur Schopenhauer, from *Die Welt als Wille und Vorstellung*, published in English as *The World as Will and Idea* and *The World as Will and Representation*. This is Campbell's translation.
3. Joseph Campbell, *Historical Atlas of World Mythology, Volume 1: The Way of the Animal Powers*, Part 1, "Mythologies of the Primitive Hunters and Gatherers" (New York: Harper and Row, 1988), 8.
4. This excerpt is from an unpublished portion of Campbell's journals.
5. "On the Apparent Intention in the Fate of the Individual" is Campbell's translation of the title of Schopenhauer's essay "Transzcendente Spekulation über die anscheinende Absichtlichkeit im Schicksale des

Einzelnen." The essay has since been translated; see Arthur Schopenhauer, *Parerga and Paralipomena: Short Philosophical Essays*, trans. E. F. J. Payne (Oxford, UK: Clarendon Press, 1974), vol. 1, 199–223.

Chapter 1. Wanderings—Paris to Pacific Grove: 1927–1939

1. For a more detailed discussion of the importance of the Orient in Campbell's studies, see the edited volume of his lectures *Romance of the Grail: The Magic and Mystery of Arthurian Myth*, ed. Evans Lansing Smith (Novato, CA: New World Library, 2015).
2. Apparently, Campbell is referring to a writing project of which we have no record.
3. "Oiseau dans l'espace" ("Bird in space") was the first in a series of abstract sculptures by Romanian sculptor Constantin Brâncuçi.
4. Jackson Sholz was an American Olympic runner whom Campbell had met at the AAU track championships in San Francisco in 1925. See Joseph Campbell, *The Hero's Journey: Joseph Campbell on His Life and Work* (Novato, CA: New World Library, 2003), 32–34.
5. "The only true success comes from the good quality of the spirit—that is to say, from the realities of the soul."
6. "The little American girl who had captured it." *Croquer*, meaning "to sketch or draw," can have the figurative sense of capturing the essence of an idea, a person, or a thing.
7. He was not in fact able to take this trip until 1954. See Joseph Campbell, *Asian Journals: India and Japan* (Novato, CA: New World Library, 2017).
8. Curuppumullage Jinarajadasa (December 16, 1875–June 18, 1953) was an author, occultist, and Freemason. The fourth president of the Theosophical Society, Jinarajadasa was one of the world's foremost Theosophical authors, having published more than fifty books and more than sixteen hundred articles in periodicals during his life. His interests included religion, philosophy, literature, art, science, and occult chemistry. He was also a linguist who had the ability to work in many European languages.
9. Campbell is referring to Angela Gregory's friezes on the Louisiana State Capitol.
10. Campbell is referring to the library in Carmel, California, where he discovered Oswald Spengler's *Decline of the West*, a pivotal book for Campbell's thinking. Campbell had begun his stint in Monterey, California. He would remain there, meeting poet Robinson Jeffers and

novelist John Steinbeck and working with marine biologist Ed Ricketts.

11. Robert Gessner, *Massacre: A Survey of Today's American Indian* (New York: J. Cape and H. Smith, 1931). The political implications of Campbell's response to the book contrast sharply with the views expressed below in chapter 5.
12. Franz Blom taught at Tulane University in New Orleans. During his tenure, he undertook several expeditions to Mesoamerica. In 1923 his studies at Palenque documented a number of features neglected by earlier researchers. In 1924 he excavated the Maya archaeological site of Uaxactún in Guatemala. From his explorations around the Isthmus of Tehuantepec, he wrote some of the first scholarly reports of a number of sites of the Olmec civilization. In 1926 he was made head of Tulane's newly established department of Middle American research.
13. Edward Flanders Robb ("Ed") Ricketts (May 14, 1897–May 11, 1948), mentioned in this letter to Angela Gregory, was an American marine biologist, ecologist, and philosopher. See page 33 later in this chapter for more on Ricketts and his friendship with Campbell.
14. The "gang" was composed of Ed Ricketts and his wife, John and Carol Steinbeck, Campbell, and the artist Richie Lovejoy ("Rich"). "Tal" was Natalya Kashevoroff, Lovejoy's girlfriend. See Larsen and Larsen, *A Fire in the Mind*, 198.
15. Alexander Archipenko (May 30, 1887–February 25, 1964) was a Cubist sculptor in New York who was the teacher of Alice Campbell (Joseph's sister).
16. This actually refers to Joseph Campbell, *The Inner Reaches of Outer Space: Metaphor as Myth and as Religion* (1986; reprint, Novato, CA: New World Library, 2002), the last chapter of which is indeed titled "The Way of Art" and does indeed quote Antoine Bourdelle.
17. See page 1 above.
18. The Southeastern Architectural Archive of Tulane University is the source of many of these letters.
19. Although this work was not published before Gregory's death in 1990, it is scheduled for publication in 2019 as Angela Gregory and Nancy L. Penrose, *A Dream and a Chisel: Louisiana Sculptor Angela Gregory in Paris, 1925–1928* (Columbia: University of South Carolina Press, 2019).
20. In the year following Campbell's death in 1987, his work gained massive notoriety due to the airing of *Joseph Campbell and the Power of Myth with Bill Moyers*. This notoriety led to both an unexpected windfall and an unexpected series of challenges that led Jean Erdman and Campbell's editor, Robert Walter, to found the Joseph Campbell Foundation in 1990.

21. John Cage would become a close friend of the Campbells' and would compose for Erdman's dance company. See Joseph Campbell, *The Ecstasy of Being: Mythology and Dance*, ed. Nancy Allison (Novato, CA: New World Library, 2017), passim.
22. This "chapter" would become Joseph Campbell and Henry Morton Robinson, *A Skeleton Key to Finnegans Wake* (1944; reprint, Novato, CA: New World Library, 2005). The collaborator mentioned below is, of course, Robinson.
23. This collection of Ricketts's essays was released posthumously: Edward F. Ricketts, *Breaking Through: Essays, Journals, and Travelogues of Edward F. Ricketts*, ed. Katharine A. Rodger (Berkeley: University of California Press, 2006).
24. John Steinbeck and E. F. Ricketts, *Sea of Cortez: A Leisurely Journal of Travel and Research* (New York: Viking, 1941).
25. This work, tentatively titled *How to Read a Myth*, would eventually be released as *The Hero with a Thousand Faces* in 1949.
26. In Sitka, Alaska.
27. "Toni" was Eleanor Susan Brownell Anthony Solomons (February 15, 1911–April 6, 2006), Ricketts's common-law wife. A writer and editor, Toni served as John Steinbeck's secretary. She later married oceanographer Ben Volcani (Jack Williams, "Toni Volcani; Writer, Editor Worked for Steinbeck," obituary, *San Diego Tribune*, April 16, 2006, http://legacy.sandiegouniontribune.com/uniontrib/20060416/news_mz1j16volcan.html).
28. Xenia Kashevaroff, who was later married to John Cage. Ed Ricketts was her first lover when she was seventeen, which was partly the cause of the split-up between Ed and his wife, Nan. See Larsen and Larsen, *A Fire in the Mind*, 175.
29. This is the portfolio edition of Jeff King and Maud Oakes, *Where the Two Came to Their Father: A Navaho War Ceremonial*, foreword and commentary by Joseph Campbell (1st edition, Richmond, VA: Pantheon, 1943; 3rd edition, Princeton, NJ: Princeton University Press, 1991).
30. That is, mothers of soldiers killed in the war.
31. A group of islands in the North Pacific Ocean, which Japan, fighting on the side of the Allies, conquered from Germany in World War I. As part of the postwar settlement, Japan administered the islands until World War II.
32. John Steinbeck, *Cannery Row* (New York: Viking, 1945). Ricketts is easily recognizable as the model for the central character, "Doc."
33. Pacific Biological Laboratories on Cannery Row in Monterey,

California, later destroyed by a fire. The site (along with the adjoining cannery) now serves as the Monterey Bay Aquarium.

34. Kay was Toni's daughter, Ricketts's stepdaughter. She would die of a brain tumor in 1947.
35. Campbell edited four posthumous volumes by Indologist Heinrich Zimmer: *Myths and Symbols in Indian Art and Civilization* (1946), *The King and the Corpse* (1948), *Philosophies of India* (1951), and *The Art of Indian Asia* (1955). See page xxx above and Chapter 2 below.
36. Ricketts would die on May 8, 1948, when his car was struck crossing train tracks blocks from his lab.

Chapter 2. Decade *Mirabilis*: The 1940s

1. Marginalia in Campbell's hand: "Oakes sections separate. 12–15 compressed. PP. 43–46 cut. P. 46 cut. P. 30 Jeff anecdote cut."
2. Mary Conover Mellon, a student of C. G. Jung, was the founder of the Bollingen Foundation. The foundation published (first through Pantheon and then through Princeton University Press) one hundred volumes of books, including the *Collected Works of C. G. Jung* and fifteen titles written and edited by Joseph Campbell, including *Where the Two Came to Their Father* (the first title in the series), *The Hero with a Thousand Faces*, and the series's final title, *The Mythic Image*.
3. Joseph Lewis Henderson (August 31, 1903–November 17, 2007) was an American physician and a Jungian psychologist. Henderson founded the Jung Institute of San Francisco, of which he was the president.
4. Here Campbell and Robinson are discussing the preparation of their essay "The Skin of Whose Teeth?" for Cousins's *Saturday Review*. The essay compared Thornton Wilder's *The Skin of Our Teeth* with *Finnegans Wake*. See also *Mythic Worlds, Modern Words*, chapter V.
5. *A Skeleton Key to Finnegans Wake* was published in July of 1944.
6. Campbell is discussing the source material for the book that would become *The Hero with a Thousand Faces*.
7. Campbell is referring to Robinson's 1950 novel *The Cardinal*.
8. This is *Oriental Mythology* (vol. 2 of *The Masks of God*).
9. Sergeant was wounded by shrapnel while serving as a nurse during World War I.
10. Heinrich Zimmer, *The King and the Corpse: Tales of the Soul's Conquest of Evil*, ed. Joseph Campbell (Princeton, NJ: Princeton University Press, 1948).
11. John D. Barrett, president of the Bollingen Foundation.
12. A handwritten note in the upper left corner of this letter reads, "Re

ESS proposed bio on Zimmer—never written—a few notes are in her papers."

13. Coomaraswamy's many notes in *Myths and Symbols in Indian Art and Civilization* are in fact marked with his initials.
14. Ananda Coomaraswamy, "'Spiritual Paternity' and the 'Puppet Complex,'" *Psychiatry: Journal of the Biology and Pathology of Interpersonal Relations* 8:3 (August 1945).
15. This would become *The Hero with a Thousand Faces.*
16. It is clear that these notes refer to the galleys of *The King and the Corpse,* and equally clear therefore that Coomaraswamy has written Gawain when he meant to say Lancelot, who famously hesitates a couple of steps before climbing into a cart offered by a dwarf.
17. In the margin to galley 15, Campbell has noted "Aitareya Aranyaka," which has to do with the philosophy of sacrifice in the Vedas.
18. In the margin to galley 27, Coomaraswamy has written "puer aeternus, Sanatkumāra" (meaning *always a youth*; Sanatkumāra is the name of one of the sons of Brahma). On the back of the envelope, Coomaraswamy has written "Loathly Bride p. 399 note 2: the source is Sir John Mandeville's *Voyages and Travails.*"
19. Coomaraswamy would die less than a month later, September 9, 1947, in Needham, Massachusetts.
20. Most likely *The Origin and Function of Culture* (Berkeley: University of California Press, 1943).
21. *The King and the Corpse,* which explored (among other things) what Zimmer argued were the Indo-European origins of the Arthurian romances and other legends.
22. That is, *bard.*
23. Jessie Laidlay Weston (1850–1928) was a medieval scholar. In her seminal work *From Ritual to Romance,* she argued for pre-Celtic origins to the Grail legend; T. S. Eliot cited it in his notes to *The Waste Land.*
24. See Joseph Campbell, *Romance of the Grail: The Magic and Mystery of Arthurian Myth,* ed. Evans Lansing Smith (Novato, CA: New World Library, 2015), pp. 82–84, 145.

Chapter 3. The Banquet Years: The 1950s

1. See William McGuire, *Bollingen: An Adventure in Collecting the Past* (Princeton, NJ: Princeton University Press, 1982).
2. His journals from this trip, which turned out to be a turning point in his career, were posthumously published as *Asian Journals: India and*

Japan, ed. David Kudler, Antony Van Couvering, Stephen Larsen, and Robin Larsen (Novato, CA: New World Library, 2017).

3. An authority on the works of Thomas Mann, Harry Slochower (September 1, 1900–May 11, 1991) wrote five books of literary criticism, including *Three Ways of Modern Man* (1937), *Thomas Mann's Joseph Story* (1938), and *No Voice Is Wholly Lost* (1945). He also contributed widely to philosophical, literary, Marxist, and psychoanalytic journals and was editor in chief of *American Imago*, a psychoanalytic quarterly, from 1964 until his death.
4. Stith Thompson (1885–1976) was an American scholar of folklore. He is best known for his motif index system for myths and folktales.
5. Amy Maud Bodkin (1875–1967) was an English classical scholar, writer on mythology, and literary critic. She is best known for her 1934 book *Archetypal Patterns in Poetry: Psychological Studies of Imagination* (Oxford, UK: Oxford University Press). It is generally taken to be a major work in applying the theories of Carl Jung to literature. Bodkin's other main works are *The Quest for Salvation in an Ancient and a Modern Play* (Oxford, UK: Oxford University Press, 1941) and *Studies of Type-Images in Poetry, Religion, and Philosophy* (Oxford, UK: Oxford University Press, 1951). She lectured at Homerton College, Cambridge, from 1902 to 1914.
6. Jane Harrison (1850–1928) was an English classical scholar, best known for *Prolegomena to the Study of Greek Religion* (1903) and *Themis: A Study of the Social Origins of Greek Religion* (1912), both of which had a profound impact on Campbell's thinking. She lectured at Newnham College, Cambridge, from 1898 to 1922. See Joseph Campbell, *Goddesses: Mysteries of the Feminine Divine*, ed. Safron Rossi (Novato, CA: New World Library, 2013).
7. Swami Nikhilananda (1895–1973), born Dinesh Chandra Das Gupta, founded the Ramakrishna-Vivekananda Center of New York and remained its head until his death in 1973. Nikhilananda was an accomplished writer and thinker. His greatest contribution was the translation of *Sri Sri Ramakrishna Kathamrita* from Bengali into English, published under the title *The Gospel of Sri Ramakrishna* (1942). Campbell helped with the editing. See Campbell, *Asian Journals*, "Travels with Swami."
8. Shirley Jackson, *Hangsaman* (New York: Farrar, Straus and Young, 1951).
9. Published by Atlantis Verlag, 1949.
10. Lawrence Law Whyte, *The Next Development in Man* (London: Cresset Press, 1944).

11. Perhaps *The Armed Vision: A Study in the Methods of Modern Literary Criticism* (New York: Knopf, 1947).
12. Most likely Carl Karényi, *Die Jungfrau und Mutter der griechischen Religion: Eine Studie über Pallas Athene* (The virgin and mother of the Greek religion: A study of Pallas Athena; 1952).

Chapter 4. *The Masks of God*: 1959–1968

1. No recordings of this public television series, titled *Mask, Myth, & Dream,* seem to have survived. However, Campbell transcribed them for his own use.
2. Probably the Hungarian poet Imre Madách de Sztregova et Kelecsény (January 20, 1823–October 5, 1864).
3. The Great Alaskan Earthquake, which took place on Good Friday, March 27, 1964, was the most powerful one recorded in American history.
4. Campbell would in fact cite Piaget's work, not in Volume 2 of *Masks of God—Oriental Mythology*—but in *Creative Mythology,* the final volume in the series.
5. The reference is to Wilhelm Gundert, ed. and trans., *Bi-Yän-Lu: Meister Yüan-wu's Niederschrift von der Smaragdenen Felswand verfasst auf dem Djia-schan bei Li in Hunan zwischen 1111 und 1115 im Druck erschienen in Sitschuan um 1300* (Bi-yän-lu: Master Yüan-wu's transcript of the Emerald Cliff, written on the Djia-shan near Li in Hunan between 1111 and 1115, published in Sichuan around 1300) (Munich: Carl Hanser, 1960–73).
6. The Sothic cycle, or Canicular period, is a period of 1,461 Egyptian civil years of 365 days each, or 1,460 Julian years, averaging 365¼ days each. The cycle, which has to do with the heliacal rising of the star Sirius, was important in Egyptian sacred chronology.
7. James Broughton (1913–1999) was an American poet and playwright who was part of San Francisco's vibrant counterculture from the Beats through the Summer of Love to the Sisters of Perpetual Indulgence.
8. This would become *The Mythic Image.* See chapter 6 below.
9. Alan Watts, *Behold the Spirit: A Study in the Necessity of Mystical Religion* (New York: Pantheon, 1947).
10. See Campbell, *Asian Journals,* "Travels with Swami."
11. Joseph Campbell, ed., *Myths, Dreams, and Religion: Eleven Visions of Connection* (New York: Dutton, 1970).
12. See Campbell, *Asian Journals,* 238–39.
13. "Der Orient der Kreuzügge in Wolframs Parzival" ("The Orient of the

Crusades and Wolfram's Parzival"), *Archiv für Kulturforschung* 2, no. 1 (1967); and "Imperial Rome and the Genesis of Classical Indian Art," *East and West*, new series, 10, no. 3–4 (Sept.–Dec. 1959). See Campbell, *Romance of the Grail*, 38–39, 168.

14. Campbell's research files show an early and sustained engagement with this book. The English version is *Love in the Western World*, trans. Montgomery Belgion, rev. ed. (Princeton, NJ: Princeton University Press, 1983).

Chapter 5. Political Matters—Thomas Mann to the Vietnam War: 1939–1970

1. Peter Dreier, *The 100 Greatest Americans of the 20th Century: A Social Justice Hall of Fame* (New York: Nation Books, 2012), 283.

Chapter 6. *The Mythic Image*: The 1970s

1. Campbell's handwritten notes on this page: "Total responsibility to be paid directly to Princeton. Jack Pictures $12,000 > $1,000 per ?? > Ideal time 6 mo—$10 x 40 = 400 / 1600 > $15,000 2yrs."
2. Campbell served as president of the American Society for the Study of Religions during this time.

Chapter 7. The Last Decade: The 1980s

1. Vernon W. Gras, "Myth and the Reconciliation of Opposites: Jung and Lévi-Strauss," *Journal of the History of Ideas*, 42, no. 3 (1981): 471–88. I [Evans Lansing Smith] am grateful to Richard Buchen, special-collections librarian at Pacifica Graduate Institute, for providing me with a copy of this letter.
2. Stanislav Grof, *When the Impossible Happens: Adventures in Non-ordinary Realities* (Boulder, CO: Sounds True, 2006), 22.
3. Quoted in Larsen and Larsen, *A Fire in the Mind*, 478. Bracketed insertion in the original.
4. Campbell retired from Sarah Lawrence in 1972.
5. Georges Dumézil (March 4, 1898–October 11, 1986, Paris) was a French comparative philologist best known for his analysis of sovereignty and power in Proto-Indo-European religion and society. He is considered one of the major contributors to mythography, particularly for his formulation of the trifunctional hypothesis of social class in ancient societies. Among his best-known works in English is *Gods of the Ancient Northmen* (Berkeley: University of California Press, 1977).

6. The underlinings in this and subsequent paragraphs are Campbell's, in red ink.
7. This paragraph has a red highlight line beside it in the left margin.
8. The letter includes the original Icelandic for this quotation, omitted here and below.
9. The Joseph Campbell Archives includes the original invitation in Icelandic.
10. The essay appeared in Joseph Campbell and Charles Musès, ed., *In All Her Names: Explorations of the Feminine in Divinity* (San Francisco: HarperSanFrancisco, 1991).
11. See Campbell's *Historical Atlas of World Mythology, Volume 2: Way of the Seeded Earth, Part 3: Mythologies of the Primitive Planters: The Middle and Southern Americas,* 377–78.
12. Donald W. Lathrap, *The Upper Amazon: Ancient Peoples and Places,* (London: Thames & Hudson, 1970), and *Ancient Ecuador: Culture, Clay and Creativity, 3000–300 B.C.* (Chicago: Field Museum of Natural History, 1980).
13. The National Arts Club awarded Campbell a Gold Medal of Honor for Literature in February 1985.
14. Bill Moyers (born June 5, 1934) is an American journalist and political commentator. Perhaps his most famous achievement is his 1988 series *Joseph Campbell and the Power of Myth with Bill Moyers,* consisting of interviews with Campbell, which Campbell refers to here. The series aired on PBS after Campbell's death. It remains, at the time of this publication, the highest rated broadcast in the history of the network.

Coda: Testimonials and Condolences

1. James Merrill, *The Changing Light at Sandover,* "III. Scripts for the Pageant" (1980; reprint, New York: Knopf, 2011), 304–5.
2. Wendy Doniger, "A Very Strange Enchanted Boy," *New York Times Book Review,* February 2, 1992, https://www.nytimes.com/1992/02/02/books/a-very-strange-enchanted-boy.html.
3. David Browne, "The Last Word: Bob Weir on Grateful Dead's Legacy, Adele, Fame's Downside," *Rolling Stone,* October 25, 2016.

WORKS CITED

Campbell, Joseph. "Creativity." In *C. G. Jung and the Humanities: Toward a Hermeneutics of Culture*. Edited by Karin Barnaby and Pellegrino D'Acierno. Princeton, NJ: Princeton University Press, 1990.

———. "Elders and Guides." In *Parabola* 5, no. 1 (1980): 57–65.

Dundes, Alan, ed. *Sacred Narrative: Readings in the Theory of Myth*. Berkeley: University of California Press, 1984.

Grof, Stanislav. *When the Impossible Happens: Adventures in Non-ordinary Realities*. Boulder, CO: Sounds True, 2006.

Hart, Mickey, and Frederick Lieberman. *Planet Drum: A Celebration of Percussion and Rhythm*. San Francisco: HarperSanFrancisco, 1991.

Larsen, Stephen, and Robin Larsen. *A Fire in the Mind: The Life of Joseph Campbell*. New York: Doubleday, 1991.

McGuire, William. *Bollingen: An Adventure in Collecting the Past*. Bollingen Series. Princeton, NJ: Princeton University Press, 1982.

McNally, Dennis. *A Long Strange Trip: The Inside History of the Grateful Dead*. New York: Broadway Books, 2002.

O'Connor, Flannery. *The Habit of Being: Letters of Flannery O'Connor*. Edited by Sally Fitzgerald. New York: Farrar, Straus, Giroux, 1979.

Paglia, Camille. "Erich Neumann: Theorist of the Great Mother." *Arion* 13, no. 3 (winter 2006).

Spretnak, Charlene. "Anatomy of a Backlash: Concerning the Work of Marija Gimbutas." *Journal of Archaeomythology* 7 (2011).

Vickery, John, ed. *Myth and Literature: Contemporary Theory and Practice*. Lincoln: University of Nebraska Press, 1966.

Winston, Richard, and Clara Winston, eds. and trans. *Letters of Thomas Mann: 1889–1955*. Berkeley: University of California Press, 1975.

Wulf, Andrea. *The Invention of Nature: Alexander von Humboldt's New World*. New York: Knopf, 2015.

WORKS CITED

PERMISSION ACKNOWLEDGMENTS

The editors gratefully acknowledge permission given to reproduce the following images in the text.

Page xxvi: Courtesy of Phil Cousineau.

Pages xxxiv, 9, 136, 228, 246, 286, 306, 362: Courtesy of Jean Erdman.

Pages 2 and 302: Photo by Clarence J. Zumwalt.

Page 3: Courtesy of H. Roger-Viollet, Paris.

Page 12: Photo from the Bain Collection at the Library of Congress (public domain): http://loc.gov/pictures/resource/ggbain.38863/.

Page 33: Photo by Bryan Fitch.

Page 64: Photo by Philippe Halsmann, 1943, courtesy of Yvonne Halsmann, © 1989.

Page 67: Photo by Louisa Jenkins, courtesy of Dr. Elizabeth Osterman.

Page 69: Courtesy of Maud Oakes.

Page 96: Courtesy of the Eranos Foundation, Ascona, Switzerland.

Page 113: Photo taken in 1922; photographer unknown (public domain).

Page 140: Courtesy of the C. G. Jung Institute, San Francisco.

Page 152: Courtesy of Sarah Lawrence College, Bronxville, New York.

Page 187: Courtesy of the Alan Watts Foundation.

Page 232: Courtesy of the German Information Center, New York.

Page 341: Photos by Janelle Balnicke.

Page 346: Courtesy of Gillet G. Griffin.

INDEX

Page numbers in *italic type* refer to photographs.

ABOUT THE JOSEPH CAMPBELL FOUNDATION

THE JOSEPH CAMPBELL FOUNDATION (JCF) is a nonprofit corporation that continues the work of Joseph Campbell, exploring the fields of mythology and comparative religion. The Foundation is guided by three principal goals:

First, the Foundation preserves, protects, and perpetuates Campbell's pioneering work. This includes cataloging and archiving his works, developing new publications based on his works, directing the sale and distribution of his published works, protecting copyrights to his works, and increasing awareness of his works by making them available in digital formats on JCF's website.

Second, the Foundation promotes the study of mythology and comparative religion. This involves implementing and/or supporting diverse mythological education programs, supporting and/or sponsoring events designed to increase public awareness, donating Campbell's archived works (principally to the Joseph Campbell and Marija Gimbutas Archive and Library), and utilizing JCF's website as a forum for relevant cross-cultural dialogue.

Third, the Foundation helps individuals enrich their lives by participating in a series of programs, including our global, Internet-based Associates program, our local international network of Mythological Roundtables, and our periodic Joseph Campbell–related events and activities.

www.jcf.org